BEAUTIFUL DEMOCRACY

Russ Castronovo

BEAUTIFUL DEMOCRACY

. . . .

Aesthetics and Anarchy in a Global Era

The University of Chicago Press
Chicago and London

RUSS CASTRONOVO is the Jean Wall Bennett Professor of English and American Studies at the University of Wisconsin–Madison. He is the coeditor of two collections, and the author of two books, *Necro Citizenship: Death, Eroticism, and the Public Sphere in the Nineteenth-Century United States* and *Fathering the Nation: American Genealogies of Slavery and Freedom*

The University of Chicago Press, Chicago 60637
The University of Chicago Press, Ltd., London
© 2007 by The University of Chicago
All rights reserved. Published 2007
Printed in the United States of America

16 15 14 13 12 11 10 09 08 07   1 2 3 4 5

ISBN-13: 978-0-226-09628-5 (cloth)
ISBN-13: 978-0-226-09629-2 (paper)
ISBN-10: 0-226-09628-9 (cloth)
ISBN-10: 0-226-09629-7 (paper)

Library of Congress Cataloging-in-Publication Data

Castronovo, Russ, 1965–
    Beautiful democracy : aesthetics and anarchy in a global era / Russ Castronovo.
        p. cm.
    Includes bibliographical references and index.
    ISBN-13: 978-0-226-09628-5 (cloth : alk. paper)
    ISBN-13: 978-0-226-09629-2 (pbk. : alk. paper)
    ISBN-10: 0-226-09628-9 (cloth : alk. paper)
    ISBN-10: 0-226-09629-7 (pbk. : alk. paper) 1. Aesthetics, American. 2. Arts—United States. 3. United States—Civilization. 4. Democracy—United States. I. Title.
    BH221 .U53C37 2007
    306.4'70973—dc22

                                            2007003728

· · · the beauty of the everyday · · ·

Maya, Julian, Leslie

CONTENTS

ILLUSTRATIONS

ACKNOWLEDGMENTS

Early work on aesthetics is all over the place. It is a global discourse that established a foothold in a range of fields from psychology to literary criticism and from philosophy to early film studies. But I intend this statement about the widespread disciplinary nature of aesthetics more literally and spatially. Largely forgotten in professors' lecture notes and research papers from a century ago, theories of art, beauty, and common feeling are strewn, rather unsystematically, across university archives. In many cases, work on aesthetics mainly shows up in the notes of philosophy professors, while in other collections it is concentrated in typewritten dissertations of psychology students. The University of Wisconsin–Madison has some of this material, but fires at the original Science Hall in 1884 and at University Hall in 1916 no doubt consumed many documents that would have proved valuable to my study. For this reason, I am grateful to the Jean Wall Bennett Fund and the Dorothy Draheim-Bascom Fund for enabling me to widen my search with visits to the University of California, Berkeley, the University of Chicago, Harvard University, the Huntington Library, and the Yale University Divinity School Library. I thank the librarians and archivists at these institutions for providing access and insight to the miscellany of aesthetic education.

Aesthetics are conceptually all over the place, too. Approaches to the topic at the end of the nineteenth and start of the twentieth centuries drew on scientific, historical, physiological, and sociological approaches, or, as was more likely, some mixture of these methodologies. Getting a handle on what "the beautiful" meant to university men and women has been a difficult task, certainly no easier than trying to figure out what beauty and art meant outside the ivory tower in places like tenements, five-cent theaters, and the wheat fields of California. I have been fortunate to have the support and insight of friends and colleagues who helped me tackle the sprawl of aesthetic discourse. Jana Argersinger, Jonathan Auerbach, Tom Augst, Mike Bernard-Donals, Colleen Boggs, Greg Jackson, Susan Gillman, Susan Stanford Friedman, Dana Nelson, Don Pease, Tom Schaub, and Yasemin Yildiz supplied everything a writer needs: key turns of phrase, searching questions, help with translations, lucid readings, leads on sources, and, most of all, encouragement to keep writing. I am grateful to Nellie McKay for taking an interest in my work on W. E. B. Du Bois: like so many in the profession, I will miss her. Since I worry that the tyranny of alphabetization might minimize his contribution, I reserve a separate sentence for David Zimmerman, who graced this project with discernment and friendship. Along the way in writing this book, I had the opportunity to co-edit with Chris Castiglia a special issue of *American Literature* on "Aesthetics and the End(s) of Cultural Studies." Working with Chris sharpened my thinking about the collective horizon of aesthetics. Caroline Levander posed extraordinary questions about this project at an important juncture, helping me to travel to the "antipodes." From day one to the final edits, this project has had the support of Wai Chee Dimock. A model of insight, generosity, and rigor, she's simply the best.

I was also fortunate to deliver portions of this book as talks where audiences energized my thinking with their responses, comments, and questions. In particular, I would like to thank Renée Bergland at Simmons College, Larry Buell and Wai Chee Dimock at the Symposium on American Literary Globalism at Yale University, James Dawes at the Center for Scholarship and Teaching at Macalaster College, Elizabeth Duquette and Stacey Margolis at the Tanner Humanities Center at the University of Utah, Bob Levine at the University of Maryland, College Park, Don Pease at the American Studies Institute at Dartmouth College, Michael Rothberg at the Unit for Criticism and Theory at the University of Illinois, Urbana-Champaign, and Laura Thiemann Scales at the American Literature Colloquium at Harvard University for opportunities to share my work. In every case, these individuals extended so much more than an invitation: they provided intellectual community, critical engagement, and good cheer.

Portions of this book first appeared as articles, and I am grateful to these journals for permitting me to draw on this material here. An early version of chapter 5 appeared as "Geo-Aesthetics: Fascism, Globalism, and Frank Norris," *boundary* 2 30 (Fall 2003): 157–84. Since its initial publication and as the book took shape as a whole, this article has seen extensive reworking. Roughly half of chapter 2 appeared in "American Literary Globalism," a special issue of *ESQ* 50 (2004): 53–93. Newly added material frames this contribution in terms of research on university aesthetics, crowds, and William Dean Howells. Finally, a shorter version of chapter 3 was published in *PMLA* 121 (October 2006) and is reprinted by permission of the copyright owner, The Modern Language Association of America. I am also grateful to the University of Chicago Archives, the Houghton and Pusey Libraries at Harvard University, and the Yale University Divinity School Library for permission to quote from letters, dissertations, lesson plans, and other documents relating to the teaching and research of aesthetics a hundred years ago.

None of this revised material would have made it into its final form here without the steady hand of Alan Thomas. I am fortunate to have the benefit of his counsel and support. Also at the University of Chicago Press, Randy Petilos helped with everything from permissions to illustrations, and Richard Allen made sure that all the details, both large and small, were in order. This book took a decisive turn when students in a graduate seminar on "Aesthetics and American Studies" decided to scrap a few weeks of the syllabus and tackle Kant's *Critique of Judgment*. Since that time, I have benefited from the research support of graduate students at Madison, and I especially want to thank Sebastian Frank and Chris Rogers.

Even as aesthetics lead us to imagine the universal, they also help us to see why the particular is worthy of admiration and wonder. For me, the particular is the long-distance support that I receive from my parents, Mike Castronovo and Frances Abelson Castronovo. Luckily, I find the beauty of the particular also close at hand, around me everyday. It is to this small collective of Leslie, Julian, and Maya that I dedicate this book.

INTRODUCTION

. . . .

Aesthetics and the Anarchy of Global Culture

How does democracy taste? This question neatly encapsulates the political uncertainty that makes aesthetics a problem without neat answers. Such messiness comes from the fact that the question is really two counter-vailing questions, each of which confuses the political with the aesthetic: How does democracy taste to the individual? How do the people, as the subject of democracy, taste? Each rendering runs at cross-purposes to the other by suggesting different levels of engagement, action, and agency. If the issue is how democracy tastes—whether aesthetic sense can shape political judgment—then the citizen seems more or less inert, a subject molded and refined in accord with common standards and forms. If, how-ever, the issue is how the multiple subjects of democracy taste—whether aesthetic perception unifies people or sets them at odds—then agency seems much less calculable, the size and potential heterogeneity of the mass creating a range of possibilities for action and association. Aesthetics reveal the political terrain of democracy as erratic and shifting: when we talk of democratic taste, are we referring to autonomy or collectivity, cool deliberation or sudden affect, universal accord or the swirl of competing beliefs and values?

In the late nineteenth and early twentieth centuries, academics, re-formers, civil rights activists, socialists, literary types, and revolutionaries asked these questions with such frequency that it is hard to believe that they did not imagine some answers. While answers ranged from the prag-matic to the utopian, citizens' engagement with the issue of democratic taste remained centered on prospects of social transformation. On the safe ground of liberal reform, for instance, if classrooms could stimulate and refine students' artistic instincts, political life might gradually become more harmonious, more patterned, more refined, in a word, more beautiful. What if aesthetics could inspire individual ethics? From a more radical perspective, if large swaths of the population came to feel the same way about an object or event, the possibility of sweeping social change would be revealed to be as imminent as human sensation itself. What if everyone felt that a strike against capitalism were a beautiful thing!

As these possibilities for social transformation suggest, democratic taste is a function of space and time. But the exact location of social transformation is hard to pinpoint since aesthetics are at once a matter of individual judgment and collective feeling. Meanwhile, at the level of temporality, the pace of social transformation becomes a pressure point since aesthetics entail both the quick reaction time of emotion and the measured pace of deliberative judgment. This book seeks to map the uneven spatial-temporal coordinates of aesthetics by examining the rise of a broad commentary on sensation, beauty, and mass culture across novels, university research, urban photography, and motion pictures in the United States from 1877 to 1936. During these years of widening class division (the clashes between strikers and Pinkertons) and unabated racial terror (the everyday fact of lynching), crowds, popular spectacles, and other collective emanations made aesthetics a critical, if indeterminate, coordinate in national discourse. Could art and beauty unify the tastes of the nation's citizens if aesthetic feeling, as many suggested, also fed the reactions of anarchists and lynch mobs? This uncertainty was only the tip of the iceberg: the universal accord associated with aesthetics makes the nation-state appear as a puny entity dwarfed by the oceanic currents found in international socialism, Pan-Africanism, and trans-Pacific trade at the turn of the century.

The looseness with which the term *aesthetics* gets thrown around makes my endeavor, what we might think of as a cultural geography of beauty, a tricky one. Alternately described as a specialized discourse about art and as the general processes through which people respond to sensation and form judgments, aesthetics have been notoriously difficult to define. Such elusiveness is prime territory for conflicting agendas, which enlist aesthetics in a progressive program that opens new conceptual horizons and just as often dismiss aesthetics as a tired elitist dodge that preserves class privilege. Conflict comes with the territory in the period of American culture that this book explores, marking aesthetics as a site that not only registers violence but also produces it in the form of urban crime, racial victimization, and widespread economic antagonism. Beauty and the sublime do not exist apart from lynching, militarism, and urban riots. Nor do these conflicts remain confined to U.S. shores. As a discourse wrapped up with the universal, aesthetics fuse violence to specific manifestations of global thinking, whether as internationalism, worldwide community, or Americanization.

By invoking the global as a material and historical horizon, this book reconfigures some of the broad debates that have characterized aesthetics. Ever since Immanuel Kant protested that Alexander Baumgarten's *Aesthetica* (1750–58) had limited its focus to specialized artistic capability, aesthetics have verged on the universal but without ever fully shedding the particularity of physical objects or material reactions. As Raymond Williams explains, this tension creates a "real mediation between (isolated) subjectivity and (abstract) universality." Despite Williams's insistence on an ongoing negotiation between abstraction and materiality, a position echoed by Theodor Adorno's emphasis on the simultaneity of autonomy and social context in artworks, the aesthetic over the last twenty years (at the very least) has been rendered a caricature of its former self.[1] Aesthetics oppose culture, whitewash social conflict, establish the dominion of formalism, dehistoricize representation, subsume all particulars under the hegemony of the universal—the list goes on but an exhaustive indictment would be exhausting. According to postmortems of the culture wars that bemoan the real and supposed maligning of beauty in the 1980s and 1990s, overzealous practitioners of cultural studies are to blame for this witch hunt, an ironic accusation given Williams's status as a godfather of cultural studies.[2] A contrasting irony comes closer to the truth: aesthetics were enlisted, thinned out, and, finally, depleted by its conservative defenders who, in their turn away from ideologies of race, gender, and nationalism, surrendered to their own desire for a formalist paradise sheltered from the tempests of materiality and history. In this defensive aesthetics, the timeless art and beauty hovering above particularities of racism, class inequality, colonialism, or any other concern deemed political and hence ephemeral was a version of the universal that, like the Matterhorns at Disneyland and Disneyworld, seemed reproduced at only 1/64 scale.

A universal aesthetic judgment in which all people would theoretically agree, as its utopian dimension suggests, cannot be built at full scale. But rather than miniaturize this concept, I seek to recontextualize the universal as a global discourse. The global materializes the concept of the universal, converting this philosophical idea into a historical phenomenon. While commentators often gesture to a "global aesthetic experience" or "global decree" legislated by aesthetic judgment, their uses of *global* function more as synonyms for *universal* than as tangible invocations of cosmopolitan politics, world systems, or diasporic populations.[3] In this book, I do not intend *global* as an equivalent to *universal*: instead, I use "global culture" to historically embed the universal horizon of aesthetics both circulating in philosophy and psychology departments of U.S. universities and animating less elevated contexts such as settlement houses, strikes, and murderous spectacle. The global, in short, allows me to set the universal on a cultural relief map dotted by peaks of foreign immigration, international socialism, and overseas trade conducted exclusively on behalf of U.S. cultural and economic interests.

The global does not replace the universal, and yet these two locations remain joined together by associations of wholeness and unity that mean different things to each. Partners in a marriage gone bad, the global and universal continually snipe at one another: complaints about being too totalizing and criticisms about being either overly empirical (or not empirical enough) fly back and forth in this relationship. While witnessing a scene is always uncomfortable, the evident tension between global and universal bespeaks a productive antagonism that adds nuance and depth to conversations about the political import of aesthetics. To discussions about philosophical aesthetics, this book supplies a cultural history of aesthetic formalism, showing how concepts such as "the beautiful" mobilize collective social endeavors from tenement reform to lynching. To readings of U.S. culture, this book offers a theoretical angle that widens the meaning of a national discourse on art and beauty, pinpointing aesthetics as a relay for international solidarity and global exchange. *Beautiful Democracy* combines these aims to show how aesthetics are a case of both more and less: more than an agenda for instilling an individual ethos confluent with national interests but less than a fulfillment of world citizenship.

THE CULTURED FEW

In the context of such high-flying claims, it may be a good idea to begin again at a more modest spot within this conflicted territory. Late in *We and Our Neighbors*, Harriet Beecher Stowe's unremarkable novel of 1875, a British literary man named Mr. Selby drops in at the Thursday evening salon arranged by a young American wife with a knack for "produc[ing] in daily life the sense of the beautiful." In case the muttonchops in the illustration of this scene are not enough to identify Mr. Selby as Matthew Arnold, his severe judgment upon the masses' incapacity to exercise taste are a dead giveaway that this guest represents the author of *Culture and Anarchy* (1869). Selby and his hostess chat amiably about the importance of a society that fosters beauty in everyday life through civic architecture, an idea being realized in the parks and squares of the City Beautiful movement, until their conversation comes to a screeching halt. When Mr. Selby begins, "The reign of the great average masses never can be so agreeable to taste as that of the cultured few," it sounds like the beginning of a longer harangue.[4] At this point Stowe provides a welcome literary fadeout that spares the reader all details of the conversation other than to say that it continued well into the evening.

My book continues that conversation by introducing a range of voices that counterbalance Selby's diatribe. The unreported dialogue between the hostess and this thinly disguised version of Arnold was one that occurred across a range of cultural institutions from colleges to moving picture shows, in different forms from philosophic treatises to political protests, and against a variety of backdrops from drawing rooms to labor strikes for decades to come. The tone was frequently academic but just as often discussions of aesthetics became raucous, animated by terror and violence. Never was beauty the sole topic; instead, the conversation about beauty invited the divisiveness of international class conflict, lynching, anarchism, and globalization. Owners against workers, whites against blacks, wild-eyed socialists against mild-mannered liberals, West against East: these antagonisms erupted from a discourse that, theoretically, was supposed to provide a basis for social cohesion.

Beautiful Democracy does more than resume the interrupted conversation in Stowe's novel; it seeks to explain why that interruption occurred. One reason has already been suggested. The violence that characterized late-nineteenth-century and early-twentieth-century U.S. culture, both at home and abroad, strained the credibility of a discourse that linked aesthetic unity to civic stability. If violence is the repressed content of this Arnoldian sermon, form is the other issue that derails the discourse about beauty. By form, I mean the aesthetic components that encase expression, making a thing recognizably "artistic" or "beautiful" because it bears familiar relation to the properties of other artifacts. Form has long been the centerpiece of aesthetic theory where, as Friedrich Schiller summed up the Kantian project in a footnote, "everything depends on freeing form from content."[5] But when aesthetic form shapes political possibility, violence appears at the edges of the discourse on beauty. Thus bound up with Mr. Selby's opening salvo is the portentous assumption that taste and other aesthetic matters provide a sure pattern for modeling the proper exercise of authority, rule, and power. His mention of "the cultured few," who presumably are to keep the "masses" in line, only scratches the surface of the antagonisms that striate aesthetics in the late nineteenth century. It is rather what Selby and the others who follow in the pages of this book take for granted that proves so troublesome: namely, the belief that aesthetic formalism can somehow express, enhance, or stimulate political judgment and collective action.

Good reason exists for this belief and its attendant optimism. Although the aestheticization of politics has incurred a fair amount of concern and contempt, especially in the responses of twentieth-century cultural criticism to fascism, "the beautiful" has just as often been extolled in democratic theory for inspiring civic feeling, educating citizens, and organizing political attachments into coherent form. With its ability to harmonize the heterogeneous interests of "the people," the polis merits description as "an aesthetic masterpiece" that every citizen, not just the custodians of taste, can appreciate.[6] For Hannah Arendt, the collectivist nature of aesthetics challenges an Arnoldian sense of culture that values art for what turn out to be narrow, self-serving ends of mere ornamentation or fussy individualism. "Sweetness and light," that memorable phrase from *Culture and Anarchy,* which, in effect, presents taste as a matter of personal enlightenment in opposition to external chaos, appears to Arendt as a "veil" that obscures true and honest perceptions of political reality. Aesthetics, by contrast, fulfill a political function by emancipating individuals from the solitude of private judgment to consider the perspective of others. Such disinterest should not be confused with the crusty reserve of "the cultured few" or the weary appreciation of the dandy: it is instead an aesthetic capacity that allows one to bracket private opinion and see the world in the multiple ways that others might. Taste acts as a public faculty that renders the subject political by overcoming the tapered limits of the self and positioning her amid other citizens who also see the world but, as is often the case, see it differently. As Arendt defines it, "taste is the political capacity that truly humanizes the beautiful and creates a culture."[7]

Although Arendt does not come right out and say it, the implication is that democracy tastes good. The good, of course, is not the sweetness of personal satisfaction but deeper awareness of a wider public realm shared with others. As in so much of Arendt's work, Athenian democracy enjoys a prominent place in her deliberations. Writing at a time when challenges to democracy—fascism, totalitarianism, anticommunist demonology, racial segregation, authoritarianism—were lined up one after another, the political theorist Arendt turned to aesthetics in order to shore up the ethical foundations of democratic thought. Aesthetics takes on the mission of political preservation, connecting democracy to its ancient moorings so that public freedoms are not set adrift on the wreckage of modernity.

Tradition and continuance, however, can overshadow an important aspect of aesthetic portraits of democracy: the creative, transformative potential that molds, reshapes, or defamiliarizes the world. Along these lines, theorists have called for a style of political representation that borrows from aesthetic representation, taking its cues, for instance, from Watteau or Cezanne and seeing people and their surroundings in new lights and from different angles. Aesthetic representation need not be held apart from political representation for, as F. K. Ankersmit argues, "political insight is not part of the realm of facts or of values, but of aesthetics."[8] W. E. B. Du Bois, as we will see in chapter 3, also invoked painters—Picasso and Matisse—as an experiment in perspective that would rewrite the political DNA of citizens. In her attempts to refashion the modern city after the classical city-state, Jane Addams grounded a radical political charge in aesthetic forms from poetry to film that represent—and, perhaps more importantly, misrepresent—social reality. Once the flavor of these entertainments is tasted, people can stage "moments of revolt against life's actualities" and search for a "possible avenue of escape" from narrow pathways of everyday existence.[9] Addams's influence, part of the larger inheritance of American pragmatism, still resonates with assessments that detect emancipatory potential in aesthetic perspectives that shift, unsettle, or otherwise change how people in common think about social and political conditions.[10] As much as aesthetic discourse orients political and social forms with respect to tradition, it also opens the door to transformation. When theorists compare politics to painting, when social reformers link democratic renewal to senses quickened by poetry or film, and when activists see in art the possibility of social transformation, the initial act of understanding the hurly-burly world of politics with reference to form constitutes a political act par excellence. Whether the conjunction proceeds by analogy or association, whether it is a convenient metaphor or a careful study in perspective, the expression of democracy in aesthetic terms introduces fundamental changes in the genetic makeup of politics. This expression alters how people perceive their polity even as it impacts how states view their citizens; it establishes criteria for legitimate action even as it encourages collective feelings that run toward insurgency. Both a tool for crafting hegemony and an instrument of change, aesthetics allow us to redraw an otherwise flat representation of democracy as a bumpy cultural topography that shows political and social life with new detail and unexpected features.

Awareness of this awesome potential can put the brakes on the optimism that people have for aesthetics. When politics are wedged into aesthetic forms, concern arises that complexity and historicity are sacrificed to the abstract dictates of seemingly timeless patterns. These worries surface prominently in the work of the Frankfurt school. After a bit of cautious optimism about the democratizing possibilities of mass art, theorists such as Walter Benjamin and Theodor Adorno were convinced by the Nazi rise to power that aesthetic technologies can be used not merely to falsify popular will but to whip it into a frenzy.[11] Benjamin detects this threat when he describes how fascism converts political violence into artistic expression. He confronts readers with the appreciation that the fascist has for war: "War is beautiful because it enriches a flowering meadow with the fiery orchids of machine guns."[12] The day after September 11, 2001 an unfortunate echo of this position was heard in the pronouncement by a European composer that the terrorist attacks on the World Trade Center and the Pentagon were "the greatest work of art ever."[13] These outrageous metaphors aestheticize violence, making destruction a point of pleasure. What happens to the content of violence—the persons killed and the bodies maimed—when its overall form is seen as a manifestation of beauty or art?

Nagging doubts about aesthetics as political misrepresentation, as enforced harmony, or as false consciousness are hard to shake.[14] It becomes necessary to revise my previous maxim: if democracy tastes good, it just as often leaves a bitter aftertaste.

AESTHETICS 101

When I started working on a book about beauty, art, and aesthetics, I was at first surprised to see how often I was also writing about violence. My research initially seemed the stuff of sober, if not dry, investigation as I began reading turn-of-the-century doctoral dissertations in philosophy and psychology to find out how U.S. intellectuals and educators sought to deduce a democratic ethos from citizens' encounters with art and beauty. Then I discovered a looser, irregular but in many ways parallel discourse about aesthetics far from the cloistered halls of academia. City streets, parks, theaters, and public spectacles in town centers provided vibrant and often contested spaces for citizens to explore connections between aesthetics and politics. And when Pinkerton detectives, the state militia, or a lynch mob closed down on these spaces, those connections became lethal. While university researchers hypothesized beauty's effects on subjects, urban reformers and social activists asked if flowers, slideshows of art's masterpieces, and "high-class moving pictures" could encourage people to act as agents in command of their own ethical destinies.[15] But for every such agent engendered by aesthetic discourse, there also seemed to be a victim: the lynched man or woman, the striker with a busted head, the prostitute ensnared by finery.

This violence splits my archive down the center. Under the rubric of "Aesthetics 101," I examine theories of aesthetics that were institutionalized in universities starting in the 1890s. Poised against this august body of learning is what the next section, borrowing a phrase from Tom Paine, calls "the popular rage." In contrast to professional and pedagogical material, mobs, strikes, and other public spectacles outline a stubbornly empirical terrain that resists the abstractions of academia. This tension between university research and popular manifestations such as magic lantern shows and other crowded venues is reproduced in the competing sets of primary material that are integral to this book. Academic studies that approached aesthetics with an eye toward producing order and systematization were shadowed by popular encounters with art and sensation whose effects were anything but neat and predictable. In my research, democracy comes together with beauty to produce a series of unstable referents. On the one hand, my archive seems a model of decorum and professional rigor with its philosophical treatises, university extension courses, and public lectures. On the other, the police billy clubs, signs of strong-arm robbery, and anarchist pipe bombs that kept intruding on audiences and crowds seem an inventory of riot and confusion. Taken together, these dissonant texts and artifacts throw the Arnoldian project into disarray. Does the "and" of *Culture and Anarchy* maintain a respectable space between the terms of the title or does it work to conjoin the two so that "culture" somehow triggers "anarchy"?

I begin with the half of my archive that falls squarely and securely within the domain of culture. Even as U.S. academics hoped that beauty would unify democratic culture, they just as often fretted that aesthetics promoted unpredictable activity, disorganization, and excess political affect. In her 1904 doctoral thesis, Elizabeth Kemper Adams argued against theories that correlated art with passive absorption and instead sought to prove that aesthetic experience resulted in action and innovation. "A fixed and unchangeable aesthetic attitude is a contradiction in terms and an anomaly in experience," her dissertation contends. This conclusion makes for certain problems, as our reading of sonnets, interest in drama, and attendance at symphonies can stimulate intense responses that cry out for regulation and control. The ancient Greeks knew the difference between an art that "uplifts" as opposed to one that "excites"—and the implicit question for Adams is whether citizens of modern democracy can exercise such judgment. While she asserts that "aesthetic experience" imbues citizens with "increased vigor" and the daring to break from old usages, she wants to ensure that this potential does not run riot.[16] She solves this problem by theorizing that ruptures caused by aesthetic experience necessarily feed the recognition that wider controls are in order. The energy released by aesthetic experience is properly rerouted into stable organization. Her post as educational secretary of the Girl Scouts (she also was Professor of Education at Smith College), it may be assumed, gave her opportunity to put her theories about organization and equilibrium to the test.

Political and social concerns intrude on scholarly treatments of aesthetics. Consider "Plato's Aesthetics," a 1915 master's thesis written by Phyllis Ackerman, a University of California, Berkeley graduate student who later became a pioneering figure in the study of tapestries and Middle Eastern art. Although much of Ackerman's thesis concerns the abstract nature of the Ideal, she also sets herself the task of understanding the reasons behind Plato's insistence that ethical considerations trump aesthetic ones. Part of the answer is historical: only by placing Plato's thoughts about beauty in the sociopolitical context of antiquity can we appreciate his "amusingly naïve . . . commendation or condemnation of art on moral grounds." But this contextualization sounds rather like a description of Ackerman's own impressions of U.S. culture beset by democratic distraction:

> Mob rule was the order of the day. That was produced which pleased
> the multitude. Any thrill was desirable, the more intense the more ac-

ceptable. The cheap spectacular excitement was morally degenerating, too appealing to the already too excitable nation.[17]

The presentist tone of her explanation postdates the threat that aesthetics pose to civilization. Instead of standing as a bulwark against "mob rule," culture incites the people, making them into a "multitude" that clamors for instant gratification and finds it in degrading forms of art and entertainment. Along with Adams's doctoral dissertation on *The Aesthetic Experience,* Ackerman's thesis registered a small but growing suspicion within U.S. academic philosophy and psychology that aesthetics, far from assuaging the mass, stirs citizens into a fever pitch. These misgivings fuel even greater doubts: is an "already too excitable nation" the antithesis of democracy—or its most complete realization? In light of such unanswered questions, the relative position of anarchy to culture lacks the surety of Arnoldian wisdom.

The work of Adams and Ackerman represents but a slice of the archive that *Beautiful Democracy* assembles. Housed in special collections at the University of Chicago and the University of California, Berkeley, their typewritten manuscripts are indeed representative of the research and pedagogical materials that I studied in order to understand how aesthetic discourse circulated in both professional and popular cultures. By examining course syllabi, outlines for university extension courses, doctoral dissertations, and textbooks in philosophy, art, rhetoric, and literature, I argue that aesthetics became institutionalized as an academic subject charged with the mission of creating and maintaining a democratic culture. Adams and Ackerman are also representative of the women at the forefront of this mission, some of them, like Kate Gordon and Ethel Dench Puffer, working in university settings and others, like Jane Addams and Jessie Redmon Fauset, taking part in wider circles of reform and civil rights. Research and writing on aesthetics by women recalls—and reworks—more pervasive associations of beauty and effeminacy. Investigation into beauty's social use served at times as an indirect inquiry into what women, feminized men, and feminized artifacts like flowers could do to enact political change. As might be imagined, hardscrabble notions of politics often belittled gendered social action. Literary salons met with contempt in the world of Frank Norris (see chapter 5), just as categories of "the literary" and "the beautiful" emasculated subjects in fiction by Fauset and Walter White (see chapter 3) dealing with white sexual paranoia and lynching. But in an era of labor strikes and racial violence, realpolitik could be graphic and combative, in other words, too real. Crusades to disarm threats of urban lawlessness by introducing natural beauty in the form of flowers and parks and by institutionalizing cultural refinement in the form of museums and art galleries turned on the belief that feminine influences could domesticate even the coarsest anarchist. This possibility, according to Adams's *Aesthetic Experience*, goes all the way back to early hunting societies where "woman was probably, to a large extent, the primitive artist."[18]

But at a time when the professional study of aesthetics had aspirations of becoming a "science," when beauty's effects were classed as both psychological and physiological, male researchers in the field generally compiled longer curriculum vitae and achieved the most prestigious university posts. By looking at hundred-year-old lecture notes, proceedings from scholarly conferences, textbooks on the philosophy of art and aesthetics, study questions, student paper topics, even unauthorized outlines intended for students who did not go to class, I demonstrate how aesthetics functioned as a civic pedagogy designed to remake individuals into disinterested, dispassionate citizens with an eye for social order and equilibrium. Stored in archives at the University of California, the University of Chicago, Harvard University, the University of Wisconsin–Madison, and Yale University, this archive I call "Aesthetics 101," both to identify recurring concerns that crop up in this diverse material and to suggest its introductory and instructive nature in training students to appreciate the American state as a work of art. By and large this body of work did not present aesthetic experience as inherently unstable or as besieged by social unrest, as Adams and Ackerman did. Instead, the task was to systematize beauty, adducing formal principles and timeless properties that governed human sensation. Divided into disquisitions on harmony, symmetry, proportion, balance, unity, simplicity, and purity of form, these materials presented aesthetics as a coherent field whose effects upon human subjects could be predicted.

Predictably enough, then, most university research and instruction did not present aesthetic experience as a likely zone of social irruption or political transformation but rather as a coherent arena for creating a citizenry ruled by its own internal adherence to form. Even where divisions did exist, aesthetic experience brought about ultimate continuity and order. In a dense contribution to *The Psychological Review* of 1908, John Hopkins University Professor William Davis Furry began by noting a fundamental rift between metaphysics and epistemology and solved the problem

150 pages later by concluding that "the aesthetic experience" bridges this gap by removing the tension between "dynamic satisfactions" and "static meaning" via an overarching act of "world-completion" that reconciles all tension. "The aesthetic," he proclaims in global terms, "has functioned always as the organ of world unification and completion."[19] Just as turgid are scientifically slanted studies that brought human subjects to the psychology laboratory at Harvard or Princeton to determine which shapes, types of geometric symmetry, and variations of color produce aesthetic pleasure. Often, though, the method of such science proved more deductive than inductive, as the results confirm Kantian tenets about universality, Platonic conceptions about the good as the highest aesthetic value, or other accepted premises. Aesthetic theory pursued broad statements about human psychology that transcended specific content. All that would be left was form. "The beautiful," as a contemporary survey of academic philosophy put it, constitutes "that portion of aesthetic value which depends solely on form."[20] Through involved psychological experiments, aesthetic theory repeatedly turned to form not just to categorize the fruit of its labors but also to regularize emotions, stimuli, and reactions churned up by beauty.

Fortunately, a sizable portion of this archive was published as textbooks for college juniors and seniors, study guides for teachers, and university extension courses. With study questions frequently tacked on at the end, these pamphlets, books, and multivolume sets activate the social and political dimensions of aesthetic discourse by appealing to and instructing ever-widening publics: underclassmen, inhabitants of rural townships, city dwellers. Remembering his years teaching aesthetics at Yale University, Henry Davies complained that the student body, instead of learning the political virtue of aesthetic disinterest, merely displayed a lack of interest in the subject. Yale students saw Aesthetics 101 as a "snap," with courses on "art and beauty . . . generally regarded as easy . . . requiring little work but gathering high marks in the examinations." This instructor was miffed that a student in his course confessed "he had never heard of the words 'aesthetics' during [the] course, and that he not the slightest idea what it meant!"[21] Rather than blame the student, Davies saw this failure as part of a pervasive trend in a modern democracy that obsessed on economic questions at the expense of aesthetic ones. From this perspective, the real loser in the end was the nation whose citizenry lacked the training in judgment to guide political decision-making.

When it came to aesthetics, the ivory tower had a verifiable interest in reaching out to the rural farm or the city street on two related fronts, the cultivation of ethical demeanor in individual citizens and the creation of universal accord. This sense of public mission underscores the potentially democratic aspect of beauty in the U.S., as political questions about the relationship between "the people" and the nation-state were referred to aesthetic criteria. If everyone shared an "art-instinct," a psychophysiological mechanism thought to be operative in all human beings, then, beauty might cement the ground for national unity. But since that instinct was a matter of general human existence, aesthetics also implied a universalism that outstripped the nation as a provincial form. In a syllabus for an extension course run through the University of Michigan, Fred N. Scott's *Aesthetics* (1890) supplies weekly study questions and final essay topics that invite citizens—remember, this course plan for "The Interpretation of Art" was intended for a much wider audience than regularly enrolled students at Ann Arbor—to contemplate interconnections between art, individual governance, and U.S. nationalism. At the end of the first week, students should be prepared to discuss the ethical benefit that works of art bestow upon viewers. In week six, Renaissance art becomes the subject, as students are asked to respond to the question, "Of what value are the frescoes in the Sistine chapel to modern citizens of the United States?" Here, world art seems destined to follow the more narrow criteria of U.S. nationalism. These inquiries prepare broad areas of investigation set for the course as a whole. Students might tackle "the political 'machine' as a work of art." Or in a related query, they might explore the role of "the art-instinct . . . in municipal or state politics." In a gesture to the City Beautiful movement, other students were encouraged to assess the "ethical effect of the average aesthetic environment in American cities." Topic #2 seems the most open and daunting, asking students to evaluate the "aesthetic environment of the American citizen." Many of these topics advise that research was to be conducted "from personal observation," right away making the student-citizen a participant in the discourse of beauty as it touched upon political life.[22] No longer the preserve of the cultured few, aesthetics were constructed as innately popular, a subject that any beginner with a little training could master.

The effect was assumed to be reciprocal. Aesthetics, as such instruction stated either implicitly or explicitly, should master the citizen by encouraging social and political behavior guided by order, unity, and symmetry. By seeking satisfaction in formal properties that encase affect and action, the citizen as aesthetic subject internally adjusts him- or herself to criteria that, as luck would have it, are also the hallmark of state-sponsored liberalism.[23] Punishment has no place in an aesthetic state, just as violence loses its attraction in a society where "sweetness and light" rule the day. As different sections of this book illustrate, this gentle program is what makes democracy beautiful: petty thieves intuit ethical standards from encounters with well-proportioned artworks; anarchists have no desire to dynamite cities that have become beautiful; disaffected populists come to appreciate the wonders of trans-Pacific trade by thinking about the totality of form, misconstruing the universal as globalization.

The search for the universal and its relation to a national civic ethos led me to the basement of the Yale University Divinity School Library. In the handwritten notebooks of Henry Davies, first a philosophy student and then a lecturer in aesthetics, nationalism seems awkwardly wedged into aesthetic theory. In his undergraduate days, the nation does not make an appearance, as his notes for "Introduction to Philosophy" for the spring term of 1894 record general relationships between ethics (what we "ought to do") and aesthetics (what "ought to be").[24] Seven years later as an instructor for "Philosophical Aesthetics," Davies imparts these same lessons to the next generation of students, lecturing on Kant to describe how "ethical considerations enter into judgments of the beautiful."[25] In a notebook from the same time, he begins to politicize these thoughts, proposing that art plays a crucial role in the cultivation of national life. Alluding to urban reformers such as Jacob Riis (see chapter 1), Davies writes that "a positive contribution to social well being has been made when the street has been beautified."[26] But these statements give him trouble, as Davies wonders about the political geography of beauty: is the public mission of art wholly encompassed by the U.S., or does it reach out toward a universal horizon that extends beyond the nation? While Davies unequivocally concludes that "so, finally, art cannot be satisfied with merely national development," it is not clear whether he conveyed this global import to his classes.[27] This aesthetic challenge to nationalism appears in a notebook that is distinct from his lecture notes, filled more with thought experiments than the orderly presentation of lesson plans and course outlines. What are the coordinates of beauty: the few students taking a class on aesthetics (five out of an original twelve students dropped Davies's 1901 course on "Philosophical Aesthetics"), groups of people traversing a beautified street, or the mass of humankind?

Uncertainty over the scale of beauty becomes visible in what aesthetic research did not study and what aesthetic textbooks did not say. Test subjects were regularly examined in psychology laboratories at Harvard or the University of Chicago in order to determine how, for instance, the muscles of the eye relaxed in situations of visual pleasure. But I seldom came across experiments that studied how groups of people responded collectively to such stimuli. Third and fourth-year college students learned how beauty awakened the individual to the ethical importance of balance and symmetry in social relations. But it seems that they did not read about how bunches of subjects, crowds, and masses were spurred on by aesthetic experiences. While the generic aspect of the "individual" appeals to humanity's broad outlines, the persistent singularity of the term works against notions of the aesthetic subject as varied, multiple, or plural. In the political geography of beauty, between the poles of the individual and the human species as a whole stands a highly contested middle ground populated by crowds and other popular associations. Consider the potentially insurgent meanings that creep into Professor Furry's journal article if its context is not the singular subject. Furry writes: "The pleasure of the beautiful is emotional and hence immediate. The secret of aesthetic construction is, that in it, the mind constructs its own objects without purpose and under its own immediate control."[28] When "mind" is dispersed, who exactly has control? Does the philosophical sense of "immediate," implying something that is intuited from within, slide dangerously toward a more popular usage that indicates action undertaken without delay? Unlike the individual studied in the psychology laboratories, this collective subject seemed susceptible to unpredictable feelings.

Proportion, balance, and, above all, form were instrumental in molding a heterogeneous mass into a collectivity unified by similar tastes. The danger, however, was that aesthetic experience could unite and organize anarchists, workers, and the dispossessed just as readily as it could lead to individual moral elevation. In contrast to the Kantian category of *sensus communis,* which implies not just common sense but "community sense," as Arendt reminds us, this era of labor strikes, lynching, and anarchist threats saw the emergence of what might be called *sensus conflictionis,* a sense of clashing judgments produced by class antagonism, racial terror, and political discord.[29] Kant had tried to guard against this possibility by shearing "aesthetical judgment" from "the culture of taste." For the philosopher who also wrote *Perpetual Peace,* the intent was not to make aesthetics an abstract disembodied realm, as many of Kant's critics have charged, but to make judgment a bloodless affair. The distinction Kant draws between "the faculty of taste" and "the culture of taste" is crucial in this regard.[30] While the first refers to a biological sensitivity that all human beings share, the latter opens a dangerous can of culturally variable conditions and subjective determinations. Because culture can never be a completely unified or universal terrain, it always threatens to introduce divisiveness into aesthetic judgment. The very agenda that Arnold as well as his U.S. compeers pushed in their different appeals to culture, if it did not sow the seeds of anarchy, at the least provided fertile ground for conflict. The collapse of aesthetics and politics introduced uncertain, treacherous content where there should have been surety of form: what sort of democracy—one governed by shared sensibility or one ruled by the shifting, undisciplined feelings of the mob—does beauty engender?

Such uncertainty led academics and cultural critics to express second thoughts about prospects for a beautiful democracy. As soon as culture becomes widely accessible and diffused, it has the potential to turn anarchic. Aesthetics, that preserve of upper-class refinement and internal discipline, may also provide the gateway to violence. The common hope among academic theorists and social activists was that aesthetics might supply the key to the democratization of culture. Their common fear was that the "science of beauty" taught in university classrooms and extension courses might fuel "immediate" struggles in the streets. To defuse the popular sense of immediacy, turn-of-the-century academics stressed the importance of form as did more practically minded proponents of taste and culture who advocated parks with clear borders, public squares with symmetrical dimensions, and cultural performances that held audiences captive in their seats. In a logic that hearkens back to Schiller, form ensured that emotions tapped by encounters with beauty did not run rampant but instead flowed into well-grooved channels cut by centuries of taste and tradition. The New Critics would accentuate this line of reasoning, as John Crowe Ransom did by explaining that when we are tempted to "lay hands on the object immediately," the "form of art" intervenes to cool our passion so that we can approach the object in a "state of innocence" and "know it for its own sake."[31] In this reading, form takes anything that is immediate—stimulus, feeling, action—and mediates it. Providing a buffer to direct action, form guides us into capacious, enduring patterns, and anything that fails to fit these theoretically universal categories is deemed illegitimate, excessive, impure, in a word, deformed.

In setting a political terrain, form appears as a mechanism that blocks uncontrolled affect, unmediated action, and other manifestations of direct democracy. It is hard to argue, though, with Elaine Scarry's graceful proposition that citizens who appreciate balance and proportion in beauty also develop a strong taste for fairness and justice.[32] But within the historical specifics of "Aesthetics 101," the professional study of form and formalism animates undecidability with respect to political action—is it to be welcomed or feared? As an assortment of college textbooks, extension courses, curricula, and research, this discourse sought to shape people into citizens who would act in accordance with established forms. At the same time, ideas about "physiological aesthetics" and the "psychology of beauty" pointed to instinctual responses and creative principles through which groups of people might shape political interaction. This fundamental incongruity expressed itself across a wider set of cultural materials than academic papers and courses, leading to the other half of my archive.

THE POPULAR RAGE

This other archive cannot be neatly summed up as though it were a college course or unified philosophical endeavor. It consists of a broad commentary on sensation, art, and mass culture across novels, urban photography, and motion pictures. As this archive spills out across the fin-de-siècle landscape to include opera houses as well as five-cent theaters, public art lectures as well as spectacle lynchings, in short, examples of "sweetness and light" as well as acts of violence, definitions of aesthetics became porous, rooted less in the domain of form and more in the shifting register of emotions, instinct, and mass feeling. Never confined to merely national subjects, these potentially universal reactions tested the borders of state identity. In theorizing art and beauty, the work of university researchers converged with the practical efforts of reformers such as Riis, Du Bois, and Addams who variously tied democratic progress to the extension of beauty to society's most powerless and victimized citizens. This experiment was undertaken in the public squares of New York's lower East Side, the common rooms of Chicago's settlement houses, and the pages of NAACP's *The Crisis,* as reformers sought to introduce the experience of beauty to wider populations. Could the "science of beauty" that was being theorized in college classrooms be activated in the streets?

Aesthetic discourse in the late-nineteenth and early-twentieth-century U.S. was always interdisciplinary and cross-institutional. Only recently has it been narrowed to connoisseurship and techniques associated with high art. Beyond academia, civic organizations, charitable institutions, and working-class associations discussed and debated uses of beauty in the public sphere. Imagine the leveling possibilities in a society where access to culture has been democratized, as did the author of "Art for the People": "Come, aristocracy; come, democracy! A first *rendezvous* at the evening museum!"[33] Academic research in our own moment is often cast in opposition to public discourse, but my examination of aesthetics suggests such a rift is a relatively recent phenomenon. When it came to theorizing notions of beauty, intellectuals found themselves engaged by the same public gardens, art galleries, museums, and nickelodeons that drew the attention of crowds. In its focus on coincident—and competing—uses of beauty among academics and social activists, this book bridges the university and emergent mass culture. Never confined to a single discipline or institutional location, aesthetics bespeak the potentially public accents of academic discourse while stressing the importance of formalist categories to everyday cultural expressions. Looking at aesthetic theory and practice from a century ago, *Beautiful Democracy* keeps an eye on the future by examining the lost overlaps that connect cultural studies, humanities research, and civic discourse. These connections are neither smooth nor level. Philosophy does not mesh readily with public spectacle; controlled experiments into individual psychology jar with the raucous nature of crowds; professional research into perception is often removed from what people outside university settings considered beautiful. This uneven but integrated landscape accounts for the split in my archive between "Aesthetics 101" and popular spectacles such as magic lantern shows, nickelodeons, and slum photography.

This schism is likely exaggerated since theorists of aesthetics devoted their professional hours to the same cultural forms to which "the people" gave their leisure time. Moving pictures, for instance, were heralded as a "democratic art" both by academics and by the popular press, though, of course, the definition of democracy in this context was up for grabs with representatives of elite institutions tending to focus on the single spectator in contrast to lay commentators, who, with a mixture of enthusiasm and repulsion, took stock of immigrant audiences that crowded the theaters. In *The Art of the Moving Picture* (1915), Vachel Lindsay made the most of this tension by ridiculing doctoral students who "work for the high degrees in the universities" all so that they can produce "a piece of literary conspiracy called a thesis which no one outside the university hears of again." In contrast to "this research work that is dead to the democracy," he urged scholarship to take the form of a "motion picture transcript" so that it "would have a chance to live and grip the people."[34] This popular project, Lindsay claimed, would be university extension in the truest sense. While university men and women brought their formal training in aesthetics to bear upon everyday cultural forms, the university itself had its understanding of aesthetics warped by shows and spectacles of the day. To cite a disconcerting example, cultural critics at times posited that lynching constituted an aesthetic experience for the perpetrators of racist violence. After an Illinois lynching, Harvard professor William James sent the Springfield *Republican* a letter that explained white vigilante "justice" against blacks as a matter of entertainment and spectator pleasure: "The illiterate whites everywhere, always fretting in their monotonous lives for some more drastic excitement, are feeding their imaginations" with lynching.[35] The connections between aesthetics and lynching are the subject of chapter 3. For the moment, though, it is worthwhile to remark that white violence forces James to reconsider criteria of universal taste.

Against this perversion of the imagination, there remained an abiding faith that aesthetics came hardwired with ethical lessons. Tenement novels, documentary photographs, and reports from charities such as the New York City Flower Mission do more than detail squalor: they also speak to the belief that beauty could turn the urban herd into disciplined citizens. In *Essays Aesthetical* (1875), George Calvert called for a city of parks, flowers, fountains, and other incarnations of "ever-present beauty" that would work "to refine, to expand, to elevate" the perspective and taste of "the masses."[36] For Calvert, the mayor of Newport, Rhode Island, this order might not have seemed as tall as it did for Addams or Riis as they looked out on the crowded thoroughfares and back alleys of Chicago and New York. Urban reformers observed that magic lantern shows created unruly crowds, flowers bedecked prostitutes, and nickelodeons encouraged larceny. Creating law-abiding citizens as well as lawbreakers, aesthetics suggest a field of transformation not confined to the campus quad or museum gallery. Overflowing the domain of the cultured few, the potential commonality of taste was always an implicit threat to ideas of culture (and reactions to it) as a members-only club barring entrance to blacks, workers, and revolutionaries.

Years before the heyday of "Aesthetics 101" and the explosion of popular entertainments and activities that are the other half of my archive, Professor James C. Moffat of the College of New Jersey had grumbled, "The term *Aesthetic* is not indeed perfectly satisfactory, but we have no better." He consoled himself with the thought that, whatever its imprecision, "aesthetics" is "a word yet unperverted by the popular tongue, and so completely in the hands of science."[37] Rather than restrict the study of aesthetics to artworks that had received the imprimatur of the ages, subsequent researchers aligned aesthetics with the endeavor of understanding human subjectivity as a set of universal phenomena. This broader agenda explains why psychology and physiology got into the act of determining aesthetic judgment for the human species as a whole. In this more expansive usage, aesthetics intend the entire "corporeal sensorium," to borrow a phrase from Susan Buck-Morss, including affect and emotion, pain and pleasure, feeling and sensibility.[38] Never merely a discourse about art, this widened sense of aesthetics comes into play in chapter 2's discussion of *aisthētēs* and the language of everyday cultural transformation. But for now I want to mark how this appeal to human reactions and responses suggests the potential force of commonality as a universal feeling that collides with and energizes political positions.

A shorthand sketch of this collision can be found in translating Kant's notion of *sensus communis,* that is, the common standard of aesthetic judgment in which individual perception tallies with general taste, as Tom Paine's revolutionary invocation of "common sense." By representing the struggle for American independence as "the cause of all mankind," Paine's 1776 pamphlet anticipates in extremist fashion the universal accord outlined by Kant's third *Critique* of 1790. *Common Sense,* we might say, radicalizes the aesthetic sensibility of *sensus communis* before the fact by converting it into a political sentiment. Just as the subject in Kant's account feels pressured to adhere to the presumed taste of everyone else, Paine's revolutionary citizen better take sides with the presumably collective decision for independence or suffer the consequences. It is thus no accident that Paine concludes with a threat, invoking the odds-on probability of "popular rage" to bully Tory sympathizers into agreement.[39] As the lines between *sensus communis,* common sense, and mob rule blur, the enlargement of aesthetics from a specialized commentary on art into a full-blown demonstration of mass feeling seems more than ever a prescription for violence.

ARTWORK ESSAYS AT THE ANTIPODES

The earliest chronological point for this study is 1877, dubbed the "year of violence," when a coast-to-coast strike paralyzed the country, breeding fears that U.S. culture lacked sufficient "sweetness and light" to withstand the crest of anarchy riding the waves of labor radicalism, immigration, and crowd politics. The Great Strike and the anxious commentary it inspired in the periodical press and serialized fiction intensified these doubts, suggesting that culture does not stave off anarchy but incites it. The year 1877 stands as a watershed moment of historical crisis when the image of crowds, the mob, "the people," the mass—contemporary observers had their pick of loaded terms—challenges ideas of the American world as a place of order and unity. At its outermost chronological limit, *Beautiful Democracy* reaches forward to 1936 and two very different commentaries on mass culture produced that year, Benjamin's "The Work of Art in the Age of Mechanical Reproduction" and Charlie Chaplin's *Modern Times,* to examine the catastrophic impact that crowd feeling, global spectatorship, and other facets of democratized aesthetics had upon political forms and possibilities. The thorny matter of aesthetic politics has remained a critical concern since Benjamin warned how aesthetics could distort democratic potential into the nightmare of fascism, but it is an issue that wells up earlier in textbooks, dissertations, and other odds and ends rescued from the dustbin of academia. Benjamin's presence in this book about late-nineteenth and early-twentieth-century U.S. democracy is neither an anachronism nor a dislocation: his focus on the convergence between aesthetics and politics suggests the necessity of historicizing aesthetics as a culturally broad discourse that cannot be separated from episodes of violence.

As conceptual brackets, then, 1877 and 1936 provide this project with a critical span to account for persistent tensions between the anarchic tendencies of fin-de-siècle democracy and the stable order that academics, activists, and reformers tried to wring out of "the beautiful." Located in this range are a series of "artwork essays" that experiment with political aesthetics. While the category of artwork essay is usually reserved for Benjamin's thesis on mechanical reproduction, I turn to university instructional material, the black press, the realist novel, and the motion picture to contend that citizens produced sustained reflections on the transformative possibilities of aesthetic experience. These American artwork essays take different forms, some immediately identifiable by their stand-alone quality as manifestoes, others so scattered and episodic that they become recognizable only by the hand (mine) of the archivist. What's more, these essays differ with respect to their positions on democracy and "the beautiful." Some have a proto-fascist hue while others adopt an avant-garde sensibility to push a perspective that departs from standard criteria of representation. The artwork essays I have gathered include studies of aesthetics by university philosophers and psychologists, William Dean Howells's treatment of mass art, Du Bois's writings on beauty and death, Norris's meditations on the global future of the American novel, and Chaplin's cinematic thesis on the mechanics of universal language. Part of the same cultural continuum, these documents collectively reveal how the capacity for judgment, the stimulation of collective affect, the power to transform matter, in short, all the central operations of aesthetic discourse, were politicized by citizens dedicated to preserving a purportedly unified U.S. social world as well as by those intent on changing that world.

My collection of artwork essays supplies a scaffolding but not one that adheres to regularities of chronology that might be implied by "1877–1936." The chapter on the strike of 1877 comes after chapter 1's treatment of later turn-of-the-century materials that attempted to theorize a "science of beauty" with broad application. Likewise, chapter 4's analysis of silent film's potential to visualize a worldwide *sensus communis* is followed by an examination of chronologically prior writings about the tandem encroachment by U.S. literary and economic interests along the Pacific Rim.

This uneven temporality directs itself towards both the past and the future. First, it serves as a methodology for excavation that connects cultural forms and practices to unlikely antecedents. What looks like democratization may be continuous with a cultish unity that seeks to incorporate and even liquidate the inherent multiplicity found in Kant's "culture of taste." What appears as universal judgment may hinge on a globalized and highly particular political economy. Thus the Americanizing promise of early cinema examined in chapter 4 depends upon an earlier image of unified form—the globe—that binds together the international crisscrossing of markets, commodities, and aesthetic theory examined in chapter 5. Second, this jagged temporality can turn historical structures inside out. Possibilities that failed to find a future can flare up, however briefly, once more. Outcomes that had seemingly put to rest lingering debates about what could have happened, in favor of what really did happen, might no longer appear so certain or final. Thus the aesthetic theory that in chapter 1 creates proper civic subjects is haunted by specters of international revolution seen in chapter 2. With its chronology out of joint, this book implicitly contends that what we take as the outcomes of history are at best provisional. As the sequence of events that lead up to the present become disorganized, the future seems less knowable, eluding the type of historians who, in Benjamin's words, position themselves as "soothsayers" to foreordain the future.[40] Aesthetics, I have been arguing, wreak havoc on such predictability, whether in terms of how citizens are certain to act, what culture must mean, or the paths democracy is destined to take.

Location matters to this book as much as skewed chronology. For *Beautiful Democracy*, that location is the global, a profoundly unstable coordinate of aesthetic discourse. Even as the global points to the universal, the compass of beauty also flips around to [the historical axis of] foreignness, international socialism, Americanization, or other partisan concerns. In this respect, the universal always contains its own antipodes. Despite the bluster about aesthetics as an abstract, formal, and unified discourse, the pretense of universalism always ensures that art and beauty enfold elements that are particular and hence discordant. "There is no art that does not contain in itself as an element, negated, what it repulses," writes Adorno.[41] So while the sky-high orbit of aesthetics seems so far above the surface of culture that all features are rendered smooth, this global position ensures that everything, even specific political and social concerns that seem alien to art and beauty, is part of the picture and comes into focus at some crisis point of history or another. The universal sows the seeds of its potential undoing: its global reach extends to heteronymous elements that often prove difficult to reconcile to an order of overarching formal unity. In the context of conversations about beauty found in the global aspirations of early film critics, socialist provocateurs, and urban reformers anxious about the influx of foreign immigrants, to name just three of this book's key players, the antipodes of aesthetic discourse suggest a geography that is as literal and historical as it is figurative and theoretical. The antipodes plot specific locations within the prospect of the universal, dimly realized as global actuality: the Paris Commune, the open door of the Pacific Rim, the international spaces in Du Bois's thinking about propaganda, and other seemingly foreign sites that widen and unsettle U.S. plans for a beautiful democracy.

With each chapter, the global becomes more pronounced, at once pointing to collective utopian possibilities while insinuating the alarming presence of the foreign right at home. This global thread emerges in chapter 1 in ways that at first seem innocuous enough, as academic theorists and progressive reformers experimented with using aesthetic notions of unity to develop a national civic ethos only to discover that an aesthetic sphere that included everything also included crime and larceny. Looking at anarchist "how-to" manuals on bomb-making and works on international socialism published in the U.S., including Howells's *A Hazard of New Fortunes*, chapter 2 argues that aesthetic discourse domesticates foreign ideas about strikes and social upheaval, installing them as familiar accents of the U.S. cultural idiom at century's end. Could translation make explosive matériel into cultural material? With his artwork essay of 1926, "Criteria of Negro Art," Du Bois, as chapter 3 shows, capped off an effort to map universal beauty according to the particularities of the Color Line. Chapter 4 examines how film, dubbed the "Esperanto of the eye," reproduces schemes to create an international language, an idea that anarchists and socialists as well as businessmen and diplomats found enticing. But as Chaplin's writings on cinema and early academic studies of film spectatorship suggest, the utopian prospect of international language and global understanding echoes the grammar of a univocal commodity culture. Chapter 5 excavates this convergence of capital and aesthetics by contending that Norris's writing reveals a logic linking literary naturalism with U.S. incursions into "the East."

All these global associations twist and invert Arnold's formula of culture and anarchy: the global makes culture anarchic. While falling short of the universal sensibility wrapped up with the beautiful, the global style of American aesthetics nonetheless includes far too much for any one nation to assimilate. Between the universal and its antipodes, aesthetic theory formulated in universities and the aesthetic practices of everyday life are credited with shaping, inspiring, even provoking different subjects from individual citizens to the more unwieldy agglomeration of the crowd. In recovering "lost" aesthetic theory produced within and beyond the ivory tower and designed, to a certain extent, to bridge that divide, *Beautiful Democracy* reveals the distance separating academic thinking and popular wisdom about social transformation as less gaping than we generally suppose. It might even be that anarchy is our shared culture. From this perspective, asking "how does democracy taste?" provides a starting point for taking the history of aesthetics as incitement to reconsider forms of the political that move unevenly back and forth between individual and collective, citizen and crowd, nation and globe.

FLOWERS AND BILLY CLUBS

. . . .

The Beauty and Danger of Ethical Citizenship

An election occurred—exactly how recently is uncertain—in which citizens did not have the opportunity to participate as they weighed in on issues of justice. This paradoxical vote without voting supposedly revealed the will of the people across generations so clearly that it might be said to constitute a mandate. So lopsided was the outcome that the need to have regular elections, let alone some sort of plebiscite in the future, is rendered superfluous. This contest is not presented as a political matter but rather as an aesthetic one. Then again, as an aesthetic matter, the issue inevitably engages politics. The political/aesthetic question creating so much fanfare is the relationship of art to justice, a relationship framed by Elaine Scarry as an election in her succinct and often elegant book, *On Beauty and Being Just.* "The vote on blossoms has already been taken (people over the centuries have nurtured and carried the flowers from place to place, supplementing what was there); the vote on the sky has been taken (the recent environmental movement); and the vote on the caves has innumerable times been taken," she writes.[1] From this transcendent polling booth, beauty has forever garnered universal accord. Hovering above private concern and ratified by all throughout the ages, beauty supplies abstract parameters and formal perspectives that underwrite a code for justice.

A century earlier, William Dean Howells also entwined art around democratic activity by comparing aesthetic judgment to voting. Unlike Scarry, though, Howells sees this election as ongoing since the public, the general, the masses, the people, the multitude, or the crowd—each of these terms was in play in an era when formative notions of mass culture were framed against the actualities of packed tenements, noisy proletarian rallies, and congested cities—is constantly voicing its likes and dislikes. When it comes to art, "the polls do not close at four o'clock the first Tuesday after the first Monday of November, but remain open forever, and the voting goes on." Results in this election are notable for their lack of fairness, inspiring neither dutiful reflection nor careful deliberation. "The common people," Howells writes, often reduce aesthetic evaluation to snap judgments so that "brute liking or misliking is the final test."[2] Remembering her own mistake in deeming palm trees pleasant but unbeautiful, Scarry instead believes that people can learn the error of their ways, revise first impressions, and evolve beyond slapdash assessments. "Equality is at the heart of beauty," which trains citizens how to value proportion, reciprocity, and symmetry in social arrangements.[3] Aesthetic sensibility, in Scarry's view, teaches ethical fairness. Whether gut instinct or reason rules the day, beauty invites electoral metaphors that render perception, taste, and other faculties of aesthetic judgment not just like politics but as political activities in their own right.

Beauty fights the good fight against social and political ugliness: "the arts . . . speak of the indomitable spirit that will forever resist an imperial power"; beauty "suggests a movement toward social responsibility"; art "inherently promotes freedom"; the aesthetic "emancipates us" by pointing "a *way out*" for identities tethered to convention.[4] While talk of equality, justice, and freedom openly declares beauty's wide ambit, the target of aesthetics is often much more near—the single self whose generality often stands in for a national or even universal population. Without art to instill an appreciation for proportion, symmetry, and harmony, the citizen lacks the instincts that lead to collective longing. Aesthetic disinterest prompts an ethical attitude since the subject who forgets his or her own idiosyncratic desires, a "radical decentering" in Scarry's terms, better appreciates the perspective of all others who constitute a polity.[5]

Before enabling an objective as lofty as political community, aesthetics do their work at more intimate and basic levels, investing citizens with freedom and moral capacity. By learning to stand outside the limits of private, autonomous personhood and apprehend the world from enlarged points of view shared by others, "the individual," according to Ankersmit, "only becomes a citizen through aesthetic representation."[6] For what sort of political community is the citizen fashioned? This question often meets with cautious responses from critics who see the aesthetic citizen as the perfect calculus of a bourgeois regime that prizes an ethos of self-regulation. But the account of possessive individualism only tells half the story; the subject of aesthetic ideology also possesses the "self-determining nature of human powers and capacities" crucial to "the anthropological foundation of a revolutionary opposition to bourgeois utility."[7] This ambivalence suggests that the outcome of Scarry's election that has people affirming beauty across centuries might not be so predictable. Beauty will always find something like universal approbation at the polling booth, but less calculable are the effects of political aesthetics upon citizens who encounter flowers, appreciate blue skies, and respond to works of art.

If aesthetics are a starting point to ethical citizenship, it is worth remembering that starting points do not necessarily lead to their destinations and that the path from aesthetic perception to democratic sensibility is not always a straight one. Even when links between aesthetics and justice seem secure and predictable, subjects whose emotions and instincts are quickened by beauty often fail to arrive at their moral destinations, their ethical baggage misplaced and their capacity for civic obedience lost along the way. For philosophers and reformers of the late nineteenth century, no less than for contemporary theorists of the last half century, aesthetics have appeared as an experiential base to start laying a foundation for social justice, political unity, or other collective project. But because this base shifts in response to historical and economic pressures, it is always in motion like the flimsy rope suspension bridges found in action adventure movies. For critics reluctant to trust politics to a domain once deemed "thoroughly tattered" and devoid of "political use-value" for all except the right, periodic backlashes that make aesthetic culture sway with conservative precepts of canon or nation fail to inspire universal confidence in that bridge.[8] When aesthetics are charged with bearing the burden of representing and cultivating the mass, the people, the proletariat, or any of the various collectivities implied by the looseness of democracy, art and beauty seem that much more rickety, that is, contingent. Can such a flimsy structure support the weight of community sense, to say nothing of the hefty ideal of universal accord?

Perhaps it is only contemporary world-weariness that motivates such pessimism. By way of contrast, the answer from several quarters, including philosophy departments and ethnic slums of the late nineteenth and early twentieth centuries, was a guarded "yes": aesthetic theorists and social activists felt that beauty could supply different people—the poor, immigrants, criminals—with a common standard. I begin with those who believed that the discourse of beauty, given half a chance, might forge not just national unity but the common feeling of the entire human species. I end up in a very different spot in which aesthetic resources reveal a population divided by class resentment and violence. The full story of aesthetics, then, involves a lot of twists and turns, as hopes for a common culture are undone by the very technologies that seemed to pave the way to that promise.

BEAUTY AND CIVIC IDENTITY

Courses in aesthetics at U.S. universities and colleges dovetailed with the pragmatist bent of American philosophy that refused to keep the social world at arm's length. Professors at Yale, Wellesley, Berkeley, and Michigan authored textbooks designed to aid college students and, in some cases, nonacademic audiences in discerning proportion and unity in social as well as artistic arrangements. Both Princeton University and Columbia University did away with town-gown distinctions and advertised lectures on aesthetics to the general public.[9] Among more specialized students of aesthetic theory, dissertators like Edwin Lee Norton of Harvard devoted long hours and many pages toward proving that "supreme ethical value" and "supreme aesthetic value" were united in the concept of the good. At a time when most doctoral theses seemed to have received tepid evaluations as either "satisfactory" or "sufficient," the faculty assessment that Norton's "The Concepts of Harmony and Organism in Ethics" (1900) merited "the grade of excellence" points to its success in adapting positivist science to idealist philosophy.[10] His colleagues spent large chunks of time in the Psychology Laboratory, examining the contraction and relaxation of eye muscles in an effort to determine how physiological stimulus conditions pleasure. Thus when Roswell Parker Angier, who later headed up the Institute of Psychology at Yale, took the question "what divisions do people like" as the central focus of his dissertation, he noticed that test subjects preferred to look at horizontal and vertical lines of equal length. His findings, later published in *Harvard Psychology Studies,* showed that eye muscles are relaxed and the individual is at rest when looking at visual representations where balance, symmetry, and equality obtain.[11] The goal of these experiments, as another graduate student put it, was "to show how the methods of experimental psychology can with advantage be applied to the study of aesthetic consciousness."[12] If college classes addressed students who want "to engage in practical philanthropic work," as the course bulletin for Harvard's philosophy department put it, then research on the perception of equilibrium and pleasure of bilateral symmetry may not have been merely academic.[13] What was happening in the Psychology Laboratory filtered down to undergraduates taking basic courses in aesthetics. "Philosophy 10" at Harvard stressed connections between the "sense of beauty" and the "psychology of facts," helping the sons of the elite (who else, after all, had the wherewithal to be philanthropists?) to intuit the relevance of aesthetic pleasure to the shaping of social reality.[14]

For those who knew a lot about social reality but little of aesthetic pleasure, university extension courses sought to disseminate ethical lessons bound up with beauty. A Harvard pedigree was not a requirement for understanding something about sensation, perception, and judgment. At land-grant institutions, two-semester sequences in Aesthetics 101 were standard fare sophomore and junior years. Along with pamphlets on dairying and milking, Midwestern universities published what were essentially philosophical starter kits on art and aesthetics. The implicit belief of *Aesthetics: Syllabus of Course of Six Lectures* (1895), published by the extension program at the University of Wisconsin, was that farmers, small-town merchants, and homesteaders could benefit from critical attention to "means, proportion . . . lines and forms."[15] In light of the larger mission of university extension to "make possible an ideal state" by realizing a university without walls that would sow knowledge and culture across the countryside as "the birthright of all," aesthetic education was an important building block of a civic ethos.[16]

Efforts to train citizens from all walks of life in aesthetic appreciation attracted publishing houses whose multivolume projects on beauty and art comprised hundred of pages and included detailed plates and engravings that make a stapled syllabus titled *Aesthetics* look positively rinky-dink. Yet even in these massive and expensive efforts, the popular tone of aesthetic education remained in full force. When Scribner's published *The Philosophy of the Beautiful* (1891), a textbook "designed to aid the University Extension Movement throughout Great Britain and America," the cultivation of disinterested judgment among the masses took center stage. But once in the limelight, beauty seemed to falter in establishing a common standard. In a world where "pleasure reaches us in the plural," how can the experience of beauty yield unity and consensus?[17] Amid the easy and quick availability of art—or at worst, commodified entertainment such as magic lantern shows, peep shows, cheap stage productions, dime novels, and shoddy lithographs of the old masters—how can emotions and instincts be channeled into predictable responses and disciplined reactions? *The Philosophy of the Beautiful* meets with mixed success in answering these questions, but perhaps such ambiguity is the point since turn-of-the-century academic research walks a fine line between codifying formal aesthetic principles and proposing art as the engine of perceptual innovation and intellectual change.

Out West, juniors and seniors taking Charles Gayley's seminar in aesthetics at Berkeley were taught that only a reductive didacticism evaluated art in terms of its ability to promote concrete reform. Subtle influence was another matter, though. Gayley theorized that "the work of art produces indirectly an effect upon the will" by recalibrating individual desire and action as social functions. The inward operation of "the beautiful," this English professor told his students, can be summed up as "an ethical effect." Yet this language proved unsatisfying, since it necessarily limited aesthetics to the borders of individual experience. New terminology was needed and that came from his graduate student, Arthur Weiss, who proposed the concept of the "coenopathic" to describe the confluence of individual instinct and social function.[18] The term did not seem to catch on. What Gayley prized, as he and his co-author argued in their 1899 textbook on the "bases in aesthetics and poetics," was the development of social criteria that would make individual judgment a function of mass appeal and public usefulness. His lecture notes express doubts as to whether such criteria could ever be discovered. Even as Gayley earnestly believed that the highest art enjoys the approbation of the crowd, he also admitted that beauty can only be perceived by members of an intellectual aristocracy, an ideal "that does not appeal to the most people, does it?"[19] The negative answer implied by this phrasing might continue to echo were it not for the fact that beauty was theorized not only in college classrooms but was also advocated in settlement houses, nurtured in tenement blocks, and activated in the streets.

In institutional contexts very different from academic discipline, social reformers, social Darwinists, socially minded novelists, and just plain socialists pinned their hopes for an ethical citizenry on beauty. Artists and activists sought to mold "the other half" into the artwork of the people, revitalizing the waning energies of civic republicanism. Assessing the rate of "Aesthetic Progress" as part of a three-part series in 1899, the *Atlantic Monthly* acquainted readers with the uplifting and unifying influence of the Public Art School League of Boston and the Art Education Society of Cleveland. Similar organizations were at work in San Francisco, Milwaukee, Denver, and St. Louis "upbuilding . . . the culture and the character of the whole people."[20] But a list of beautiful cities does not a civic pedagogy make. To link aesthetic cultivation and democratic feeling, the *Atlantic* looked back to ancient Athens and quoted Pericles—"Make Athens beautiful, for beauty is now the victorious power in the world"—to exemplify how aesthetic sensibility shapes and governs the political sentiments of modern urban dwellers.[21] The moral resolve to create the "City Beautiful," as turn-of-the-century movements in urban planning, flower missions, settlement houses, public architecture, and civic beautification were called, invites questions about the relationship between democracy and "victorious power." Such power in 1899 clearly had imperial dimensions in the wake of the U.S. declaration of war against Spain the previous year. Yet the target of "victorious power" is also more intimate and private, namely, the perception and use of pleasure by the single citizen.

As the city becomes beautiful, people become "happier." Surrounded by public parks, gardens, and exhibitions, people "will become better citizens . . . filled with civic pride." Exactly how do art and beauty encourage citizens to recreate Athenian democracy as an American inheritance? Although the plan for of aesthetic progress remains vague as to this precise point, the *Atlantic* does specify that the people will be "instructed."[22] This response raises more questions than it answers. Does instruction straighten people out, making them into citizens? If instruction fills them with civic pride, does it first empty out some other set of contents from their subjectivities? Do scenes of instruction coincide with sites of discipline and punishment forcing universal taste on every last soul? But, perhaps, this line of interrogation presumes that aesthetics are guilty of all sorts of things from disseminating middle-class values as ideal to palming off the class structure as the height of social symmetry and balance. Less suspicious questions are in order as well. Might not beauty enhance the citizen's perception of social justice? Is it possible that its power would lead not to scenarios of discipline and punishment but to what Michel Foucault called "an aesthetics of existence"?[23]

To attempt answers to such questions, it is not necessary to look back as far as Pericles, although the Greek orator's speech that oscillates between defining democracy as the "administration [that] favors the many instead of the few" and mapping the "empire which we now possess" certainly speaks to the manic history of U.S. domestic and foreign policy at the turn of the century.[24] Flipping back a few pages to the previous article is far enough: in "The Tenement House Blight," photographer, public lecturer, moralist, autobiographer, and urban reformer Jacob Riis leads a tour of ugliness, guiding genteel readers of the *Atlantic* through the dank passages of a Polish capmaker's home. Riis invites the reader in, introduces the weary tenants, and walks about the decrepit rooms while dropping statistics about public health. Part sociology and part sentimental narrative, this interdisciplinary portrait mixes aesthetic lessons and political moralizing. Beauty, suggests Riis, can bring light, air, and hope to scenes of immigrant despair while organizing the immigrants themselves into a civic-minded body. Riis's plan for civic embellishment passes itself off as preeminently organic, relying on metaphors of soil, sunlight, water, and growth to outline a regimen for molding the slum's youngest inhabitants into productive members of society. The language of gardening is more than metaphor to Riis: if sunlight can brighten the cheerless rooms of the capmaker's tenement, if his children can romp in the open space of a park, if slum dwellers can tend flowers and learn to cultivate beauty, living conditions will improve and democratic attachments will take root among the foreign-born and their sons and daughters. Setting his sights a little below the level of the universal, Riis still charges beauty with a mission of national incorporation. When Riis speaks of creating "a good soil for citizenship to grow in," he at once refers to public institutions that nurture U. S. democracy and actual public spaces, especially parks and squares, which instruct citizens to love their city.[25] New York discovers its Pericles in Riis.

Flowers smooth the way to beautiful politics. The hope of the capmaker's daughter—to walk among "grass and flowers and birds and soldiers" just as she did in Warsaw—finds its champion in Riis, who announces the "time is at hand" to thaw the frozen hearts of building owners, cut through the red tape, and clear space for

> a park, with flowers and grass and birds to gladden the hearts of those to whom such things have been as tales that are told, all these dreary years, and with a playground in which the children of yonder big school may roam at will, undismayed by landlord or policeman.[26]

He leaves the little girl's wish for "soldiers" off his list, sensing that militaristic pomp is out of step with public feeling. Neither patrolled nor privately owned, the park is public, a post-Athenian version of Arendt's space of appearance where members of the city-state enact freedom through interactions with each other.[27] Authoritarian figures are as unsuited for the park's soil as European soldiers for U.S. shores. Civic instruction and Americanization seem as easy and as natural as child's play. Howells picked up on this association between nature and state naturalization by likening sprigs of celandine, wood-sorrel, and dwarf larkspur poking through cracks in the city pavement to ideological messengers of the nation. Rather than refer to these blossoms with Latinate nomenclature, Howells insists on their common names, stating that he "should like to get them all naturalized here" under names abbreviated and adapted to U.S. principles—just as surnames were shortened and standardized at Ellis Island. In a context where even nature, as Howells jokes, needs to be naturalized, snapdragons and baby's breath reveal "how bountifully the world is equipped with beauty, and how it is governed by laws which are not enforced by policemen."[28] While Howells chooses a less programmatic approach than Riis, both writers act as social ecologists who look to flowers, green space, and nature as pleasing alternatives to the rule of law.

Riis's call for a park practically implements aesthetic principles set out in a series of lectures given uptown from the capmaker's home. Speaking at Columbia University during the fall term of 1894, Henry Rutgers Marshall theorized aesthetics as the grist that holds society together. Art promotes attachments, the "attraction of others to ourselves," not through any express or deliberate code but through unconscious reactions that make social feeling pleasurable.[29] A century later, a similar idea popped up at the 1996 Ryle Lectures when the keynote speaker began by musing that "the arts somehow sustai[n] the fabric of the society" and ended by declaring that "aesthetics will always be with us, like a mildew that we scrub away but reappears every time the weather is wet and warm enough."[30] While this pronouncement airs contemporary doubts (is the culture that withstands anarchy really more of a fungus than a refined tradition?), back at the turn of the century Marshall's voice did not waver when it came to assessing the desirability of aesthetics. Academic discipline is the key to Marshall's surety. Drawing on his earlier work, *Pain, Pleasure, and Aesthetics* (1894), Marshall propounds the quasi-biological hypothesis that subjects instinctively congregate around beauty, thereby promoting interaction and ensuring the continuation of the species. People naturally gravitate toward pleasurable sensations created by art as part of a social ethos. "The art instinct," Marshall explains, teaches the subject to abandon individuality and throw his or her lot in with collective life.[31] This logic anticipates Scarry's claim that beauty at a fundamental level ensures human survival. Observing that beauty inspires copies, Scarry sees reproduction as fulfilling the most basic of desires: beauty "prompts the begetting of children: when the eye sees someone beautiful, the whole body wants to reproduce the person."[32] Beauty supplies a sort of come-hither look, a pheromone for the soul that endows human beings with an aesthetic instinct that seems bound up with the impulse for collective social interaction.

Human beings pursue biological preservation as an aesthetic principle, which is also to say that aesthetic taste is as universal as human biology. Just as the listener of Wagner's music, to follow Marshall's example, is "very often lost in the totality" to the point that "all particulars seem to be forgotten in the general effect," so, too, the particular person is absorbed by a larger belonging to the "race" and the "whole system" of existence. Biology underpins psychology, which explains aesthetics, which accounts for the politics of human organization on a grand scale: "I think we may surely say that the *function of art in the development of man is social consolidation*."[33] The quaint beauty wished for by the Polish capmaker's daughter, Riis's practical response to that vision, and Marshall's theoretical investigation of aesthetics all converge around the pleasures of community and associative life.

This convergence of university lecture and reform journalism, especially with a few choice selections from late-twentieth-century academic work on aesthetics thrown into the mix, should not obscure the very different institutional context of each. It is doubtful that Riis developed reform tactics by first brushing up on aesthetic theory, and college professors probably did not begin teaching aesthetics in explicit response to some perceived social crisis. Still, Thorstein Veblen, who would go on to found the New School for Social Research, wrestled with Kantian aesthetics in *The Journal of Speculative Philosophy* in an effort to theorize a coherent social world, while Professor Davies at Yale invoked flowers, the beauty of tulips in particular, to provide an example of universal consensus.[34] Even though reformers rarely saw occasion to frame their actions against Kant or Schiller, just as university lecturers seldom spoke of flowers with the same materiality as did Howells or the New York City Flower Mission in its crusade of urban beautification, each assumed aesthetics as a point of ethical intervention. Exactly what amounted to an ethical intervention was of course open to debate, not simply between theorists and activists but within each group itself. But on one question academics and reformers were united, perhaps because it spelled a problem that was at once theoretical and practical: what happens when flowers cannot be separated from police billy clubs, that is, when beauty cannot avert and even incites violence?

BEAUTY AND SCIENCE

The pleasures of collective association were not to be confused with law-lessness or anarchy. Although Riis invokes nature and although Marshall's *Aesthetic Principles* roots aesthetics in instinct, neither abandons citizens to the law of survival. Crime statistics and infant mortality rates in the slum argue that there is already enough Darwinism at work among the poor. Stability instead lies in the ascendancy of natural law over the law of nature. The distinction is subtle but important: whereas the individual, under the law of nature, succumbed to the influence of stale beer dives and gambling dens, the ethical citizen, guided by his or her own instincts, enjoyed an inner rectitude that made social cohesion with others not only possible but pleasurable.

A far cry from the dens of iniquity portrayed by Riis, college class-rooms and public halls rented for university extension courses supplied the lesson that art ordained law in a natural and pleasing fashion. Ethel Dench Puffer's course in aesthetics at Wellesley College outlined a "sci-ence of beauty" that revealed "a system of laws" based on physiological reactions to inspiring scenic vistas, mellifluous sounds, and masterful art-works.[35] While neither a musical composition nor painting is natural, hu-man response to an artwork is biological since judgments about beauty are governed by fundamental stimuli. In *The Psychology of Beauty* (1905), Puffer turned to "the instinctive, involuntary part of our nature" to argue for the existence of predictable, universal responses whose eternal quality ensure that aesthetic—and social—experience is one of equilibrium and harmony. Beauty reveals law as an internal proposition: there is no need, as the *Atlantic* had advised, to instruct subjects, since aesthetic instincts are already hardwired in our neural processes. Because "laws of beauty" ordain that "physical reactions . . . are practically changeless, even as the human instincts are changeless," aesthetics never tempt subjects to run amok as they stroll among the flowers and birds of the city park that Riis imagines for the Polish capmaker's daughter.[36] As Puffer explained in her own contribution to the *Atlantic*, a painting that takes balance and symmetry as the principles of its composition will likely produce these results within spectators.[37] A hundred miles to the north of Puffer, John Bascom lectured students at Williams College that aesthetic form guides individuals, counseling against excess and ensuring obedience to the law of beauty. Located in the inwardness of subjects, this lesson stemmed not just from moral philosophy but from notions of science, as the title of Bascom's *Aesthetics; or, the Science of Beauty* shows. The untutored longing of the capmaker's daughter for beauty is ushered by the academy into the domain of institutional aesthetics.

Except that capmakers' daughters did not often have the opportunity to attend Wellesley or Williams. Still, if aesthetics were a matter of instinct, college classrooms were not absolutely necessary to awaken ethical feelings among the populace. The physiological nature of aesthetics, bound up with species survival, allowed that the nervous system of any subject could respond positively to beauty. Mixing John Ruskin and Charles Darwin, Grant Allen suggested as much in his *Physiological Aesthetics* (1877), arguing that scientific investigations of beauty must consider "the average human being," the human organism that seeks pleasure and avoids pain. The baseline for the species will not be determined by examining the artistic genius of Raphael, Mozart, or Milton. Instead, as researchers turn to everyday effects of color and sound on the "cerebro-spinal nervous system," biology indicates that a capacity for beauty resides at large in the mass qua species. But fundamental human capacity is not a guarantee of the universal: although "aesthetic matters are the necessary result of natural selection," not everyone wins in the struggle for survival.[38] Aesthetic science, as a matter of Darwinian evolution, postulates a food chain of taste in which the most discriminating subjects set formal criteria that the rest of the herd feel compelled to follow. Even with this disdain for the masses, physiological aesthetics still resound with social optimism, since even the most uncivilized subjects can evolve if their instincts to recognize, feel, and consider beauty, common to the human species at large, can be stimulated. While this hypothesis did not send Riis to the slum, progressive cultural reform and university aesthetics, despite their different institutional locations, did occasionally look to one another for authority. "Esthetic Nature of Thugs to be Subjected to Old Art" ran a headline to a *New York Times* article on a display of oil paintings at Sing Sing. Citing clinical research in psychology and physiology, the article believed it worthwhile to see what effects "harmonies of line [and] color" will have on prisoners' dispositions.[39]

More common were university researchers' references to public architecture and public gardens as examples of how harmony and unity worked upon the nerves, brain, and finally, the soul. Tending a flower garden, like the cultivation of artistic talent or sensibility, improved the subject, pruning the soul of excrescences as surely as unsightly weeds were pulled from a garden path. While the parallels of cultivating soul and garden remain imprecise and figurative, George Lansing Raymond's *The Essentials of Aesthetics* (1906) credited "the flower garden with straight and rectangular pathways" with grounding "emotional impressions" in regularity, precision, and proportion.[40] In making such pronouncements, Raymond, an instructor at George Washington University and Princeton, was not alone in concentrating on gardens as sites of instruction. Water-lilies, for instance, were heralded as communicants of a "silent lesson": if such beauty could emerge "heavenward even from the black oozy depths below," then perchance decent citizens could also rise out of squalid conditions of the urban cesspool.[41] Ordered beds, symmetrical walks, and graceful blossoms, it was hoped, would encourage human nature to develop in accordance with aesthetic form.

The science of beauty finds its corollary in Riis's sociology of the floral. Observing the "rough young savage" who inhabits the slum, Riis assesses the possibilities for aesthetic evolution:

> Let him [the social observer] take into a tenement block a handful of flowers from the fields and watch the brightened faces, the sudden abandonment of play and fight that go ever hand in hand where there is no elbow-room, the wild entreaty for "posies," the eager love with which the little messengers of peace are shielded, once possessed. . . . I have seen an armful of daisies keep the peace of a block better than a policeman and his club, seen instincts awaken under their gentle appeal, whose very existence the soil in which they grew made seem a mockery.[42]

Nature (in the form of flowers) quells nature (in the form of urban savagery) by awakening nature (in the form of "instincts"). The process would be confusing were it not scientific: aesthetics police the wilder side of human subjectivity to promote social tranquility and internal order. This science is highly metaphoric, dependent on a logic of substitution that replaces the harshness of the law's enforcer, the police billy club, with nature's delicate offering, flowers. Tap the art instinct, nurture its growth, cultivate its bloom, and witness the degraded species of slum dweller evolve into a respectable citizen. In Riis's metaphor, however, the policeman's nightstick never vanishes completely, its repressive force sublimated as petals of a flower. Beauty does not offer an alternative to the ugly, uninspiring face of the law so much as reshape threats of force and retaliation as beautiful, as law with a pretty face.

University professors also theorized exchanges between flowers and police, but these conversions were sentimental in a much more professional way, relying on the field of psychology for intimate access to the self. Harvard professor Hugo Münsterberg, who would later author an important early study of motion pictures and spectatorship (see chapter 4), explained to readers of the *North American Review* that rules of artistic composition "do for real beauty and art just what police and the prisons . . . do for real morality." Yet art instruction and social planning should not rely exclusively on disciplinary power. The "aesthetical psychologist" teaches that while regulation and threat of punishment will almost certainly make people cower and cringe, only an appeal to interiority can produce subjects who will act virtuously even when the police are not present. How to gain access to the will and conscience? That mission falls to art, which inspires children toward moral reflection and behavior. The problem is that art education has been tied to an orthodoxy that makes "every drawing-teacher" into "an aesthetical policeman" who saps the spirit out of his or her pupils and converts creation into a mechanical process. Instead of establishing laws for art in the belief that "aesthetical life needs . . . the policeman's function," educators should see that art itself, in its ability to communicate fundamental values, provides a code of ethical conduct.[43]

Despite efforts to splinter off aesthetics from police work, the two remained intertwined to the extent that persons stopped in their tracks by the unexpected appearance of flower boxes outside tenement windows were exposed to a sort of racial and ethnic profiling. Different nations and nationalities, according to physiological and psychological aesthetics, possess differently evolved instincts and tastes. In Riis's urban polis where "esthetic starvation" is the general condition of the masses, beauty is not fitted for survival among all ethnic groups.[44] In the grafting of natural selection onto presumptions about national types, some are more ardent than others in their support of flowers:

> The German has an advantage over his Celtic neighbor in his strong love for flowers, which not all the tenements on the East Side has power to smother. His garden goes with him wherever he goes. Not that it represents any high moral principle in the man; rather perhaps the capacity for it. He turns his saloon into a shrubbery as soon as his backyard. But whenever he puts it in a tenement block it does the work of a dozen police clubs. In proportion as it spreads the neighborhood takes on a more orderly character. As the green dies out of the landscape and increases in political importance, the police find more to do. Where it disappears altogether from sight, lapsing into a mere sentiment, police-beats are shortened and the force patrols double at night. . . . The changing of Tompkins Square from a sand lot into a beautiful park put an end for good and all to the "Bread or Blood" riots of which it used to be the scene, and transformed a nest of dangerous agitators into a harmless, beer-craving band of Anarchists.[45]

Emblematized by flowers, aesthetics exert metaphoric power that acts as and substitutes for discipline, serving as both carrot and stick. Still, the art instinct provides no surefire counter to the force of "ethnic instinct," which, in the case of the German beer guzzler, makes a mockery of beauty by adapting artistic touches to the overall economy of the saloon. Where aesthetics hold undiminished sway, taste and judgment instruct and citizens, remaking then internally into an artwork of "orderly character." The same principles that characterize artistic composition typify an ideal citizenry. Make no mistake, however: this citizenry should not be political, certainly not if it is to be considered ideal. "Political importance" appears excessive and chaotic, a negative quality that necessarily invites the repressive arm of the law. Beauty is inversely related to politics; as aesthetic resources become scarce, politics intrudes more and more on the scene, resulting in the ugliness of agitation and anarchic passion. Aesthetics seem an antidote for politics, but Riis is no dandy who insists on art for art's sake. Taking care to sidestep violent agitation, Riis uses art as a progressive medium for grappling with material conditions that trap subjects in poverty.

Riis's attraction to the socializing force of aesthetics distinguishes him from more skittish reformers who saw art as a nonpolitical haven from collective activities that included everything from organizing in public to gathering in stale beer dives. Art propagates an ideology of escapism— which for many of Riis's contemporaries was a good thing, the only thing the hopeless had left to hope for. Reformers basked in data showing that the New York City Flower Mission distributed 100,000 bouquets and that the Boston Young Men's Institute took the time to attach a bit of up-lifting scripture to each bunch of flowers.[46] While rescuing the poor from poverty proved impossible save by revolution (and there were plenty of anarchists advocating exactly this plan of action), efforts to "beautify pov-erty," as one social missionary put it, could make harmless visions of so-cialist millennium seem that much more real.[47] Or, what is more likely, if the millennium was never to appear, then the seamstress who "begged for lilies-of-the-valley" might be induced to find contentment sewing piece work "with the delicate white flowers keeping her company."[48] This seam-stress's perspective is confirmed by one contributor to Harper's, who only identified herself as a "A Working Girl," an appellation that rings rather dubiously in a forum such as Harper's. Her 1883 short story presents aes-thetic education as a source of social harmony and moral salvation. En-titled "An Aesthetic Idea," the narrative begins with the facial disfigure-ment of a young girl in a circus accident. What is she to do, especially after the troupe moves on without her? Her own beauty gone, she is retrained to provide "aestheticism in the kitchen" and "intelligent service in com-fortable homes" that creates, not the City Beautiful, but a "House Beauti-ful" for others. Although a well-run domestic space takes the place of a beautiful polis, this solution comes none too soon, as the circus girl's raw instincts start to show themselves in impromptu performances that have become sexually inappropriate with her maturation. Left to run wild, the art instinct can devolve into animalistic urges. Fortunately, though, her ability to keep a "home orderly and beautiful" restores her injured self-hood while simultaneously endowing her with traits that make her part of a contented servant class.[49]

For his part, Riis rejected the mission to beautify poverty, protesting that "New World poverty is not often picturesque."[50] His crusade to intro-duce flowers, parks, and open spaces to the slums rarely lost sight of the fact that aesthetics were matters of material conditions. Light and air, for instance, are every bit as fundamental to sanitation and progressive urban design as they are to pleasing panoramas. "Tenement-houses have no aesthetic resources," he writes.[51] Fetid airshafts and stagnant pools of water both offend aesthetic sensibilities and present a danger to biological survival, a fact confirmed by the high rates of infant mortality that Riis cites in *How the Other Half Lives*, which is just as often a study of the how half dies. Aesthetics, in short, are not just the icing on the cake but the stuff of basic sustenance. Given its deep connection to the senses and instinct, "the functional centrality of the aesthetic in keeping us alive," to borrow Isobel Armstrong's language, strikes not just a psychological chord not but biological one as well.[52] Similarly, when Richard Shusterman writes that "art's pleasures by their very pleasure have evolutionary value in that they make life seem worth living, which is the best guarantee that we will do our best to survive," his language intimates how close to the existential abyss human beings teeter if they are not ethically anchored by senses attuned to beauty, pleasure, and collective judgment.[53] Early-twentieth-century academics employed more convoluted terminology to express this same idea. The "coenopathic" aspect of aesthetics, as Weiss's Berkeley dissertation described the theoretically universal response to the beautiful, aligned self-preservation with the continuation of society as a whole. Riis's photographs of "Bottle Alley" (fig. 1) and other trash-strewn cityscapes never escape this context of survival, the overflowing sacks of waste creating a visual analogue to the human wrecks cuddled up in doorways in other shots. Rooted in feelings, instincts, and sensation, aesthetics are entrenched in the sociality of the human body. Riis communicates this material sensibility, his camera rarely shying away from the dirt and squalor of narrow alleyways that an idealist discourse on aesthetics, one limited to the beautiful, would readily exclude from portraits of reality.

More than a few reformers, however, were generally all for leaving behind such grim facts, relying on aesthetic experience to guide subjects along broad avenues of escape and transcendence. No doubt clean drinking water, ample sunlight, and improved air circulation are very fine things, but so is illusion. Anxious that urban despair might erupt into revolutionary action, Charles Loring Brace in *The Dangerous Classes* (1872) prescribed healthy doses of escapism to allay the anarchist discontent that he saw smoldering in a growing army of the poor. Buffeted by "the sweet odors of hyacinth and heliotrope, sweet-william and violet," beauty overcomes the stench of the city sewers to the point where olfactory power overcomes the subject as well so that "a poor child could stand and fancy herself, for a moment, far away in the country."[54] Illusion is to be freely consumed; fantasy, no matter how temporary, is all that the poor have

FIGURE 1. Jacob Riis, "Bottle Alley, Baxter Street" (ca. 1890). Museum of the City of New York, Jacob A. Riis Collection. Offering a gritty contrast to picturesque representations of poverty, Riis's photographic perspective supplied viewers with a realist aesthetic.

and, as anyone mindful of Riis's besotted anarchists knew, far better to have the poor drunk on fantasy than organizing or acting. The illustration (fig. 2) to this scene, "Poor Children among Flowers," depicts flowers in vases, hanging from ceilings, and redoubled in mirrors, surrounding the downtrodden with aesthetic resources that counteract the unpleasantness of their social condition. The Rivington Street Lodging House portrays the

POOR CHILDREN AMONG FLOWERS.

(T   on Street Lodging-House.)

FIGURE 2. "Poor Children among Flowers," from Charles Loring Brace, *The Dangerous Classes of New York, and Twenty Years' Work among Them* (New York: Wynkoop & Hallenbeck, 1872). The small children at the center of this drawing are getting much more than a flower. As the desks, books, quaint verses about "Truth" imply, to be "among flowers" is to be firmly situated amid moral instruction.

power of aesthetics, capturing a moment of instruction in which beauty is seen forming subjects. But with the exception of the one child with Sid Vicious hair turned around in his seat, none of the students pictured seem "far away in the country" or transported to some other innately ethical locale. Instead, their gazes are riveted to the floral arrangements at the front of the classroom. The children look at flowers, allowing teachers to eye them. In their looking, they forget that they are being watched. Beauty has the power to create subjects. And not just any subject: guided by natural laws, subjects become affectively bound to civic authority, intuitively recognizing their city as beautiful much as Athenians loved their city because it, too, was beautiful.

BEAUTY AND CROWD CONTROL

The creation of artwork draws on but a fraction of beauty's power. Subjects, citizens, and collectivities are also the product of form, perception, and sensation. "Beauty only concerns men," Kant writes, explaining how aesthetics establish us as subjects endowed with capacity to render judgments that make sense not simply to ourselves but also to the larger mass of humanity.[55] In this transit from self to others and from individual satisfaction to collective accord, aesthetics mold individuals and organize communities. These different results point up irresolvable tensions within aesthetics, which, at one moment, carve out a bourgeois subject who is perfectly suited to liberal forms and, at the next, generate "a community of subjects now linked by sensuous impulse and fellow-feeling rather than by heteronomous law."[56]

Between the formation of singular bourgeois identity and the stirrings of collective feeling, Riis adduces a third possibility: aesthetics invent subjects who have the luxury to hide their agency. Especially in modern mass society where seeing and being seen correspond to varying degrees of knowledge and regulation, the ability to expose others, which is literally the mechanism at work in Riis's urban photographs, and bring them into focus either as individuals or as part of an ethnic group is a tremendous asset. If aesthetic judgment inspires fellowship and potentially universal tastes, what about the person who wants to remain apart from the mass, or perhaps, more prosaically, the unwashed masses, and hold up this population as an object of study without subjecting his or her own self to scrutiny? Here is where Riis's deployment of aesthetic technology comes powerfully into play, as he uses the camera to construct subjects like "the thief" or "the burglar" and to mold collectivities like "the desperate poor," all the while keeping distance from his creations. Shots of tenement lodgers, roused from sleep, eyes shut to the explosion of flash powder, withhold volition, awareness, and even consciousness from these objects of sociological study and moral concern in *How the Other Half Lives*. Setting the scene for his portrait of sleepers crammed together in a tenement (fig. 3), Riis dryly observes:

> From midnight till far into the small hours of the morning the policeman's thundering rap is heard, with his stern command, *"Apri port'!"* on his rounds gathering evidence of illegal overcrowding. The doors are opened unwillingly enough—but the order means business, and the tenant knows it even if he understands no word of English—upon such scenes as the one presented in the picture. It was photographed by flashlight on just such a visit. In a room not thirteen feet either way

FIGURE 3. Jacob Riis, "Five Cents a Spot: Unauthorized Lodgers in a Bayard Street Tenement" (ca. 1890). Museum of the City of New York, Jacob A. Riis Collection. The camera simultaneously provides access to the poor and keeps them at a distance.

slept twelve men and women, two or three in bunks set in a sort of alcove, the rest on the floor.

Passive voice occludes both the subjectivity of tenement sleepers and Riis's agency as a photographer. His rhetoric creates the impression that the slum presents itself, preserving his disconnection from the scene, as the photograph manages space in such a way that the slum's inhabitants are driven further into their dens. Like so many of the images in *How the Other Half Lives*, "Lodgers in a Crowded Bayard Street Tenement" pushes its subjects to the back of the frame, concentrating on the foreground, usually strewn with debris, that provides a buffer between the middle-class viewer and the objects of charity.[57]

Glad in *How the Other Half Lives* to have the police along for protection, later in his autobiography Riis declared their presence incidental, going so far as to say that the police accompanied him out of "curiosity."

Photography packs its own threat of violence: "The flashlight of those days was contained in cartridges fired from a revolver. The spectacle of half a dozen strange men invading a house in the midnight hour armed with big pistols which they shot off recklessly was hardly reassuring, however sugary our speech, and it was not to be wondered at if the tenants bolted through windows and down fire-escapes wherever we went." The police, Riis concludes, "were hardly needed . . . our party carried terror wherever it went." But the threat of force is useless (otherwise the reformer is just preying upon the powerless) unless one takes pains to imagine the situation of those who are subjected to the art of photography. Riis refines practices accordingly: "I substituted a frying pan for the revolver, and flashed the light on that. It seemed more homelike." [58] Just as flowers and law substitute for nightsticks and violence, frying pans take the place of revolvers. Feelings of social fellowship rest on a particular formal device that first allows for the conversion of police clubs into flowers: metaphor. Metaphor is not the effect of deception or an alibi of brute power; rather, the introduction of aesthetic resources (via photographic documentation of slum conditions) domesticates the tenement, forcing it into "homelike" patterns. The substitutions among frying pans, cameras, and revolvers are not merely ideologically fraudulent but instead offer a portrait in transformation. In its capacity to transfigure concrete objects of physical reality, aesthetics perhaps can reshape all sorts of matter, from individual subjects to collective social reality. Pistols become kitchen implements and thugs become citizens. Such modification explains the attraction to aesthetics because implicit in the exchanges that photography and metaphor make among reality and image is the promise that materials and people can be reinterpreted, reworked, and, in effect, changed.

The softening of billy clubs and revolvers is not something to be taken lightly; such reshaping of the real entails ethical considerations. To view Riis's crusade for public parks simply as another ideology to beat the immigrant poor into submission would be to distort the progressive elements of aesthetic reform. And yet, many of his contemporaries did use notions of beauty and taste to bully the ethnic underclass. Riis's ethic of aesthetic transfiguration contrasts with the mission of other reformers who had no problem embellishing the urban landscape but stopped short of a more adventurous program committed to changing the material conditions (for instance, by razing tenements and building public parks) of the slum. Consider the case of Arthur Pember, better known as the "Amateur Vagabond" for his undercover journalistic forays into the lives of tramps and beggars, who sees aesthetic activity as little more than an effort to slap a new coat of paint over the ugliness of the slum. Intrigued by a hand-bill asking, "WHY WEAR A BLACK EYE?" Pember enters the Tombs one Monday morning "in search of a subject" and exits with Mary, a battered wife. Elated to be "in possession of a 'subject,'" Pember brings Mary to the address on the handbill and sits her down before an artist who prepares brushes and palette with a range of flesh-tones. On seeing Mary, the artist at first demurs: "I don't paint any but the upper classes," he says with "a slightly offended air." Pember prevails on the craftsman to democratize his art and turn his hand to Mary's bruises. "As though he was about to begin the head of a Madonna for the next exhibition of the Academy of Design," the Bowery artist disguises Mary's black eye. As the allusion to the atelier of high art implies, the operation is more than disguise. Pember muses in tongue-in-cheek fashion, "What a benefactor to suffering humanity must that man be" who, like the literal painter of human faces, advertises his skill in covering up scars, blotches, and marks left by "personal encoun-ters." Irony soon slides into sarcasm, and by the conclusion of this slum portrait entitled "Painting *à la Mode*," Pember deems a painted woman after this fashion no better than a painted woman after another fashion. Though the Bowery artist reminds him of the Old Masters in their studios, Pember is "disgusted at such a horrible prostitution of so glorious an art as painting."[59] The transformative power of art proves false and deceitful, its ethical bankruptcy figured as a sexual commerce that corrupts innocence and destroys purity.

Riis's position is more nuanced than this view of art as deceptive adul-teration. He instead intuits that the quick exchanges among flowers and policemen's clubs fail to coalesce into singular or predictable configura-tions. From one perspective, the new art of photography easily fell in line with police work and a carceral mentality, as Riis's inclusion of criminal portraits (fig. 4) from the Rogues' Gallery attests. From a broader perspec-tive, however, photography might also exercise ethical influence by famil-iarizing citizens with true-to-life examples of taste, high culture, or moral-ity that before had been remote or unavailable. Hence the popularity of magic lantern shows staged in settlement houses and public parks where audiences could, theoretically, be uplifted and unified by the projection of glass slides illustrating instructive Bible scenes, harmonious natural panoramas, or perfectly proportioned European architecture. Defensively

FIGURE 4. Jacob Riis, "Typical Toughs from the Rogues' Gallery" (ca. 1890). Museum of the City of New York, Jacob A. Riis Collection. Riis includes an early version of the mugshot in *How the Other Half Lives*, here showing an alleged thief and burglar. Pember's Mary gives evidence of photography as a police mechanism when she agrees to sit for a face painter but not a photographer. In explaining her hesitation to enter the artist's studio, she says, "I was lookin' to see if there was any of them photograph tings about. I don't want to have my portrait took for no rogues' gallery" (*Mysteries and Miseries of the Great Metropolis*, 293–94).

stating that "my pictures were real work [*sic*] of art, not the cheap trash that you see nowadays on street screens," Riis casts his magic lantern exhibitions as an effort to redistribute aesthetic resources. Although his autobiography acknowledges that his real works of art were often product advertisements, the images projected, Riis asserts, can reform the "hoodlum" who is "driven into mischief by the utter poverty—aesthetically I mean—of his environment."[60] Riis privileges aesthetic conditions over economic ones, yet the stark and intrusive photographs in *How the Other Half Lives* refuse maudlin sentimentality. Art would make the tough less tough, as it were, more responsive to what the science of beauty identified as the instincts underlying social cohesion.

If the hoodlum were freed of an ugly environment, he would soon evolve into an ethical subject, and, as aesthetic science proposed, this initial step exerts a "coenopathic" or collective influence leading to social fellowship. Real differences separate Riis from fin-de-siècle readers of Kant who, like Veblen, spoke of "subsum[ing] the particular under the general" in order to achieve "the form of a connected whole."[61] The particular in Riis's writing and photographs appeared with a brutal materiality rarely found in the speculative works of philosophers and psychologists; nevertheless, socially minded theorists and aesthetically minded reformers emphasized the beautiful as a gentle force that would do the subsuming, coaxing particulars (such as hoodlums) into the embrace of the general (white middle-class liberalism).

Socially minded socialites, too, dispensed scraps of beauty and called it ethical reform. In Hjalmar Hjorth Boyeson's novel of high society and slum life, *Social Strugglers* (1893), magic lanterns shed moral influence not just on the poor who lack aesthetic resources but also on the wealthy who squander their privileged access to music, drama, and other arts. When a party of debutantes, properly chaperoned of course, gets into a carriage for a night on the town with the specific purposes of touring an Italian-American ghetto, the drama fails to provide any glimmer of social justice and, in fact, only exacerbates the gulf between elitism and squalor. The girls who attend this slumming party "had the sensation of sitting in a high-priced box, looking out upon a play which had been gotten up for their benefit, and pity was not their uppermost feeling. Even the children, who held out their hands to them, asking for 'fiva centa,' and the women, who sent volleys of sonorous but happily unintelligible observations after them, seemed to be separated from them by invisible foot-lights, and to be part of the play." Certainly a stirring spectacle, but its quality as unrehearsed theater readily represents class cleavages as a matter of overdone aesthetic performance. It comes as no surprise, then, that the novel's title refers not to people who struggle against poverty but rather to the heroine of finer sensibilities, Maud, whose heart rebels against the cloying conventions of her set. Even though the slumming party witnesses outward "faces [that] spoke of privations, sordid effort, and passions easily unleashed," the struggle does not take place in the streets; instead, the conflict wages at the most fundamental scene of instruction, Maud's soul.[62] She combats elitist perception, which, far from inspiring feelings of social cohesion, drives a wedge between the classes and permits the hoi polloi to feel self-satisfied about that distance.

The climax of the poor's unwilling performance comes as the carriage clatters to a stop and the party descends to watch a magic lantern show at a settlement house. It just so happens that the exhibition's impresario is Maud's true love, a specimen of muscular Christianity who narrates slides of Bible stories. His lecture instructs not only the downtrodden seeking shelter in the mission. Maud learns a valuable lesson as well:

> It was obvious to Maud, as she sat listening to his stirring discourse, that he had not arrived at this perfection of *artless art* without earnest endeavor and deep and painstaking study. There was not a particle of condescension in his manner, nor of the usual clerical, God-bless-you-my-children air; but rather the tone of an affectionate elder brother who claimed no other authority than that which was freely accorded to his ampler experience and his sincere desire to do good.[63]

Although she does not confess to a new understanding in so many words, Maud adopts a position taken by Boyeson in an 1893 essay complaining about the lack of social responsibility in writing that tries too hard to be clever. Artless art, in contrast, militates against "what the critics call art," a set of dainty judgments that "removes the book from the intelligence of ordinary people."[64] Artless art rejects the class connotations of aesthetic discourse while retaining its affective, transformative power. Stripping away suffocating layers of pretentiousness, artless art returns beauty to the theater of natural government, where it works on the soul's ethical instincts. Police clubs will not do for the upper classes. While it is impossible to instruct the members of the slumming party with nightsticks, it is within bounds to use more gentle means and pack ethical lessons into a magic lantern show and its reception.

If art replaces violence, it seems possible to reverse the process. Metaphoric substitution can always be undone: police clubs, once made superfluous by flowers, reappear at scenes of aesthetic instruction. When Riis stages a magic lantern show in a "little public park," the collectivity formed is anything but civil. Aware that some individuals in the crowd may prove insensible to beauty's influence, Riis supplements art with a show of force:

> I hired four stout men who were spoiling for a fight, and put good hickory clubs into their hands, bidding them restrain their natural desire to

use them till the time came. My forebodings were not vain. Potatoes, turnips, and eggs flew, not only at the curtain, but at the lantern and me. I stood it until the Castle of Heidelberg, which was one of my most beautiful colored views, was rent in twain by a rock that went clear through the curtain. Then I gave the word. . . . We made one dash into the crowd, and a wail arose from the bruised and bleeding hoodlums that hung over the town like a nightmare, while we galloped out of it, followed by cries of rage and a mob with rocks and clubs.[65]

Even though theorists of beauty and purveyors of art saw their various activities as democratic pedagogy, it is the mob that best imparts a democratic lesson in this instance. The toughs protest artistic representation as the reproduction of European affluence and aristocracy, their missiles an assault on both the Castle of Heidelberg and Riis's ideology of aesthetics. The crowd's unruly members negate interpretations (such as those found in Raymond's *Essentials of Aesthetics*) that value gardens as an aesthetic realm to be lingered in or walked through. What matters in this public encounter with beauty are a garden's products, its potatoes and turnips used to rout attempts at aesthetic instruction. The slippage from projecting pleasing images to wielding "good hickory clubs" illustrates the easy interchangeability between art and violence, between beauty and punishment.

Hickory clubs and other signs of violence are nowhere seen when Riis next brings his traveling magic lantern show to Elmira, New York. How Riis got there is not exactly clear, since striking railroad workers had ripped up the tracks. Riis is clearer in specifying that he and his colleagues "are noncombatants and engaged in peaceful industry."[66] His autobiography explains this about-face by contextualizing aesthetic performance: Riis prepares his projection screen by unfurling a white sheet that flaps about in the wind, readies his canisters of gas that will be used to illuminate the glass slides, and gathers a crowd of onlookers all during summer 1877 as bayoneted soldiers patrolled the Erie Railway. On July 22, 1877, the governor of New York issued a proclamation from Elmira, warning that "unless the State is to be given up to anarchy," swift measures must be taken to restore order.[67] Although law did prevail, afterimages of violence do not escape the photographer's eye, prompting Riis to report that "there had been dreadful trouble, fire, and bloodshed." With his slide exhibition midway on a bridge, "a crowd of strikers" at one end and a delegation of merchants and shop owners at the other, aesthetic instruction inevitably becomes political—and perceived as dangerous. A sheet become screen become white flag does not convey submission or surrender; the town's business interests suspect this fluttering *tabula rasa* as a seditious signal. Even though Riis attempts to identify with the forces of law by speaking collectively of "our end of the bridge," the blank screen's sheer ability to convey information paints him as a subversive, a co-conspirator, sending not-so-covert messages to striking workers.[68] Never mind that his original purpose in coming to Elmira had been to advertise publication of a city directory, his mission a careful blend of the civic and the commercial. What the authorities and a scary sounding "committee of citizens" see in the language of images trumps all: aesthetic education doubles as popular agitation. In terms of democratic meaning, the vignettes of Riis's magic lantern experiences, one a battle by aesthetics against the rabble and the other an inadvertent alliance of aesthetics and the crowd, are as confused as policemen's clubs become flowers—and back again. Now, however, one more signifier gets added to the mix: glass slides etched with pleasing images replace hickory clubs, but it is a substitution that requires the presence of bayonets. Invited to leave on the next train out of Elmira, Riis did not refuse the offer. The alternative, it seemed, was to get caught up in this signifying chain and experience personally the pleasure and pain of metaleptic substitution and reprisal.

Riis's problem at Elmira was that he expected images to establish *sensus communis,* a common understanding in which individuals, though divided by different interests with respect to capital and labor, could overcome class antagonism by effectively imagining themselves in the place of others. In his view, strikes erupted precisely because of a lack of common understanding between employer and employee: if they could only see their "common interests," then "the man who does the work and the man who hires it done so that he may have time to attend to his own" would recognize each other as "workmen."[69] An awareness that each engages in similar economic activity will create community among opposed individuals, previously trapped in the subjectivity of private judgment. By sensing "common interests," individuals will attain something like a universal view of the greater social needs they all share. Although Riis casts a strike as an atomized confrontation between owner and worker, he is not dealing with individuals. Rather, aesthetic language is positioned amid two crowds that have been created, or, at least, put on alert and stirred up by images from a magic lantern. Not *sensus communis* but *sensus conflictionis:* aesthetics are a battleground in which judgment incites violence.

This history puts a wrinkle in aesthetic theory by plotting a third co-ordinate on the cultural map of beauty. University philosophers and psy-chologists had no problem talking about the individual in the abstract, just as they effortlessly jumped from there to the general terrain of the uni-versal. But Riis points to an unreconciled social force, one greater than the individual but not quite universal, which makes groups, crowds, and mobs a worrisome emanation of collective feeling. In colleges, men and women learned that aesthetic judgment could, theoretically, subsume the particular under the general and create worldwide community; in the streets, Riis learned the slightly different lesson that aesthetic judgment could pit the particular against the general. In each case, beauty expands beyond individuals to form collectivities, but the crucial difference con-cerns the issue of scale and whether the collectivities formed represent universal accord or a more localized and potentially combative grouping such as the crowd.

BEAUTY AND DANGER

From the ethical dimension of the magic lantern show in Boyeson's *Social Strugglers* to Riis's illuminated pictures flashed at park-goers and strikers, aesthetic value seems as fungible as flowers become billy clubs. Encom-passing parables of moral enlightenment and scenes of unwitting work-ing-class alliance, the potential implications of extending art to the masses are as mobile as the moving images of the magic lantern itself. Eagleton captures this dynamism well, depicting aesthetics as at once fighting on the side of an "inarticulate rebellion against the tyranny of the theoreti-cal" while conspiring with universalist claims that suit repressive power all too well.[70] This dialectical energy revolves around aesthetic theory de-veloped by the academic professional class at the turn of the century. On the one hand, the philosophy of beauty abounds with imperatives. "Ev-ery realization of the ideal of beauty . . . *ought* to be admired and sought by all rational beings," declared a Yale philosophy professor.[71] University researchers aspired to global and categorical statements when it came to setting out the scientific laws of aesthetics: "Beauty must be for all minds alike. . . . It is offended by multiplicity."[72] On the other hand, aesthetics open up into fluidity and unpredictability: "It is an obvious psychological truth that there is no unity in pleasure," stated *The Philosophy of the Beauti-*

ful.[73] While unity remains indispensable, Raymond's *Essentials of Aesthetics* holds that human perception without variety is oppressed by monotony and singularity. The political ramifications of this tension, like the standoff between universal human community and conflictive formations of mass subjectivity, were not lost on Professor Gayley and his colleague from the University of Michigan, Fred Scott, who sought to reconcile idiosyncratic neurological response with global sensibility by giving aesthetic judgment a quasi-socialist tinge that made "the people" the true arbiters of taste. Gayley and Scott wonder broadly about the relationship of art to the social body and social progress, reworking what seem to be purely academic debates over unity and multiplicity as deeply political concerns. "Is the best art that which appeals to the people—the masses? Or that which appeals to an aristocracy of intellect and emotion?" they asked.[74]

In lectures at Harvard, John Dewey had no difficulty answering such questions once he wrested art away from the narrowness of "self" and claimed its power on behalf of "the common world" and "public world." As artwork stimulates collective sensibility, it acquires a transformative force that results in unexpected changes to political structures and social arrangements. For Dewey, "the work of esthetic art satisfies many ends, none of which is laid down in advance." This openness jibes with the multiplicity of human experience by refusing to command a precise set of reactions, a prescribed habitus, or a "limited mode of living." Art experienced in this manner makes subjects restless, unwilling to accept customary and stultifying social patterns as either pleasurable or desirable. Art spurs "the first stirrings of dissatisfaction," inciting interrogations of convention, precept, and established order.[75]

Dewey's emphasis on art's disaggregating effects seems a far cry from the attention that academics a generation earlier gave to beauty's role in promoting social cohesion. Whether aesthetics render subjects quiescent or excite the senses, fuel homogeneity or foster diversity, or lay down the law or flout it, these possibilities all emerge from recognition that beauty packs many forms of power—psychological, ethical, affective, and political. The question for theorists and practitioners of aesthetics becomes: how to feel and what to think about that power? Is this power to be jealously guarded lest it fall into the grimy hands of hoodlums who, at the very least, will not esteem its true value or potential? Or, in a moment of nationalist optimism, should this power be directed at those hoodlums to promote civic education and Americanization? Riis had less of a problem when he confronted this issue in 1901: "We all love power—to be on the winning side. You cannot help being there when you are fighting the slum, for it is the cause of justice and right."[76] Riis dispenses with ethical considerations—all that matters is a victorious outcome—only to have notions of justice return to retrospectively sanction the end result as fair and just. He enlists artistic technology in a bid for power because he well knew that magic lanterns, flash powder, and cameras potentially shaped the social world, generating citizens, making them, in an echo of his autobiography's title, into Americans.

Theorists of beauty who had none of Riis's devices at hand and instead relied only on abstract formulations drew conclusions about aesthetics and self-making similar to those of the urban photographer. When professional men and women at the turn of the century investigated the psychological dimension of aesthetics, they readily implied the cultivation of individuality as a beautiful undertaking. "Beauty, we learn, is to bring unity and self-completeness into the personality": according to a newspaper review of Puffer's *Psychology of Beauty,* this dictum constitutes the central lesson of the Wellesley professor's work, and many felt that this general principle could be fitted to the particular goal of national social cohesion.[77] Such wisdom suggested that life, instead of merely imitating art, is shaped, managed, and given purpose by beauty. For any number of reasons from the aestheticization of politics to the regulation of conduct, the intimate association of aesthetics and governance sets off alarms. But this convergence need not get our hackles up: the "aesthetics of existence," a concept Michel Foucault explored in his later writings and interviews, endows subjects with the capacity to govern themselves in ways that produce their lives—and, just as importantly, the lives of those around them—as works of art.

This productive—as opposed to the merely repressive—facet of aesthetics would seem to lead, naturally enough, to Foucault. Before taking up that discussion, an examination of these ideas also leads, historically enough, to Kate Gordon's *Esthetics,* a college textbook for junior and seniors published in 1909. Under the section heading "Life as a Work of Art," her book draws together psychological studies of feeling and ethics to theorize three modes of existence, each tightly structured around a formalist sense of aesthetic style. In the romantic mode, the subject pursues life on the edge, acting in accord with impulse, instinct, and private conviction. Basic principles of harmony and equilibrium, like caution, are thrown to the wind under this style, rendering it of dubious value to projects of ethical self-construction. Gordon appreciates a realist mode even less, since its adherents tend to obsess over miniscule details at the expense of forgetting the big picture that connects subjects to broader patterns of the social. *Esthetics* reserves esteem for a mode of existence based on "the classical ideal," which encourages a life patterned after a Greek temple so that "order, proportion, symmetry, balance, perfection of detail" predominate. As a work of art, life never strays from formal principles that underlie justice. "Beauty," she concludes, "is an essential aspect of the ethical ideal. . . . So it is with art and life; each takes its turn as leader of the other, and life could no more spare art in the wide sense of that term than art could spare life."[78] Wrapped around one another, art and life are negotiable, their interchangeability powered by a logic of substitution that ultimately is about power in its productive aspects, aspects that have little do with power as out-and-out subjugation.

As Gordon hopscotches from aesthetics to ethics and from art to justice, she acknowledges that beauty exerts a power both so basic and transcendent as to be simultaneously prior to and beyond considerations of morality. Rooted in fundamental human emotions and feelings, the ethical stimulus derived from beauty precedes logical proofs about goodness. If beauty is only what everyone else feels, the universal accord that it inspires can also lead to a "moral regularity" synonymous with conservatism.[79] Like her mentor, Dewey, Gordon does not want to surrender the transformative potential of aesthetics. Without this capacity, there is no point to treating life as a work of art since doing so would immobilize the subject and put existence under glass. *Sensus communis* seems overrated; for Dewey and Gordon, social progress depends on a robust sense of conflict that seems like a theoretical rendition of the opposition that Riis encountered in showing pictures to crowds of hoodlums and strikers. Art apart from conventional morality: *Esthetics* arrives rather inadvertently at a position, which from the perspective of Elmira's concerned citizens who hurried magic lantern showmen out of town, no doubt smacks of anarchism.

An "absence of morality," as Foucault would insist almost a century later, need not negate the presence of ethics.[80] An aesthetics of existence hinges on ethics but not in the usual sense that implies adherence to rigid social formulas or pre-given moral expectations. Instead, by ethics Foucault intends an art of living that has no truck with juridical, religious, or other disciplinary structures. As a subject undertakes the project of a beautiful existence, treating "the *bios* as a material for an aesthetic piece of art," ethics and aesthetics embellish one another.[81] Like Gordon's "Life as a Work of Art" or the City Beautiful crusade that invoked Pericles and the Parthenon, Foucault's investigation cruises the archive of Greece, but his visit to the classical past nets markedly different results. The difference lies in the recourse to instinct among turn-of-the-century theorists of aesthetics as opposed to the deep sociality uncovered by Foucault's genealogy. Gordon's "Life as a Work of Art," as with most efforts in her day to describe a psychology of beauty, trades heavily on an interiorized subjectivity that experiences citizenship as a code of conduct, as an art of governance. Foucault guards against the impulse to channel ethics into an intense personal examination of self that requires a turn away from the public political world. An aesthetics of existence does not predispose the subject to the mortifications of conscience—although early Christianity, according to Foucault, would soon rush down that solitary path of abnegation. Practicing life as a work of art instead functions as "an intensification of social relations."[82] Art of this sort demands context: in Foucault's version of the Hellenistic world, enmeshing the self amid others provides texture and meaning to the ethos of a beautiful existence. Pursuit of beauty in this sense does not aestheticize life but rather politicizes it by revealing the subject as ethically—but not morally—situated among others.

No pretty picture is this, however. Always involving relations of power and frequently wrought up with mastery and even domination, the cultivation of the self as an ethical subject is a project that touches upon others, "blend[ing] into preexisting relations, giving them a new coloration and a greater warmth."[83] Treating the *bios* as a work of art after this fashion is a non-Kantian project in which the absoluteness and regularity that come with harmony and ideal proportion are out of place. Foucault suggests "dissymmetry" and "nonreciprocity" as criteria for an "aesthetics of existence" because these lopsided formal principles keep life beautiful by rendering it out of step with the authoritarian need for order and moral clarity.[84] Other people provide context to the art of one's life, making the politics that appear between individuals more vivid, deeper in meaning, richer in association, more powerful in its effects, and, finally, less manageable in terms of its outcomes.

Yet the Greek example, no matter how laden with past promise, will not serve as a model for modernity. Foucault acknowledges as much in a 1983 interview when he refused to hold up life in classical antiquity as a fix for contemporary social arrangements. "I don't accept the word *alternative*," he tells his interlocutors. The past comes burdened with its own problems, too weighted down by historical specifics to offer solutions for the history of the present. But Foucault is interested a "genealogy of problems" in which solutions are scarce and risks common. "My point is not that everything is bad," Foucault explains. "But that everything is dangerous, which is not exactly the same as bad. If everything is dangerous, then we always have something to do." Such danger stalks Foucault's conceptualization of a beautiful existence that intersects with others on an ethical basis since that intersection is equally prone to subjection as care. "Couldn't everyone's life become a work of art?" he asks, even though he has already admitted that only a select subset of citizens was empowered to undertake an aesthetics of existence. Ethics after this fashion "was not a question of giving a pattern of behavior for everybody. It was a personal choice for a small elite."[85] The disjunction between "everyone's life" and *not* "everybody" marks the danger: democratic longing trips over antidemocratic restriction.

This danger that is the accomplice of Foucault's aesthetics lurks around the history of reformist and academic aesthetics. For Riis, as we have seen, the deployment of aesthetic resources creates multiple public bodies, assembling audiences of well-heeled citizens but also gathering rowdies to public parks, intriguing store merchants but also exciting crowds teetering on the edge of working-class unrest. Aesthetics are not always pretty or predictable. Illuminated glass slides and other materials of beauty that were supposed to create culture in the face of anarchy seemed just as likely to breed riot. The unsteadiness of aesthetic discourse in this historical context, engendering an ethical subject but also priming the passions of collective bodies, far outpaces the sociality that characterizes Foucault's notion of a beautiful life. The aesthetics of self-creation, as Thomas Augst illustrates in his study of diaries by middle-class young men in the nineteenth century, intensified an individual accounting of morality. Social feeling and connections to others, insofar as such impulses figured into this ethical culture, seem rather airy, a nice but rather vague gesture that "linked the individual student to the collective memory of *humanitas.*"[86] In parks, tenements, even in university classrooms at the turn of the century, the prospect of collectivity was much more than a memory; it was an insistently material context that could lead crowds and other public subjects, such as strikers and criminals, to act dramatically.

The art of self-government can not be held apart from suspicions of moral anarchy. Aesthetic resources designed to instruct and elevate subjects posed inadvertent dangers to ethical citizenship. In addition to bestowing moral influence, flowers came laced with seduction, as distributing blossoms on the city streets provided a dodge for prostitutes. Girls selling bouquets, contemporaries of Riis observed, were no doubt selling much more, using anemones and violets as "cover" for "places of vile resort."[87] The flower mission that encouraged "innocent and attractive recreations" remained in close proximity to "bad habits and pernicious customs" that grew like weeds in the urban wilderness.[88] The problem with using beauty to mold subjectivity was that it might in fact mold subjectivity: while the beautiful polis transforms disconnected private persons into publicly concerned citizens, the prospect of having citizens out on the streets desiring equitable living arrangements, justice, or anything else for that matter could not always be trusted to link up with conventional notions of morality. The risk of turning to aesthetic feelings as a basis for social association was that this gambit might accomplish its purpose, encouraging unlooked-for and unlicensed couplings.

"Hundreds of bouquets are distributed every day. They prevent crime," a Boston matron in Howells's *The Minister's Charge* (1887) states with matter-of-fact irony.[89] Howells follows this irony with accusation, implying that the real crime occurs among upper-middle-class persons who imagine that distributing flowers actually amounts to meaningful social intervention. Bouquets, as it happened, seemed to abet crime, according to one Boston publication lamenting the plight of "those little girls who sell flowers at the doors of houses of bad repute."[90] Aesthetics resources cannot be controlled nor their effects predicted. As Riis observes derogatorily, "the ordinary aesthetic equipment of the slum"—by which he means dime novels, cheap theater productions, and the paint on painted women—often leads to the reformatory or worse. Boys with an appetite for "literature of the Dare-Devil-Dan-the-Death-Dealing-Monster-of-Dakota order" are seduced by fantasies of petty thievery and assault.[91] Life as a work of art can be replaced by a life of crime—but the situation is more insidious since art paves the way for criminality.

Even the camera and photograph, trusty friends of the police and surveillance, enhance an aesthetics of lawless conduct. In *The Battle with the Slum*, Riis recounts an episode of two muggers who, styling themselves outlaws of the territories, pose for a crude Bowery tintype, taking on roles of hold-up man and victim (fig. 5). Once apprehended, the bandits confess that they staged this scene of strong-arm robbery as a "rehearsal" to commemorate how one of their more successful jobs went down.[92] Dramatic and visual arts coincide in a *tableau vivant* of larceny. Riis discovered as much when he went down to the docks at West 37th Street to photograph

FIGURE 5. Jacob Riis, "Two Bowery Lodgers in Character, Practicing a Hold-Up" (ca. 1890). Museum of the City of New York, Jacob A. Riis Collection. Aesthetic resources, as this tintype from Riis's *Battle with the Slum* suggests, could provide a dress rehearsal for crime.

a street gang and saw firsthand how the presence of the camera encourages the performance of crime. The members of the "Montgomery Guards" clamor to have their portraits taken, completely unfazed by any associations that photographs have with police mug shots. In fact, the petty thieves play up these associations by wishing to appear as brazen criminals

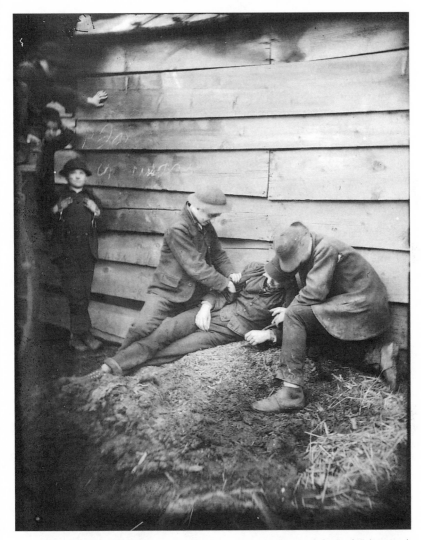

FIGURE 6. Jacob Riis, "Members of the Gang Showing How They 'Did the Trick'" (ca. 1890). Museum of the City of New York, Jacob A. Riis Collection. Soon after the image was taken, the gang reenacts this scene for real by mugging a passerby. In this shot, the gang members extend beyond the frame, suggesting how photographic representation bleeds into the world of crime.

who welcome the documentary lens of the camera as a means of preserving and accentuating their moral trespasses. Riis's art inspires a rendition of highway robbery as the gang gets "in character" and stages a mugging with one of their own members adopting the role of victim (fig. 6). Riis leaves no doubt that this performance amounts to more than harmless method acting. Half an hour later and three blocks over he walks into a police station to face the very gang members he has just photographed, now in jail for theft and battery after jumping a Jewish peddler and "trying to saw his head off."[93] Connections between aesthetic technology and crime remain suspect. Is the photograph a rehearsal for violence? Can the performance of crime be distinguished from its enactment? Because Riis's mission is in part aesthetic, it is also dangerous, leaving him on some rather shaky ethical ground, as it appears his actions and equipment may have abetted vice.

Lessons of aesthetics are not schematic, which is precisely why they are dangerous. Approaching beauty through Aesthetics 101 as well as progressive cultural reform, researchers and reformers learned how much they did not know about their topic or the human subjects it supposedly nurtured. For all its grounding in moral philosophy, the science of beauty might prove a "gay science," which Nietzsche tells us is a system that cannot be trusted, let alone taken at face value. And, as we might imagine Riis adding, neither could a photograph. As a model for social arrangements, art spurs on suspect groupings (such as a strike in Elmira) that may not be so well arranged; as a practicum for moral citizenship, aesthetic training leads to the practice of immoral activities (such as prostitution or theft); as a design for democratic tranquility, beauty seems to traffic in haphazard violence (such as billy clubs). If immigration, labor conflict, and urban disarray often made it seem that culture was in a battle against anarchy, it was never certain which side was winning. Even more disturbing, it was never clear which side art, aesthetics, and beauty were on.

AMERICAN LITERATURE
INTERNATIONALE

. . . .

Translation, Strike, and the Time of Political Possibility

The irony about the installment of "Aesthetics 101" as a fixture in so many U.S. colleges was that the readings assigned and examples invoked tended to be non-American. The 1896 course catalogue for the University of California, Berkeley is heavy on Kant.[1] The papers of Yale undergraduate and then Yale professor Henry Davies mention U.S. contexts rarely. Davies's "Data of Aesthetics," a handwritten notebook on beauty from a "psychogenetic standpoint," is filled with pen-and-ink drawings of cornices, facades, and cathedral arches associated with European cultural treasures.[2] For some at Harvard, aesthetics may have had a less psychological cast, but the content of the field still seemed outside the nation. In his stint as a University Lecturer at Harvard, William Dean Howells framed his comments on style, technique, and art in the context of Italian literature. When he searched for precedents to realism, the novels of Jane Austen, not those of Brockden Brown or Hawthorne, came first to mind because their exacting social perspective made them nothing short of "beautiful."[3] So, too, as we will see in chapter 3, Matthew Towns in Du Bois's *Dark Princess* will have his head momentarily turned by Croce and Italian aesthetic theory before regaining his bearings in the sorrow songs. If taste was a matter of aesthetics, its flavor was distinctively international.

This chapter considers several connected variants of "the international," ranging from issues of translation to the specter of worldwide working-class revolt. Its archive is the most traditional and literary of all the chapters in this book with chunks of analysis devoted to Walt Whitman and Howells. At the same time, however, the competing attention that I give to texts about dynamite, bomb making, and socialist revolution leads this chapter unapologetically in a different direction toward the radical dissolution of tradition. These diverging trajectories each gain initial impetus in aesthetic forms associated with crowds, collective pleasure, and shared pain. Such spectacles and feelings gave proof of the organic unity of national culture even as they veered toward undeniably foreign elements that stood in anarchic opposition to social order. This skid toward the foreign represents a road seldom taken in U.S. cultural politics. As a result, this chapter is perhaps more speculative than actual, asking how an alternative literary history can provide an account in which translation appears, neither as a tool of linguistic conversion nor as a progenitor of babble, but as a revolutionary engagement with the idea of the common.

TRANSLATING AESTHETICS TO THE COMMON

During his U.S. lecture tour, Matthew Arnold put a finger on what Howells, Du Bois, and others felt instinctively about the logical inconsistency of discussing America and aesthetic achievement in the same breath. As it turned out, though, Arnold failed to strike a sympathetic chord in Howells, who rather resented interlopers from across the pond taking potshots at U.S. culture and calling it one shade better than anarchy. Aware that the middling state of American arts and letters did not make for easy refutation of Arnold's criticism, Howells accepted—and then twisted—the Englishman's evaluation of the American novel as an undistinguished, plebeian affair: "Such beauty and grandeur as we have is common beauty, common grandeur, or the beauty and grandeur in which the quality of solidarity so prevails that neither distinguishes itself to the disadvantage of anything else." Howells counsels his fellow citizens to embrace the ordinary, equalizing aspects of American culture rather than feel embarrassed by its shortcomings. Whereas Arnold mounts his attack on purely aesthetic grounds (though, of course, politics are everywhere evident in the class anxieties of *Culture and Anarchy*), Howells doctors aesthetic criteria to include social and political factors so that "solidarity" becomes the responsibility of fiction. "The arts must become democratic" if only so it will be proven that "the reproach which Mr. Arnold was half right in making shall have no justice in it."[4] Let us welcome the accusation that "our" literature is common, Howells argues, because American provincialism provides the basis for social unity. For all Howells cared, the Euro-trash of his day could be damned.

This rejection of snobbery as a foreign attitudinal import bolsters Howells's advocacy of "common beauty" as a homegrown product. Literary realism hinges on what Amy Kaplan identifies as an "aesthetic of the common," which stresses shared perceptions in an effort to craft a single national culture that is broadly accessible.[5] College lectures for "Aesthetics 101" shared this emphasis on the common, imbuing it with a psycho-evolutionary strain by positing aesthetic instinct as a species-wide trait that led to everyday sociality and cooperation. In James Hayden Tufts's course in aesthetics for seniors at the University of Chicago in 1902, the necessary prerequisite of Introductory Psychology ensured that students would be primed to understand the beautiful in terms of human social function. From this perspective, aesthetic instinct was as momentous as any element in human evolution, since the "exploration of aesthetic categories" in terms of "social psychology" indicates that art, throughout the history of civilization, has "served social ends in the struggle for existence." Tufts's association of aesthetics with "the joys of common glory, common victory . . . or the grief of the common loss" seems of a piece with Howells's attention to an "aesthetics of the common," although this developmental account of a timeless social impulse seems rather bloodless, deprived of the international and collective resonance that adds tension to Howells's portrait of the common.[6]

Howells made a case for everyday aesthetics even as he lavished attention on foreign writers whose names did not roll readily or easily off American tongues. In a famous September 1886 installment of his "Editor's Study" column for *Harper's Monthly*, he introduced readers to the soul-stirring sufferings of Dostoyevsky's *Crime and Punishment* only to aver that the American literary gallery requires no grim portraits of hunger, misery, or political executions—although the sentencing of the Haymarket anarchists to death on August 20, 1886 would seem to have already contradicted Howells's musings before the September column ever made its way into print. For now, though, Howells claims that

> very few American novelists have been led out to be shot, or finally exiled to the rigors of a winter at Duluth; one might make Herr [Johann]

Most the hero of a labor-question romance with perfect impunity; and in a land where journeymen carpenters and plumbers strike for four dollars a day the sum of hunger and cold is certainly very small, and the wrong from class to class is almost inappreciable. We invite our novelists, therefore, to concern themselves with more smiling aspects of life, which are the more American, and to seek the universal in the individual rather than the social interests.[7]

A mild expression of literary nativism, Howells's sketch surveys foreign writers to better acknowledge that international themes do not suit his countrymen's—and especially countrywomen's—tastes. The aesthetics of the common are reduced to the common denominator of the individual, the privatized calculus of a contented self cut adrift from class relationships and the earlier talk of "solidarity," its gesture toward collective action or, at the very least, collective feeling if action seemed too threatening, nowhere to be seen. Because of this conviction that the drama of the individual could speak for the multitude, social realism does not result in social expression. Simultaneously contracted to the individual and exalted to the universal, realist aesthetics imagined "solidarity" by conflating the fantasy of a homogenous people under the sign of the abstract person. But like other critics of the social landscape, including Jane Addams, George Santayana, and Jacob Riis, Howells was forced to admit that heterogeneity—in the form of strikers, crowds, and anarchists—gave "solidarity" a Janus-faced aspect, both smiling and unsmiling. It all depends on how one translates the idea of "solidarity."

The blithe indifference to class strife embedded in Howells's "smiling aspects of life" incurred him the scorn of Sinclair Lewis and, later, a generation of literary critics. As Gore Vidal puts it, Howells "rather absently dynamited his own reputation for the next century" by palming off an evasive and maudlin justification of the status quo as though it were an aesthetic manifesto of the common opposed to artificially ornate modes of sentimentality and melodrama.[8] Vidal's canny assessment alludes to Howells's passing invocation—and immediate rejection of—Johann Most, a German anarchist who urged U.S. workers and their European counterparts to manufacture explosives in basements for use in the coming revolution against capital. In light of the homemade bomb lobbed into the ranks of police four months earlier during a workers' demonstration in Haymarket Square, Howells's attempts to defuse the radical critique of capital, as though any anarchist could harmlessly be written up as "the hero of a labor-question romance," sounded not just blithely indifferent but callously so.

Although sunny portraits of American life could not be more different than the extremist views of an anarchist such as Most, Howells's aesthetic proclamation resembles the agitator's portentous politics in an important respect: each invokes the common. While Howells celebrated ordinary and unpretentious individuals, Most devoted his attention to everyday objects. "Take a piece of iron pipe, as commonly used for water and gas mains, and cut it into short lengths" and you are on your way to making pipe bombs, Most explained in his *Science of Revolutionary Warfare* (1885). Or, construct homemade grenades using "hollow spheres of zinc," which "have the advantage that they can be made in an ordinary apartment." Obtaining potassium chlorate, a crucial ingredient of explosives, is never a problem because it is commonly available at "any drugstore" for "very cheap," usually no more than 35 cents a pound. Best of all is highly flammable gun cotton, loads of which can be stuffed into sofas and mattresses and carted around in public "under the noses of the police." Most had successfully disguised his own person within the everyday when he moved to Jersey City Heights and, pretending to be an ordinary workingman, was hired on at a dynamite factory. When he quit, he did not take any dynamite with him but something far more dangerous: knowledge of how to make explosives. Formulas previously available only in "expensive textbooks meant for professional chemists," now were put at the disposal of "the layman."[9] Armed with this know-how shared by comrades in a proletarian army of the dispossessed, the fed-up layman would soon be prepared to drive a stake through the hearts of "capitalistic vampires" so that property, the means of production, in short, everything, and not just beauty, would be held in common.[10]

Notions of the common, as deployed by an anarchist and a fixture of the literary establishment, strike vastly different chords. This difference between Most and Howells can appear as mainly stylistic: as Dick Hebdige's study of subculture suggests, style marks an aesthetic terrain that always bears traces of conflict and antagonism. The Sex Pistols and The Clash, according to Hebdige, turned to "the language of the common man" in order to prepare an "armoury of frontal assaults" on bourgeois tastes that limited art and entertainment to class-bound registers. Language of the common can be spoken with a range of intonations from Howells's optimistic notes about human solidarity to the "vulgar" in-your-face tones with which punk subcultures advocate anarchy in the U.K. For his part, Howells emphasizes stylistic difference in *A Hazard of New Fortunes* by making the novel's anarchist speak with a thick German accent that mangles socialist "principles" into "brincibles." However disaffected or angry, style has a knack for pushing its way into the cloistered halls of culture. With punk make-up in the 1970s "faces became abstract portraits . . . meticulously executed studies in alienation," much as the anarchist's face of the 1880s serves as an exemplum of intensity and zeal for the artists in *A Hazard of New Fortunes* who use him as a model.[11] Despite sharp stylistic contrasts among late-twentieth-century punks, a late-nineteenth-century revolutionary like Most, and a respectable novelist like Howells, each enlists the common as a locus of aesthetic tension in an effort to redraw the landscape of social possibility.

Just in case stylistic differences were not pronounced enough, when Howells reworked his thoughts about common aesthetics and homegrown American fiction as a showcase for the "smiling aspects of life," he omitted all reference to the foreign anarchist. It was one thing to state indifferently that contented, well-fed U.S. publics "may nevertheless read Dostoïevsky" without too much harm and quite another to insert ironic jabs about foreign dynamiters.[12] In the final tally, however, were the two invocations of foreignness all that dissimilar? University and extension courses invoked a German Romantic tradition that was not always easy to distinguish from German social radicalism. Although aesthetic judgment complements middle-class pursuits, Eagleton reminds us that this tradition is "double-edged," laced with affect, sensuousness, and collective impulses that are "exactly what it [the social order] has most cause to fear."[13] Still, aesthetic ideology's role in fashioning a well-heeled subject of the state often renders these notes of social insubordination barely audible. As a faintly legible trace from a copy of James Hayden Tufts's *On the Genesis of the Aesthetic Categories* shows, such stirrings appear quite literally in the margins. Next to a passage rehearsing Kant's notion of subjective judgment as the basis of objective sense, a much-faded scrawl, the artifact of what seems to be handwriting contemporary with the text itself, reads "public thought."[14] This connection between aesthetics and collectivity prompted hesitation in others: Davies wrote that "art is undoubtedly a social function dependent on social motives, social ideals, and social activities" but then returned to this sentence and penciled in "quasi" to modify "social."[15] Hardly the stuff of revolution, these bits of marginalia nonetheless invest aesthetic education with a collectivist trajectory. What public accents do aesthetics acquire in their dissemination? In the internationalization of philosophic tradition, how does German idealism intersect with the currents of American pragmatism? How do aesthetics become "socialized" in their translation to U.S. shores?

Translation, as Walter Benjamin would later remark, operates as a mode of upheaval that fragments meaning into shards of the text's original language. True enough: translation converts texts to an alien tongue, creating new meanings, often sacrificing the fullness of signification that inheres in the original. But it would be a mistake to believe that translation affects the original as a matter of loss or deficiency. Instead, translation can radically alter "the mother tongue of the translator," introducing new ideas, concepts, and sensibilities to a language that had abandoned its users to the same old idiom, not simply of expression, but also of social possibility.[16] In some notes for a radio dialogue, Benjamin suggested that the effort to perfect translation as an "autonomous art form" kills off social possibility by leaving no room for "bad translations" that would engender "productive misunderstandings."[17] From this perspective, the effects of "Aesthetics 101" lay not in what this discourse communicated about art to college students, Wisconsin dairy farmers, or immigrants visiting Jane Addams's Hull-House. Rather, the social charge of aesthetics resides in the more fundamental fact that matters of form and feeling serve as an inexact conduit between the American and the un-American. With frequent mention of Arnold, Schiller, and Kant, "Aesthetics 101" could not deny the transatlantic pull of British culture and German Romanticism. German radicalism, in contrast, was something to deny, but this insurgent meaning always lay dormant in a discourse concerned with common tastes, human solidarity, and universalism.

Keeping its eye on the rise of "German socialism in America," the *North American Review* traced the crisis back to a variety of influences including "the philosophic mind of Kant."[18] Art and beauty were not that innocent after all. Aesthetic discourse repositions American literature on an international axis, but those coordinates are also crisscrossed by the specter of "the Internationale," the movement that emerged from the International Workingmen's Association (also known as the First International of 1864) to promote the worldwide interests of the dispossessed over and beyond the barriers of language, ethnicity, and nation. Such repositioning is foremost an act of geographic translation, as in the etymological sense of *translāt-us* in which something is "carried across," "transferred," or "transported."

As in Benjamin's rendering of the act of translation, that "something" may not be an object so much as a mode of understanding. What matters is not the thing carried but the movement itself, the minor adjustments as well as tectonic shifts that result from rephrasing and replacing. Ending the inaugural address to the First International, one member of the General Council sounded a familiar global imperative that also registers a mandate for translation: "Proletarians of all countries, unite!"[19] This exhortation requires translation to enlarge the possibilities for expressing new formations of community.

Collective formations emerge when American literature is understood as a site of translation. What new constellations come to light when literature is recognized not simply as international but also as Internationale in the sense of a revolutionary project that employs a language inflected with accents of mass subjectivity? This question immediately invites a second that undercuts the implicit progressivism of the first: does not the specter of a revolutionary language sound a counterrevolutionary alarm to ensure that American expression remain fixed in place? The answer to both queries lies in a focus that is not so much transnational as *translational:* according to Benjamin, translation is systemic—"it intends language as a whole"—modifying the contours of what can be thought and said. Rather than narrowly construe translation as equivalence between tongues so that "house" equals *haus, maison,* or *casa,* "translation must in large measure refrain from wanting to communicate something, from rendering sense."[20] The task of the translator is not to pin down meaning but to open up as-yet unimagined possibilities for both the original and the language to which it is carried. This theoretical account acquires historical texture in late-nineteenth-century culture as American aesthetic discourse sought to adjust itself to seemingly foreign ideas about crowds, mass meetings, and anarchist activity.

Howells found himself drawn into the aesthetics and politics of internationalism when he took the unpopular stand of protesting the legal machinery that convicted the Haymarket martyrs on rather flimsy evidence. The press lambasted Howells, telling him to keep his nose in books and magazines where it belonged. U.S. newspapers, he later recalled, "abused me heartily as if I had proclaimed myself a dynamiter."[21] From overseas, there came at least one show of support when a translator enclosed a note with some recent specimens of Norwegian fiction that she thought Howells, in light of his efforts to secure an appeal and amnesty for the Haymarket anarchists, might appreciate. She saw no split between the author's fiction and his public protests against the state's rush to judgment. In her eyes, Howells is both a "true artist" and a "brave and just man." The letter writer had her doubts whether Howells would recognize her name, so she reminded him that just two years before the Chicago bombing she and her husband had toured the U.S. giving speeches on socialism. In case that still did not ring a bell, she was certain that her maiden name would be familiar: "my father's name I am sure you know—Karl Marx."[22] As it turns out, Eleanor Marx-Aveling's letter to Howells was not the first time that someone with the last name of Marx had written to America to discuss aesthetics and politics.

THE TIME OF AMERICAN LITERATURE

The same year that witnessed the publication of Melville's *Pierre* and Hawthorne's *The Blithedale Romance,* a German immigrant named Joseph Weydemeyer living in New York laid out forty dollars to print a lengthy pamphlet analyzing the aesthetic dimensions to the revolution and counterrevolutionary aftermath of the 1848 socialist uprising in France. Its author, Karl Marx, urged quick publication since the events were fleeting, but he seemed pleased when one thousand copies of *The Eighteenth Brumaire of Louis Bonaparte* were printed in 1852. As Marx's wife prodded Weydemeyer, it was best "not to delay matters too long . . . for the matter is extremely timely."[23] While Jenny Marx's concerns for timeliness are reasonable, they nonetheless underestimate the ability of *The Eighteenth Brumaire* to propel itself forward and act as a template for evaluating the usefulness and bankruptcy of aesthetics as a political tool in times of revolution. Marx's 1852 text resonates, to follow Wai Chee Dimock's urging that reading practices break free from restrictive notions of literary chronology, well beyond its temporal moment.[24] This provisional installment of Marx in the panoply of the American Renaissance reveals an international dimension to the aesthetic language welling up from the waves of strikes and domestic terrorism sweeping the late-nineteenth-century U.S.

The *Eighteenth Brumaire* supplies an unexpected global context to American literature that reorders the timeline of literary production. Chronologies do not suddenly need to be ditched; the sequence of literary history remains unchanged by injecting Marx into the American canon. What is altered, however, is the present and future of American literature, specifically, our understanding of language's capacity to effect sociopolitical or cultural change. Literary history unfolds as it always has; Melville still published *Moby-Dick* in 1851 whether or not Marx's *The Eighteenth Brumaire* is added to the American Renaissance. Literary production, in contrast, undergoes some fairly significant changes within this model, for what Marx encourages is renewed attention to the political possibilities that language creates. Insertion of Marx skews the time of American literature, implying that political possibility does not await some future construction of a city upon a hill but instead lies in the language of the here and now.

With its scathing mention of farces, props, and facades to signal scorn for the ultimately hollow nature of a socialist revolution co-opted by bourgeois interests in mid-century France, *The Eighteenth Brumaire* contains some of Marx's most theatrical writing. Terrell Carver describes Marx's language as "technicolour writing" whose attention to costuming, performance, and dramatic effects "were the closest that Marx could get to the movies."[25] The bourgeoisie, always eager to save its own skin, turned in a B-movie performance for this revolution. Aesthetics become the brush that tar the bourgeoisie as blackguards for betraying a socialist revolution by courting the rule of Louis Bonaparte in a low-comedy remake of the tragic history of the 1789 revolution and Napoleon Bonaparte. Thus Marx begins famously by proclaiming that history occurs "the first time as tragedy, the second as farce" and goes on from there to indict the bourgeois counterrevolution as an impromptu staging in which even the actors fail to take their own roles seriously. Armed with a variety of costumes, poses, and theatrical sleight-of-hand, the leading man, Louis Bonaparte, uses army detachments to impersonate "the people." Marx glosses this bit of artifice behind Bonaparte's coup d'état by referencing *A Midsummer Night's Dream*, drawing a parallel between impersonators who "play the part of the people" and "Nick Bottom" playing "that of the lion."[26] The result is the same in each performance: the buffoon confuses private comedic delusion for the real stuff of world history. Marx's contempt for theater analogizes his disgust with the revanchist role that bourgeois actors play upon the public stage of national politics. In sum, aesthetics front a falsified history.

But Marx's study also implies that theatricality is more than false, just as the language of facades and artifice is more than true. "Oh, Marx's love for Shakespeare!" exclaims Jacques Derrida in recognition of the theatricality and staging that everywhere accents revolutionary possibility.[27] Never merely counterfeit, aesthetic language is instead productive, engendering the world it describes. Discourse, no matter how decked out in allusion or metaphor, can have world-historical impact and even articulate new forms of social reality. As *The Eighteenth Brumaire* tackles revolution and counterrevolution, it intuits linkages between language and radical political knowledge and practice. It is a connection that requires a simile about translation to explain how new, revolutionary speech comes into being: "In like manner a beginner who has learnt a new language always translates it back into his mother tongue, but he has assimilated the spirit of the new language and can express himself freely in it only when he finds his way in it without recalling the old and forgets his native tongue in the use of the new."[28] Progressive thinking is at core a question of speech in which prior forms are outmoded by a new language that does not seem strange or unfamiliar. New or radical ideas appear as a matter of course much in the same way that a people express themselves in their native tongue (even if the nativeness of that tongue is an invention). New or radical ideas become revolutionary when they can be enacted immediately and without translation.

In contrast to Benjamin, who later claimed that translation involves a lot of waiting around since it comes after the original, Marx synchronizes revolutionary translation with expression itself. "Works of world literature," Benjamin states, "never find their chosen translators at the time of their origin," but Marx wonders what if they did? What if revolutionary speech were so familiar and immediate that it needed no laborious cross-referencing to a more ancient idiom? Between Benjamin and Marx lies a different temporal vantage, with Benjamin stressing the "continued life" or open future that the original acquires in its delayed effects upon the translator's tongue and with Marx concentrating on the revolutionary possibilities of simultaneity that forgetfulness of "the old" provides.[29] Benjamin looks to the future; for Marx, the time is now. No time lag exists between thought and action because the desire for social transformation embedded in revolutionary consciousness requires neither mediation nor translation. What previously required mediation to translate a new terminology to old political limitations now becomes immediate. As Marx puts it, this revolutionary speaker "can freely express himself" *(frei in ihr zu produzieren)*[30] without stutter or delay because he or she is already conversant in a new language of political possibility. The speaker does more than simply express himself; the German *produzieren* implies that the speaker also produces freely in this new language and one of the first things he or she produces is a new identity fluent in a language that has no debts to a politics of dead precedents and bourgeois traditions. Revolutionary speakers automatically double as revolutionary actors. If citizens are intent upon "revolutionizing themselves and things," to use Marx's formulation, then expression and production must become one and the same, occurring at the identical instant.[31] There is no need to wait around for social transformation while this actor fiddles with that transformation, taking time to bring it in line with antiquated thoughts and ideas. Such tweaking saps revolutionary ideas of their force because the old idiom lacks the vocabulary to express anything that is literally unheard of within the language of the status quo. The payoff is that new ideas cease to seem "foreign" and need no adjustment to the customary lingua franca of political possibility since they make sense "without recalling the old." As the language of innovation and change appears as society's default position, revolutionary consciousness takes hold.

This consciousness arises out of a radical temporality—a rupture in time. The production of new social conditions depends on an amnesic episode in which people interrupt the continuity of the vocabulary that ties their lives and their world to established forms and usages. Memory loss is crucial to the revolution; otherwise citizens will only think of what has come before, never daring to imagine alternatives to arrangements and relationships that they always already know. Without amnesia, people cannot "produce freely," cannot create new political identities or social landscapes, because they are constantly remembering—and are bound to—the grammar of prior existence. As Marx's analogy between revolutionary change and language acquisition implies, the actor who "forgets his native tongue in the use of the new" breaks with a past that always holds new possibilities, radical ideas, and alternative methods at arm's length by mediating them in terms of what came before.

Learning a new language may be more than an analogy or metaphor: unfamiliar locutions can transform what people say, think, and do. If citizens can forget that a lexicon accented by strange phrases such as "social equality," "communal action," "mass democracy," "strike," and "anarchy" sounds foreign, the likelihood of producing these conditions seems less farfetched, sliding over into the domain of the possible. This orientation does not demand a language of revolution so much as treat revolution as a linguistic act that alters consciousness by making the foreign familiar. International renderings of American literature or, better yet, an American literature Internationale would thus be written in a language that forsakes prevailing meanings of culture and forgets rather tame notions of democracy that have governed political sensibilities in the U.S. Standing on the nearside of a temporal rupture that divides citizens from an ancestral tongue that limits democracy to predictable events and formal outcomes, an American literature Internationale accustoms us to once-threatening and alien ideas about terror, crowds, and mass subjectivity. Possibly, within a new language of democracy, guarded rationality and safe liberalism will make way for the unmeasured yearnings of the multitude. Not wholly romantic but more than a tad speculative, this receptiveness to "as yet unheard-of ideas and entirely alien expressions" that readers such as Thomas Kemple have discerned in Marx suggests that internationalizing American literature can make literary history less historical, as it were, not as fully bound by what happened and more open to the possibility of what could happen.[32]

The Eighteenth Brumaire slams the Revolution of 1848 for degenerating into a second-rate comedy, but the figurative language employed by this "American" text to account for political devolution also packs a performative power that can produce the very revolutionary energy that aesthetic discourse at first seems to dissipate. Through an "imaginative anachronism" in which a radical idiom appears as old hat, language "enacts the requisite changes" that bring about new ways of describing and shaping society.[33] The language of aesthetics, which had seemed so retrograde, now lines up on the vanguard, or more accurately, just beyond the vanguard at the temporal location where the vanguard has become as common as everyday speech. A sustainable revolution entails thinking about a world in which discourse is both cause and verification of sociopolitical change. Despite its initial rejection of aesthetic language as the stuff of bad bourgeois drama, Marx's project remains dependent on such embellishments and, as Peter Bellis suggests, the text "ends by entangling action and discourse instead of separating and opposing them."[34] Even as a revolutionary account is sapped by its own susceptibility to aesthetic figuration, it nonetheless remains open to unpredictable meanings. For this 1852 analysis of revolution written by a foreigner and first published on U.S. soil by an immigrant, international currents ground a revaluation of aesthetics that sloughs off old associations with simpering elitism. Citizen-speakers become conversant in alternative methods—crowd politics, unruly agitation, strikes—for changing historical conditions and effecting social transformation.

International aesthetics pivot not so much on geography as on translation, especially in its ability to conjure a language of civic disorder and mass identity. International American literature, then, bleeds into American literature Internationale, creating performative traffic between aesthetic work and revolutionary social thought. This invocation of the "Internationale" involves more than a thematic searching out of connections between American writing and the European radicalism witnessed, for instance, in Whitman's "O Star of France" (1872) or Robert Chambers's *The Red Republic* (1895), where an American dilettante of the Left Bank admits his status as "rotten painter" and abandons his easel to join the Communards.[35] It is also an approach that exceeds direct historical connections that made the U.S. a point of interest for socialists and Marxists, seen most spectacularly in the address of the First International to Abraham Lincoln, which praised this "single-minded son of the working class" for staring down a "counter-revolution" led by slaveholders.[36] Certainly the sight of American phalanxes of the International drilling with weapons in the streets of Chicago, New York, and Philadelphia was not to be taken lightly.[37] Internationalism begins with such historicist connections but, as a conceptual tool for literary and cultural study, it quickly outstrips specific empirical links to enable an evaluation of the revanchist consequences as well as radical possibilities within aesthetic discourses of revolution. In Derrida's terms, this space is spectral, haunted by shadows of ideas that have not yet come into being but whose possibility of existence frightens the governing social order. This incalculable potential emanates from *The Eighteenth Brumaire* by not confining the text to its chronology. So while the serendipity of publication that makes Marx's text part of the American Renaissance provides the springboard for this reconceptualization of literary production (both as product and as productive agent), I hope it is clear by now that this approach, with its emphasis on language and form, is not so much classically Marxist as figurative and transfigurative, concerned with the political possibilities of translational aesthetics.

Cued by Marx's attention to translation, American literature Internationale emphasizes possibility as the temporal condition of language. Unexpected meanings strike anywhere—even in aggressively reactionary texts of the late nineteenth century that sought to paint labor struggle as outside American values. Admittedly, though, unexpectedness runs counter to Marx's teleological view of history as proceeding ineluctably toward revolution. Finding consolation in a long-term view of human history, *The Eighteenth Brumaire* refuses to cast the farce of 1848 as failure: mired in

an era of bourgeois restoration, "the revolution" may be "still journey-
ing through purgatory" but it is also waiting in the wings to complete the
second half of a world historical drama. Turning again to Shakespeare,
Marx draws comfort from *Hamlet,* alluding to the "old mole" that burrows
steadily and surreptitiously beneath the ground, always moving forward.
Marx's allusion, as Margreta de Grazia points out, is layered and double,
referring to Hegel's use of Shakespeare's "old mole" as shorthand for the
progressive unfolding of spirit toward "the freedom of full consciousness."
Not only does Marx replace "consciousness" with "revolution" but he also
rewrites Hamlet's "well said, old mole" as "well grubbed, old mole" to pri-
oritize material conditions over discursive ones.[38] Relentless, eventual,
even formulaic, this view of history seems locked into a trajectory with
no wiggle room for fragments of resistance, episodic irruptions, or other
aleatory events that do not readily fit the big picture. Seizing on *Hamlet's*
disjointedness ("the time is out of joint") to offset an otherwise iron teleology of Marxism, Derrida explodes temporality so that the future, instead
of appearing as a foregone conclusion predicated on the present and con-
firming present conditions, veers off into the "not yet" and "the perhaps."[39]
History may switch direction at any time. Where and when will the future
next appear? Not knowing for sure, people may now think and say things
that heretofore have not been possible.

Uncertainty and unpredictability, as components of an internationalist approach, invite an anarchist rendering of American literary history.
A faint echo of the International, this anarchist sensibility forces an examination of the time of American literature. Political aesthetics require a
temporality that rethinks the timeline of change, whether aesthetic, literary, or social. As opposed to highlighting ruptures or avant-garde sensibilities, what would it mean to locate newness within the familiar and common? Revolution is not about waking up one day and discovering that one
suddenly speaks revolution. Instead, changes in cultural consciousness are
always present within the vocabulary of culture. As Ralph Waldo Emerson
put it in a burst of popular energy tinged with condescension, "I embrace
the common, I explore and sit at the feet the familiar, the low. Give me insight into to-day, and you may have the future and antique worlds." Taken
spatially, Emerson's declaration is tame enough, creating impression of a
scholar who abandons books to walk within realms of wider experience.
But in striking a temporal chord, his words resonate more sharply with
the demand that the present, now "bristling" with opposition and "lurk-

ing" with possibility, not be subsumed under the glories of yesterday or deferred by the prospects of tomorrow. Emerson's demand for the "insight" of "to-day" rejects the standard time lag that postpones new knowledge either until it can be framed in terms of tired precedents or until it finally catches up with an always-distant dawn when conditions, at long last, may be ripe for change. Emerson, in short, wants it now—and the "it" for him is the "topics of the time," the quotidian stuff of familiar sentiments and routine use, which, because they are held in common, inject "new vigor" into men and women so that society can take "a great stride." As Emerson asks, "If there is any period one would desire to be born in,—is it not the age of Revolution"?[40] His answer is not to sit idly by, waiting for an auspicious birth; he looks to generate favorable conditions now by radically condensing time into a temporality that refuses the remoteness of the past or the suspension of the future.

Or, to preview an example developed in the final sections of this chapter, the crowd does not suddenly spring to life but has always been lurking within individual citizenship. Such ever-present possibility emerges at the horizon of some future moment when the people, the mass, the crowd speak of these possibilities so often that they seem routine. Howells addresses these concerns in his novel of aesthetics and the mass market, *A Hazard of New Fortunes,* which attempts to pinpoint the instant when consciousness is altered and even revolutionized. Replete with an impassioned German anarchist, an aesthetic poseur, and rather picturesque episodes of urban poverty and violence, the novel is, above all, about timing. At what point will democracy in America be ready for foreign ideas? When will a new political idiom no longer need translation back into an acceptable tongue? Does fiction speed up—or slow down—social transformation? These questions, posed from an international (and Internationale) time zone, suggest that cultural change occurs when the future seems to have already happened and become as familiar as the everyday.

Before tackling these questions, it is necessary to consider the methodological implications of thinking about the time of American literature. Since possibility always seems to fall short of actuality, no guarantee exists that reconfiguring American literature in terms of a global "now" that views the future as immediate will eventuate in change or innovation. It indeed seems more likely that ever-present possibility can hold democratic energy in suspended animation, placing the productive aspect of language in a perpetual deep-freeze. A temporal realignment of American literature therefore calls for a good amount of unease. Does a timeline that ignores dramatic shifts implicitly sign on to the position that change is really un-noticeable, having become so unremarkable that human actors will not even recognize it as change? How will we recognize political newness if the idioms of expression and action do not appear as new but instead seem part and parcel of the language we've been speaking all along? Might not the familiar even be touted as new and revolutionary when it is nothing more than the same old language? Claiming the familiar as new has all the marks of a bad faith strategy that persists in seeing the status quo as something other than it is. Even with these misgivings there remains something worth holding onto: a rethought temporality makes change imaginable by suggesting that newness need not come from some future cataclysm in consciousness but is instead lambent in the here and now.

The possibilities of newness play off the aesthetic surface of *The Eighteenth Brumaire*, perhaps despite Marx himself. The figurative language, theatricality, and artifice that derail revolution unexpectedly indicate that political newness and cultural innovation do not exist elsewhere but lie right here in front of a civic audience even if at first unrecognizably, shrouded by degraded forms of bourgeois representation. Undoubtedly, aesthetic discourse can defuse radicalism and lend order to otherwise chaotic events. But, in its internationalist mode, aesthetic discourse also threatens to spin out of control. As *The Eighteenth Brumaire* extends beyond its American Renaissance moment, it reveals that aesthetics often add fuel to the flames that beauty and art are supposed to quell. In 1877, as an unprecedented wave of strikes spread across the U.S. and officials looked to the police and government troops for order, more than a few observers suggested, as I show in the next section, that local, state, and national authorities might want to examine aesthetic discourse as a means of minimizing threats of working-class revolt. But this strategy seemed liable to backfire for two reasons. First, as contemporary accounts and histories explored what was called the "Great Strike" in aesthetic terms, they raised the possibility that seemingly random social chaos was in actuality part of a plot so well-planned and organized that the spectacle of strikers clashing with bayoneted soldiers might become a familiar sight. Second, while social reformers and housing authorities advised that urban beautification could allay the discontented masses, such projects also called the masses into being.

In the section that follows, I take up these possibilities by reading histories of the 1877 strike, which compulsively return to scenes of international terror as a way of understanding civic unrest and social upheaval in the U.S. The next section extends this focus to consider why the time of American literature seems to invite unpredictability even when aesthetic components of that literature are engineered, theoretically, to cultivate formal stability. The concluding section explores the effects of the unstable connection between beauty and democracy on the citizen-subject. Among these effects are a series of substitutions that produce the crowd, replacing the citizen with mass subjects.

1877: *The Time is Now*

In summer 1877, as strikes spread from Pittsburgh to Galveston, the labor crisis afflicting the nation was blamed on international contexts. Angry denunciations of capital, industrial sabotage, and pitched battles between strikers and police were branded as acts of terror. Such extreme language is the staple of quickly produced histories of the Great Strike such as Alan Pinkerton's *Strikers, Communists, Tramps, and Detectives* (1878), which likens U.S. labor strife, crowds, and mass meetings to the revolutionary terror of France that off and on for two centuries had served as a point of cathexis for Americans anxious about democratic excess. Foremost in Pinkerton's mind is the 1871 civil war in France, which established the Commune and supposedly revealed the full extent of the International, with socialist cells joined together in a conspiracy of transatlantic sweep. And nowhere was the International more deeply entrenched than in the U.S., as an 1877 report on the American strike claimed.[41] Phobic estimates that the International had an American membership of 600,000 workers supported Marx's claim that the civil war in France revealed the "international character of class-rule" so dramatically that "working people all over the world" saw the struggle of the Communards as their struggle, too.[42] If the First International had sought to inculcate the masses with a "duty to master themselves the mysteries of international politics," then the great railway strike and the literally thousands of smaller ones that recurred every year afterward suggested that the Commune stood unveiled in America.[43]

Just as federal troops were leaving the South to abandon blacks to the failure of Reconstruction, the White House called out the army to restore order in a nation rocked by the most dramatic and bloody struggles between workers and owners in its history. Work stopped at train depots, coal yards, stockyards, ports, tanneries, quarries, and mills as the Great Strike spread westward, leaving in its wake scores of dead strikers, burning railroad cars, looted stores, and echoes of violent denunciations against capital. By the time the unrest arrived in the heartland, soldiers were recalled from the war against the Sioux to battle protestors in Chicago. The soldiers, according to Pinkerton, were "quite as ready to meet communists as to follow Sitting Bull."[44] Warships from the North Atlantic Squadron sailed up the Potomac to protect the Capitol, and marines landed in Philadelphia as striking workers on the Pennsylvania Railroad fired back at the bayonets. Governors of ten states called out the militia to keep order against what seemed a rising sea of democratic terror, specifically *le Terreur* of French revolution become international in its transit to places like Philadelphia and Baltimore. Women in places like Pittsburgh were compared to the *pétroleuses* of the Commune who firebombed the boulevards and avenues of Paris. Strikers in St. Louis hummed the "Marseillaise" as they took to the streets. "The Commune had found a place in America," asserted J. A. Daucus in *Annals of the Great Strike*. "Who could say that the Red Lady might not soon appear to garner a ghastly harvest of bodiless heads?"[45] Journalists and clergy joined government officials in denouncing workers' rallies as handiwork of the Commune that revealed the long shadow of the International. In the aftermath, homeland security became paramount: proposals were made to enlist more troops and reorganize deployments so that the military might respond more quickly to civil unrest. Armories still stand in many major U.S. cities that were constructed in specific response to 1877 so that the militia might have bigger weaponry such as Gatling guns for use against the mob.

Perhaps most important was the psychological aftermath, which fueled suspicions that the terror of 1877, what one historian has called the "year of violence," was orchestrated by a vast network of international socialists.[46] Political paranoia appears as the content of aesthetic form: commentators such as Pinkerton speak of labor radicalism and civil strife as a theater in which communists plot behind the scenes, directing once sober-minded workers to play the role of insurgents. "When the curtain may be raised" and the "actors in the scenes" unmasked, writes Pinkerton, the International will show its hand, revealing itself as the same "blood-red figure which 'cried havoc and let slip the dogs of war' in Paris, in the day of Robespierre in 1793 . . . and again, in the same city, in 1871, when the rallying-cry was, 'Paris against Versailles.'" Theatricality plays a post-revolutionary role for Pinkerton, much as for Marx, by providing coherent form to and boxing in the swirling histories of revolution and terror. In *The Eighteenth Brumaire*, aesthetic discourse only goes so far in capturing the movement from revolution to counterrevolution, necessitating exaggerations that replay tragic historical reality as farce. But for *Strikers, Communists, Tramps, and Detectives,* performance, metaphor, and literary allusion go too far, endowing events with the transnational force of repetition, as 1877 seems the revenant of the Paris Commune and "the Internationale." Where Marx cites Nick Bottom, Pinkerton invokes Banquo's ghost to describe a secret organization that "will not down," its adherents constituting a "force as large as all the standing armies of the world."[47] The bourgeois aestheticism that had pulled revolution down into farce now seemed capable of becoming tragedy once again by ripping apart U.S. society at the seams of commerce, industry, and ownership. More than one postmortem of the Great Strike suggested how narrowly the country had escaped a second reign of terror and, indeed, many feared that that the International might be still alive and kicking behind the scenes. What if summer 1877 were only the first act?

And as an act, summer 1877 seemed particularly threatening in its linguistic dimensions. Violence required no arsenal other than language. In their cultural anthropology of Basque separatism and Euskadi ta Askatasuna (ETA), Joseba Zulaika and William Douglass assert that "whatever else it might be, 'terrorism' is printed text."[48] From this perspective, the performative quality of Pinkerton's history of domestic unrest becomes as volatile and as unpredictable as the crowds that assembled that summer. Impassioned language and spectacular description fill the pages of *Strikers, Communists, Tramps, and Detectives* so thoroughly that this account of the Great Strike can do little more than follow—and repeat—the angry protests of workers and the unemployed. Pinkerton's text is controlled by the strike, with each chapter ending and another beginning as quickly and as randomly as the violence erupts across the U.S. The only rhyme or reason to *Strikers, Communists, Tramps, and Detectives* is supplied by the strike itself. The book moves westward from city to city much as the strike had done the year before. Any attempt to deal with the causes behind the spread of "the accursed communistic spirit" leads to the foreign contexts of "Dr. Karl Marx," the Internationale, and the Paris Commune. Such incendiary markers of ideological difference become less alien-sounding as this counterrevolutionary history unfolds—just as the secret rituals, passwords, and countersigns of anarchist cells and clandestine societies of radical workers lose their strangeness in the reports filed by Pinkerton operatives who claimed to have successfully infiltrated socialist brotherhoods. *Strikers, Communists, Tramps, and Detectives* reads as an unwitting translation of Marxist historiography: like *The Eighteenth Brumaire*, which claims the Revolution of 1848 as the second performance of Revolution of 1789, Pinkerton presents the pitched battles at rail yards, depots, and public squares in 1877 as a nearly successful attempt to "repeat the savages scenes of massacre in republican America that visited Paris in 1871."[49] Except that where Marx finds plenty to laugh at Louis Bonaparte's farcical revolution, Pinkerton confronts the grim prospects of international class warfare at home. Etymology reveals the terror of translating the international and the foreign: *translāt-us* threatens to carry, bear, or transport radicalism undiluted across the Atlantic. In effect, the translation of "Paris Commune" could have been "Pittsburgh," "Baltimore," "Martinsburg," or any number of railway towns where violence flared up during the summer of the Great Strike.

As a specimen of American counterrevolutionary history, *Strikers, Communists, Tramps, and Detectives* reveals that the expression of terror is also its production. International time embodies this radical simultaneity of speech and action. Much as expression and revolutionary practice get conflated in Marx's sense of *produzieren*, in the history of late-nineteenth-century U.S. anarchy and terror it is difficult to distinguish enactment from repetition. Describing the "inchoate language" of anarchist bombings in fin-de-siècle Paris, Howard Lay contends that terrorism merges speech and action to the extent that action becomes a form of speech.[50] If such claims seem inflated or extreme, consider the state's evidence at the trial of the Haymarket anarchists, which was solely textual in nature. The defendants were arraigned for what amounted to bomb-talking, much in the same way that in the recent past speaking of bombs while in an airport or on a plane counts an actionable offense. "The majority of the 136 exhibits entered into evidence by the state at the anarchists' trial were words the indicted men had spoken or published in the years leading up to the Haymarket bombing," writes Jeffory Clymer.[51] It is not just that language precipitates terrorist acts; the true threat of linguistic terrorism is its ability to install the possibility of such acts as the ordinary cultural idiom of society. Zulaika and Douglass underscore that the printed text of terrorism can appear just as readily in the headline of the daily newspaper as in the militant's training manual or a government report.[52] Once terror becomes the stuff of everyday parlance, it slides from threat to possibility. The proximity and potential of terror only heightens the threat. Linguistic acts of terror attain the unremarkable status of a mother tongue; as they imagine or even take measures promoting radical political possibility, the people who speak this language do so immediately and "without recalling the old." Political upheaval requires this sort of simultaneous translation.

If a secret global organization stood behind a summer of rock throwing, fusillades, running street battles, and inflammatory speech, its reputed aim was "social disorganization" and the eventual "political death" of the U.S.[53] Were it not for aesthetics, however, no larger pattern could be discerned beneath this spreading anarchy. By processing events through the language of performance as Marx had in *The Eighteenth Brumaire*, observers such as Pinkerton adduced an intelligible form out of the chaos. Clashes between strikers and soldiers often seemed like grand spectacles, as crowds gathered on overlooks to watch—and participate—in the melee. The American characters in Chambers's *The Red Republic* repeatedly look down on the barricades and battles as though such sights were bits of street theater. Tableaux vivants of revolution seem to spring up everywhere in the novel, most dramatically when a prostitute, striking a pose inspired by Eugène Delacroix's 1830 canvas, *Liberty Leading the People*, rallies her comrades by waving the tattered tricolor. Reporting on the Paris Commune for *Century Magazine*, noted war correspondent Archibald Forbes described the action as a "blood-and-thunder melodrama" in which anarchists and socialists consciously exaggerated their violence in response to the "handclapping from the 'gallery'" of spectators.[54] In "What an American Girl Saw of the Commune," a sketch from the same issue, the writer remembers watching the violence through opera glasses.[55] Drawings in Pinkerton's *Strikers, Communists, Tramps, and Detectives* visibly betray aesthetic perspective as murderous by placing rampaging strikers in the position of spectators. A crowd gathers on a Pittsburgh hillside to watch the railroad roundhouse burn while rioters hurling bricks from a viaduct are arranged like a theater audience (figs. 7 and 8). The crossfire that pins down the troops seems so deadly because in this urban amphitheater every seat offers not just a clear view but also a clear shot at the forces of order.

At this level where historiography meets narrative, the same aestheticism that looks at urban unrest in Paris, Baltimore, Pittsburgh, Chicago, and San Francisco and comes up with a pattern also raises the possibility

Futile attempt of the mob to cannonade the Pittsburgh Round-house during the night of the Great Riot.

FIGURE 7. "Futile Attempt of the Mob" from Alan Pinkerton, *Strikers, Communists, Tramps, and Detectives* (New York: G. W. Carleton, 1878).

that there is a pattern, a conspiracy of international scope. What if the articulation of an aesthetic pattern also stands as the enactment of a political plot? What if events that read like a drama complete with curtains, revolutionary costumes, directors behind the scenes, and tragic outcomes give evidence of a rank and file following a script laid out by internationalists? The answer to these questions provides cold comfort: instead of being defused by aesthetic discourse, politics may find in the art of performance a method to organize the madness of revolution. If the civil disorder of summer 1877 were new and unexpected, might not aesthetics allow such scenes to appear familiar? The language of tragedy and performance is redolent with the possibility of giving radical thought and action an intelligible form so that radicalism does not seem all that new but rather a natural default position. Just as accomplished students of a second language learn to use an adopted tongue with all the fluency of native speakers, so too American workers on the vanguard can learn to couch "foreign" or putatively international ideas about class warfare with all the familiarity of homegrown American ideology. Histories of the Great Strike are about nothing so much as temporality, condensing the retrospective of European radicalism and the prospect of future terror into the language of the present.

Rioters assaulting Soldiers in the cut at Reading, Pennsylvania.

FIGURE 8. "Rioters Assaulting Soldiers," from Alan Pinkerton, *Strikers, Communists, Tramps, and Detectives* (New York: G. W. Carleton, 1878).

ART FOR THE POST-REVOLUTION:
Whitman and Santayana

Deducing aesthetic theory from *The Eighteenth Brumaire* and the language swirling around the Great Strike is all well and good, but it ignores the efforts of those who, convinced that art and beauty were anything but volatile or unpredictable, promoted beautification in cities and industrial centers that had been the scenes of violence. In addition to sending troops to quell what Secretary of War George McCary in 1877 called an "insurrection," many thought it necessary to enlist aesthetics as well.[56] Against a backdrop of several hundred strikes every year in the late nineteenth century—in 1886, the year of the Haymarket bombing, workers staged 1,572 strikes—it seemed fairly clear that bayonets and billy clubs were failing to bring order and form to the urban landscape.[57] Reformers redoubled the efforts of the City Beautiful movement, hoping that public architecture and art galleries would elevate rioting masses into civic subjects. Culture in the Gilded Age was "exercised as paramilitary force," according to James Livingston, its values and lessons deployed along a second front of museums, symphonies, and other institutions that gently consolidated the authority of the upper class.[58] If the "art instinct," as the *Atlantic Monthly* advised, appeals to socialists seeking inspiration for change, then capitalists and other defenders of the social order would do well to give serious consideration to beauty as a tactic for achieving unity and public accord.[59]

This need to muster beauty in the cause of social reform, as chapter 1 showed, corresponds to efforts to professionalize aesthetics as an academic discipline whose ethical effects could be predicted and controlled. Discipline, of course, is always more than an academic matter of classifying facts and organizing branches of knowledge; it also affects the moral nature of the subject, as critics as diverse as Kant and Schiller on one side and Emerson and Whitman on the American side have noted, where matters of taste, beauty, and art come into play. Each recognizes the power of aesthetics in producing a range of effects that includes influencing, soothing, constituting, activating, and governing individual subjects. In this era of crowds and public ferment, could not aesthetics do more than inspire the subject by shaping the mass?

In the same year—1871—that the Paris Commune burst on the scene as mass spectacle, Whitman called for an "esthetic democracy" to stabilize a nation that had just emerged from the devastation of civil war. Entire cultural orders rest on aesthetics, according to Whitman. Searching for "the main support for European chivalry," he identifies "esthetics" as the foundation of society, "forming its osseous structure, holding it together for hundreds, thousands of years, preserving its flesh and bloom, giving it form."[60] Whitman's purpose here seems conservative in the sense that he wants to conserve a republic, still raw from civil war and now exposed to oligarchic forces associated with industrial capitalism ratcheted up to corporate complexity. Supplying a vital and invulnerable social bedrock, aesthetics ensure that American democracy will last for eons. On closer inspection, though, Whitman's purpose is as productive as it is conservative; his hope is that aesthetics will not only safeguard what already exists but also produce a new political language. Betsy Erkkilä's assessment of *Leaves of Grass* as a "language experiment" that privileges newness—the poem contains 14,000 different words, many of which are used only once—suggests how Whitman's aesthetic democracy seeks to enact the new social and political possibilities that it describes.[61] As Whitman puts it in *Democratic Vistas*, the goal is for Americans to articulate a "new aesthetic of our future." To be truly revolutionary, however, this new world should not be so strange or unexpected as to paralyze the people with self-doubt about their ability to express themselves as a body politic. Only when citizens become fluent in a new language and literature that no longer seems new but instead appears as natural as their own bodies will their expression produce the very conditions it describes. "Democracy," Whitman writes, "remains unwritten"; its history will be written when it is "enacted." As with the one bright spot in Marx's history of failed revolution, language and literature familiarize people with new concepts, making it so that what Whitman calls the "syllables" of democracy are pronounced as they are lived.[62]

Lecturing on aesthetics at the end of the nineteenth century, George Santayana credited Whitman as one of the few thinkers to connect beauty and democracy. But the Harvard philosopher found the Brooklyn poet too undisciplined to provide more than a "momentary pulsation" of insight into the discursive attributes of political psychology. Santayana's unease consists in his discernment of a "terrible leveling" in Whitman's aesthetic democracy that does not produce new forms so much as ignore all form to delight in a "liquid and structureless whole."[63] Liquid has often been a problem for readers of Whitman, who have sought to sidestep the political import of lines about "delirious juice" and "my own seminal wet."[64] Perhaps because Santayana has in mind *Leaves of Grass* and not *Democratic Vistas,* he does not mention how Whitman's concern for language and literature is intended both to stabilize the social order and to bring more democratic forms of democracy, as it were, into existence. It is at this level, however, that Santayana shares Whitman's belief that aesthetics play a post-revolutionary role in legitimating the regime that revolution establishes, making its rule seem disinterested, ordered, proportioned, in a word, beautiful.

As he describes the post-revolutionary function of aesthetics, Santayana turns to international contexts, conjoining French and American radicalism. Rather than cause alarm, this conjunction demonstrates that neither beauty nor art can act as the wellspring of revolution. "Nothing could be more absurd," he argues, than to posit that sociopolitical change has an "aesthetic . . . basis" or to imply that people found class inequalities and aristocratic excess so ugly that they rebelled with a French Revolution.[65] What aesthetic discourse does supply, however, is a lack of historical context that proves supremely useful in subjecting the new political order to amnesia, allowing its arrangements and structures to appear perfectly symmetrical and balanced. With its preference for "abstract forms," Santayana's *The Sense of Beauty* (1896) condenses the French and American revolutions to discern a similar psychological mechanism operating across world history. French aristocracy seemed in perfect taste to aristocrats just as a marketplace freed of monarchical restrictions and colonial dependency appears beautiful to American subjects after 1776. In democracy no less than tyranny, an "aesthetic consecration" sanctifies the sociopolitical system, making its order appear beautiful and hence fair and just. International aesthetics mop up after the revolution so that its leveling seems less terrible. Santayana shrewdly understands beauty as a form of political displacement that overlooks the terror of *le Terreur* to bring the past excesses of popular democracy in line with stability and predictability. Here is the time of international aesthetics: beauty supplies a temporal language that accustoms citizens to the consequences of revolution.

In this improbable traffic from Marx to Pinkerton and from Whitman to Santayana, we see that democracy, rendered as an aesthetic matter, returns compulsively to revolution even when sociopolitical change is exactly what beauty and art are supposed to make unimaginable. When aesthetics become international, anarchy enters the picture whether as Whitman's "terrible leveling" or as the rumored plots and conspiracies of the Great Strike. Connections between internationalism and threats to the nation gained new relevance at the start of the twenty-first century. Since September 11, 2001, art and terror have taken on heightened meaning. As in 1877, beauty is pressed into active service. In celebration of National Arts and Humanities Month, George W. Bush in October 2001 touched on all the flashpoints that lend art a special purchase on democracy. Much as Whitman and Santayana invoke aesthetics as means to sort out the relationship between the nation and its citizen-subjects, Bush recognizes the political uses of aesthetic formalism, stating that art acts as a "unifying force" without trampling "individual expression." Public demonstrations of art, Bush hopes, will engender a discourse indispensable to "maintaining . . . a strong democracy," presumably because such expressions recall the principles of distribution and symmetry through which individuals understand their place within the larger body politic.[66]

White House aesthetics fall in line with an American literature that associates aesthetics and democracy. But this convergence only goes halfway, as Bush does not voice the more volatile possibility of possibility itself. There are no surprises in an address that invites citizens "to participate in activities" befitting National Arts and Humanities Month, which in this case apparently means "proudly singing 'The Star-Spangled Banner' and 'God Bless America.'" Citizens become spectators who experience art as the maintenance and celebration of a national culture besieged by inter-

national terror. While citizens may not now understand the larger significance of their various acts of aesthetic commemoration after 9/11, the artifacts they produce will surely provide "a lasting historical record for future
generations."[67] As art becomes an effect of history, it also mortgages the
future, ensuring the nation's "lasting" form. Such permanence prohibits
an open-ended future; once tethered to the nation-state, the future offers
nothing other than confirmation of present conditions rather than the risk
of untold possibilities. The distance between American literature Internationale and national arts is a temporal one in which endurance takes
the place of enactment. Citizens under this schema never have the time
to achieve fluency in a new political language and instead are advised to
brush up on a national idiom they already know.

THE HAZARDS OF NEW TRANSLATION

While Bush's address may be predictable in its lack of surprise, aesthetics do become surprisingly international in the labor rallies, protests, and
strikes of the American scene. At least that is how Marx saw matters in October 1877, when he wrote to contacts in the First International, requesting
information about "the long strike of 1875" in the Pennsylvania coalfields,
a region that had been dubbed "The Commune in Pennsylvania."[68] Marx
was not the only one making these connections. Urban reformers worried
that immigrant ghettos bred not just despair but also the fever of international socialism. The year after the Commune came to a bloody end in
France, Charles Loring Brace warned in *The Dangerous Classes of New York*
(1872) that "the same explosive social elements [lie] beneath the surface
of New York as of Paris." While proposals that the defeated Communards
of Paris be shipped off to the American Southwest stoked fears of contagion, the prospect of expatriating 40,000 French radicals never loomed as
large as the Jewtowns, Bohemias, and other ethnic quarters in cities like
New York and Chicago. As Brace surveys pockets of foreignness on American shores, his thoughts run anxiously to "European *prolétaires*" bent on
lawlessness.[69]

Precautionary force was an obvious response to the threat of socialist cells taking root in America. Urban planning, as Riis cynically noted,
consisted of "bullet-proof shutters, the stacks of hand-grenades, and the

Gatling guns" ready for use against the horde teetering on mob rule. To avert the barricades and bloodshed that many thought imminent, Riis proposed a more aesthetically pleasing stockpile for preventing a second civil war that would pit not slaveholders against unionists but capitalists against workers. In place of the latest weapons, he suggested that slum denizens, workers, fallen women, the jobless, rowdies, and youth gone bad be met with images. Jane Addams shared his optimism, believing that "the object of art" could "connect" the worker to a "larger world outside of his immediate surroundings," replacing the biological individual trapped in an animalistic struggle for survival with an ethically minded subject who weighs the needs of others.[70] But, as chapter 1 argued, on more than one occasion Riis and his reformist colleagues were surprised by the propensity of aesthetics to produce as much anarchy as peace. By presenting images of the dangerous classes to genteel viewers, Riis revealed the barbarian threat at civilization's gates in an effort to impress middle-class audiences with the urgent need for tenement reform. By presenting images to the uncontrolled masses, he devised a pedagogical mission to ennoble and uplift the rabble. Keeping these aims distinct proved a difficult task, as the display of images often encouraged individuals to mill about and congregate, in short, to form themselves as a crowd. Aesthetic appeals to individual subjects could metastasize into spectacles of mass subjectivity.

Crowds had welled up long before Parisians flocked to the barricades or railroad workers flooded the streets of Baltimore. By the end of the nineteenth century, however, the crowd appeared as a unique expression of modernity for early sociologists, who endowed it with an important attribute: psychology. Seeking to understand criminality, Gabriel Tarde and Scipio Sighele confronted the Paris Commune as a "crowd event" that impelled normally law-abiding individuals to recklessness.[71] Like the subject of Kant's *Critique of Judgment*, the individual subject of the crowd acts with disinterestedness but, as Gustave Le Bon theorized in his landmark psychosocial study, *The Crowd* (1895), this demeanor can change in a heartbeat, inducing people to consent to and commit "every kind of crime." Rationality flies out the window, moral sense evaporates, and "confused anarchy" reigns the instant that the crowds reveals itself as a mob.[72] Le Bon claimed to know full well what he was talking about: the Paris Commune, an event he witnessed firsthand, supplied him with ample fodder to present the crowd as organically primitive, impulsive, and violent.

U.S. academics were not far behind in identifying the dangers of collectivity. Writing on "the psychology of crazes," G. T. W. Patrick of the University of Iowa worried that the "American mind" may be highly susceptible to hysteria. While France underwent "revolution crazes," the fervor surrounding the Spanish-American War proved that the U.S. had its "war craze." Patrick, it seemed, saw potential frenzy everywhere: even a group as patriotic and demure as the Daughters of the American Revolution "collectively are an uncontrollable mob."[73] Not all researchers followed suit. University of Michigan sociologist Charles H. Cooley asserted that "the shrewd farmers and mechanics of American democracy" could never be grouped with "Le Bon's *foules*."[74] Yet Le Bon's characterizations of the crowd, despite (because of?) their reactionary nature, relied on a latent aestheticism. Explaining how the "conscious activity of individuals" erupts into the "unconscious action of crowds," Le Bon employs visual language, postulating that masses depend on images, not ideas. "A crowd thinks in images, and the image itself calls up a series of other images, having no logical connection with the first," writes Le Bon.[75] Collective expression proceeds without syntagmatic association: it is jumbled, confused, productive of rash and even murderous conclusions.

Aesthetic judgment, so long theorized as key to individual subjectivity, in an era of American labor radicalism operates at the level of crowds. From the outset of Kant's *Critique of Judgment*, beauty appears as a subjective determination that serves as a foundation of the subject and his or her "feeling of pleasure or pain."[76] But what about the mass subject? Is mass subjectivity productive of pleasure or pain? The answer is not as simple as the billy clubs that rained down on strikers' heads during the summer of the 1877. Instead, the possibility exists that a crowd may create and find pleasure in any number of forms (the experience of solidarity, the sight of its own magnitude, or a new political vocabulary) that also occasion pain. Not "pleasure or pain" but pleasure and pain: because the crowd enjoys a common sensibility that progressive sociologists expressed as "the democratic mind" but also breeds irrationality, mass feeling was celebrated every bit as much as it was demonized.[77] As an episode of democratic sadomasochism, the simultaneity of pleasure and pain echoes the coincidence of flowers and billy clubs in Riis's loaded metaphor. Whereas Kant's individual receives either pain or pleasure, these powerful stimuli are combined in modernity's mass subject. As Michael Warner argues, images of disaster and public trauma produce an "erotics of a mass imaginary" by fulfilling desires for self-abstraction.[78] This transfer between singular and collective experience is not wholly foreign to Kant's individual, whose private aesthetic judgment shares in a universal sensibility of *sensus communis*. Can the line between common feeling and crowd mentality be drawn with any surety?

Kant specifies that "common sense" emerges not through concepts but through feeling, just as Le Bon contends that crowds think not in ideas but in images. Individual subjective judgment, because it rests on a "ground that is common to all," prepares the "agreement of everyone" and therefore extends beyond its own particular nature.[79] The crowd also overrides individual feeling but to such an extent that people commit acts and atrocities that the singular person would never countenance. The distinction is only skin deep: *sensus communis* and collective popular feeling wind up having similar effects by identifying the subject's judgment and the crowd's lack of judgment each as a matter of taste, affect, and images, that is, as a matter of aesthetics. As subjects of feeling and inclination, individuals are unpredictable, as ready to consent to Kant's "agreement of everyone" as they are likely to respond to the primitive unconscious of Le Bon's crowd of *foules*.

Le Bon could have told Riis that he was playing with fire by using a gas flame to illuminate and project images. Describing the disconnected, nonsyntagmatic language of mass consciousness, Le Bon warned that "image-like ideas . . . not connected by any logical bond of analogy or succession" worked on the crowd's collective spirit "*like the slides of a magic-lantern which the operator withdraws from the groove in which they were placed one above the other.*" Suddenly and without explanation, the crowd arises. The threat posed by the crowd's visual thinking lies in its free association, not of ideas, but of images. Images "always have an enormous influence on crowds," writes Le Bon. "It is only images that terrify or attract and become motives of action."[80] Just as Marx's revolutionary people speak "without recalling the old," the crowd is encouraged by images to produce new meanings without regard for the sequencing of logical thought. No matter what has come before, each image contains within it an equal likelihood of incendiary use; each image exists as ever-present possibility. The episodic time of the image annihilates the past in ways that, instead of signaling the deprivation of meaning, suggests its unruly plenitude. Without syntagmatic sequencing, previous expressions no longer hold sway or lord it over present speech. The crowd can now express and produce (*produzieren*) political meaning freely. In a radical temporal shift, the here and now takes precedence over all prior articulations—we might even say that it precedes the past—thereby enabling discursive enactments that far outstrip what has been imagined. Newness is always here and its temporal location is the image of the crowd.

Academic research gave unlikely support to the political potential of crowds. In his 1904 doctoral thesis written at the University of Heidelberg, the pioneering American sociologist Robert Park stitched together loosely Kantian notions and crowds: the "personal disinterestedness" experienced as a "crowd characteristic" allows for each individual to identify with a "collective being." But here is where any fondness for Kant ends, as this new agglomeration embodies "anarchy in its purest form." Even though Park's dissertation splits the crowd off from the public, his research invests collective frenzy and rational public opinion equally with the potential of social transformation. In these collective forms, "individuals cut themselves loose from society and join together around a new nucleus of feelings and ideas." For Park, strikes are no socialistic bugaboo but rather a social organism that makes intelligible the interests of workers that cannot be expressed in the customary language of institutional stability. When Park describes how people in a crowd are "caught up so strongly in emotional and mental currents that they are swept along, as if caught in a flood, towards an unknown goal," his impulse is not to throw out an ideological life-preserver and reel the mass back to solid ground.[81] He calmly evaluates strikes and crowds as forms of mass communication whose suddenness demands listening for new social possibilities. The "unknown" does not frighten the sociologist who has an ear for the sense of a new language, even one accented by anarchy.

In less scientific studies than Park's, mass subjectivity coincides with the image-making capacity of visual technology. The fast-paced illogic of the crowd makes collective subjectivity appear, in the words of the best-selling nonfiction book of 1913, as "a moving picture of democracy." Its author, Gerald Stanley Lee, fused impressionistic sociology to modern media, invoking film to describe the rapid succession of images that characterizes thought and action in an era of mass art, mass demonstrations, and mass feeling. A crazy sort of book, Lee's Crowds invokes Whitman's oceanic feelings for humanity, posits an anachronistic socialism in Jesus Christ, and seeks to blend "Karl Marx and Emerson" in the figure of a poet-lawgiver who will make society beautiful by harmonizing collective desire and individualism. Anticipating Benjamin's thesis on mechanical reproduction, Lee argues that the lithograph, photogravure, and motion picture are especially suited to democracy because these technologies vanquish the past by prioritizing the here and now, modernizing culture by radically altering its temporal and spatial structure. As opposed to the restricted compass of Renaissance art, "crowd civilization" uses "the beautiful [to] minister day and night to crowds": at every instant, mass art addresses a global humanity (but one that looks suspiciously like an Anglo-American public) because no prior cultural knowledge is required for this aesthetic experience.[82] Democratic beauty has neither time nor leisure for the accumulations of tradition but instead must keep pace with the continual unreeling present of the crowd, which thinks only as far back as the most recent image that excites its collective psyche. As Lee wrote in 1901 for the *Atlantic*, the art of antiquity got away with celebrating mere individuals but modern society demands a "modern art to express the beautiful in endless change, the movement of masses, coming to its sublimity."[83]

Modern art needs to be immediate, popular, universally accessible, and, above all, transformative on an unprecedented scale. *Crowds* views the challenge of industrial modernity as the task of making civilization beautiful, which, as far as Lee is concerned, seems a rather tall order since the entropy of the mass tends inevitably toward inarticulateness, ungoverned passion, and ugliness. Lee would like to see transformation take place as a bloodless social upheaval, but he recognizes that, in a world of science and money, people "have not the time for revolutions nowadays." To make matters worse, reformers and radicals lack proper judgment, "rushing about the world trying to get up exact duplicates, little fussy replicas of a revolution" whose original form no longer suits new modern conditions. Agendas for change are but copies of the past, and although the U.S. polis needs reform, what it really needs is an overhaul that is "precisely the opposite of the violent, theatrical French-Revolution way." The shortcomings of 1789, 1848, and 1871 are aesthetic: none of these democratic movements made the French people beautiful because these uprisings remained dependent upon excessive affect and show. Lee shares Marx's impatience with display and performance, but his solution calls for an alternative aesthetics that will recognize the president, for instance, as "the portrait painter of the people," that is, as "an artist in a nation." When citizens at last have a "poet in the White House," its leaders will revolutionize people and things by "taking Karl Marx and Emerson and Hamilton and Jefferson and melting them down" into a unitary being who embodies the crowd.[84] The aesthetics of crowd theory lump together the socialist mass together and the fascist leader. If Lee anticipates the importance that Benjamin would give to mechanical reproduction and its potential democratization of culture, his aesthetic solution for the crowds generated by that democratization also prefigures the logic of fascism.

In a world where the ideal politician behaves as an epic poet who gives the people a grand single voice, the novelist stands forth as a consummate social manager. Since "the crowd will not make itself beautiful" on its own, the artist shapes the inchoate popular mass, lending form to social and political chaos. "What kind of artist will he be?" asks Lee. "He will be a novelist."[85] Not just any novelist will fit the bill, certainly not authors who address the coterie. What is needed is a novelist who, to borrow a formula from Howells, cherishes intimacy with "the mass of men" and uses his talents to promote "democracy in literature."[86] But talent only tells half the story; the novelist of mass culture must also demonstrate familiarity with modern technology. Although Lee condemns political projects that would seek to copy the original of French terror, by no means does he reject mechanical reproduction out of hand. Crowd civilization demands artists who "shall produce art for crowded conditions," using the printing press, photogravure, lithography, and motion pictures to create "the kind of beauty that can be indefinitely multiplied." Prone to none of Benjamin's melancholy over the withering of tradition, Lee would have the U.S. enter the age of mechanical reproduction and represent democracy through "art that can be produced in endless copies, that can be subscribed for by crowds."[87] In this calculus of political aesthetics, originality and authenticity seem overrated.

If Lee were searching for a candidate up to the challenge of crowd art, he might well have nominated Howells. Howells's public statements about producing anti-aristocratic art, treating novelists as members of the working multitude, and creating an aesthetics of the common seem to certify him as an artist who can fulfill Lee's mission of making the crowd beautiful. For Howells, though, the ugliness of governmental injustice stood in the way of this mission. His crusade to save the Haymarket anarchists from a legal railroading dramatized his belief that literary figures needed to shore up civil liberties that were fast being eroded by the state. To this end, he wrote John Greenleaf Whittier to join his defense of the anarchists, but the famed abolitionist poet refused to entertain any comparisons between reputed bomb-throwers and fugitive slaves. Neither the Illinois courts nor the court of public opinion accorded the accused much sympathy or legal fairness, and on November 11, 1887 the Haymarket anarchists, save those whose sentences were commuted to life in prison and the one who allegedly committed suicide in his cell, were hanged. For his part in publicly supporting a fair trial and appeals for the anarchists, Howells was branded in the press as a "dynamite thrower."[88] The "smiling aspects of life" that once made forced exile or political execution unimaginable in the U.S. were nowhere to be found in the faces of anarchists who could not receive a fair hearing. The irony surely was not lost on Howells: now he resembled the foreign dynamiter Johann Most, whom he had once represented as wholly alien to American values.

Even though state institutions and public opinion dealt with the Haymarket anarchists in ways that left no doubts about the reception that un-American talk should expect in the future, the class strife that had seemed to have been safely quarantined in "old" Europe was fast becoming a familiar American sight. Strikes, mass meetings, rallies, and other episodes of popular unrest, as earlier sections of this chapter show, appeared as instances of *translāt-us* that gave U.S. social conflict an international accent. The fallout from this grim political awakening permeates the cosmopolitan universe of *A Hazard of New Fortunes*, where the Marches absorb New York City as though it were a stage show or a painter's canvas, experiencing scenes of urban despair with alternating fascination and revulsion. Basil March pronounces the spectacle of peeking into apartment interiors from the elevated train "better than the theater."[89] Wandering into a tenement district, the couple find themselves unable to adopt "a purely aesthetic view" that would entail "saying that it was as picturesque as a street in Naples or Florence and with wondering why nobody came to paint it" (55). Such wonder does last long; the Marches' reverie is deflated by undeniable sensory encounters with the street's crowds, drunks, and garbage. They no longer have the comfort of picturing the world through the romantic filter of tourism and insulating themselves from the more jarring aspects of the cityscape. What they feel is immediate: the stench of the street cannot be ignored. Two competing senses of aesthetics come head to head at this moment: an aesthetic discourse of taste and refinement that enfolds the world into formal patterns derived from the arts is pitted against the etymologically older meaning of *aisthētēs*, a meaning rooted in fundamental sensuous perception. The latter notion wins out, as the rarefied meaning associated with genteel art gives way to a common sensibility shared, theoretically, by all human subjects, no matter their class position, educational background, or professional training. This victory of a potentially universal aesthetics temporarily defeats the Marches: they do not want to smell, see, or touch things foreign and strange, especially when those things are not on another continent but are found right around the corner. The conditions that the magazine editor and his wife attempt to bracket as foreign taint their taste for culture—and, for the Marches, "culture" is by invitation only—with unwelcome sensory perception. The expansive notion of *aisthētēs* refuses to recognize aesthetics as a private enclosure.

Yet cavalier attitudes die a slow death. Still discombobulated by what she has seen, Isabel March, formulating her own version of Nikolai Chernyshevsky's question of "what is to be done," insists that poverty and filth are not inevitable. "We must change the conditions," she tells her husband. But March demurs, "Oh no; we must go to the theater and forget them" (60). March admittedly has a difficult time connecting aesthetic activity with ethical responsibility. Challenged whether the mass-market magazine of art and illustration that he edits can "do some good," March answers the question with questions of his own that show his confusion: "Some good? . . . What do you mean by good? Improve the public taste? Elevate the standard of literature? Give young authors and artists a chance?" (131). At first glance, March hits all the right notes, understanding aesthetics as a matter of public access and uplift. But the problem with March's aesthetic mission is that it remains purely aesthetic, constrained by a narrow professionalism that limits aesthetics to art. Unable to connect aesthetics to broader human sensations, March refuses to believe that art and beauty, not to mention the grotesqueness of urban squalor, can provide a point of common understanding in a world where huge gulfs between rich and poor give the lie to notions of universal accord. Reflecting on this conversation about social responsibility, he confesses to feeling "a little ashamed . . . for having looked at the matter so entirely from the aesthetic point of view"—as if there were only a single aesthetic perspective—instead of considering "ethical intention" (133).

Things continue pretty much in this vein for two hundred pages, with March traipsing about the city, reconciling unfamiliar sights and sounds to an urban aesthetic that evaluates, or better yet, under-evaluates social conditions as specimens of "gay ugliness," "reckless picturesqueness," and "frantic panorama" (163–64). These ambivalent phrases capture his struggle in maintaining an attitude of poetic tourism when it comes to foreign scenes and alien sensations. For the most part, he is winning this

battle: the literary man transplanted from quaint Boston likes the cosmopolitan flavor of New York. And, in return, New York seems to like him, if
the public's approval of his tastes in art illustration and magazine writing
are any indication. The city itself becomes the scene of actual battle, however, when various characters in *Hazard,* including the anarchist Lindau,
the self-denying socialist Conrad Dryfoos, the self-consumed artist Beaton,
and the mild-mannered editor cross paths with striking workers. Modeled
on a New York City streetcar strike in winter 1889, this conflict assumes
larger proportions both specifically in terms of the Great Strike and in general since transportation stoppages "have a special visibility because they
can bring the everyday operations of the city to a halt," as Kaplan states.[90]
March at first witnesses no evidence of disruption, finding himself interested in the public's lack of interest in the conflict. To his eyes,

> the mighty city . . . kept on about its business as tranquilly as if the
> private war being fought out in its midst were a vague rumor of Indian
> troubles on the frontier; and he realized how there might have been a
> street feud of forty years in Florence without interfering materially with
> the industry and prosperity of the city. (373)

On the hunt for some sign of "great social convulsion," March seems alternately relieved and disappointed not to come across lines of police holding
off the mob. After reading so much buildup about the strike in the press,
he wants both to see and close his eyes to the extraordinary spectacle of
public violence. But everything looks ordinary, which precisely suggests
the scale of the threat: a major U.S. city can be brought to a standstill and
the event will have all the familiarity of the mother tongue of everyday
life. All set to follow in Pinkerton's footsteps and excoriate the strikers as a
ruthless mob, March encounters only "very quiet, decent-looking people"
dressed in their "simple Sunday best" (373). What if these men, ordinary
and commonplace, represent the first emanations of a culture in which
radicalism appears in the guise of the normal?

March responds by depicting the nonexistent mayhem as exotic and
foreign, locating conflict at the nation's borders and beyond. The violence
he has read about but not seen he likens to "Indian troubles on the frontier," but this denial seems rather tenuous after 1877 when U.S. troops
fighting the Sioux were recalled to restore order to Chicago and after
Haymarket when, as Clymer argues, newspapers talked of the "race war

against 'red men' in the West" in ways that "metaphorically paralleled the class war against the 'red devils' in Chicago."[91] In the next breath March pushes signs of public discord even further away in geographic and historical terms, going back to his and Isabel's favorite tourist spot—Renaissance Italy. But this tactic proves even less reassuring than the attempt to remove conflict to the frontier: the lesson of Florence backfires by suggesting that hostility and aggression can become daily aspects of social life. So March makes a third stab at displacement, comparing his observation of a policeman riding shotgun on a cross-town streetcar to "the ferocity which he had read French troops putting on toward the populace just before the *coup d'état*" (374). Reading would seem to do the trick by allowing March to substitute the threat of imminent contact with the rabble to reading about the rabble. His memory fondly calls on a counterrevolutionary sense of aesthetics, which esteems the French forces, not for their "ferocity," but for their knack for "putting on" a show of "ferocity." March takes pleasure in feeling duped; he likes intimidation never more keenly than when he is able to generalize, in skewed Kantian fashion, from his subjective experience to assume that the entire public feels as he does and accordingly is cowed by the police. If everyone feels as he does, then there is nothing to worry about.

But what about the threat of a reciprocal identification? What if March feels like everyone and what if that everyone goes by the name of the crowd? As March compares the policeman to a government *soldat*, his metaphor enlists him in the partisan struggle but on the side of the Communards, marshalling his sympathies on behalf of those who would challenge the wisdom of owners who think they owe nothing, perhaps not even a living wage, to workers. Upon making this involuntary comparison, March "began to feel like populace," which should not be too much of stretch since he has already proven he is not simply going to roll over and give in to the capitalist who bankrolls the magazine he edits. The oppositional stance emanating from popular feeling momentarily jostles March's detachment and disinterest, and accordingly "he struggled with himself and regained his character of philosophical observer" (374). March's success would be Howells's downfall in the eyes of critics who evaluate Hazard as a mealy-mouthed expression of socialism in which capitalism gets little more than a slap on the wrist.[92] Such conclusions echo the peculiar formulation lodged at the center of this passage in which March "began to feel like populace" as opposed to "feeling like a populace" or "feeling like the populace." The lack of either article prevents a concrete public from congealing. The mass remains amorphous and undefined, a site of abjection perhaps not at all unlike "feeling like shit" as opposed to "feeling like the shit," which as students tell me, signifies the best, something tremendously cool or great.[93] "Feeling like populace" and "feeling like the populace" register completely different qualities of social affect: in the first, March relishes subjection and timidity while in the second he flirts with an empowering collective identification.

This prospective collectivity remains strongly accented by the Paris Commune, inciting March's fear that radicalism and terror are festering just beneath the smiling surface of U.S. democracy. Within the logic of mother tongues and translation supplied by *The Eighteenth Brumaire,* it is tempting to claim *Hazard's* toothless portrait of Americanized socialism as a progressive sign of the foreign becoming familiar, an indication of once radical ideas accustoming themselves to everyday life. Rather than risk a smiling assessment of the novel, a more exact read on the foreign and the familiar, the American and un-American, lies in the literal figure of the translator—Lindau. An immigrant, socialist, and an "old dynamiter" (129), Lindau scours international journals for articles to translate for March's magazine and gives March's son German language lessons. He communicates new ideas, helping young Tom March get his tongue—and mind—around the notion that state-supported capital ravages the poor. Translation, as Colleen Boggs suggests, produces a "counterknowledge" that unsettles the fullness of national identifications such as Tom's.[94] Even though March browbeats his son into dismissing Lindau's extremism, he cannot gainsay the fact that Tom has translated simultaneously by deploying Lindau's radicalism "without recalling the old" or adjusting it to the native idiom of Americanism.

Tom is neither a reformer nor a radical and seems bound to enter Harvard as he takes the first steps toward reproducing his parents' class status. He thus sacrifices few principles in telling his father that he disapproves of Lindau's wild talk. He prefers an enduring national optimism: "I don't suppose this country *is* perfect, but I think it's about the best there is, and it don't do any good to look at its drawbacks all the time" (271). Tom contemplates the "time" of cultural critique. He approves of present conditions, esteeming the U.S. to be "the best there is" even as he highlights the imperfection of the now. If "is" marks conditions that are not so great, how does the "could be" or the "will be" look? Tom is not looking to join a den of anarchists. Safe, studious, and respectful, he's a good kid. Still, this solid citizen entertains the idea of a different temporal order as a way of imagining an alternative present—even if he ultimately associates that possibility with Lindau and rejects it as a "bad cause." He accepts his father's counsel about the necessity of preserving law and order with an air of resignation, asking, "What's the use of our ever fighting about anything in America? I always thought we could vote anything we wanted" (409). March can rest a little easier; his son is off to polling place, not the barricades. Where Tom is now, however, is the brink of disillusionment. He "always thought" that legality was not at odds with social change, but his words also suggest that whatever he may have "thought," he is not thinking this way now and is on the cusp of questioning his most fundamental beliefs about his country. His thoughts about the futility of violence cannot be separated from frustration and impatience with the social order. Frustrated with the present, impatient with the glacial pace of change, people often act.

NOVELISTS FOR (AGAINST?) CHANGE

People may act but Tom never will because he is not even a person. He is a character in a book. Howells reminds us of this inescapable fact via some metafictional moments in which Basil and Isabel March discuss novelists, character, and change. Forget about wide-ranging social change: March and his wife have their sights set on the scaled-back issue not of whether people can change conditions but of whether conditions can change people. "Does anything from without change us?" March wonders. Commonsense wisdom dispensed by "novelists," he says in answer to his own question, tells us that external forces do affect inner constitutions, but March himself is not so sure. He doubts whether any event, especially one of "cataclysmal" proportions, can dislodge individuality from its regular course (439). We remain insensible to social upheaval, March avers, with our resistance becoming more resolute as the extent of turmoil increases.

Howells in turn may not be so sure of March. Making a distinction between active and mechanical translators, Brook Thomas suggests that March incurs Howells's disapproval for refusing to view himself as anything other than an autonomous agent immune to dialogue or exchange.[95] The novelist's ironic distance from his character allows him to think, however obliquely, about the connection between literary strategy and change. At first glance, March's pessimistic outlook about change is the best news for the status quo:

> I suppose I should have to say that we didn't change at all. We develop. There's the making of several characters in each of us; we *are* each several characters, and sometimes this character has the lead in us, and sometimes that. (440)

Although March discounts novelists' ability to influence "people's thinking," he associates the literary with the multiple possibilities that characterize human beings as ethical actors. From within a novel, March invalidates novels just as he is a character who explores the relationship between character and change. These nifty enclosures accentuate the extent to which the inwardness of the subject takes the place of social conditions in the economy of *Hazard*. In the process, the mass subject disappears from view, leaving Howells and his readers with only a wishy-washy ("this character . . . and sometimes that") sense of direction that looks a lot like immobility.

Yet the conceit of a novelist writing about a character who disregards novelists serves as an ironic reminder that novelists shape characters and their actions. March's fixation on character—both in literary and moral terms—draws attention to Howells's belief that character can be skewed, redirected, and profoundly altered. It is a belief that returns us to the moment of subjective judgment that for Kant forms the basis of aesthetics. For Kant, the subject's taste becomes both the fantasy and foundation of a much wider collective sensibility, one that ideally would be valid for the human species as a whole. Howells seems to be running in the other direction, fleeing from the spectacle of mass subjectivity and toward the isolation of character. The theoretical conduit between the subject and the mass is broken; individual feeling will never be translated into collective social action. The hazard of literature is nothing less than this negation: in imagining a potential world of different choices and new outcomes, literature may be forced to say that such possibilities will never come to pass.

BEAUTY ALONG THE COLOR LINE

· ·

Lynching, Form, and Aesthetics

Theories of beauty, when put into praxis, invoked the specifics of daisies, sweet william, and hyacinth as true missionaries of the City Beautiful movement. For two years running from 1913 to 1914, a flower garden remote from narrow alleys and cramped tenements received accolades for the social work its beauty performed. Its owner, Alexander Hughes of Springfield, Massachusetts, donated blossoms to area hospitals and, in a more intimate gesture, urged flowers on "strangers having no friends near."[1] Beauty, it seems, possessed curative power along with an ability to inspire feelings of community among the alienated.

This award-winning garden does not grow only in Springfield. It blooms along the contested ground of the Color Line. As *The Crisis* remarked, Hughes is "a colored citizen" whose horticultural achievements are also simply cultural, packed with larger representative significance for a people seeking redress in an era of lynching and murderous race riots.[2] Beauty offers an implicit political statement: aesthetic sensibility jars with the ugly social treatment that black citizens received in U.S. culture. Set against the reporting of narrow prejudices appearing monthly in *The Crisis*, beauty constitutes an expansive geography. As an emblem of beauty, this flower garden puts into practice a style of black cultural nationalism identified by Wilson Moses as a conservative discourse bound by Anglo-American notions of gentility.[3]

Theory proved much harder than practice. "In aesthetic theory and criticism, the Negro has not yet made any worth-while contribution," announced *The Crisis* of September 1924.[4] This statement, however, ignored the history of *The Crisis* itself, which almost from its inception had provided W. E. B. Du Bois and others a venue for exploring the status of "the beautiful" in relation to social justice. With columns on "Music and Art" that often ran side-by-side sections on "Lynching," *The Crisis* staged monthly confrontations between aesthetics and black print culture. The inclusion of artwork and news about black artistic achievements no doubt worked to embellish a journal that chronicled and fought against black victimization. The effects worked the other way, too: with each issue, aesthetics were retheorized so that beauty no longer appeared as an ideal beyond practical purpose but was instead revealed as a formal matter saturated by the historical content of racial atrocity. At a time when some black intellectuals found safe harbor in the doctrine of art for art's sake, *The Crisis* as an agent of black print culture pushed a confrontational aesthetics that revalued traditional categories of "the beautiful."

Du Bois sought to compensate for this deficiency by inviting Charles Chesnutt, Countee Cullen, Jessie Redmon Fauset, and other leading figures in black and white letters to participate in a forum about race and aesthetics. Dissatisfied with the responses he received, Du Bois took matters into his own hands, using *The Crisis* to develop an uncompromising aesthetic theory. The result—his 1926 provocation entitled "Criteria of Negro Art"—culminates in the equation of art to a political tool, famously defining art as propaganda. To observers at the time, such as Claude McKay, who wrote Du Bois that "nowhere in your writings do you reveal any comprehension of esthetics and therefore you are not competent nor qualified to pass judgment upon any work of art," the editor of *The Crisis* had approached art using all the subtlety of an ideological jackhammer.[5] To readers since, Du Bois's prescription has often seemed old fashioned, constrained by a party line of culture that slighted black vernacular expression in order to demand, as Darwin Turner puts it, a single "standard for all blacks—at least for all cultivated blacks."[6]

When Du Bois declared propaganda as the criterion of African American art, he did not insist that art be created in strict accord to some preexisting cultural orthodoxy. What matters instead is the instrumentality of beauty and art for political confrontation. This approach uses aesthetics to redefine propaganda, which in both Du Bois's day and ours tends to be discredited because of its overt ideological imperatives. As an endeavor "ever bounded by Truth and Justice," to use the lofty description of

"Beauty" in *The Crisis*, aesthetics overhaul propaganda so that it no longer connotes vulgar partisanship but rather operates as "the one great vehicle of universal understanding." Aesthetics make propaganda true by coloring the concept with the history of race in ways that people, including white people, are compelled to recognize. Beauty is not a matter of perception but an arena for crafting hegemony. "All Art is propaganda and ever must be, despite the wailing of the purists," Du Bois explains. "I do not care a damn for any art that is not used for propaganda." And it's high time that black intellectuals develop an aesthetic theory that encourages expropriation: "But I do care when propaganda is confined to one side while the other is stripped and silent."[7] This pronouncement seems muddled: how can "all Art" already be propaganda while "any art" has the potential to be propaganda? The answer lies in the difference between "Art" and "art." Whereas "Art" implies aesthetic forms that receive the cultural validation of unassailable tradition, "art," a much more ductile category, does not abide prescribed understandings and instead questions the constitution of such judgments as universal.

Du Bois was led to these rather fine and orthographic distinctions from his work with *The Crisis*, experimenting with the political uses of formalism. Starting with Du Bois's 1926 manifesto and reading in reverse chronological order every issue of *The Crisis* to its first issue in 1910, I have attempted to re-create a critical narrative that traces the development of an aesthetic theory among African American writers associated with the NAACP's national magazine. Month after month, *The Crisis* assembled short notices about black achievements in painting, music, and sculpture as an overall aesthetic of racial uplift whose mission "would end when Negroes were rightfully placed in the pantheon of American civilization."[8] But any smooth tracing out of this narrative is interrupted issue after issue by the ghastly reporting of lynchings that make attention to beauty seem misguided at best and frivolous at worst. Had not James Weldon Johnson in *The Autobiography of an Ex-Colored Man* (1912) already written about beauty and racial consciousness, only to end with a renunciation of aesthetics? Johnson's ex-colored man seeks to ennoble black life by expressing "all the joys and sorrows, the hopes and ambitions, of the America Negro, in classic musical form." As he collects material from the Deep South, the ex-colored man is poised to fuse race to aesthetic form, implying that African American identity, like music, can be arranged—and rearranged—into universally pleasing compositions that transcend the provinciality of racism. But a spectacle lynching derails his goal of aesthetic reclamation. Frightened and ashamed, he boxes up his transcriptions of black popular music and decides to pass as white, turning his back on art and rejecting his racial heritage. Black life cannot be made over into classic forms of "universal art" when its content is infused with the racialized specifics of murder.[9]

The Autobiography of an Ex-Colored Man suggests the difficulties facing Du Bois and his colleagues at *The Crisis* as they attempted to articulate an alternative aesthetics whose principal criterion centered on propaganda. Johnson's novel also indicates the ethical difficulty that this chapter's association of beauty and lynching poses. Du Bois argues for the necessity of this disturbing conjunction because of his belief that aesthetics, as a broad endeavor that includes propaganda, counteracts the narrowness of spectacle violence. Surveying the early history of this monthly magazine, this chapter uncovers an aesthetic theory that locates beauty at a site of "crisis" where violence is aestheticized even as aesthetic formalism is linked to social transformation. If "literary form itself," as Elizabeth Maddock Dillon writes, "can speak . . . of the creation and distribution of political power," Du Bois's interest in aesthetics speaks volumes about how specific content—particularly African American personhood—often fails to meet putatively universal criteria that underwrite justice.[10] By attending to form in an era of lynching, Du Bois rearticulated the initial delimitations of "the beautiful" whose abstract parameters disallowed black lives from having merit both in the national sphere and in international settings of colonialism.

Although Du Bois's "militant journalism," according to David Levering Lewis, clearly follows in the tradition of Frederick Douglass's *North Star,* the intellectual inheritance linking African Americans to the tradition of Western aesthetics seemed tenuous if not antagonistic.[11] Aesthetic philosophy could be downright hostile, stipulating that general precepts about beauty always met their limit in blackness, the Negro, or Africa.[12] For a people that *The Souls of Black Folk* defined as the "problem" of the twentieth century, the eighteenth-century neologism "aesthetics," infused with weighty philosophical matter first by Baumgarten and by Kant, seemed a long way off. Never daunted by history's rejection, Du Bois read Kant at Harvard and deepened his knowledge of German aesthetics in Berlin. By starting with *The Crisis* and moving outward to consider black writers' engagement of art and propaganda, including Du Bois's own novelistic examples, I bring an alternative aesthetics into focus. The problem is that other issues—most notably the aestheticized violence of lynching—enter the frame as well. This friction led to Du Bois's experiment with propaganda in defiance of colleagues at *The Crisis*, who did not feel comfortable with such overt politicization. As this chapter ultimately argues, Du Bois reacted by pushing his agenda even more strenuously via a sort of political alchemy that tried to wring an activist methodology out of aesthetic formalism.

AESTHETICS VERSUS ART

In rearticulating "the beautiful," the men and women at *The Crisis* walked dangerous ground, trying to recuperate forms of representation that had done so much injury to black people. Worse still, they risked their own irrelevance, opening themselves up to the accusation that effeminate dabbling in art did little to abate black victimization. At the forefront of the crusade for federal anti-lynching legislation, *The Crisis*—as the urgency of its name suggested—had little use for racial accommodation. This stance set it apart from competing African American monthly magazines, which owed allegiance to Booker T. Washington and routinely attacked *The Crisis*. At the helm, Du Bois stood for nothing less than "arousing and edifying his audience . . . reshaping a race's image of itself, and . . . serving a resounding notice to white people of a New Negro in the making."[13] Through it all, the belief that beauty was instrumental to social justice remained a poignant chord in the writings of Du Bois and other *Crisis* staffers, including Walter White and Jessie Redmon Fauset. Their principled stand recruited new subscribers in droves, to the alarm of the Tuskegee machine: after selling out the inaugural issue of 1,000 copies, Du Bois increased the print run to 2,500 for the December 1910 issue, and by April 1912 distribution was at 22,500.[14]

Each month *The Crisis* ran a regular section entitled "Along the Color Line," featuring short notices about both black achievements and victimization, which taken together served as a record of racial progress—or lack thereof—at home and abroad. Grouped under the headings "Education" (showing black students outperforming white peers in oratorical contests, science fairs, and overall graduation rank), "Economics" (tallying the combined deposits of black-owned banks or the wealth of the black bourgeoisie), and "Music and Art" (publicizing black singers performing classic opera), these snippets located "Along the Color Line" documented the importance of intellectual, economic, and artistic uplift. Yet categories such as "Crime" and "Lynching" offset these encouraging signs in the battle against discrimination. Amid this constant tension, the banner for "Along the Color Line" remained the same issue after issue: rows of corpses stretch into the distance, the horizon broken only by a corpulent white figure, an allegory of mob "justice," who holds fast the ropes that strangle human beings (fig. 9). The February 1914 *Crisis* exemplifies the antagonistic confrontation between aesthetics and murderous ugliness. While "Music and Art" applauds "the ease and freedom" that characterized the vocal performance of an African American tenor and acclaims Alexander Hughes's "beautiful flower garden," the column "Crime" recorded that David Lee "was lynched" by "a dozen masked men" and that Mary Marshall narrowly escaped a lynch mob after she "kill[ed] a white boy under provocation."[15] The layout of *The Crisis* illustrates that "Music and Art" are always positioned against other forms of black life and against death. Art for art's sake does not exist when aesthetic acts remain adjacent to columns of crime and categories of injustice, especially murder. Art always exists for the sake of something else. To assert otherwise, to claim that art exists for its own autonomous purposes, would be to give art a freedom that the American world so clearly denies its citizens.

This placement of beauty along the Color Line at first seems to follow the dictates of Anglo-American aesthetics. William Morris, for instance, imbued art with democratic potential by identifying beauty as "the solace of oppressed nations."[16] Yet the idea of beauty as compensation for defeat hardly seems consistent with Du Bois's activist sense of art as embattled among the materialist contexts of racial life. A generation earlier, John Ruskin, for his part, had allowed that "beauty . . . [might] be sought for in the forms which we associate with our every-day life," but he strictly limited this search to "the drawing-room."[17] Johnson's ex-colored man betrays how adherence to such criteria traduces racial consciousness when he likens his son, who knows nothing of his African bloodline, to "a little golden-headed god, with a face and head that would have delighted the heart of an old Italian master."[18] The ex-colored man literally reproduces European classicism as racial amnesia. For writers who imbibed these precepts, the task was difficult and the payoff dubious, as Nathan Huggins first argued: "The black artist had to convince himself that he had

THE CRISIS

| Vol. 7—No. 4 | FEBRUARY, 1914 | Whole No. 40 |

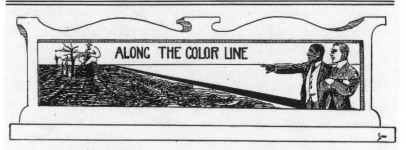

MUSIC AND ART.

A T the annual meeting of St. George's Club, of New York, Mr. Harry T. Burleigh, the distinguished baritone-composer of New York, in recognition of his twenty years' service as baritone soloist of St. George's Episcopal Church, was presented with a Tiffany watch bearing the inscription: "The Brotherhood of Men to Harry T. Burleigh, as a token of esteem from his fellow members of St. George's Club, November 29, 1913." The presentation was made by the rector, the Rev. Karl Reiland.

¶ The program for the series of artists' recitals which the Washington Conservatory of Music (Mrs. Harriet Gibbs Marshall, director) undertakes annually in Washington, D. C., at the Howard Theatre, began on December 13, when Mrs. Marjorie Groves Robinson, pianist, and Mr. William Speights, tenor, were heard in piano and song recital. Among their selections were numbers by Clarence Cameron White, Rosamond Johnson, Will Marion Cook and Coleridge-Taylor. Miss Beatrice Lewis was the accompanist. Mrs. Robinson and Mr. Speights are both graduates of the New England Conservatory of Music in Boston, and have lately joined the faculty of the Washington Conservatory. The concert series for 1914 will include a concert by the Conservatory Folk Song Singers in January, a lecture recital by Mrs. Maud Cuney Hare, pianist, assisted by Mr. William H. Richardson, baritone, in February, and a comic opera to be presented by Mr. Speights in March.

¶ A series of five recitals on folk songs, folklore and folk dances in costume have been presented at the Brooklyn Institute of Arts and Sciences by Mrs. Alexina Carter-Barrell, an American singer of Boston, Mass. Negro and Creole folk songs were given on December 3. Dr. W. E. B. Du Bois was the lecturer; Mrs. Barrell, soprano; Mellville Charlton, organist; Walter Craig, violinist, and Henry L. Jeter, violoncellist, with Mrs. Dora Cole Norman, solo dancer. On December 10 an Indian and Mexican program was presented, with the addition of Miss Lucille Perry Hall as solo dancer.

¶ On December 14 Mr. Julian F. Adger, organist, gave an organ recital under the auspices of the Philadelphia Organists' Alliance, at Cherry Memorial Church, Philadelphia, Pa. The assisting artists were Miss Blanche Williams, soprano, and Miss Elizabeth Benson, pianist.

¶ On December 29 the Philadelphia Concert Orchestra gave the first of a series of concerts for the season 1913-1914, at Philadelphia. The soloist was Miss Lydia C. McClane, soprano, of Philadelphia. The orchestra, which is in its ninth season, is the first incorporated colored symphony orchestra in the United States.

¶ Mr. T. Theo Taylor, pianist, and Mr. Harrison Emanuel, violinist, of Chicago, Ill., were heard in a joint recital on November 20, at Springfield, Ill.

¶ Cloyd Boykin, the artist of Boston, Mass., sailed on November 29 for London. Mr.

FIGURE 9. "Along the Color Line," *The Crisis* (1914). This graphic depicts black and white activists joining the crusade against lynching even as it implies their different responses. The white observer needs to have this outrage pointed out to him, as if lynching would go unnoticed if his black companion did not draw attention to the lynching tree. The white man wears eyeglasses, his ability to perceive social injustice always in need of adjustment, and his arms are crossed, suggesting relative complacency with what he sees.

something to say worth saying, and that he had the skill to say it; then he had to defy the white eyes which were too often his eyes as well. All so that he could end with a work of art."[19] Traditions of Anglo-American aesthetics, it would seem, fold art back on itself, so that it is never positioned among other historical categories.

Du Bois's innovation was to see this fold as a tear in aesthetic formalism. Just as the orthographic distinction between "Art" and "art" alludes to Du Bois's nuanced dissent from Anglo-American aesthetics, so too the repeated juxtaposition of beauty with lynching in the columns of *The Crisis* bespeaks the impossibility of cordoning off "the beautiful" from the content of racial life. Formalism, in effect, is never as formal as it pretends to be; it is always a historical category. If, however, beauty appears removed from historical striving, it can provoke self-doubt, leading race men and women to wonder, "After all, what have we who are slaves and blacks to *do with* Art?"[20] Plenty, would be Du Bois's response. Du Bois could answer so sharply because art—much of it specious and injurious—had already *done* so much *to* slaves and blacks. *Doing with* as opposed to *done to*: the difference between transformative use and passive receipt of art lies in an interventionist methodology that treats aesthetic formalism as debatable ground on which judgments are made, criteria established as universal, and hegemony treated as the common sense of the majority. Aesthetics interested Du Bois not because of its subject matter—that subject matter was white enough—but because it provided him a form to reconstruct social and political categories.

The sticking point in this assertion about Du Bois's radical aesthetics is his finicky attitude toward new and popular art. *The Crisis* under Du Bois's leadership "hardly concealed its disdain for jazz, the blues, and the popular gospel song . . . [and] seldom questioned the artistic criteria of the white world," as Arnold Rampersad observes.[21] Such statements are not contradicted by Du Bois's ambivalence toward the Harlem Renaissance, evident in his confusion over formal experimentation in Jean Toomer's *Cane* and discomfort with working-class vulgarity in Claude McKay's *Home to Harlem*.[22] Little payoff exists in interpretative backflips that would square Du Bois's tastes with his aesthetic theory, for instance, by claiming his artistic preferences as more adventurous than generally assumed. Just as it would be pointless to explain away his parochial convictions, it would be disingenuous to pretend that Du Bois's own literary efforts are not, in the words of Rampersad, "dated" and "bombastic."[23] In contrast to his pronouncement that the Color Line is the problem of the twentieth century, Du Bois's artistic productions seem stuck in the Victorianism of the nineteenth. But to accept this judgment is not to surrender the terrain of aesthetics. Only by using propaganda to cut a distinction between art and aesthetics can Du Bois ask: what does art do to people and what can people do with art?

Construed as a political discourse about form, aesthetics theorizes what art does: the subjects it creates and limits, the analyses it forecloses and enables, the historical linkages it reveals and obscures, and the justice it promises and the injustice it legitimates. Propaganda, above all, represents an aesthetic concern about the form politics should take. By cutting a distinction between art and aesthetics, propaganda does not separate these two densely intertwined categories so much as turn the tables on their relationship to imagine different criteria that give primacy to aesthetics, usually a second-order discourse, as a field of investigation devoted to understanding art as one *historical form* among the many forms—legal, institutional, national, gendered—that constitute social possibilities and political horizons. Rather than attempting to unlock the meaning of an artwork, aesthetics probe the exclusions, effects, and uses of form. Aesthetic formalism gave Du Bois necessary leverage to exert pressure on— and think about doing something with—art. While the stilted aspect of his fiction did little to trouble established standards of representation and, in fact, probably confirmed New England ideals of refinement, his concern with historicizing aesthetic formalism, that is, with locating and situating "the beautiful," strikes at assumptions about art's role as disinterested and socially irrelevant.

If his artistic tastes never shed certain niceties, Du Bois's politics also never strayed too far from what Adolph Reed identifies as a mode of "inquiry linked to strategic action." Reed identifies such inquiry as anti-aesthetic, contending that Du Bois's political vision was unclouded by literature or idealistic philosophy. This assessment hinges on a rigid disciplinarity that upholds politics as "an autonomous domain of social activity" that, as far as Reed is concerned, is thankfully immune to literary hermeneutics, which are often nothing other than empty exercises in "formalist aestheticism."[24] Neither formalism nor aesthetics, however, is as formal or as historically empty as assumed: the content of aesthetic form, especially in the first decades of the twentieth century when "Aesthetics 101" was standard in many university curricula, is always a political matter that entails asking how the aesthetic field is delimited and defined in the first place. This recognition offers insight into the unequal relations that structure not only art but also any field (such as politics) or endeavor (such as justice) that relies on formal criteria. By disentangling art and aesthetics, Du Bois steps outside the category of "the beautiful" to consider art's uses and effects.

By foregrounding issues of placement—where does "Music and Art" belong in relation to "Lynching"?—*The Crisis* mapped aesthetic theory onto a geography of racial difference. The journal featured a "multimedia format" made possible by advances in halftone reproduction that allowed for cheap and easy combination of lynching photographs, illustrations by black artists, and editorials about political action.[25] Print culture brought Du Bois to the radical edge of Kantian critique by revealing the contingency of form, both in terms of its specific location and its historically composite nature. The subject, according to Kant, "judges not merely for himself, but for everyone" by adopting a perspective that everyone else is presumed to already share.[26] Hannah Arendt discerns deep political significance in this axiom, as aesthetic judgment rouses "the fundamental abilities of man as a political being" who "orient[s] himself in the public realm, in the common world."[27] But to say that individual judgment prepares the ground of collective sensibility—what Kant labels *sensus communis*—does not put the case strongly enough. Aesthetic judgment requires obligation, decreeing a shared sensibility for all people. This strenuous discourse that tells people to agree with universal feeling is redeployed in Du Bois's instruction to *his* people that "until the art of the black folk compells [*sic*] recognition they will not be rated as human."[28] His word for this instruction, of course, was *propaganda*. By connecting propaganda to aesthetic judgment, Du Bois reactivates the "the beautiful" as a democratic imperative to revise the forms that encompass what *The Crisis* each month identified as "the darker races."

Du Bois's turn to aesthetics seems surprising and counterintuitive, given that symmetry, balance, and unity became intense topics of academic study even just as those same qualities were receding ever faster from black-white relations. But because he understood aesthetics, not as a set of abstract propositions about Beauty or Truth, but as a historical category determined by the Color Line, he came to see propaganda as vital to democratic struggle. As an alternative aesthetics, propaganda provides an insistent reminder that beauty always has a location. Mapping aesthetic formalism onto a zone of political "crisis," Du Bois and *The Crisis* redrew the landscape that hemmed in the lives of black people. When extralegal terror seems in accord with national criteria, as Du Bois first recognized, a partisan beauty supplies a methodology that pits the narrow geography of such judgments against the possibility of universal form.

AESTHETICIZING VIOLENCE

The decades that witnessed the greatest toll of black victims at "the hands of persons unknown" (a convenient legalistic cliché of the era expressing the willful failure to seek indictments against lynchers even though the perpetrators were often commonly known) also saw a flurry of academic research to codify beauty as an aesthetic "science." Educators sought to establish links, ranging from the philosophical to the physiological, between the perception of beauty and the citizen's capacity for ethical behavior. More difficult to establish is a relation between beauty and lynching. Would a critic or theorist be so incautious as to stretch the limits of political good taste by associating ritualized murder with the philosophical discourse of aesthetics? Du Bois took this chance because the linkage of beauty and lynching provided an analysis of white injustice as well as a means of countering such ugliness.

As university research grounded the Kantian project in psychology and physiology, theories of universal taste stumbled against the "the darker races," whose specific history seemed far removed from the vague generalities of *sensus communis*. When neo-Kantians like Henry Rutgers Marshall, author *Aesthetic Principles* (1895), peered across the Color Line, the tendency was to correlate the "development of notion of beauty *pari passu* with the development of racial life" in ways more invidious than this vaguely romantic and anthropological appeal to race would at first suggest.[29] A universal sensibility shared by humanity may be a worthy ideal, but cultural differences in judgment suggest it is neither practical nor likely. This attention to difference is the "neo" that makes a neo-Kantian: whereas Kant sidelines anything that would particularize aesthetics, the textbooks for "Aesthetics 101" stressed the importance of climate and geography, each a codeword for race, upon people's capacity to create and appreciate beauty. In *The Philosophy of the Beautiful* (1895), William Angus Knight stipulates that universal aesthetic sensibility cannot map onto the actualities of the globe since only "the temperate zone," not the tropics, has produced great works of art. How to defend against "scattered judgements" which would esteem the Hottentot Venus to be as beautiful as the Venus of Melos or the Castellini Aphrodite? Not a problem for Knight because as "world-wide" pronouncements of taste "approach toward a common standard . . . the crude taste of the savage will yield, in a perfectly normal way, to the insight of the civilized."[30] If the "darker races" were to join the community of world civilization, then, in the eyes of aesthetic science, the contents of "racial life" that seemed too specific for universal forms of beauty could not in any way be countenanced.

Beauty and lynch law exist at different ends of the Color Line, each appealing to justice as either imminent in a formal world where individual difference does not signify before more global concerns about proportion, symmetry, and purity or as long deferred in a world so out of proportion that human beings are burned alive. At the same time, aestheticized representations of racial subjects cannot be held apart from the history of lynching. "Rituals of aggression and negation" remain even today the inevitable context of "beautiful black male bodies," according to Kobena Mercer.[31] These comments, made on looking at Robert Mapplethorpe's photographs, stem from a history in which the two ends of the Color Line—lynching and beauty—meet up in spectacles of violence. Lynching and beauty can be examined together only through a politicized methodology—might we use the term propaganda?—that takes aim at national criteria that evaluates white violence as though it were a work of art.

Activists working for the NAACP experimented with this sort of methodology, debating the extent to which beauty could facilitate visions of a just world. The risks of this experiment were by no means incidental: in the face of mounting statistics that "on the average a black man, woman, or child was murdered nearly once a week, every week, between 1882 and 1930 by a hate-driven white mob," an aesthetic strategy seemed not only implausible but also dangerous by potentially legitimating a turn away from ugly social realities terrorizing U.S. black populations.[32] Even worse, such a solution could aestheticize the violence that was the mainstay of that terror. Du Bois's undertaking required vigilance lest "Music and Art" beautify violence, making murder seem a thing of common sense. Writing in the context of a different terror, Walter Benjamin in his famous artwork essay would pinpoint this danger as an aestheticization that makes destruction beautiful. In an artwork essay of his own, Du Bois seeks criteria that will differentiate between an outlook that aestheticizes racism and one that uses "Beauty to set the world right," a distinction that Benjamin would later reproduce as the difference between the politicization of aesthetics and the aestheticization of politics.[33] Benjamin attempted to hold the line between the two by, on the one hand, valorizing the role of Communism in "politicizing art" and, on the other, denouncing aesthetic politics as the watchword of fascism.[34] Du Bois faced a very different task, if only because the repressive aspects of U.S. culture remained fused to a liberal ideology of rights, not to rigid state control. Unable to draw neat distinctions, Du Bois conflated aesthetics and politics by imagining the possibility of doing something political with art. The payoff was small and the risks enormous since U.S. media had no qualms about doing something aesthetic with politics by presenting African American dehumanization as a source of white pleasure. The market never can stock enough "Uncle Toms, Topsies, good 'darkies' and clowns," writes Du Bois.[35] Too plainly, the campaign of extralegal terror against black people, promoted by literature such as Thomas Dixon's romances of the Klan, justified in film by D. W. Griffith, and accepted by the mainstream press, was in accord with national taste.

Du Bois felt sufficiently dogged by these pitfalls to begin his "Criteria of Negro Art," published ten years before Benjamin's 1936 artwork essay, by ventriloquizing the concerns of those who doubted the usefulness of drawing methodological links between efforts to create beauty and protests demanding respect for blacks as citizens and human beings. "How is it that an organization like this [the NAACP], a group of radicals trying to bring new things into the world, a fighting organization which has come up out of the blood and dust of battle, struggling for the right of black men to be ordinary human beings," wondered Du Bois, "how is it that an organization of this kind can turn aside to talk about Art?"[36] No great leap was needed to imagine this anti-aesthetic position because Du Bois and his comrades had long asked such questions of themselves and each other. In their more sanguine moments, workers at *The Crisis* would make the case that a turn to aesthetics as a discourse "about Art" was never a turn aside but rather a mode of confrontation. But optimism was often difficult to come by, and Du Bois, White, and Fauset frequently asked when beauty had ever stopped a lynching. Did not the aesthetic aspects of lynching itself—its cruel drama, ritual orchestration, and spectacular atmosphere— invalidate political aesthetics even before it got under way?

The aesthetic dimension of lynching comes through in the work of historians who describe the systematic persecution of blacks as "theater," "festival," and stage show.[37] In his haunting collection of picture postcards of lynchings, James Allen confronts the grisly aesthetics of torture. Likening the photographic record of strung-up bodies to *"nature morte,"* which typically displayed ripe fruit or fresh game up for viewers' pleasure, Allen implies that visual art played an important role in commercializing and publicizing atrocity.[38] Connecting the troubling aesthetics of violence to classical representation, Michael Hatt reads a photograph of one lynching victim as a "grotesque parody of Parmigianino's *Vision of St. Jerome*," the twisted, murdered body an eerie citation of the saint's posture.[39] The spectacular nature of racial victimization established lynching as public art, what Philip Dray calls a "'folk pornography' that made for welcome, titillating reading" in the morning newspaper. Macabre orchestrations of mob injustice render murder fit for public consumption. In his disquieting book *At the Hands of Persons Unknown: The Lynching of Black America*, Dray refuses to shrink from these aesthetic aspects when discussing the spectacle lynching of Henry Smith before a crowd of 10,000 people in Paris, Texas in 1893. Apprehended in Arkansas, Smith was being dragged back to the scene of his alleged crime when the train stopped in Texarkana, and the crowd at the depot urged that the lynching take place then and there. If not for the intervention of city officials, including the district attorney, to ensure Smith's safe passage to his murder, the town of Paris would have forfeited its "right to *stage and enjoy* its own lynching."[40]

Newspapers that publicized the time when a lynching would take place, specially scheduled trains to shuttle white folk from the countryside to the event, schools that let out early, and onlookers that gathered at spectacle lynchings made racial horror a grotesque distortion of *sensus communis*. As an aesthetic object, the victimized black body becomes the focal point of white subjectivity. Lynching's performative nature produces a drama of white community that, as Hatt argues, erases potential class antagonisms among whites. In short, the collective nature of aesthetic judgment that Arendt defines as crucial to the shared endeavor of political life becomes the terrible standard of white community. The Kantian subject who feels that he or she *ought* to accord with presupposed tastes reappears in monstrous guise at lynchings where many spectators reportedly felt unable to turn away. "I was fixed to the spot where I stood, powerless to take my eyes from what I did not want to see," confesses the ex-colored man of his behavior at a Georgia lynching. "It was over before I realized that time had elapsed."[41] Only afterward can the ex-colored man extricate himself, the retrospection of his telling separating him from the crowd. Arendt's account of spectatorship describes his situation: "Spectators exist only in the plural. The spectator is not involved in the act, but he is always involved with fellow spectators. . . . The faculty they have in common is the faculty of judgment."[42] The ex-colored man's experience puts a horrific twist on Arendt's portrait of public viewing: judgment is exactly what the lynchers have in common, their decision that a black person must die a public death providing confirmation of their social cohesion as white people.

Difficult as it is to say, lynching was an aesthetic performance. This point is driven home by the *New York Times*'s coverage of the lynching of Will Porter in a Kentucky opera house in 1911. After he shot and killed a white man, Porter was hauled off to the city jail. Suspecting that a mob would overrun the jail to enact its summary justice, the city marshal hid his prisoner beneath an opera-house stage. The mob tracked Porter there and quickly hit upon the play of executing him on stage. Turning on the house lights and setting their captive before stage scenery and props, the mob "silhouetted against the theatre walls," upon a given signal, fired two hundred bullets into Porter's body. The *Times* made the most of the event's aesthetic possibilities in describing the lynching as a "melodrama" that was "staged" in front of an "audience of half a hundred determined avengers." When the performance was over, "the lights were extinguished, the curtain lowered, and the mob then filed out."[43] Dramatic sensibilities lend order to the scene, giving this revenge play closure and organizing the mob into an audience. By the next day's edition, the sarcasm of the *Times* soured the aesthetic possibilities of lynching:

> Whatever else may be said about the inhabitants of Livermore, Ky., it cannot be denied that in them the dramatic sense is strongly developed. For, when they deemed it expedient to lynch a negro, they managed to do the familiar deed in a way not only entirely new, but highly picturesque.[44]

Aestheticization revealed that beauty and art could not be trusted in the campaign against white injustice. Too easily, the "picturesque" nature of violence overshadowed the reality of Porter's death, so that murder became melodrama.

The sheer fact that the *Times* could describe lynching, no matter how mockingly, as theatrical spectacle suggests the urgency of politicized aesthetics. Where Du Bois supplied "criteria of Negro art," Walter White's analysis of lynching functions as a scathing corollary that might be entitled "Criteria of White Southern Art." Although White never organized his exposé into a bold treatise on the scale of Du Bois's artwork essay, he explained the mutilation and murder of black bodies as fulfilling aesthetic criteria common to the rural backwaters of the South. As assistant secretary of the NAACP, White used his light skin to go undercover and investigate the Ku Klux Klan. Posing as a white newspaper reporter, he duped Governor Charles Hillman Brough into giving him a letter that served as a passport to interview whites in the aftermath of a campaign of terror against black sharecroppers in Arkansas that left, by NAACP estimates, at least two hundred blacks dead.[45] His investigations later led to *Rope and Faggot: A Biography of Judge Lynch*, a 1929 psychosocial study that diagnoses the public shooting, hanging, and burning of black people as an instinctive aesthetic response among poor Southern whites. Just as researchers in U.S. universities and colleges theorized the appeal of the beautiful as psychological instinct, White discovered what he called "lynching-psychology" to explain why lynching seizes white imaginations. For the white subject of the unindustrialized South, lynching provides pleasure by interrupting the dreary uneventfulness of small-town life. Literary allusion underwrites White's brand of cultural psychology: the "leaden colours" that Sinclair Lewis and "countless of his imitators" have used to depict the bleakness of middle-class existence in Midwest prairie towns seem a chromatic explosion when set against the "endless routine of drab working-hours and more drab home life" of the "average small town in the South." In this cultural landscape, its horizon unbroken by the existence of "the merry-go-round, the theatre, the symphony orchestra," lynching satisfies an instinctual "human love for excitement."[46] Lynching fills the void of aesthetic pleasure and, in the process, becomes less a surrogate for amusement than an aesthetic activity in its own right.

Years later Du Bois gave credence to an unofficial criteria of white art as injury to black people by attributing "the increase in lynching in 1915" to *Birth of a Nation*.[47] This peak soon leveled off, according to White. But while *Rope and Faggot* contends that the incidence of lynching declined somewhat in the 1920s, the savagery of the mob intensified. "Human love for excitement" made lynching still more ghastly: "Against this gratifying decrease in number of victims is the greatly aggravated brutality, often extending to almost unbelievable torture of the victim, which has marked lynchings within recent years." As the bonfires rose higher and mutilation of the lynched corpse entailed ritualistic dismemberment, shock and outrage were harder to come by. Aesthetic disinterest—the sign of mature reflection and appreciation—literally makes for a lethal performance. Excitement created an imagined public that, paradoxically, proved indifferent to lynching. As White charged, "an uncomfortably large percentage of American citizens can read in their newspapers of the slow roasting alive of a human being in Mississippi and turn, promptly and with little thought, to the comic strip or sporting page. Thus has lynching become an almost integral part of our national folkways."[48] Aesthetic disinterest manages Southern horrors so that the local practice of terror seems abstractly American.

"National folkways" are a false universal that limits aesthetics to the theatricality of ritualized violence. For Du Bois, politically useful aesthetics depend not on false universals but on the avowed partiality of propaganda. "I want to make a fight for art freedom," Du Bois wrote in 1925 as he was gathering material for his artwork essay.[49] Such freedom was partisan—Du Bois always saw art as a matter of taking sides—and those who took part in the fight, he believed, would do well to arm themselves with propaganda. Thus rather than neutralize murderous regionalism with an abstract aesthetics that pretends to be beyond location, The Crisis set columns about "Music and Art" against reports of lynching under the banner "Along the Color Line." Beauty has a location, and it's not pretty.

ORGANIZED PROPAGANDA

The geography of beauty in The Crisis invites dissonance, assembling evidence of black achievements in painting and performance while confronting readers with accounts of injustice that kept at the forefront the NAACP's emphasis on political action. Aesthetic theory envisioned by The Crisis insisted on something still more: artistic achievement not only may temporarily counteract the mounting record of abuse suffered by black citizens, but also, as a Kantian endeavor twisted by the materiality of racial violence in America, the political dimension of aesthetic judgment would establish African Americans' sense of right as the common sense of the nation.

The problem, as The Crisis itself acknowledged, was that black forays into aesthetic theory seemed almost nonexistent. Its chiding that "the Negro" had not yet made "any worth-while contribution" to aesthetics did admit of single exception, one that had been "adopted as a standard text book."[50] Joining the academic materials listed on college syllabi and housed on library shelves was a volume by William S. Scarborough, president of Wilberforce University and the first African American member of the Modern Language Association. While it turns out that the book in question is a Greek grammar and not a formal treatise on aesthetics per se, Scarborough had on more than one occasion encouraged political uses of art. Art, he explained, marshals "strenuous opposition to the spirit of the age," specifically when a state's imperial adventures threaten to hijack a body politic's ability to provide justice for its own people. Rather than an indictment of U.S. domestic or foreign policy, this accusation comes as part of Scarborough's literary interpretation of Aristophanes. The imperial state he has in mind is Athens but the lesson is intended for the U.S.: "the drift of the democracy—what it is bringing the people to" can be righted by attending to the implied critique of classical art. For Scarborough, poetry stands as the guardian of "the freedom of democracy."[51] Earlier, in a speech delivered at the Colored Men's Inter-State Conference in April 1884, he placed classical aesthetics and political critique into sharp proximity by attacking the Democratic Party as a deceitful Ulysses that "caresses and cajoles the poor colored man until it has made him drunk with wine, then it commits terrible crimes" just as was done to the Cyclops in his cave.[52]

The Crisis valued such efforts to politicize aesthetics, and its columns ventured beyond the obliqueness of an academic conference paper such as Scarborough presented. From time to time, articles would pivot off specific black achievements in the arts to broach abstract discussions of aesthetics and politics. An exhibition by the sculptor Meta Warrick Fuller prompted one reviewer, quoted in *The Crisis*, to proclaim, "art is the purest democracy in the world—ever has been, and ever must be."[53] But democracy in this instance hardly signified the collective agency of black people. Instead the example of Fuller's work releases—rather than addresses—racial tension by applying the balm of individual accomplishment, advising other members of "this young sculptor's race" that a "way out" of presumed inferiority "lies through the fine arts."[54] Or, to take another example, this one from the "Votes for Women" issue of August 1915, an essay on "Democracy and Art" pushed past homilies about a "way out." Refusing to legitimate notions of meritocracy by holding up an artistic genius or two, *The Crisis* posits beauty as a potentially revolutionary discourse that confronts head-on bias and caste prejudice. "Art is bringing democracy face to face with beauty," thereby initiating an expansive discourse in which universal judgment will vanquish petty distinctions that keep women from voting and blacks from receiving fair treatment.[55]

Aesthetic theory being developed by hook and by crook at *The Crisis* in reviews, manifestos, and literary contests lacked the rigor of a professional academic inquiry into beauty. With faculty members such as George Santayana and John Dewey, Harvard College could claim to be a major contributor to American aesthetics for three decades. It is by no means incidental that Santayana served as Du Bois's tutor and that Dewey's pragmatism influenced Du Bois. Despite these lines of affiliation, it is difficult to say whether the seeds of Du Bois's interest in aesthetics were planted in his student days at Harvard, to sprout later in the pages of *The Crisis*, or whether Harvard was catching up with the preeminent African American publication of the day. Certain it is, however, that Dewey invested aesthetics with a transformative capacity to emancipate people from stultifying convention. Affecting people's instinct and sensory experience, art inspires social change at the foundational level of thought and attitude. The closing lines of *Art as Experience* express this sentiment: art exerts a "liberating and uniting power" that is "looked upon with the eye of suspicion by the guardians of custom. . . . Art is a mode of prediction not found in charts and statistics, and it insinuates possibilities of human relations not to be found in rule and precept, admonition and administration."[56] Dewey's meditation goes global at this juncture, as he hypothesizes a "common world" that would be not national but cosmopolitan, a community expanding beyond U.S. citizens to include geographically unspecific "human relations." His impression of aesthetic experience echoes the discourse of Pan-Africanism that had been appearing regularly in the pages of *The Crisis*. Did Harvard educate Du Bois or was *The Crisis* making an impression among leading intellectuals in the U.S.?

"When we enter into the spirit of Negro or Polynesian art," Dewey writes, we experience a refreshing dislocation that frees us from the bias of a first-world perspective. Stilted tastes, stuffy preconceptions, and cloying criteria prized by Western subjects "melt away" in the encounter. As the barriers that prop up ethnocentrism dissipate, "we become artists ourselves." Global culture widens access to aesthetic sensibilities, although the question remains if that experience is only available to first-world tourists who consume *objets d'art* alienated from Oceania or Africa. "Polynesian" and "Negro" cultural productions acquire significance only for white subjects in need of a vacation from the cold chambers of industrial consciousness. As he rejects excess ratiocination in favor of "melting," Dewey slips into primitivism, accepting the belief that life forces enervated by mechanization and standardization can be revitalized by contact with "tribal" influences.[57] This exoticism reveals that Dewey's transformative aesthetics may not be all that transformative.

World art had been a touchy matter since the advent of world war. When the director of the Psychology Laboratory at Princeton University, Herbert Sidney Langfeld, made the trip to Cambridge to deliver a series of lectures at Harvard, he began by invoking "the aesthetic attitude" as reason enough to explain U.S. involvement in World War I. Why would a "free nation" allow itself to become entangled in what many viewed as a conflict among European powers battling over the last shreds of feudal privilege? "The sense of beauty," Langfeld declared, drew the U.S. into the war on behalf of cultural treasures threatened by military aggression. Art appreciation justifies military force:

> It required no organized propaganda to arouse the indignation of neutrals when ancient churches, libraries, and town halls were leveled by the invaders. The indignation was immediate and almost universal, as is the case in the arousal of a primitive instinct, and it was not because these were useful buildings, or because they were devoted to worship, but evidently and undeniably for the reason that they were works of art.[58]

Beauty awakens citizens to injustice, working at an instinctual level to fuse ethical concern to artistic appreciation. "Organized propaganda" is superfluous because the inborn psychological response to "the beautiful" justifies U.S. intervention in making the world safe for democracy. State-sponsored propaganda is unnecessary because, as university research claimed, aesthetic judgment is already hardwired with the criteria of the state; the universal feeling of *sensus communis* has a decidedly American cast.

The campaign against lynching, in contrast, required organized propaganda. Activists at *The Crisis* were not willing to trust in art and await a solution that would bubble forth from aesthetic instincts. Left to its own devices, the "art" of lynching, as White argued, had been hard at work in the South, victimizing black populations while entertaining whites. Even so, academic theorists resisted the imperative to organize art as propaganda. Langfeld's *The Aesthetic Attitude* (1920) draws the line at using art to rally supporters around a cause: "Aesthetics can merely indicate that as soon as a work of art communicates nothing but a lesson to the observer, it ceases to be for him a work of art. . . . It seems futile from the standpoint of aesthetics to ask the purpose" of art. Langfeld assuredly is no anarchist who believes in the free play of meaning or judgment, and he finds comfort in the Kantian *ought* that makes unity paramount to aesthetic pleasure. Lest aesthetics foment agitation in place of harmony, Langfeld locates repose at the heart of beauty. When "one views an object aesthetically," symmetry, proportion, and balance provide an intrinsic code for the self. Aesthetic power overwhelms the individual who encounters these precepts, internalizing them as the beautiful alignment of subjectivity to form. No struggle takes place since the individual's participation in bending self to form occurs "without any opposition upon one's part."[59] Langfeld embraces this paradox, stipulating that the self should be active in cultivating an attitude of aesthetic repose. For the theorist who sees "no organized propaganda" as freedom's negative condition, aesthetic repose delays political engagement.

If anything, then, aesthetic theory in universities was a bundle of contradictions that, on the one hand, encouraged aesthetic repose as a precondition for deliberate action and, on the other, discouraged politicized uses of art as doctrinaire and less than beautiful. Aesthetic repose avoided this latter pitfall by taking art as an instinctive ethics—as opposed to the artificiality of "organized propaganda"—that arises without regard to external crisis or purpose. The authority of his alma mater notwithstanding, Du Bois was moved to challenge this wisdom and ask in 1926, "What has this Beauty to do with the world?" Writing at the height of the Harlem Renaissance, Du Bois charged that aesthetic repose not only provided a rationale for white disinterestedness but also encouraged indifference among a younger generation of black artists. "'Nothing,' the artists rush to answer," was the anemic response that Du Bois imagined as coming from this cohort.[60] He proposed instead an aesthetic strategy that took the idea of beauty's connection to "the world" as a geopolitical provocation toward global thinking, using aesthetics to open a wedge between nationalism and internationalism.

After this caustic portrait of the artist who fails to weld beauty to action, Du Bois calls off his attack to confess:

> They may be right. I am but an humble disciple of art and cannot presume to say. I am one who tells the truth and exposes evil and seeks with Beauty and for Beauty to set the world right.[61]

Under cover of a temporary truce, he cuts a distinction between art and aesthetics. When it comes to art, Du Bois admits his disadvantage. "Beauty" is quite another matter because it is *global* in a double sense, suggesting at once a comprehensive philosophical discourse on art and a geopolitical discourse on "the darker races" worldwide. It is only taking Du Bois at his word to view beauty as connected to "the world" in literal geographic fashion. While art seemingly interpellates Du Bois as the subject of aesthetic repose recommended by Langfeld's *Aesthetic Attitude*—he affects diffidence and appears hesitant to stake an opinion—beauty's relationship to propaganda implies a herculean force that first shoulders and then shifts humanity's collective perspective. If the world is out of whack, then only a universal discourse will do the job and "set the world right."

Often pushed to the margins by civil rights issues, aesthetics survived in *The Crisis* largely as a global discourse that lent diasporic energy to its pages. In a series of letters mailed to *The Crisis* from the Soviet Union, the Jamaican-born Claude McKay credited Marcus Garvey, no doubt to Du Bois's chagrin, with recognizing the significance of "organized propaganda" for countering decades of "white American propagandists." In contrast to Langfeld, who saw no need for organized propaganda and assumed that art would do its political work spontaneously, McKay takes propagandistic art as direct action to stem a flood of "misinformation" that begins with *Uncle Tom's Cabin*. Organized propaganda, McKay argues, can be useful precisely for organizing blacks to advance "racial interests . . . on a world scale, to combat their white exploiters and traducers."[62] Du Bois had long operated on "a world scale," and his attraction to propaganda rescued him from the instinctual beauty of nationalism backed by Langfeld and other defenders of Western civilization. In a January 1924 article on neocolonialism and Pan-Africanism, Du Bois stated: "Nothing is more interesting than to read the carefully prepared propaganda upon which the British Empire thrives."[63] As he examines alibis for imperialism, Du Bois responds with a mixture of icy condescension and fascination, viewing propaganda's sleight of hand as "interesting" because what had come to interest him was the power of representation—and misrepresentation—to achieve hegemony. At this point, however, his aesthetic theory conceptualizes propaganda not as a tactic of transformation but only as a force aligned with domination. Hence the difficulty of articulating politicized aesthetics. The presence of staffers at *The Crisis* intent on salvaging art from what was perceived as blatant overpoliticization did not make things any easier. Thus, if 1924 began with Du Bois's warming up to political aesthetics, the line against propaganda was as fixed as ever by February when *The Crisis* condemned Dixon's *The Leopard's Spots* for "viciously" trespassing the "Color Line type of fiction" for "purposes of propaganda."[64]

Conflict came with the territory: the staff of the NAACP encouraged propaganda, deplored the intrusion of politics into literature, and called for more activist writing, disagreeing with one another each issue. Arnold Rampersad takes stock of this uncertainty, noting that Du Bois "had written so ambivalently and confusedly about the relation of art to propaganda that misinterpretation on this subject was inevitable."[65] Nevertheless, Du Bois's appreciation of propaganda steadily grew in proportion to his impatience with nationalist criteria of art. As Du Bois makes global connections between imperialist struggles among European powers over Africa and the continuing exploitation of Western working people, he condemns propaganda as a threat to democracy. His condemnation, however, is laced with awe as he recognizes that propaganda is a "tremendous weapon in our day."[66] This mixed assessment raised the possibility of revaluing propaganda so that prejudice against art with overt agendas might be temporarily set aside and beauty construed as a politically pragmatic form. Not for nothing would Du Bois look back on this stage of his career and remember it as a time of training for his "role as a master of propaganda."[67]

GENDERING AESTHETICS

Despite Du Bois's gradual reevaluation of political aesthetics, Walter White persisted in viewing propaganda as a shameless tool of the South's master class. "NEGROES ANXIOUS TO RETURN SOUTH" and "MAGNOLIA STATE INVITES WANDERING NEGROES HOME" ran headlines in Southern papers trying to halt the exodus of black labor to Northern cities. White cited these journalistic "untruths" as proof of the "mythical and slanderous propaganda" that, together with specious assertions about Southern blacks' inability to adapt to harsh economic conditions and cold winters, attempted to keep slaves' descendents quite literally in their place.[68] Given his uncompromising view of propaganda as an alibi for Southern peonage, White would no doubt have bristled at Du Bois's book review of his first novel, *The Fire in the Flint* (1924). Reportedly written in just twelve days, White's story concerns a Harvard-trained black physician who returns to practice his profession in a small Georgia town where working-class whites practice intimidation and lynching with a professionalism all their own. Du Bois praised the novel generally but found fault with White for having imbibed the cant of the former planter class to the extent that *The Fire in the Flint* lets Southern gentility off the hook by casting white poverty and ignorance as sources of black victimization. Having absolutely no use for such class nostalgia, Du Bois criticized this aspect of *The Fire in the Flint* as "based on the propaganda which sons and daughters of slave-barons have spread." [69]

Viewing propaganda as merely negative, White undercut art's use for democratic struggle. In *The Fire in the Flint* and *Flight,* his novel two years later, he invalidated aesthetics by gendering aesthetic interest as a feminine preoccupation. In a world where black masculinity is under attack, beauty is hardly the weapon of choice, for it represents a debilitating detour from hands-on politics. Art jeopardizes black masculinity by inviting suspicions that the doctor in *The Fire in the Flint,* an avid reader, is not only "decadent" and "effete" but also "a little queer in the head," disposed to "moral turpitude and perversion."[70] The charge of queerness at once hypersexualizes and emasculates black men, raising the troubling implication that art in the context of lynching is responsible for violence. Like lynching, art incites panic over black male sexual deviance and then punishes black men for that accusation. White exposes the addictive unreality of this sexual-gender mythology by speaking of beauty in both novels as an "opiate."[71] The best the doctor can do is use literature as a narcotic to stupefy political consciousness when life in a Georgia town under Jim Crow becomes unbearable. Mimi, the heroine of *Flight,* turns a more sympathetic ear to art, taking it in as "an opiate to forget hard circumstance."[72] Art becomes dangerous in Mimi's world as it spreads, finding a new population of addicts in Harlem's vibrant mecca of nightclubs and literary salons. She patronizes such hot spots but only while passing as white, indicating her disconnection from any affective—or effective—criteria of Negro art. Instead of finding a use *for* art, she simply uses it, becoming strung out on opera taken in from the cheap seats at Carnegie Hall, the sopranos and tenors affecting her "as drugs or liquor to addicts—they swept her up, up above her narrow, difficult existence to a world where cares and sorrows and toils did not exist."[73] The novel pushes a "just say no" attitude toward aesthetics, fearful that all beauty leads to illusions of escape and empty transcendence. After a program of aesthetic detox, Mimi no longer craves such fine-grained junk as opera but neither can the speakeasies or juke joints of Harlem's nightlife offer her solace. White's novels spoke for many writing about art and literature in *The Crisis* who, because they did not believe in propaganda, saw little value in aesthetics.

This rejection remains consistent with the deprecatory gendering of aesthetics. Jessie Fauset, usually a staunch ally of Du Bois, elaborated on the social inefficacy of beauty by associating it with feminine weakness in her novella of passing, "The Sleeper Wakes." Appearing serially in *The Crisis*, Fauset's narrative asks just how much social power beauty can exert. Not much, is her answer. Only through the deracialization of beauty does her heroine, Amy, achieve social status; by passing as white, she finds a husband who showers her with jewelry. Though cozy with white economic power, Amy recognizes her powerlessness to curb her husband's virulent racism; she ultimately judges her own beauty as weak—indeed, as effeminate. She correctly judges her personal attractiveness to be a valuable sexual commodity in the eyes of white men, but she errs in investing it with any political valence. When she tries to cash in on that asset to purchase social justice, all she receives is proof of beauty's lack of value. Stepping between her husband and a black servant, who are about to come to blows, she desperately clings to the white man to prevent him from fulfilling his promise to have the black man "hanging so high by midnight."[74] For a decade, *The Crisis* had been counteracting the ugliness of black victimization with occasional remarks on African American artistic accomplishments. Now in Fauset's novella of 1920, beauty goes head to head with lynching—and comes up short in the contest.

Bent on lynching, her husband pries apart her arms, leaving Amy clutching at only self-accusation: "How, *how* could she keep him back! She hated her arms with their futile beauty."[75] Stigmatized as feminine, beauty has no role to play in the defense of black masculinity. Overvaluing beauty, specifically her own physical attractiveness, Fauset's heroine blunders in thinking that a racist husband would prize feminine allure over deeply held racism. Once beauty is asked to justify something other than its own existence, once a race woman tries to put it to use in the belief that art may be for something other than its own sake, it fades. Amy's attempt to defend black humanity rests on a fundamental error: the equation of beauty solely with white standards of attractiveness. She understands beauty as "Art" but not "art," to recall the terms of Du Bois's 1926 manifesto, wholly subscribing to standards that are at once the impersonal criteria of white institutions and the personal criteria of white men's sexual desires for exoticness.

Shocked that her beauty has no use, she renounces it by confessing her racial origin to her husband (what white man would publicly admit black heritage under the category of beautiful?) as he prepares to carry out the threat to lynch. Yes, beauty fails her but has it really come up short? Renunciation is also use: exposing the racial truth behind her beauty inverts white assumptions about purity. While Du Bois's complaint about the "the wailing of the purists" obviously refers to aesthetic debates, the anxiety surrounding purity as a matter of racial origin and mixing cannot be forgotten in this context. If Elaine Scarry defines beauty as a generative form of desire—"when the eye sees someone beautiful, the whole body wants to reproduce the person"—then the specter of miscegenation frustrates that desire when it its historicized as white, male, and economically privileged.[76] Amy's disclosure of racial heritage undercuts the exotic femininity prized by white masculinity, leaving her husband pale and temporarily stricken at the thought—and threat—of being married to a Negro. He becomes powerless to follow through on his mania to lynch. By racializing her attractiveness, Amy employs beauty only to deflate it, making the white male passion for vengeance go flaccid, as it were.

Amy's expenditure of beauty buys a temporary cessation of violence, but it has no lasting legitimacy. White male desire remains the same as it ever was. Still fixated by her beauty, Amy's husband asks her to patch things up but on his own terms by stipulating that she come back to him, not as his wife, but as his mistress. The October 1920 installment of "The Sleeper Wakes" begins, "Amazingly her beauty availed her nothing. If she had been an older woman . . . she would have been able to gauge exactly her beauty over Wynne [Amy's husband]. . . . She was a little bewildered at her utter miscalculation."[77] Amy's judgment is a "miscalculation" precisely because it is a calculation; she devalues "her beauty" by valuing it economically. The final lesson of "The Sleeper Wakes" is that beauty has no social use value: it is an outcome that looks a lot like the fussy doctrine of "art for art's sake" that impelled Du Bois to develop a "Criteria of Negro Art." In publishing Fauset's novella, *The Crisis* undid its own attempts to distill a political methodology from aesthetics. This contradiction moved Du Bois to action in subsequent issues.

ALTERNATIVE AESTHETICS

Announcing the criteria for the NAACP's literary prizes of 1926, *The Crisis* offered this advice to aspiring writers:

> We want especially to stress the fact that while we believe in Negro art we do not believe in any art simply for art's sake. We want the earth beautiful but we are primarily interested in the earth. We want Negro writers to produce beautiful things but we stress the things rather than the beauty. . . . Use propaganda if you want.[78]

Although these guidelines came with no list of examples, Du Bois's novels *The Quest of the Silver Fleece* (1911) and *Dark Princess* (1928) would have fit the bill. Du Bois was among those who wanted to use propaganda, and he did not deny himself that pleasure when he turned his hand to fiction. While it is easy to see these novels as overtly, even blatantly, political, a lot of work—perhaps too much—must be done to claim these novels as artistic by conventional academic standards. Du Bois had few qualms about downplaying the artistic value of *Quest* and years later favorably evaluated the novel not as a literary artifact but as "an economic study of some merit."[79] It may be wasted effort to claim these novels as artistic, but locating them as aesthetic interventions is another story.

Aesthetics saturate these "inartistic" novels. In the first crisis of *Dark Princess*, Matthew feels at a loss when a reference to Benedetto Croce's *Aesthetic* flies over his head. With perfect aplomb he recollects himself and belts out a Negro spiritual to convince a congress of the world's "darker races" that African Americans are ready to take part in worldwide revolution. His aesthetic range—diving into the depths of African American culture to resurface with the "Great Song of Emancipation"—makes an eloquent case for the political capacity of his brethren. He demonstrates that capacity himself by becoming a player in the Chicago machine, succeeding to the point where he is poised to make the jump to U.S. congressman. Soon disgusted by electoral corruption, he turns instead to art, hanging prints by Picasso, Gauguin, Matisse, and Cezanne on his walls, "half-consciously trying to counteract the ugliness of the congressional campaign." Testing the limits of aesthetic representation, he questions standard forms of political representation that entail graft and compromise. Does art encourage a flight from the nitty-gritty realities of U.S. politics, to say nothing of the global revolutionary organization that appears from time to time at the novel's outer edges? Art provides solace for the "esthetic disquiet" Matthew feels at bartering away principle in the "political game" he must play in his bid for Congress, but in no way does art displace politics. Matthew more than simply uses art as Mimi does in *Flight*; instead, he uses art to conceptualize alternate criteria of political engagement. Abandoning the usual precepts of "ideal beauty, fitness and curve and line," he develops an iconoclastic interest in the imperfect beauty of Picasso—"a wild, unintelligible thing of gray and yellow and black."[80] An avant-garde sensibility refuses the regularities of the Color Line: his expanded palette highlights the global canvas of Asian and African decolonization movements in *Dark Princess*.

Matthew's work as a ditch digger actualizes Du Bois's advice to aspiring writers that art should be "primarily interested in the earth." Art, like Matthew's days in the tunnels, is untranscendent, never escaping the conditions of its production. The politician-turned-day-laborer knows exactly how much he has paid for the Picasso painting, a price he measures in the toll that backbreaking labor takes on his body. At the least, Matthew consoles himself, he is not forced to pay for art with his soul as he was forced to do in the "esthetically" ugly world of politics. Looking at the artwork on his walls, Matthew has a revolutionary insight: "I was a more complete man—a real unit of democracy!"[81] His appreciation of iconoclastic visual forms raises questions about how boundaries and identities are drawn in the first place. No process is more political than this initial delimitation; too often the drawing of political lines bypasses the basic "units" of democracy. An alternative aesthetic is not about beauty; that topic is the property of a conventional discourse on Art. Instead, radical aesthetic judgment concerns the forms that politics takes—whether as personal "unit," nation-state, or more cosmopolitan entity. Matthew's focus on his individuality is actually a global recognition that all other people also exist as units of democracy. His avant-garde tastes encourage an identity that expands beyond boundaries of state citizenship. This universal thinking sharpens his interest in the subaltern revolutions on several continents hinted at in the novel. With this worldwide alliance, Du Bois imagines a politics of universal form, dramatizing Wai Chee Dimock's claim that aesthetics severely question the taxonomy of the nation-state.[82] Matthew's perceptual revolution pries *sensus communis* away from the sham universality of the U.S. Critique in *Dark Princess* is formal: by thinking about units, Matthew exposes the American nation-state as an idiosyncratic form that fails to be common to all. Aesthetic judgment activates an insurgent lesson that tests the narrowness of the nation; it is a political lesson that Du Bois expresses as a question of form.

Discerning an alternative aesthetic is harder in *Quest* because beauty is bought and sold relentlessly in the novel. Beauty in this case is cotton grown in an Alabama swamp, appropriated by local white gentry, and converted into commodities by Northern venture capitalists. Following the cotton crop from its cultivation to its manufacture as textile, *Quest* models an aesthetic judgment that refuses to transcend the circumstances of beauty's production. The symmetry of lawn, flowers, and trees at a white landowner's estate is duly recognized by the Yankee schoolmarm, but her appreciation of these formal qualities does not diminish the content of history. "But it was all built on a moan," she reminds herself as she surveys the grounds of the former slave plantation. By such criteria, the cotton that Bles and Zora grow in the swamp is "the beautifullest bit of all" because it recalls the "brown back of the world"—both the earth and African American labors—from which it sprang. As with the NAACP literary contest of 1926, making the earth beautiful is important, but that effort should never overshadow the earth itself. What applies to the proletarian world of cotton also applies to the genteel circles of the art world. When Caroline Wynn takes first prize at an all-Southern art exhibit, she refuses to withdraw politely from the competition when her African American ancestry proves an embarrassment to the exhibit's organizer. She will not be bought off: "I do not want money; I want justice."[83] In each setting from cotton field to fine art gallery, aesthetics are alternative to Art because they prepare a judgment that historicizes and contextualizes beauty.

Since the discourse on beauty, which brings black students into contact with white schoolmarms, is so full-blown in *Quest*, lynching is never distant. As a topic of conversation that momentarily unites black men and white women, beauty also provokes white paranoia and threats of violence. When Bles regales a white woman, Mary Taylor, with a vivid description of cotton fields in bloom, his words convert the landscape she had seen as "desperate prose" into "poetry" that begins to work on her soul—and her body. His talk about the color and form of the Silver Fleece produces aesthetic repose in the rapt listener: "'Ah! that must be beautiful,' sighed Miss Taylor, wistfully, sinking to the ground and clasping her hands about her knees." Mary behaves as academic research on aesthetic science dictates that a subject should, rendering herself passive before Bles's beauty. But in the racialized contexts of Alabama, aesthetic repose is loaded with the myth of the white woman's vulnerability to black male physicality. As Bles becomes aware that two white men are witness to his discourse on beauty, a discourse that Mary sexualizes by going down on her knees before a black man, he recognizes the peril of his situation. While *Dark Princess* experiments with non-national, global forms, *Quest* reminds us that universal forms still have a location, which, in the historical setting of white male paranoia, is on the Color Line where black men are criminally sexualized and white women are not, despite the massive cultural buildup around purity, beyond desire. Beauty in the cotton field encourages Mary to forget these contextual factors, and she realizes with a start that "the fact of the boy's color had quite escaped her."[84] Bles does not enjoy that luxury. His discourse on the beauty of cotton never outstrips violence and death in the South; to forget the location of aesthetic experience is to risk one's life.

· 4 ·

"BOMBS OF LAUGHTER"

· ·

Motion Pictures, Mass Art, and Universal Language

From daisies that rendered police billy clubs superfluous to blossoms praised by *The Crisis*, flowers seemed beautiful tools for cultivating ethics. Echoing the overblown epics of wheat and cotton produced respectively by Frank Norris and W. E. B. Du Bois, flowers suggested an optimistic spin on naturalism, operating at an instinctual level, subduing aggression, competitiveness, and other crudely biological drives while awakening higher moral senses. Distributing flowers to combat urban blight was often more an act of faith than a proven strategy of uplift and reform. Fragile and impermanent, flowers were altogether too time-consuming to cultivate, too singularized in their address, and, finally, too seasonal to supply a lasting remedy for citizens whose ethical consciousness had been blunted by modern times. The success of the New York City Flower Mission, for instance, depended on individuals voluntarily gathering wild flowers near an outlying train station, traveling into the metropolis, trekking down to Mulberry Street on the lower East Side, and scattering their bouquets among the immigrant poor. "If we cannot give them [the city's dispossessed] the fields, why not the flowers?" Jacob Riis asked. "If every man, woman, or child coming in should, on the way to the depot, gather an armful of wild flowers to distribute in the tenements, a mission work would be set on foot with which all almsgiving of this wealthy city could not be compared. . . . Let us have the flowers."[1] But Northern winters are harsh, and the Flower Mission operated only from May to November. Were the needy to be left to their own devices during the cruelest months?

While flowers could not be outmatched for the purity or simplicity of their moral appeal, nature could have stood with some improvement and modernization. Daisies remained as important as ever, but reformers' growing reliance on stereopticons, magic lanterns, illustrated lectures, and other visual technologies surpassed inherent limitations of the natural world by allowing for the aesthetic cultivation of subjectivity not only en masse but again and again without cessation. Without a doubt, so it seemed, a flower might stir something in the prostitute or pickpocket, its tender blossom reminding predators and victims alike of the duty owed to the unsuspecting and innocent. But as the audience in this case was singular, the subject of ethical awakening encompassed no one other than the individual. What if beauty's effects could be addressed to the crowd? And what if the crowd wanted to be addressed and, indeed, clamored after pleasure? When aesthetic education, defined loosely enough to pass for entertainment, crosses into the realm of mass culture, the possibility emerges that beauty could become an active agent in promoting the democratization of national life. Best of all, the mass might pay for the experience of democratization, even if only at a nickel a pop. To put it another way, philanthropy might have a greater draw than the limited sphere in which genteel reformers operated if citizens qua consumers jumped on the bandwagon of commercialism, allowing pleasure to take the place of duty and self-sacrifice. If aesthetics became entertainment, if art emerged as a truly popular medium, cultivation of democratic citizenship and Americanization might proceed at an unparalleled clip and turn a profit to boot. Such possibilities arrived full force with moving pictures.

Writing from his "Editor's Easy Chair" in 1912, William Dean Howells believed that the jury was still out about these possibilities, as "that younger sister of vaudeville, the cinematographic show" packed "potentiality for good and evil." His choice of topic required explanation: just what was the "Dean of American letters" doing talking about an entertainment whose morality seemed as questionable as its artistic merit? Howells reminded readers that the "Easy Chair" resists pretension so energetically that "there is nothing too high or too low" for consideration. In a climate where "the moving-picture show has dropped to zero in the esteem of most self-respecting persons," Howells gladly sacrifices self-respect to align himself with the masses that give their attention and money to this new and imminently global form. Proclaiming that the West has fallen to the movies and that "Asia, Africa, South America, and Oceania" are next, Howells only feels out of step with a Massachusetts village whose school board voiced concern that public education cannot compete with public amusement. Senseless are any attempts to extirpate cinema from one particular locality since it is soon to be a worldwide fixture. Howells instead believes that time and energy would be better spent examining the moving-picture show and figuring out "not only what it esthetically is, but what it ethically may be." If school boards can move from reaction to acceptance, public education can work with cinema, combining ethics and aesthetics to produce films that will provide lessons in "ethnology" by capturing shots of third-world peoples or in sociology by featuring "strikers and strike-breakers in a street fight."[2] The movies pick up where, as we saw in the previous chapter, *A Hazard of New Fortunes* leaves off.

Although no anarchist such as Lindau appears in this installment of the "Easy Chair," socialism enters the picture via some closing irony. Howells professes concern that the idea of public schools producing moving pictures smacks of socialism, and "socialism is the last thing we would advise." As a parting shot, though, he reminds readers that "our whole public-school system is a phase of socialism." Public partnership between educators and filmmakers need not be viewed as "immediately anarchistic" but rather as an innovative solution in adapting aesthetic technologies to the training of future citizens.[3] Tax dollars currently devoted to subsidizing public education could be reallocated to support the film industry in an endeavor to produce public aesthetics, and, as Howells's argument goes, young people would then hard pressed to discern the difference between education and entertainment. In Howells's logic, culture and anarchy no longer stand opposed. The conflict that pitted a Massachusetts village against the rest of the fun-loving world resounds with Arnoldian echoes, as Howells and other advocates of film "attempted to forge a cultural consensus that would incorporate rather than repress disruptive forces such as workers and immigrants by extending a vision of sweetness and light across the boundaries of race, gender, ethnicity, and class."[4] In the face of such social optimism, Howells introduces a note of doubt: what may not be "immediately anarchistic" may nonetheless prove so in the long run; anarchy may persist within formations of culture that appear to be generative of well-behaved citizens. This chapter listens for such doubts that recur in assessments of film both in the nickelodeon era and even afterward, when film becomes much more of a middle-class venue.

While anarchy, such as we might understand it, never really loomed on the horizon (or on the projection screen) in the first decades of the twentieth century, debates over moving pictures were played out against a larger backdrop that treated aesthetic discourse and practice as a flash-point of political crisis. The crisis entailed uncertainty over the nature of "democracy," which served as a catchall for varying claims that film catered to working-class and immigrant interests, offered an egalitarian cultural experience, promoted Americanization, or supplied a pictorial grammar for a universal language. Democracy in these senses rarely referred to iden-tifiable government institutions or even to discrete political ideals. What it did signify, however, was a loose set of connections between aesthetics and politics that since at least the 1890s had been the stuff of theoretical investigation in university philosophy departments as well as the stuff of practice in social missions. With the advent of film as a wildly popular aes-thetic medium, theory and practice drew closer together in ways that led to significant reevaluations of art's role in democratic life. Among the most significant of these reevaluations were coincident and competing sugges-tions that beauty—when reproduced for the mass—provided the possibil-ity for worldwide *sensus communis* as well as for world markets.

Any discussion of early film raises problems of periodization. "Early cinema historians have sliced and diced the years preceding classicism's entrenchment in 1917 into myriad phases," writes Charlie Keil.[5] Appearing first at fairgrounds and vaudeville houses, motion pictures by 1906 found a home in nickelodeons frequented by working-class and immigrant audi-ences. But by about 1912–14, the emergence of the feature film and movie theater begins to push the nickelodeon phase into the wings. The "nick-elodeons [that] multiplied like cockroaches," to borrow Charles Musser's vivid language that hints at the objections of religious conservatives for whom cinema represented a moral infestation, started to die out around 1915 when nickel storefronts gave way to the more imposing movie "pal-ace."[6] That same year the film industry began encouraging patrons to speak not of "movies" but of the more respectable-sounding "photoplays" in an effort to help cinema shed its dodgy background of immigrant and working-class contexts.[7] For Keil, early cinema comes to a close during a transitional era that lasts from 1907 to 1915; others such as Tom Gunning see the window between early films of boxing matches, travel sequences, and optical tricks (a "cinema of narrative attractions") and later films that highlight character and storytelling (a "cinema of narrative integration") as more narrow, pointing to 1908 as the beginning of narrative cinema.[8] This proliferation of dates underscores Ben Brewster's point that "periodization is a dubious enterprise" and that historical "phases are not watertight": nickelodeons did not pack up shop overnight, just as one-reel films hung around even as they were being replaced by feature films.[9] Nonetheless, by sectioning cinema into rough brackets (1896–1904/5; 1906–15; 1915–29) and eras (early; transitional; classic), film historians have added considerable nuance to accounts preoccupied with 1929 as a dividing line between sound and silent eras. Besides creating the false impression that "silent" movies were hushed spectacles, accompanied neither by songs nor chatter, this fixation with the development of sound neglects rapid changes in cinema up to 1929.

Perhaps because they were living through these periods, contemporary observers did not always take note of such changes, often tending to speak of film as a form whose meanings remained consistent over time. Howells, for instance, writes that the "moving-picture show . . . 'has come to stay,'" holding film in a sort of suspended animation that presents socialist and anarchistic potential as always imminent. Five, ten, or even twenty years after the egalitarian aura associated with early film viewing had worn off, writers and theorists who followed Howells's lead by discussing the aesthetics and ethics of cinema hung on to the myth of the movies as a democratic cultural institution. Many who spoke about film in the 1920s and 1930s filtered their impressions through a nostalgia that allowed them to talk about the present as though it still had all the potential of the past while ignoring historical developments in cinema that would have made their nostalgia, well, a thing of the past. In this respect, I am more interested in the political-aesthetic discourse that surrounds film rather than in reading motion pictures as aesthetic artifacts. With the exception of Charlie Chaplin, I do not undertake readings of individual films, if only because scholars such as Jonathan Auerbach, Jane Gaines, and Miriam Hansen, in addition to the film historians I have already cited, bring much more expertise and insight to that endeavor than I can.[10] My use of Chaplin, moreover, does not present a reading of an early film, since I am concerned with treating *Modern Times* (1936), a film whose date of production makes it anything but an early film, as an artwork essay that provides a retrospective commentary on the vanishing prospect of motion pictures as a collective, even global, aesthetic medium. Looking at assessments of cinema as a democratic institution, and, really, these assessments are much more fictions and impressions than reliable sources of data about movies and their audiences, I explore how social activists, psychologists, actors, and filmmakers invoked aesthetic principles to adduce political possibilities from what was heralded as a new, universal art form promising to inaugurate worldwide *sensus communis*.

CLASSIC BEAUTY FOR MODERN TIMES

Reformers' flowers wither after a few days. Mass-produced beauty, in contrast, could function year round, at large, and, perhaps most importantly, without stopping. While by no means devoted to beauty, the popularity of movies took off among immigrants, working classes, urban youth, and, eventually, middle-class audiences concerned with respectability. Nickelodeons were flush with stirrings of a heterogeneous public sphere that embraced working-class culture amid strivings for middle-class acceptance, furthering diverse audience reactions while promoting a standardized notion of spectatorship.[11] As the sum of these contradictions, film invited predictions about the advent of a truly democratic art, one whose popularity did not sacrifice quality or taste. For a nickel, individuals could purchase a ticket to the picture show and in the company of others watch what a 1926 study of motion pictures trumpeted as a "genuine art" like no other in its singular capability of "appealing to and serving the multitudes."[12] Surely, an art form—or was it only a degraded amusement?—that by 1927 could boast 100 million patrons a week had something to do with democracy.[13] Just what exactly remained unclear: as certainly as mass popularity implied democracy, so too democracy implied more than sheer numbers. Here's where aesthetics enter the picture by theoretically providing the millions with enlightenment as well as enjoyment.

Prospects of democratic art had long been shot through with antinomies: in the first place, the inescapable mediocrity of popular culture deflated any pretensions that media pleasure and distraction could qualify as art; in the second, the high-toned category of art operated with limited appeal, roping off avenues of expression that presumably were too elevated for the tastes of the herd. Motion pictures seemed destined to smooth out these rough spots in the quest for democratic art. "Aesthetics 101" bolstered the impression that the refined compass of art and the common tenor of democracy could be reconciled at the movies. Academics and public intellectuals had a lot to say about this aspect of film, as they commented on its technological significance, social effects, and utopian possibilities. According to a Harvard professor who regularly offered courses in psychological aesthetics, the combination of camera and celluloid ushered in "a new form of true beauty in the turmoil of a technical age."[14] Movies, in other words, ensured that aesthetic principles would not be left behind in the march of progress. But neither would this march bring the masses to the barricades. In a 1910 article in *The Harvard Monthly* on the cinematograph, alumnus Horace Kallen (B.A. 1903; Ph.D. 1908) predicted that the "coming of the 'cinema'" would dispense an Arnoldian pabulum of "sweetness and light" to a public tired of "fire and iron."[15] Likewise, Howells saw in the movies a method for "sugar-coating the pill of learning so that the youth of this fair land will eagerly swallow it."[16] *The Outlook* hit this note as well, suggesting that motion pictures would lead "the audience on 'a path of sweetness and light.'"[17] Aesthetics, in short, would ensure that culture prevailed over anarchy.

But at the movies where art and entertainment often were confused, culture did not always seem that far from anarchy. Moviegoers did not exhibit the rapt silence cultivated at today's cineplex. Conversation, dialogue, singing, and laughter animated the scene. When the projectionist changed reels, the audience chatted back and forth, and if an illustrated song was in the mix, everyone who knew the words joined in. What was happening in the seats was as significant as what was unfolding on the screen. Movie audiences were not just patrons transposed from the theater district. In comparison to the limited range of people who could purchase pricey theater tickets, a 1910 survey of film audiences in New York City concluded that 72 percent of all moviegoers came from working-class backgrounds.[18] Despite this breakdown, early movie audiences could not be standardized, as they are today, into the singular identity of an absorbed spectator but instead remained something much more uncertain and much less calculable: the crowd. Not only did films feature scenes of "crowd splendor" and not only might crowds be dubbed a "moving picture of democracy," as we saw Gerald Stanley Lee doing in the last chapter. Movies were not simply for or about crowds; this new art form might be productive of them.[19]

The nickelodeon featured publicness in ways that departed radically from the hierarchical, class-bound segmentation of vaudeville. As Roy Rosenzweig reports in a study of leisure activities among the industrial working class, in contrast to "cheap forms of entertainment such as the melodrama or vaudeville [that] had often resisted this 'radical' leveling" implicit in open seating, movies catered to patrons who exhibited no especial fondness for social stratification and appealed to impresarios of the five-cent shows who tended to share the economic and ethnic identity of their customers.[20] By documenting the availability of mass culture—theater seats nearly tripled in Worcester, Massachusetts from 1900 to 1910—Rosenzweig shows how nickelodeons, with pricing that was easy on the pocket and show times scheduled around a laborer's long day, readily found favor with working-class people. Unlike the opera house, dance hall, or ballpark, neither private boxes nor box seats were to be had in the nickelodeon. "The nickel bought a seat anywhere in the house," writes Tom Gunning.[21] And a vibrant, lively house it was—for a short time until about 1915, when the potential of the movies as popular entertainment begins to fade once "the motion picture [was] being prettified," as one observer regretted in 1924, in ways calculated to bring audiences as well as film itself more in line with middle-class expectations.[22]

Even in the face of such facts, what nonetheless endures is the story that Hollywood spins about itself, a story based in large part on a "myth of origin that would advertise a giant corporate enterprise as a genuinely democratic, popular culture."[23] The Christmas Day 1915 heralding of motion pictures as "the greatest popular aesthetic phenomenon in the world" found more than a few acolytes: university psychologists, Progressive reformers, actors, producers, and drama critics subscribed to this myth of filmic democracy.[24] Calling the cinema democratic may be putting the case too mildly even where myth sets the tone. "There was a sense of anarchy as the crowds came and went at will, since the stories followed each other without a set time sequence," creating a schedule that appealed to workers, downtown shoppers, and schoolchildren.[25] From cheap distribution costs to audiences that gobbled up cinematic fare by the millions every week, film promoted itself as a people's art well after its democratic possibilities had been absorbed by conglomerates and reined in by censorship boards. These assessments echoed in film history until not too long ago, as the titles of books such as *Film: The Democratic Art* (1976) indicate, despite the fact that there is good evidence that a subset of movie producers and exhibitors in the opening decades of the twentieth century strove to cultivate audiences who would appreciate film as culturally elite. As the production of "quality films" and "high-class moving pictures" suggests, talk about the aesthetics of film was designed to curb cinema's overly popular appeal. Even as the movies were advertised as aesthetic experience for the millions, many in the industry hoped that gracing film with mantle of art could protect the movies from too much democracy.[26]

Rapturous assessments of film's democratic potential did not always issue from on high. In *The Spirit of Youth and the City Streets* (1920), Jane Addams begins in a mildly progressive vein by suggesting that five-cent theaters could be instrumental to civic reform. Mildness soon gives way to the more insouciant contention that the sexual adventurousness of the cinema where men and women sat in the dark, absorbed by images of a young swain "snatching a kiss from . . . ruby lips," was just the thing to bring "beauty to the prosaic city and connect it subtly with the arts of the past as well as with the vigor and renewed life of the future."[27] By this time a veteran of thirty years' work in Chicago's slums, Addams had witnessed more than one old-fashioned plea for piety fall flat with the ethnically diverse population of the ghetto. For city dwellers beset by the shocks of modernity where labor was hard and pleasure so fast that it was eclipsed only by the speed at which it was commodified, publicly available art needed to be attuned to the sprawling dimensions, dizzying pace, and frequent dislocations of urban experience. Lumping together "sights and sounds from disparate times and from all parts of the world . . . in an assembly-line-like progression of lightning perceptions," the movies confirmed, rather than transcended, the limits of everyday life under industrial capitalism.[28] Beauty must adapt to modern times, and film promised to do the trick by reconciling art to mass culture. But Addams attached an important proviso to this plan: the movies first needed to be brought under governmental control. She urged reformers to take a good long look at socializing the nickelodeon, what one chapter title in *The Spirit of Youth* dubbed "the house of dreams," as "municipal art" where images would blossom into a civic pedagogy that enjoyed all the quaint charm of immigrant folk culture while "stirring emotions" of the public at large.[29]

Previously when Addams had laid out the ethical conditions crucial to democracy, she assailed the primacy of individualism in limiting the horizon of moral expectations and public expression. Democracy faced no obstacle larger than this tendency to substitute "individual relationships" and "individual morality" for truly social practice. In *Democracy and Social Ethics* (1902), she advises citizens to seek collective experience in the most unlikely of sectors—commercialism. In a world of specialized labor, sharp class divisions, and ethnic boundaries, only commercialism could lay claim to the universal: "Its interests are certainly world-wide and democratic, while it is absolutely undiscriminating as to country and creed, coming into contact with all climes and races." The task now was to distill this egalitarian potential and capture it for public use. It was a task that required reformers to turn to the everydayness of culture. Too often, people try to fix democracy by operating only in formally political spheres, confining interest and action to governmental matters, which they then "detach in a curious way from the rest of life." But democracy, Addams insists, is not a "thing set apart from daily life."[30] She briefly considered in 1902 that the novel might adapt lofty political aspirations to ordinary existence by wrapping social lessons between the covers of an entertaining book. Two decades later, the novel in Addams's thinking had been replaced by the picture show. Film renovates her ideas about creating a democratic culture: what could be more commercial—and thus more universally accessible—than moving pictures? But by 1920 as nickelodeons were giving way to more middle-class theaters and Hollywood was consolidating control over film production and distribution, Addams was holding onto a vanishing possibility that the collective spirit inspired by cinema could be liberated from dollars and returned to an urban polis.

In light of this untapped potential, city officials should not simply turn to the motion picture; they should take over the industry and make it public property. Intentions to elevate public morality and foster "civic righteousness" are all well and good, but, unless reformers can compete with the allure of mass culture, their message is destined to obsolescence.[31] Without abandoning the ethical core of the mission to remake the industrial city in the image of the ancient polis, Addams sees that this undertaking needs to be gussied up and modernized in order to attract the heterogeneous agglomeration of immigrant Scandinavians, Greeks, Russians, and Chinese to the banner of a common culture. Cosmopolitan hopes for "world-wide" democracy seem to have been scaled back to Americanization. And it is film that supplies a new technology for making American citizens: neither preachy nor boring, moving pictures and illustrated lectures, two regular venues at Hull-House, can vie with the saloon. If this gambit proved successful, then the photograph of the Acropolis that hung at Hull-House might not seem so out of place.

Might not film be the medium of a new Athens? Civic discourse cannot take the high road or even the well-traveled puritanical one and cede pleasure to the barbarians who have no qualms about commercializing sex and crime. If reformers want to awaken the soul and inspire social ethics, they had better pay attention to what is happening on the screens as well as in the seats. An alarmist approach—and on this point Addams cites the research of a prominent Chicago psychiatrist who traced any number of abnormal pathologies to the movies—will not revitalize the sagging democratic consciousness of an industrial era. What stirs the soul or, at least, excites the passions of youth is romance, transporting him or her to an idealized plane of social feeling. In tracking "this fundamental sex susceptibility which suffuses the world with its deepest meaning and beauty," Addams runs the gamut of the cultural register, invoking Plato on the beauty of soul in the same breath that she sympathizes with the feelings of "the most loutish tenement youth" for "his 'girl.'"[32] Classical ideals have not totally disappeared under the layers of dirt and coarse sentimentality of slum life. Street music, public festivals, vaudeville, and especially the uninhibited sexuality of moving pictures can nurture budding aesthetic instincts, which, Addams hopes, will supply the bedrock of virtuous conduct, social ethics, and collective feeling. Civic values need modernization, and film is just the art to do the job.

Perhaps the movies could successfully translate classical democracy to audiences nearly two millennia later because film, despite its status as a hallmark of *fin de siècle* modernity, never really seemed that distant from premodern media. For the author of "The Great American Art" (1926), film actually surpassed "the sculpture of the Greeks, the painting of the Renaissance, the drama of Elizabethan England" because it spoke to "the hearts of the people" on a previously unimaginable scale.[33] This scale was the globe itself, and Americans should rest proud knowing that this fourth largest business in the U.S. produces 90 percent of films shown worldwide.[34] Such success fueled the optimism of progressives who concluded that the fate of not just American but global democracy, as we will see with the case of Chaplin, was bound up with the masses. For now, though, what sticks out is the belatedness of this 1926 view of film as democratic art. This recidivism enabled observers to see film as it perhaps never was—as an aesthetic medium combining high art and popular culture so successfully that "the people" would benefit from what they consumed.

Although this emphasis on commercialism gives Addams pause, her study of the industrial polis is unwavering in its longing for a new classical era, one which will treasure public art and thereby ennoble citizens. For the Greeks, the amphitheater was as much an institution in its own right as the agora and the temple, and as the story goes, this autonomy freed art from the marketplace and religion so that imagination, play, and ethical self-culture became embedded in the architecture of existence. In Addams's snapshot of an urban scene where "daily life is continually more monotonous and subdivided," might not entertainment perform a civic function by once more acting as the source, outlet, and custodian of imagination? Unfortunately, public culture lags behind the modern metropolis of dollars: as long as productivity is booming, municipal life need not concern itself with the soul's nourishment. In the few cases where public culture has not disappeared entirely—gin-mills, musical theaters featuring "the most blatant and vulgar songs," and nickelodeons palming off images of crime as diversion—the impressionable minds of youth are at risk.[35] But if culture could be rescued from commercialization and privatization, specifically, if film could be developed as "municipal art," then the boon would be twofold, as pleasure would become public property and public life would become pleasurable. Although schemes for public ownership of the movie industry never really caught fire, Miriam Hansen's remark that "the cinema belongs to the classical public sphere" affirms the openness and accessibility that Addams first discerned in the house of dreams where shadows flickered with political possibility.[36]

In terms of classical political promise, cinema did the Greeks one better. Movie houses engendered community and conviviality, as the heterogeneous audiences that thronged to nickel storefronts often made a mess of traditional class, ethnic, and sexual divisions. By bringing art to "the people," the movies theoretically reproduced sociability and equal access ad infinitum—though, of course, detractors insisted that such "art" was really tasteless trash that reproduced promiscuity and vulgarity ad nauseum. Cinema supposedly projected a common culture to a degree unimaginable in the classical city, with its small population of citizens set against slaves and women. It would be easy to confuse this common culture with U.S. culture, for what was at stake was nothing less than an Americanized world that would not stop at rendering the idea of the "universal" in its own particular idiom. With unstopped repetition and exact replication, the revolutionary technology of motion pictures ensures that there is no variation within this American image.

Always more than a celluloid strip, film promised to resolve several nagging contradictions about the conjunction of art and democratic culture. Could what seemed an oxymoron, the ideal of mass art as opposed to the reality of mass tripe, exist? Could highbrow registers of art provide aesthetic instruction for the people? With little concern for actual exhibition practices or audiences, many observers responded positively. Even skeptical observers such as *The Outlook* of 1914, writing about white slave films, proclaimed that "the 'movies' are intensely democratic—emphatically more so than the legitimate stage or even the ubiquitous novel," because mechanical reproduction seemed to make a common culture that much more accessible.[37]

No matter how much social feeling stage melodrama might inspire, its effects were limited to the audience size and location. Price also presented a hurdle since the cheapest vaudeville seats started at 25 cents and rose in value in accord with hierarchical divisions between pit, gallery, and box seating. With theater performance, no amount of illusion could dispel the impossibility of ever addressing the mass in its sheer size and heterogeneity. At the movies, in contrast, the myth of democratic origins and universal accessibility took hold even though the nickelodeon era was in its twilight by 1915. Culture, while not in its highest form, could be offered at prices cheap enough and in showings often enough to invite the participation of workers after the factory whistle blew in the evening, middle-class women during the day, and children whenever school was not in session—and even when it was. Just as picture "palaces" and feature films were making the nickelodeon obsolescent, its utopian import caught the attention of Harvard faculty whose lectures on aesthetics had been packed with examples from classical Greece and Renaissance Europe. Professor Hugo Münsterberg, whose interdisciplinary work in philosophy and psychology led to *The Photoplay: A Psychological Study* (1916), one of the first theoretical investigations of spectatorship, announced: through motion pictures the "theater can thus be democratized" precisely because their form necessarily involves "cheap multiplication."[38] *The Outlook* went one further to propose that moving pictures are not simply suitable topics for academic research but that films could increase their "educational value" if shown to "freshman classes in college."[39] It was simply scratching the surface for "Aesthetics 101" to study the movies when this new art form could render aesthetic education cinematic.

On faculty with Dewey and Santayana, Münsterberg joined in their explorations of aesthetics. But where his colleagues in the philosophy department preferred to engage the subject in the abstract, Münsterberg as a psychologist relied on film to ground his claims that art in the twentieth century reached the public on a scale more massive than ever before. "A new esthetic cocoon is broken," he proclaimed. "Where will the butterfly's wings carry" the movies? To the people, was his answer. Münsterberg was eager to mine the psycho-political implications of a cultural medium engineered for the pockets and tastes of the mass. Reproduction brings a newly classic art within the reach of "everybody's purse."[40] While claims about film and the multitude, as Hansen points out, disavow the working-class accents of early cinema in favor of bourgeois values that are ascribed to the false generality of the masses, Münsterberg's enthusiasm anticipates assertions that film can spread pleasure across a landscape otherwise stratified by factors such as region, class, and educational background.[41] Less optimistic critics charged that film supplies only the veneer of human presence, an effect that Benjamin hauntingly described as the fading of the "aura," an exquisite uniqueness possessed by all persons and objects by virtue of their inimitable location in time and space. Benjamin's comments on the cinematic reproduction of human presence are not wholly clouded by gloom, for he, like Münsterberg, clearly perceived the democratizing possibilities of technology that translated aesthetic experience to a mass scale. With equal clarity, however, Benjamin also recognized the nightmarish potential of an art whose limitless appeal made it a perfect medium for "contemporary mass movements."[42] And exactly what are "contemporary mass movements?" Benjamin's lack of precision is strategic, ambivalently invoking a reference point that could just as easily signify fascism as democracy.

Did Münsterberg's exuberance prevent him from recognizing the threat to human uniqueness posed by motion pictures? Like Benjamin, he acknowledged that something was missing from even the most perfect copy and that film could reveal but the shadow of the real. After all, the sound and dialogue of the stage translated only imperfectly to the silent screen. But for Münsterberg this difference did not connote a shortcoming. Instead, the incommensurability of film and theater signaled that film had matured into an aesthetic form all its own. Elevated to the level of art, the movies attained respectability without ostensibly forsaking connections to the common and the popular. For "many respectable Americans, who saw little difference between a mob of strikers and the unruly patrons of cheap amusements," the effort to make the film more "aesthetic"—that is, less popular, less ethnic, and less working-class—grew out of the belief that art could lead the masses from the trough of anarchy to the pastures of culture.[43] Münsterberg, however, ignored the extent to which anxieties about social class impinged upon motion pictures, preferring instead a neo-Kantian perspective that enabled him to set up a closed circuit between movies and individual viewers. Having to make no allowances for the social and economic pressures shaping the film industry, he declared cinema's "esthetic independence" that made the medium answerable only to "esthetic laws of its own."[44]

"Esthetic independence" fuels a perceptual revolution. Ever since cinematic crosscutting and flashbacks introduced around 1908 overturned dramatic conventions about the unity of time and space, motion pictures rebelled against the "temporal structure of the physical universe." The film spectator defies both matter and moment to achieve psychological liberation: "The freedom of the mind has triumphed over the unalterable law of the outer world," announced the psychologist as moviegoer. For Münsterberg,

> [film] is artistic just in so far as it does not imitate reality but changes the world, selects from it special features for new purposes, remodels the world and is through this truly creative. To imitate the world is a mechanical process; to transform the world so that it becomes a thing of beauty is the purpose of art.[45]

Where Benjamin pondered the dark fate of art in an age of mechanical reproduction, Münsterberg's pioneering psychology of the movies bridged the gap between aesthetic uniqueness and soulless duplication by suggesting that mechanical processes allow subjects to act upon—to "remode[l]" and "transform"—the material world. Mechanical reproduction is not an "age" that shrouds the "work of art" but is instead an aesthetic development that enables the mind to transfigure social reality.

Despite this attention to the mechanical, Münsterberg's *The Photoplay* rather shares much more with Dewey's *Art as Experience,* which credits aesthetics with the power to transfigure knowledge and custom. For Münsterberg, this power is driven by a generalized subject—the spectator—whose anonymous contours limn a space that anyone can occupy. Of course, not every person can assume the status of "anyone," since the mass subject enjoys an unstated biography saturated with the details of middle-class whiteness that leaves few seats for the ethnic and working-class audiences that first made the nickelodeon popular.[46] Still, the identity of "anyone" remains alluring because it is theoretically available to everyone. This anonymity augured a democratization of culture unlike any other: as film became a mass commodity, art was not cheapened but politically fortified because of its wide availability and endless duplication.

Theories about how crowds absorbed images seemed more beautiful when film was conceptualized at a remove from specific audiences filled with people talking, singing, chewing, spitting, and touching in the house of shadows. It is in this context that one of the very first film textbooks assigned in university courses, Vachel Lindsay's *The Art of the Moving Picture* (1915), celebrated cinema as high culture for the mass. The director of the Denver Art Association asked in a foreword to the 1922 edition of Lindsay's effusive study:

> With the creative implications of this new pictorial art, with the whole visual-minded race clamoring for more, what may we not dream in the way of a new renaissance? . . . What possibilities lie in this art, once it is understood and developed, to plant new conceptions of civic and national idealism? How far may it go in cultivating concerted emotion in the now ungoverned crowd?[47]

Rather than cause for alarm, the crowd's primitive nature ensures that the universal language of moving pictures can govern and improve the mass. As Lindsay sets up the analogy that follows, film "is as great a step as was the beginning of picture-writing in the stone age." With the mentality of Neanderthals, the crowd thinks in pictures, reading the photoplay as cave paintings or, better yet, hieroglyphics that suggest motion pictures as an almost sacred technology. When modern cave men go to the movies, the result is a "new renaissance." Lessons in architecture, ethics, and the wisdom of presidents can all be put to the screen and presented to the mass. Lindsay's list does not end here. Most powerfully, moving picture art will ignite national pride much as "trappers in their coon-skin caps were fired to patriotism by Patrick Henry."[48] While aesthetic sensibilities reawakened by cinema may have the heft of European culture, this renaissance remains fiercely American in terms of cultural politics.

Lindsay's fantasies about the reach of motion pictures are beside the point, since the work of cinematic art theoretically enjoyed endless showings bounded neither by time (nickelodeon programs ran at all hours of the day with no set schedule) nor space (theaters seemed to pop up in any empty storefront). In short, the social horizon of the movies as a medium of democratic culture seemed as expansive as Münsterberg's optimism and as deep as Benjamin's prophetic despair.

DU BOIS AT THE MOVIES:
Ugliness, Endlessness, and Jim Crow

What if instead of copying artworks without end, mechanical reproduction replicated social dysfunction so that what became eternal was not beauty but ugliness? What if film's ability to inspire passionate commitment to U.S. values, as Lindsay predicted, propagates not cultural independence but personal degradation? These questions haunted W. E. B. Du Bois when he went to the movies. His attempt to answer them resulted in "On Beauty and Death," a painful recollection that makes aesthetic experience coincident with victimization.

"I seek the universal mistress, Art; the studio door is locked," wrote Du Bois with characteristic sharpness.[49] Even when Du Bois sought entrance to a less high-minded atelier and looked for diversion in the byways of culture, he experienced the humiliation of restricted seating, separate accommodations, and segregation. Jim Crow stood in the way of claims that the market could equalize culture, placing it within reach of all citizens, even those with only a nickel to spare. Du Bois saw the situation in still more insidious terms: Jim Crow did not simply restrict access to museums, operas, and picture palaces; rather, the slights and stigma of U.S. apartheid were what American mass culture reproduced in limitless supply. Each hurt seemed a replica of the last, leading him to suspect that American democratic culture was adept at reproducing only pain and insult instead of beauty. As Du Bois charged, "Ugliness to me is eternal."[50]

His pronouncement is cinematic. Du Bois comes to this determination after being denied orchestra seating at the picture show. At the ticket booth, he is told that seats remain only in the smoking gallery, an arrangement that recalls the Jim Crow railway car's double function as seating for blacks and smoking section for white men. Still, Du Bois wants pleasure;

he desires to consume the moving images that people find so entertaining. Pleasure triumphs over principle. So "you beat back your suspicions" and accept what the ticket girl has to offer; perhaps she is not lying and few spaces are left in the crowded theater.[51] If consumers can overcome this minor inconvenience, a vast potential of cultural belonging and mass citizenship awaits. This dilemma condenses the larger ambivalence of urban black spectatorship that, according to Jacqueline Najuma Stewart, promised African Americans access to the distractions of modernity while insulting them with racist film images and segregated seating.[52]

We know from Benjamin that film theoretically offers a universal point of address by capturing in the camera lens any one of the thousands of subjects strolling about the city. However illusive this social promise might eventually prove, the prospect that "any man might even find himself part of a work of art" once he is recognized as a cinematic subject remains an attractive fiction.[53] Within the arena of mechanical reproduction, anyone can be in motion pictures but not every one can go to the movies. In this chapter from *Darkwater* (1920), Du Bois never sees the utopian possibilities that later flit at the edges of Benjamin's artwork essay. An excursion to the movies becomes a crisis for "you," his use of second-person address forcing the moral compromises of Jim Crow's deceit upon his readers. "You," too, can be refused entrance to the nickelodeon. Here, at last, is the democratic potential of mass culture unveiled: each African American consumer can experience rejection and shame. Citizens who inhabit the lowest strata of the social order will certainly get their turn again and again. The irony, of course, is that such humiliation is reserved for blacks who are informed that no seats remain other than in the smoking gallery, as a white man pushes past "you" and purchases three tickets in the orchestra. Benjamin's dictum that "any man today can lay claim to being filmed" momentarily freezes the classless, unrestricted aspect of mass culture before the specter of fascism overtakes its potential, but Du Bois rejects even this split-second image of utopianism.[54] He instead charges that within forms of art and entertainment directed at everyone and anyone, only some are repeatedly forced to lay claim to the unequal treatment that is the enduring effect of mass culture.

Still, the lure of the silver screen remains. Why not convert this racial slight into an opportunity by redefining exile to the smoking section as the chance to enjoy the fantasy of social fellowship with a movie star? "After all, a cigarette with Charlie Chaplin," muses Du Bois, as he prepares to accept the ticket to the smoking gallery, ready to swallow his self-respect and the stale atmosphere as just another part of the illusion. Ultimately, though, the price of mass culture is too high: "you" are confronted with the dreadful possibility that

> right there and then you are losing your own soul; that you are losing your own soul and the soul of a people; that millions of unborn children, black and gold and mauve, are being there and then despoiled by you because you are a coward and dare not fight! Suddenly the silly orchestra seat and the cavorting of a comedian with funny feet become matters of life, death, and immortality; you grasp the pillars of the universe and strain as you sway back to that befrilled ticket girl.[55]

While many black moviegoers interacted with screen images and each other to create alternative viewing experiences as part of what Stewart calls "reconstructive spectatorship," for Du Bois individual consumption betrays "a people."[56] The movies promote feelings of community immobilized by schizoid effects that, on the one hand, invite the commingling of spectator and screen icon and, on the other, force that spectator to participate in his or her estrangement from larger currents of humanity.

Du Bois's trip to the movies is a low-budget remake of the moment in *The Souls of Black Folk* when John Jones buys an opera ticket only to be removed from his seat when a white man takes offense at the presence of a Negro. Without a doubt, the song of Lohengrin's swan provides a revivifying aesthetic charge that counteracts the pettiness of such racism, its music illuminating a world "so strangely more beautiful than anything he had known . . . an infinite beauty."[57] The ugliness of Jim Crow returns with a shock when an usher rouses John out of his absorption and escorts him from the theater. This incident from "The Coming of John" repeats itself almost twenty years later in *Darkwater* when the realities of second-class citizenship ruin the attempted purchase of a few moments' fantasy in a darkened movie theater. Even so, a movie theater is not an opera house and the rapturous tones of Wagner are not the herky-jerky walk of Chaplin. In the beauty of opera, the cycle of violence comes to an end. As John faces the lynch mob, the music of Lohengrin runs through his head. However stoically John awaits the "coiling twisted rope," however much the aura of high art reconciles him to a grisly fate, ugliness for him will at last end.[58] Not so with the mass art of cinema, which continues reel after reel, repeated without cessation. Du Bois's principal objection to cinema is not that it caters to "cheap and tawdry idiots" who have no problem sacrificing self-respect for enjoyment. He instead objects to film itself, which in its production, distribution, and effects whets the appetite for racism. Although Du Bois sloughs off the ticket girl's insult, he cannot square his soul with this new aesthetic form that mass culture supposedly offers each and all. As he remembers that he actually wanted to purchase a ticket, he is filled with revulsion: "To think of compelling puppies to take your hard-earned money; fattening hogs to hate you and yours." Democratic art breeds gluttony for prejudice that never ends. The sickening thing about the mechanical reproduction of mass culture, especially in the case of film, is that it goes on and on. Although Du Bois does not cement the connection between cinematic form and racism, film becomes the perfect medium for social ugliness that never ceases, forever waging an "endless battle to days without end" whose unvarying effects are the "same human ill and bitter hurt."[59] Motion pictures attract the public again and again; scenes of racism are replayed as though they were a film; swine keep eating for no purpose other than to consume more.

Ugliness continues unabated, but beauty defies reproduction. Departing from idealist aesthetics, Du Bois locates beauty in a historical world of dollars and prejudice. Beauty becomes transitory, as it is hounded out of the lives of black people. Yet this impermanence, this inability of beauty to replicate itself, also implies that the world need not simply continue to reproduce the conditions of its own production. In contrast to ugliness that endures over time, beauty is always changing and thus inspires change. Even though everyday slights incurred at the opera or the movies belie the universality of aesthetic experience, Du Bois is not immune to sublime sensations and in this vein he recalls a journey that disclosed to his eyes "the unveiled face of nature, as it lies naked on the Maine coast" out of which "rises a certain human awe." Just as keenly he feels the repugnant aspect of a "'Jim Crow' waiting room" along a Georgia railway line. The expansiveness of one setting does not merely negate the narrow prejudice of the other. Awe and disgust are structurally interrelated. How, after all, are "you" supposed to travel up the coast from Georgia? Geography and temporality always crosscut beauty. Awareness of such contingency does not mean that beauty must give up on the overblown mission of discovering the truth. But this truth must also include the fact that

> there is not in the world a more disgraceful denial of human brotherhood than the "Jim-Crow" car of the southern United States; but, too, just as true, there is nothing more beautiful in the universe than sunset and moonlight on Montego Bay in far Jamaica. And both things are true and both belong to this our world, and neither can be denied.[60]

The issue is not whether these truths exist but instead whether these truths, each differently localized along the black diaspora, should be perpetuated. Unlike the natural splendor of Montego Bay, which fades every dawn, the demeaning squalor of Jim Crow segregation continues day in and day out because human laws and customs sustain it. Ugliness, too, may seem exceptional since there is nothing "more disgraceful," but these social conditions are duplicated across the South so that one Jim Crow car looks depressingly like another. While the beauty of Montego Bay is particular to both time and place, the blight of Jim Crow exists as a general, sadly repeatable feature of the social landscape.

One way of summarizing these post-Romantic meditations on truth is to say that Du Bois does not want to see beauty made into a movie. If film "as a means of mechanical reproduction . . . can be duplicated endlessly" to boast a "mass potential through enormous exhibition outlets and viewing audiences," it is precisely this endlessness and ubiquity that troubles Du Bois.[61] The implications are just too daunting: if reproduction continues without end, does that mean that within mass cultural forms social conditions, especially their most dehumanizing aspects, will go on and on? If film lends itself to effortless replication in which there is no change between original and copy, does it implicitly justify an unchanging social order? Du Bois considers the dangers of any experience that persists with no end or prospect of change in sight:

> There is something in the nature of Beauty that demands an end. Ugliness may be indefinite. It may trail off into gray endlessness. But Beauty must be complete—whether it be a field of poppies or a great life,—it must end, and the End is part and triumph of the Beauty. I know there are those who envisage a beauty eternal. But I cannot. I can dream of

great and never-ending processions of beautiful things and visions and acts. But each must be complete or it cannot for me exist.

His perspective resists the cinematic. He seems unable—though it is more likely that he is unwilling—to consume a chain of epiphanies, a "never-ending" procession that strings together images and deeds like a film. Du Bois interrupts the ongoing repetition of ugliness by forcing an extreme conclusion: beauty is not the stuff of life's truth but instead a matter of death. "Beauty is fulfillment," he writes. "Its end is Death—the sweet silence of perfection, the calm and balance of utter music."[62] Beauty finds completion when it fulfills its task, awakening consciousness, enlarging perspective, and transforming our image of the world. Ugliness, in contrast, is condemned to "eternal unfulfilment": it must keep going, unreeling in a ceaseless onslaught that uncannily evokes the mechanical apparatuses that allow "a comedian with funny feet" to amble along without end. In other words, what mechanical reproduction democratizes is access to ugliness.

THE SOUND OF THE IMAGE:
Chaplin and International Laughter

Rather than regret his failure to embrace mass culture, Du Bois finds consolation by taking the high road and suggesting that the pantomimic art of Charlie Chaplin falls below the epic quest for beauty. Only a misplaced sense of priority allows "that silly orchestra seat" to assume transcendental significance, giving "the cavorting of a comedian" more heft than it deserves. But for Chaplin, the age of mechanical reproduction itself represented an epic juncture in the creation of international culture. His career suggests that the age of mechanical reproduction is simultaneous with "modern times," to invoke the title of Chaplin's 1936 film that seesaws precipitously between sound and silence. If adjustments are made between Benjamin's philosophical medium and Chaplin's cinematic one, *Modern Times* exerts the status of an artwork essay that critically reflects on the slender utopian tissues that connect mass culture to community feeling on a global scale.

Despite Benjamin's warnings about film's susceptibility to fascist appropriation, he praised Chaplin, who "has directed himself toward both the most international and most revolutionary affect of the masses—laughter."[63] The same year that Benjamin published the final version of his artwork essay, Chaplin wrote, directed, and starred in *Modern Times*, a cinematic "essay" that self-reflexively comments on mechanical reproduction and historicizes the place of the movies in popular entertainment.[64] In contrast to Benjamin's messianic sensibility, Chaplin looks back wistfully at popular art and entertainment eclipsed by the rise of Hollywood film. Belatedness marks the condition of both *Modern Times* and modernity that have seen the image of a universal culture burn itself out trying to keep pace with global commodity culture. For Chaplin, to be modern is to be obsolescent. His estrangement seems all the more keen in light of his iconic status: although he had been celebrated for decades as a democratic everyman that "the people" took to their hearts and funny bones, the silent film star becomes aware that he inevitably must speak the language of commodity capitalism. By the time of these two artwork essays of 1936, international possibilities were well on their way to being retrofitted to the particular accents of U.S. economic and cultural hegemony.

In 1931, five years before Benjamin's treatment of copying, W. Dodgson Bowman's biography of Chaplin associated the British-born movie star with techniques of reproduction that converted the Tramp into a global icon imbued with an international presence. The public, according to Bowman, sees no separation between the comedian and his screen image; popular feeling guarantees that Chaplin's aura is intact. Both in person and persona, Chaplin expresses broad sympathies for the downtrodden majority in ways that strike a chord with the multitudes no matter on which continent they reside. With audio broadcasts, there remains an insurmountable obstacle to the idea of artistic representation as political mass representation since "the radio makes the speaker's voice familiar to millions—but it is his voice only." But with film, the "camera multiplies the vast audience by tens and hundreds, and shows the man himself, not his pose only but the changing expressions of his face, his movements and actions—and if he be a genius, the passions that move him in the character he portrays, and the hopes and fears and thoughts that inspire his actions." Although Charlie, as Bowman affectionately refers to his subject, is not expressly invoked in this passage, his life history stands in for the history of cinema itself. His biographer makes much of the fact Chaplin was born in 1889, the same year that "Thomas A. Edison invented the Kinetoscope, the forerunner of the modern motion-picture camera," as though man and machine were predestined for one another.[65] With this splicing of man and apparatus, Chaplin emerges as the perfect subject of the mass culture.

Chaplin is, in fact, a "public institution." Such acclaim echoes with ambiguity: is Charlie an institutional identity shaped by the public, or is he himself an institution that performs a public function? The answer, of course, is both, a nod to film's doubly strategic role in reflecting as well as producing mass culture. The camera makes Chaplin public and, at the same moment, his cinematic persona projects an interiority that seems to authenticate the public's identification with the Tramp. What Chaplin reproduces, if contemporary accounts by Bowman and others are any indication, is nothing newfangled or mechanistic but rather the timeless profundity of the human condition itself, the "hopes and fears and thoughts" that lend depth to subjectivity. The people "recognize him as one of themselves," encountering no schism between the "Charlie of the screen they love" and the private person who presumably exists apart from the role.[66] In the simultaneous performance of celebrity and ordinariness, Chaplin confirms cinema as a public institution, validating its status as democratic art, not in spite of reproduction, but because of it.

According to Chaplin, however, "the word 'art' never entered my head or my vocabulary," even from his youthful days in vaudeville.[67] No sense of calling leads him to the career of a screen star. Nor does he retrospectively justify his attraction to the movies as part of a conscious strategy to reap the sociopolitical potential of mass media. "Why should I stick to show business?" Chaplin asked himself. "I was not dedicated to art. Get into another racket!" (125). Instead, the driving force is the desire to become a millionaire, and the quickest way to that goal, it first seemed, lay in hog farming, not acting. Connecting Du Bois's figurative remark about white mass entertainment (the redundancy of "white" and "mass" should not go unnoticed) as a theater for "fattening hogs" and Chaplin's literal scheme to breed swine lies a common association between consumption and sordidness. Overwrought by plans to buy two thousand acres of land in Arkansas and start breeding livestock, Chaplin remembers that he "ate, slept, and dreamed hogs" until "a book on scientific hog-raising" graphically depicting the castration of hogs caused him to abandon his intentions (128). Finding animal reproduction too brutal, he decides to give mechanical reproduction a shot when a telegram for "A MAN NAMED CHAFFIN . . . OR SOMETHING LIKE THAT" comes from the producers of Keystone Comedies (141).

While Chaplin's beginnings in the motion picture industry did not begin along the aesthetic high road, by the end of *My Autobiography* he grows melancholy over the commercialization of everyday life. Dismayed that existence has become subject to economic and governmental systems beyond the citizen's control, he concludes that "we have gone blindly into ugliness . . . and have lost our appreciation of the aesthetics" of living (509). For a man whose every move was photographed, whose private life was dissected in the press, and whose political comments invited the suspicions of the House Un-American Activities Committee, threats to privacy and autonomy must have appeared endless. But feelings of persecution do not fully explain Chaplin's cynicism. His thoughts on ugliness, like Du Bois's aesthetic theory on the eternal nature of viciousness, gather force as a sociopolitical critique of mass culture that in his view has left democratic possibilities by the wayside. Where Chaplin once reveled in being hailed as "the great people's artist of America," the movies, especially with the advent of the talkies, seemed to have abandoned both him and "the people" (445). Undoubtedly American cinema remained as popular as ever, but, in Chaplin's thinking, its potentially universal appeal—the very source of film's aesthetic merit—had been betrayed. *Modern Times*, as we will see, is a history of this betrayal.

As grandiose as Chaplin's claims about cinema and his role within it may seem, a wide swath of observers including prime ministers, socialists, Nobel laureates, theater critics, scientists, and college professors variously credited him with staging political art for the multitude. For fellow film star Douglass Fairbanks Jr, Chaplin might have enjoyed the favor of Hollywood moguls but he never forgot his position as "the champion of the oppressed even when he is on the side of the oppressors."[68] Winston Churchill, Gertrude Stein, François Truffaut, Walter Benjamin, Theodor Adorno, and Siegfried Kracauer were all struck at some point by Chaplin's ability to embody everydayness, inflect social (and quasi-socialist) criticism, and achieve mass affection. Such appreciation came well before Chaplin reached the pinnacle of his career. *Harper's Weekly* in 1914 saluted the twenty-six-year-old comedian for having "made the world laugh. Quite a beautiful thing to do!"[69] Eating tarts with Albert Einstein, Chaplin delighted in the witticism of the physicist's son who explained, "You are popular . . . because you are understood by the masses. On the other hand the professor's popularity with the masses is because he is not understood."[70] Moving on from this snack with Einstein in Berlin, Chaplin recounts his world tour as a series of teas with Marlene Dietrich, George Bernard Shaw, and H. G. Wells, culminating with rapture over a Japanese tea ceremony: "To the practical western world the tea ceremony might seem quaint and trivial. Yet if we consider the highest object of life is the pursuit of the beautiful, what is more rational than applying it to the commonplace?"[71] Posing as a cosmopolitan traveler, Chaplin boasts a global knowledge that surpasses mere hemispheric consciousness, allowing him to uncover affinities between his craft and world art everywhere. East meets West in his valorization of the "commonplace" as the height of beauty. The aesthetics of the tea ceremony stand out because the implicit appeal to the ordinary echoes the criteria that justify his screen antics as art. Wedged between globetrotting and philosophizing, Chaplin's showy embrace of the common as beautiful yokes together more than one contradiction, leading one early film history to dub him "a Walt Whitman of the screen"—this despite Chaplin's own confession that he found *Leaves of Grass* tiresome.[72]

This propensity to do beautiful things and undertake the "pursuit of the beautiful" at the level of everyday carried a political charge, according to *ruta*, a communist literary monthly published out of Jalapa, Mexico. Chaplin's art detonated "bombs of laughter—he was a dynamiter who provoked tremendous explosions." At last, here was a form of anarchy that the middle classes could laugh at. A generation after the Haymarket Square bombing, the critique of capital need not feed fears of anti-American conspiracy. Slapstick and comic pantomime exert disruptive energy in Chaplin's spoofs on industrial efficiency, civic bluster, and self-important philanthropy. Ultimately, though, *ruta* believed that such satirical dissent amounts to a "timid anarchy" in which the radical actor becomes complicit with the very social structure he protests, as his extremism actually makes the status quo appear balanced, rational, and normative.[73]

For the author of this critical assessment of Chaplin, Lorenzo Turrent Rozas, a Latin American socialist art critic, this constant threat of cooptation explains the tepid public reception of Chaplin's 1931 picture, *City Lights*. Consider the film's opening sequence. Beneath a drapery, the Tramp lies asleep on a neoclassical sculpture unawares that dignitaries and a crowd of citizens have assembled to dedicate this self-congratulatory work of municipal art associated with the City Beautiful movement. The unveiling of the monument is scandalous: the sheet is drawn back to reveal Charlie cradled amid a trio of pseudo-Greek stone figures intended to allegorize the sober virtues of industry and patriotism. His dishevelment and nonproductive leisure mock the ceremony's formality and the monument's symbolism. The city officials are outraged while the crowd erupts in silent laughter. Realizing his predicament, Charlie attempts to remove himself from the spectacle in which he now unwittingly takes center stage. Of course, however, his fumbling, slips, and pirouettes to extricate himself undercut the seriousness of occasion even more. The monument strikes back when the Tramp, unable to stop from sliding down its smooth surface, backs up into a raised sword held by one of the figures. Charlie is ignominiously impaled by the seat of his pants; he gets it up the ass from the martial spirit of public art. The epitome of the common man is suggestively violated by emblems of civic bounty and virtue. Bawdy and juvenile, this bomb of laughter ridicules extravagant public symbolism, which, like Nathaniel Hawthorne's vexatious federal eagle outside the Custom House door, offers cold comfort and unyielding hospitality to the common man. Such comedy, according to Rozas, ignites the signature effect of a film artist "who shaped projectiles to hurl at the squat edifice of capitalism."[74]

Yet, Rozas wonders, is not Chaplin also "an accomplice of capitalism?" His identity as an artist and a celebrity, after all, makes him cozy with the industrial society that he critiques, damning him as a partner in crime with the system in which "hunger attacks the masses" and "anguish grips the working class."[75] Art, as far as Rozas is concerned, remains irredeemably the province of decadence, its studied mannerisms ultimately too far removed from action to bear upon organized struggle. It is unlikely that such criticism would have caught Chaplin by surprise. His close friend, Douglas Fairbanks Jr, recognized the inevitable compromise that bedeviled the actor-director who could not decide between social criticism and commercial success: "He is at heart a rebel to society, yet insists on living within its bounds."[76] Chaplin expressed familiarity with notions of containment during his tête-à-tête with Einstein by remarking that the process of mechanization, while ostensibly unshackling workers from drudgery and increasing access to consumer goods, nonetheless "stands resolute against any fundamental change in the capitalistic system."[77] Just as Chaplin might have thus recognized his inescapability from the business that is show business, Rozas candidly acknowledges his susceptibility to the cinema's false revolution, shamefacedly recalling the delight he experienced in playing hooky to "take refuge in a Chaplin film" so that he could "enter the first grade of the revolution." Even though Chaplin's oeuvre provides the young Rozas with a socialist primer that "should have been studied in proletarian moving-picture houses," this contribution to the arsenal of laughter is itself factored into the windfall of capitalism.[78] As a more mature Rozas writes in 1934 in the midst of economic depression, Chaplin just does not seem funny anymore.

Two years after Rozas predicted Charlie's imminent decline, Chaplin produced an artwork essay on mechanical reproduction, which responds to accusations that he had become a lapdog of capitalism while more broadly considering the fading flicker of film's utopian promise as democratic art. Entitled *Modern Times*, the feature was shot with the working title "The Masses," an echo of the American Communist Party newspaper, *The New Masses*. Reports that Boris Shumiatsky, the director of the Soviet film industry, visited Chaplin during production contributed to the air of suspicion that surrounded the project even before its release. Shumiatsky breathed this air exultantly, championing *Modern Times* as a denunciation of American capitalism, citing his own influence on Chaplin as the backstory to the film's political message. Studio executives, worried that such rumors would hurt box office receipts, countered with press releases describing Charlie as an auteur who did not need advice from anyone, especially a Russian filmmaker. The studio's efforts at damage control take a blow in light of Chaplin's publicly stated interest in Communism, an interest he located not so much on political grounds as aesthetic ones: "I am an artist. I am interested in life. Bolshevism is a new phase of life. I must be interested in it."[79] This statement, perhaps making socialism merely a phase of individual genius, nonetheless conjoins aesthetics and politics to signal the influence that revolutionary Soviet cinema had upon the U.S. film industry, film criticism, and film techniques in the 1920s.

These techniques left their mark on *Modern Times*. Employing montage that transforms factory workers into sheep, strategic editing that indicts the mechanization of human perception by aligning the buttons on a woman's blouse with knobs that Charlie cranks with his wrenches, and shots of assembly lines that equate the speeding up of Fordism to sadism, *Modern Times* satirizes industrial production. No one is safe: ministers' wives, dope fiends, factory foremen, mechanics, and the police are all ridiculed in the larger assault on respectability, efficiency, and law. Yet for all its portrayals of callous owners and scenes of police officers raining down billy clubs on the melons of strikers, the film exempted neither union organizing nor the Soviet system from criticism. Just when the factories reopen and workers, heartened by the prospect of finding self-respect in earning a living wage, return to their jobs with gusto, a strike sends them back into the streets. Unions appear to be as fickle and as arbitrary as the owners they oppose.

FIGURE 10. Charlie Chaplin, *Modern Times* (1936). The human body becomes a film strip fed into the industrial machine.

In addition to dropping bombs of laughter on the U.S. labor movement, *Modern Times* with its scenes of machines and workers stuck in compulsory overdrive, according to French film critic André Bazin, "created . . . a certain cold spell in Moscow as well" by parodying Soviet stakhanovism, a program begun in 1935 that encouraged workers to follow in the frenetic footsteps of Aleksi Stakhanov, whose team of coal miners exceeded quotas by 700 per cent.[80]

Modern Times aims its critical comic energies at more specific targets than the mechanistic calculation of human labor, whether in the U.S. or the USSR. As Garret Stewart states, "Chaplin's frontal assault on industrialization" becomes most incisive when *Modern Times* trains its critical lens on the film industry, self-reflexively examining the mechanisms that establish the mass-produced image as a technology of power.[81] In perhaps the movie's most famous scene, Charlie is ingested by this technology, channeled along a series of wheels, rollers, and cogs as though he were himself a strip of film, routed through the entrails of a giant machine that resembles nothing so much as a movie projector (fig. 10). The parallel be-

FIGURE 11. Charlie Chaplin, *Modern Times* (1936). The human body fed by the industrial machine.

tween the film industry and heavy industry was not at all unwarranted, as film historian Charles Musser explains, since the principles of scientific management had been changing how movies were scripted and shot.[82] Before Charlie is swallowed up into the belly of the industrial beast, he finds the machine inside his belly when he is strapped to a time-saving feeding contraption, which goes haywire and forces food down his gullet (fig. 11). Echoing Rozas's descriptions of the explosive laughter caused by Chaplin, Siegfried Kracauer described this sequence as a "delayed time-bomb."[83] Machines feed people just as people are literally fed into machines: the critique of mechanization implicates the mechanisms of film, which constrain human potential precisely because the cameras, projection screens, intercoms, and other audiovisual equipment portrayed in the film are designed for surveillance and control even as they facilitate mass communication. Risking a self-critical commentary on its own reliance on machinery, *Modern Times* theorizes the uncanny convergence between the production of mass culture and impersonal, dehumanizing factory labor.

Modern Times historicizes mass culture in reverse, moving backward from prophetic scenes of video surveillance to vaudeville performance in an effort to trace the deterioration of cinema's utopian promises. Film historians generally agree with this narrative of deterioration, contending that early cinema's ability to play across class, ethnic, and national borders was an ephemeral phenomenon that died out long before Chaplin's entrance upon the scene, having earlier succumbed to moral and socioeconomic imperatives that made film into a commodity pitched to audiences concerned with middle-class respectability.[84] Once this popular bubble burst, a new mythology took its place. This tale of modern media proclaimed the movies as an international form that could address people anywhere no matter their spoken language, national affiliation, or hemispheric location. Chaplin was as familiar in the Far East as the Lower East Side; the *New York Times* reported that "hundreds of men and boys" were recently "swarming the streets in Oriental imitations of the comedian" when a contest for the best Charlie Chaplin was held in Japan.[85] The visual nature of motion pictures makes spoken language irrelevant, leaving plenty of space for the image of the Tramp who, as Chaplin reminds readers in his autobiography and travel writings, enjoyed global popularity from Europe to Asia to the South Pacific.

What threatens global art is sound, which, as far as Chaplin is concerned, represents a destructive provincialism that balkanizes the image by tethering it to the specific borders of national language and diminishes silent film's artistry by absolving actor and director from the responsibility of communicating universal emotions with elaborate gestures or practiced facial expressions. The withering of the aura does not worry Chaplin: his artwork essay instead protests that sound technology will burden the movies with geopolitical markers that scale back global horizons to provincial accents. Chaplin's optimism for wordless ubiquity jars with Benjamin's respect for the unique time and space that insulates sacred art. But in ways also consistent with "The Work of Art in the Age of Mechanical Reproduction," *Modern Times* expresses deep concern over the fate of uniqueness in the age of reproduced sound. While audible speech can enhance the image of human presence, sound, according to Chaplin, drains the visual of its power and limits the range of its address, translating what was once a potentially universal aesthetic into local national idioms.

Although replete with the stylized movements of silent movie actors and intertitles quoting what the Tramp has wordlessly uttered in the previous frame, *Modern Times* is not a silent movie.[86] Sound everywhere intrudes upon the image. Factory whistles peal. Gears grind. Time clocks ring. Police sirens clang. Dynamos hum. A phonograph reproduces the voice of a "mechanical salesman" who pitches an automatic feeding machine. A radio announces the Tramp's release from jail. A two-way video screen amplifies the voice of the factory president so that he can reprimand workers at all times and in all spaces even when they, like Charlie, sneak off to the bathroom for a smoke. Despite the cacophony of mechanized noise, it would be incorrect to assert that sound *exists* within *Modern Times*. Sound is almost always mediated by technology; it is not something that human beings produce but a capacity possessed largely by machines. Chaplin anticipates Jonathan Sterne's point that sound, as it is captured, reproduced, and distributed, becomes a commodity.[87] Seen (and heard) as an artwork essay, *Modern Times*, in tones as melancholy as any of the more equivocal passages in Benjamin's artwork essay, theorizes how the potential for motion pictures to democratize culture on a mass scale is traduced by sound.

Sound represents a twofold threat. First, in keeping with Chaplin's overt political critique of an industrial complex that ravages human dignity, sound becomes authoritarian when it is manufactured and deployed by commercial interests. Workers in the film run, jump, halt, and cower automatically in response to alarms, whistles, and buzzers. When the factory president spies on his employees via strategically positioned projection screens that act as cameras, his control is not only panoptic but also pan*sonic*. Surveillance would lack any bite without sound, which empowers the company president to bark out commands and issue reprimands from afar. While video is two-way, allowing worker and manager to see and confront one another, no one in the film speaks back to orders that production be speeded up. Sound, unlike vision, lacks reciprocity and remains thoroughly hierarchical, a possession of the few. Without sound, the company president carries little authority. A two-shot sequence establishes his identity, as the image of a frosted glass office door, stenciled with the words "PRESIDENT Electro Steel Corp," dissolves into the picture of a slight, graying man working on a jigsaw puzzle. His work is leisure while that of his employees inexorably remains labor. He seems inefficient and harmless enough, a victim of boredom (he throws a puzzle piece in frustration) and mild dyspepsia (his secretary brings a medicinal tablet and water). It requires sound to convey his power to direct other men's lives. Only when he puts down the newspaper and fiddles with his audiovisual intercom does Electro's president become a captain of industry. As an image, the president is powerless to order Charlie back to work when he is slacking in the bathroom, sitting on the sink with his back to the screen. In order to jolt this goldbricker back into action, the president must speak and be heard, his voice descending mechanically from the mountaintop of his executive office: "Hey! Quit stalling. Get back to work!" Vision cannot do the job of management. Sound is required to interpellate this everyman with the identity of an industrial subject. Where Althusser's cop needs two words— "Hey you"—to hail his subject, the president gets by with a simple "Hey" to identify Charlie as a malingerer. Sound prescribes meaning, instructing laborers both what certain things mean (a bathroom is not a safe place to evade work) and how little human beings, as social industrial units, mean.

Second, sound endangers citizens' ability to communicate and have meaning in mass culture. As speech becomes subject to technological mediation, individuals forfeit public voice. Chaplin's filmic artwork essay explores this paradox when, after years of resisting the talkies, his character speaks. But that's not quite right: the Tramp does not talk; instead he sings. Unable to keep a job in heavy industry, Chaplin's everyman lucks into a gig in the entertainment industry. There is only one catch: can he remember the words of the song he is hired to perform? Wrapped up in this question is an acknowledgment of the pressures faced by Chaplin as a globally recognizable commodity who, with the rise of the talkies, may no longer be able to speak to the world. As a dancehall performer, the Tramp retraces Chaplin's own path in becoming a celebrity by getting a start in vaudeville, returning to amusements now eclipsed by cinema. Such nostalgia encompasses more than a trip down memory lane: in this retrospective glance at early entertainment, *Modern Times* mourns a present in which silent film is already an anachronism. Vaudeville is but a screen for this loss, allowing Chaplin to meditate on the demise of the pantomimic art of the silents without having to confront the obvious incongruity of making a "silent" film in 1936.

The arc of *Modern Times* encompasses more than its star's insecurities within the spectacle of mass consumption. The film also suggests that the mass itself, the viewing public, is at far greater risk because it is entertained by the spectacle of its own debasement. "Bombs of laughter" go off in the audience once people begin to consume sound. The Tramp's performance, when audiences hear his voice at long last after more than ninety films, dramatizes this threat. With the words to the musical number written on his shirt cuffs, Charlie rushes on stage, swings his arms, off come the cuffs,

FIGURE 12. Charlie Chaplin, *Modern Times* (1936). As Paulette Goddard demonstrates, the human mouth seems better suited to silent pantomime than to the production of audible meaning.

and goodbye go his crib notes to the song. The music plays on but Charlie literally cannot find the words. He stands doubly speechless, once before the on-screen patrons in the dancehall and again in front of the film's audience. His befuddlement fulfills Addams's judgment that "apparently the workers of America are not yet ready to sing" after a Hull-House competition for the best labor song netted disappointing results.[88]

"Sing! Never mind the words," reads the intertitle quoting Charlie's female partner standing in the wings. She points at her open mouth as though Charlie simply does not know that this is what a mouth is for (fig. 12). But like the Tramp, when Paulette Goddard, playing the role of the gamin, gestures to her own mouth, no audible words come out. This hurried pantomime speaks to the potential power of the voice but it just as clearly attests to its emptiness.[89] Always a quick study, Charlie obeys by singing in a language invented on the spur of the moment—and the dinner crowd laps it up. The people who have come to the dancehall to eat and be entertained by singing waiters fill up on nonsense; in an age of sound reproduction, the mass will consume any old tripe. The audience is as much a herd as the workers who morph into sheep in the film's opening montage. Specifically in *Modern Times* as well as generally in modern times, the audible words coming out of the individual's mouth steer audiences to a public performance without meaning. It is fitting that Garrett Stewart calls Chaplin's song "hogwash."[90] Like Du Bois's hogs, the people in Chaplin's theater consume only so that they may consume.

This return to Du Bois unveils the racial claptrap that is central to sound in this scene. The singing waiters perform "In the Evening by the Moonlight," a nostalgic plantation melody whose chorus recalls a past when "you could hear us darkies singing/ . . . you could hear de banjo ringing."[91] Surely this false memory—and the audience's enthusiasm for it—is the height of nonsense. White baritones sing a "black" song for white consumption: when sound supplements the image, the result is a legible racial divide that fondly stigmatizes one component of humanity as simple, uneducated, and homesick for their own slavery. The soundless image that "speaks" a universal language is nowhere in sight. In light of this implied critique, it is tempting to think Chaplin would have appreciated Du Bois's reasons for dismissing "the cavorting of a comedian with funny feet." The specific sounds behind potentially universal images reveal that mass art is as cheap and accessible as it is empty of ethical import. The laughter that erupts among the dancehall audience packs no redeeming social meaning. As Horkheimer and Adorno put it in their acerbic critique of the culture industry, "there is laughter because there is nothing to laugh about."[92] *Modern Times* as artwork essay charges that mass art—especially film—democratizes access to a theater of ethically unfulfilling consumption.

Although *Modern Times* undercuts the romance of moonlight and magnolia, Chaplin is not immune to a different nostalgia. With vaudeville as a noisy set, *Modern Times* delivers an elegy for the pantomimic art of the silents. The silent film icon laments his own obsolescence—and not without good financial reason.[93] And, as an ideological concern, his suspicion of sound spliced political principles with aesthetic criteria. Hoping to put to rest rumors about Chaplin's favorable opinion of Bolshevism, his 1931 biographer aligned the "artiste" with counterrevolution:

> Whatever his opinions on social or political affairs, in matters of art he [Chaplin] is a die-hard Conservative. The revolution that has taken place in the cinema world during the last three years, leaves him unchanged, and he believes as fervently as ever in the efficacy of the art of pantomime.[94]

Not a Russian revolution but a technological one finds Chaplin playing the role of traditionalist. The ominous conflation of aesthetics and politics presaged by Benjamin (politics become aesthetic under fascism) is untangled by relegating politics to the back seat so that formal artistic concerns take center stage. But in explaining his opposition to sound technology, Chaplin corrected his biographer by citing political principles, equating the advent of sound with the lost possibility of universal understanding. As synchronized sound enhanced individual characterization, supposedly deepening impressions of psychological depth, the collective subject of film is evacuated. Once the film actor assumes a particularized voice, the space of the multitude retracts. Chaplin worries that when the Tramp speaks, he will no longer exemplify everyman. Sure, the Tramp could talk, but once he opened his mouth sound "would transform him into another person" (397). More exactly, sound would transform him into *a* person whose singularity, discreteness, and privacy do not match the biography of the mass subject. His artwork essay inverts Benjamin's anxiety over mechanical reproduction. For what Chaplin dreads is the reestablishment of a withered aura that will fix Charlie both in a historical moment and in the culturally particular space of language, forcing him to surrender a theoretically global identity rooted in soundless images.

Endowed with speech, the articulate subject comes closer to expressing human fullness. The ability to make known desire, motivation, and intention cannot be underestimated. But what can be overestimated is the public political function of that speaking subject, especially when compared to the everydayness expressed by Chaplin's mute figure of modernity. Brooks Atkinson perceived Chaplin's predicament: "In these modern times of the audible screen he still realizes that the little tramp will lose immortality if he speaks in the tongue of common men."[95] In *Modern Times*, Paulette Goddard's character of the gamin vividly realizes that sound poses a mortal danger to Charlie. As he dons a blindfold and roller-skates on the top floor of a department store, the Tramp, unawares, glides precipitously near an open balcony from which the railing has been removed. How to warn him of his peril? Clamping her hand over her mouth, she realizes that an audible warning will startle him and send him over the edge (figs. 13 and 14). Sound will be the death of Chaplin's everyman—just as the nonsense that the Tramp babbles to the delight of his public signals the end of any hopes that this cinematic artwork essay had for an enlightened culture that would be common to all.

FIGURES 13 AND 14. Charlie Chaplin, *Modern Times* (1936). Only pantomime can make visible the "danger" of sound. Sound, it seems, will push the Tramp over the edge.

ESPERANTO OF THE EYE:
Anarchy and Internationalism

Sound imperils the mass public as well. The brink that the mass teeters on is the sharp edge of its own propensity to gobble up nonsense. But Chaplin's song is not necessarily gibberish. Clearly the audience understands something when Charlie sings:

El pwu el se domtroco
La spinach or la tuko
Cigaretto toto torlo
E rusho spagaletto
Senora ce la tima
Le jonta tu la zita
Voulez vouz la taxi meter
Je le tu le tu le twaa. . . .[96]

Enhanced by Charlie's suggestive pantomime, these lyrics flirt with a bawdy message of seduction and pregnancy. The Latinate aspect of the invented song echoes utopian projects to devise a universal language such as Neo-Latina, Occidental, Parlamento, and most prominently, Esperanto. Chaplin sings in mock Esperanto, alluding to commonplace assertions that the movies provided a universal language in their function as an "Esperanto of the eye."

Lillian Gish, who at age nineteen began starring in silent films, explained, "the motion picture . . . [is] a species of aesthetic Esperanto." Internationalism now comes in pictures—and there will be no need of subtitles. In an essay on "A Universal Language" written for the *Encyclopedia Britannica* of 1929, Gish voiced Kantian enthusiasm for the "common human understanding" enabled by "a picture pantomime" that would cross borders and cultures in ways that acoustic performances such as a Strauss waltz, which remains "alien and unassimilable to the musical ear of the Chinese," never could. The problem lies not with the Chinese people since an aesthetic exchange could not function in reverse either, as Chinese music will forever be "strange, peculiar, and incomprehensible to the Anglo-Saxon ear." True cosmopolitanism lies not in sounds but in images, and to support this global assertion Gish invokes the silent film actor whose name was routinely coupled with notions of universal language: "the motion picture art of Charlie Chaplin will inevitably make a Japanese laugh as heartily as a Dane."[97] In musings on universal language, whether as motion pictures or Esperanto, China and Japan invariably mark the outer limits of global understanding, indicating the last frontier of difference that stands in the way of worldwide communication. If nonwestern speakers could laugh at Charlie, he was surely intelligible anywhere—an impression that Chaplin encouraged in travel writing recounting his popularity in Japan, Bali, and elsewhere in Asia. Esperantists were susceptible to the same mythos, and delegates to international conventions eagerly testified that representatives from Peking and Tokyo mastered this new language even though it represented "the quintessence of the chief Western tongues."[98] Synthesizing the movies and Esperanto, Gish contends that the aesthetics of slapstick surpass orientalist obstacles to universalism.

While advocates of Esperanto boasted that students attained fluency in this universal tongue within a year, human proficiency in pictures was innate and instantaneous. If Esperantists reported that knowledge of Latin or a modern European tongue considerably shortened the learning curve, cinema went one better since no advantages of education, class, nationality, or culture supposedly made a difference in grasping the meaning of moving images—precisely because there was nothing to be learned. It all depends, however, on what sense one makes of *nothing*. Devoted to what Gish labeled "primitive instincts, primitive impulses, primitive human peace and alarm, happiness and ache, ambition and dream," motion pictures required neither formal training nor specialized knowledge. *Nothing* supplies the conditions of universal access. When Ludwik Lazar Zamenhof, writing under the *nom de plume* "Dr. Esperanto," laid out the principles for a universal language in 1889, he tried to avoid stepping on the toes of cultural nationalists by limiting his invention to informational purposes. Esperanto, he stipulated, makes no pretension of *"entering at all into the inner life of these peoples"*; its psychological emptiness guarantees universality.[99] Gish, on the other hand, claims that the movies, as an Esperanto of the eye, enjoy transnational play because they are primarily focused on interiority, an emotional baseline whose naturalistic vagueness is designed to appeal to all. In this respect, the *nothing* of film, an emptiness exemplified by Chaplin's nonsense in the dancehall, assures commonality for everyone.

Even people who were seen as irredeemably primitive could share in the global community supposedly ushered in by the movies. No less a defender of Anglo-American values than Winston Churchill, writing on "everybody's language," championed silent film as "the true universal tongue." The comedy of the down-and-out Tramp was no laughing matter in Churchill's opinion. The fate of empire demands opening a cultural front, with the movies leading the charge:

> The primitive mind thinks more easily in pictures than in words. The thing seen means more than the thing heard. The films which are shown amid the stillness of the African tropical night or under the skies of Asia may determine, in the long run, the fate of empires and of civilizations. They will promote, or destroy, the prestige by which the white man maintains his precarious supremacy amid the teeming multitudes of black and brown and yellow.[100]

Churchill reorients Addams's vision of a municipally controlled film industry that would serve overdeveloped urban locales by instead imagining that film can secure colonial hegemony by providing pleasure for the underdeveloped masses of the global South. In the case of mass culture intended for Africa and Asia, moving pictures are fitted with a Western colonial vision just as the universality of Esperanto is always inflected by European romance languages. The work of art in the age of mechanical reproduction doubles as administrative technology in the age of colonialism. Under this logic, Du Bois should not be turned away from the picture show and the younger Rozas should not have to skip school to take in a movie. Invite them in; show these "others" a good time by all means. Similar to Le Bon's crowd, the nonwhite world thinks as savages or children do, jumping to unwarranted and irresponsible conclusions upon seeing a continuous strip of images. Film thus has a global job to do in shouldering the white man's burden lest civilization break down into anarchy and the "darker races" run riot.

But a universal tongue—whether as an actual language or shared fluency in mass culture—also ignites suspicions about radical equality and revolutionary association. One must travel some slightly kooky pathways for evidence of this possibility. Although Esperanto was conceived to grease the wheels of international capitalism by keeping the pace of trade humming, its hostility to provincial forms such as the nation-state and private ownership suggest that less subservient currents run through the notion of universal language as well. In a 1922 report to the League of Nations, the General Secretariat resolved to keep an eye on Esperanto as a formidable means of promoting "the moral unity of the world."[101] Within the compass of Esperanto's global promise lurks the menace of conspiracy: "the 'Universala Esperanto Asocio' . . . [is] spread over five parts of the world like a spider's web. The organization has delegates in a thousand towns of 39 countries." Quickly and cheaply, Esperanto pamphlets "can be circulated throughout the whole world." Information can pass unnoticed across national borders. The Universala Esperanto Asocio has connections to a worldwide network of members everywhere and can "obtain information with regard to all countries." What's more, "a circular pamphlet printed in Esperanto can be circulated throughout the world at very slight expense," reported the General Secretariat, a prediction confirmed the following year when an Esperanto translation of *The Communist Manifesto* appeared. Placing speakers on "a footing of the most complete equality" and leaguing adherents in a vast global organization pledging loyalty to no national governments, Esperanto inadvertently raises the specter of worldwide anarchist conspiracy.[102] While the League of Nations intends nothing so shadowy or clandestine, telling the difference between the language of the International and an international language is not always easy.

Such suspicions were exactly on the mark, as anarchists claimed Esperanto as an invaluable tool in worldwide emancipation. At the International Anarchist Congress convened in Amsterdam in 1907, delegates hailed Esperanto as a "new revolutionary weapon" ready for use by "our militant comrades." Propaganda would flow more easily. The education of workers could take place across national lines. And in a world dominated by a "daily Press, which, as everybody knows, is in the pay of capitalists," Esperanto would liberate information so that international news would become truly Internationale. Users of this universal language accrue psychological benefits as well. Revolutionaries shunned in their own countries, radicals in exile, and all other "victims of reactionary fury" including conscientious objectors, propagandists, and rejectniks could at long last find comradeship in a common language of struggle. To be an Esperantist is to be an anarchist: the authors of *Anarchists and the International Language* consider international socialists seeking to unite humanity to be no different than Esperantists who literally speak a "universal solidarity" undivided by "a multiplicity of tongues."[103] The goals of the Internationale and international language become one and the same.

It is perhaps difficult to believe that Charlie Chaplin's singing "Voulez vouz la taxi meter" alludes to international language and world citizenship. At best, such nonsense is a parody of Esperanto. His delightful song pokes fun at the notion that any verbal medium, working independent of the visual, could enhance global understanding. Playing the ethnolinguist, he argued that "talking pictures necessarily have a limited field, they are held down to the particular tongue of particular races." He is in all seriousness, however, when it comes to silent media such as moving images, pantomime, and hieroglyphics, which he believes unite people across time and space. Turning to ancient Egypt and Greece, Chaplin postulates that all cultures use images to communicate the most sacred meanings. Convinced that humanity will always desire a universal language, Chaplin predicts silent film's eventual triumph even though sound was clearly in Hollywood to stay: "the future will see a return of interest in nontalking productions."[104] Behind Chaplin's utopian future lies a good amount of nostalgia.

As Chaplin's 1931 biographer wrote, "China, Japan, and India all understand him. The whole world is still his market so long as he does not talk."[105] The reality of international form was neither aesthetic nor anarchic but economic and capitalist: it is the market, not universal culture, which counts as global. Seen from this perspective, *Modern Times* cannot account for its own status as a commodity. And neither could Chaplin. In one of the more improbable episodes from his autobiography, he tells how during a visit to Tokyo he was targeted for assassination by the Black Dragon society. An informant explains the thinking behind this plot: "Chaplin is a popular figure in the United States and the darling of the capitalist class. We believed that killing him would cause a war with America" (406–7). Chaplin chuckles at this logic, reminding readers that he is by birth a British subject. The joke allows him to duck larger accusations about his loyalty to Western capitalism. Most of all, he dodges the realization, one he expressed twenty years before *Modern Times*, that universal language echoes, not with the radical tones of international socialism, but with the ka-ching of profit. In a 1916 contribution to the little magazine *Soil*, Chaplin represents cinematic comedy as a field of anthropological discovery. Whereas "a few years ago we did not know that the Chinaman had a sense of humor," Chaplin and the film industry now know that the U.S. public and the "solemn Jap" laugh at the same images of whiskers being yanked, hats falling off, and a tramp shuffling along in a drunken walk.[106] This knowledge is worth its weight in gold—or, more precisely, the $670,000 that the Mutual Corporation pays its star. Chaplin suggests it would be too difficult to justify his exorbitant salary if the U.S. were his only market. But because the Tramp "makes the Chinese laugh, rocking the roof in all sorts of dingy little theaters along the Yang Tse," he creates a market that "makes the whole word kin," aligning a global community around the commodity that is Chaplin himself. In the nostalgia that runs through *Modern Times* and *My Autobiography*, Chaplin would forget his role in making a marketplace of the world.

For all its ironic self-awareness, the blindness of *Modern Times* to its own commodity status ultimately provides the biggest insight into global mass culture. It is not the aesthetics of motion pictures that have limitless appeal. The prospect for radically inclusive mass culture instead lies in the production and consumption of commodities—no, not simply in that but in the overproduction and overconsumption of commodities to the point where the market is found everywhere, accessible by all, at hand in all moments. If commodities might speak, to invoke Marx's bewitching supposition, they readily do so in Chaplin's not-so silent essay about silent film. Commodities are the new Esperanto. Defeated by the entertainment industry every bit as much as by the heavy industry of factories, Charlie and the gamin walk off empty-handed toward the horizon at the end of *Modern Times*. They possess nothing other than themselves—which is precisely the point. The Tramp recedes from view doing his famous trademark walk—by this time "Chaplin walk" contests and accompanying sheet music had been around for two decades—because he is his own commodity, recognizable in any latitude. When *Modern Times* was still sporting the working title "The Masses," press releases reported that it was "designed to amuse Hottentots in Africa as well as filmgoers in London, Patagonia, and Siam."[107] If Dr. Esperanto had looked to offer a common "*living tongue*" to "*the masses*," then, film as the "Esperanto of the eye" fits the bill by animating the commodity that goes everywhere.[108]

Chaplin liked to see himself as cosmopolitan, making such statements as "patriotism to me is nurtured in local habits: horse racing, hunting, Yorkshire pudding, American hamburgers and Coca-Cola—but today such native yams have become world-wide" (387). This tally that begins with a set of gentrified activities ends with items of mass consumption. For the cosmopolitan who is also an internationally recognizable commodity, the signposts of universal language are indistinguishable from items on a grocery list. The ascendancy of "world-wide" forms does not mean that there

is no local, however. On the contrary, there is only the local, one culturally specific form of Western commodity capitalism marketed to everyone.
This despairing realization from Chaplin's autobiography fulfills early predictions about the eventual ascendancy of sound. As *A History of the Movies*
(1931) put it:

> Talkies will appear, within one or two generations, in, let us say, a dozen
> or so of the world's principle languages and dialects. They will *not* be
> presented in the hundreds of tongues that now plague mankind. The
> enjoyment of screen entertainment will spread farther and farther into
> the minds of all masses, and the world will settle down to the use of the
> languages employed by the screen. And finally, before many generations
> have passed, one common tongue will dominate the globe.[109]

Motion pictures whittle the "masses" down into the singularity of "the
world," moving from a multilingual reality to the univocal fantasy of a linguistic imperium. Film is so much more than the new Esperanto; it is the
aesthetic medium that translates the particularity of American English into
a universal language. The movies represent the triumph of the local over
the global to the extent that the local usurps the position of the universal
to speak for everyone. In the terms of Chaplin's cinematic artwork essay,
the utopian dream of international accord is translated to the singularity
and dominion of American commodity form. And in terms of this chapter's
listening to motion pictures, democratic mass culture fails by succeeding
as it invites everyone to participate in an aesthetics that sounds the same
everywhere.

GEO-AESTHETICS

. . . .

Fascism, Globalism, and Frank Norris

A man walks into bar. So begins the bad joke that Frank Norris plays on an aspiring painter who squanders his artistic talent amid scenes of animalistic gratification. This bar, however, is not simply some stock setting for a sordid tale about the loss of talent and taste to sensual pleasure. Instead this bar is known as the Imperial, located in downtown San Francisco at the turn of the century. Situated along the Pacific Rim, this bar alludes to the pressures created in a prototypical imaginary of globalization when aesthetics—in the guise of the would-be artist—stops in for a drink. To tell properly the joke of *Vandover and the Brute,* one must begin again: a man walks into a highly specific and evocatively named bar. After this point the story becomes rather predictable as Norris's hero-artist descends the evolutionary ladder to wind up groveling on the floor. Less predictable is the novel's ability to communicate a failed critical insight that is the subject of the artist's uncompleted masterpiece, a salon picture of a British cavalryman lost in the Sudan, which renders legible the deep connections between aesthetics and global vision.

This concluding chapter attempts to complete Vandover's half-finished artwork by rounding out the ideological impulses that led the artist to the Imperial for drink and diversion in the first place. My examination explores how conceptualization of the globe as a single geo-economic unit depends on a historically specific aesthetic formalism exemplified by Norris's fiction. The contradictory nature of this project—that is, a contextual history of aesthetic formalism—captures the logic that ushers an Americanized global sensibility into being. Norris's career sits astride developments in market capitalism that led to an era of global commodities. The story of one historically specific commodity—wheat—encapsulates this transition: as Richard Hofstader reported over a half century ago, U.S. wheat farmers in the 1890s increasingly relied on world markets to export surplus grain, changing the nature of economic risk. Buoyed by news of failed crops in India and Australia, "wheat gamblers in New York and Chicago" were sent into a frenzy, driving the price of grain up 80 percent, but, according to an 1897 survey of economic literature, this bubble created risk for farmers once it became clear that "the speculators . . . overshot their mark."[1] Excitement rose as prices climbed, enticing farmers with hopes of paying off debts while exposing them to the perils of speculation (fig. 15). "Agrarian depressions, formerly of local or national character, now became international, and with them came international agrarian discontent," writes Hofstader.[2] With the radical political project of the Internationale nowhere in sight, the possibilities of strike and anarchy that appeared in chapter 3 give way to a world in which there is no foreign, only the same of a commodity culture on course to becoming universal. As Charles Conant forecast in *The United States in the Orient* (1900), global investment opportunities would inoculate the nation against economic depression and labor unrest by creating an outlet for surplus goods and providing U.S. workers with steady employment.[3] The unpredictability of economic speculation on a world scale could also appear as the saving grace of the West.

Readers will quickly notice that this final chapter seems out of sequence. The previous chapter on film ended in 1936, while my discussion of Norris and global form hovers around the turn of the nineteenth century. This recursive temporal arc provides an excavation of an initial collision between capital and aesthetics, a collision that becomes a happy marriage in the universal language of film. The last of the artwork essays that I discuss, Norris's articles on the U.S. novel, expressly link literary naturalism with early globalization along the Pacific Rim. By moving backwards from Chaplin and film to Norris and wheat, this final chapter is self-consciously and problematically "expansionist," taking *Beautiful Democracy* down a problematic path where aesthetics give shape to global discourse. It is hard to imagine a humanities project that would want to identify itself with terminology that conjures up imperialism, but such scruples did not seem to trouble William Dean Howells, who ended an 1899 essay by invoking Norris's work as sign of "expansion in fiction."[4] While Howells did not

WHY IS IT THAT THE WHEAT NEVER LOOKS SO GOOD TO THE LAMBS AS
WHEN IT IS SO HIGH THAT IT'S DANGEROUS?
—Bartholomew in the Minneapolis *Journal*.

FIGURE 15. "Why Is It That Wheat Never Looks So Good to the Lambs As When It Is So High That It's Dangerous?" *Literary Digest* 29 (1904): 249. Reaching after the profits of international trade, wheat farmers and grain merchants were exposed to the precipitous risks of a fluctuating market driven by speculation.

understand Norris's capacious vision as geopolitical, he did commend the author of *McTeague* for pushing beyond the niceties of the drawing room. This flattering review emboldened Norris to write Howells and confide his plan for a trilogy "around the one subject of *Wheat*."[5] "The Epic of the Wheat" began in 1901 with Norris's publication of *The Octopus*, a novel that does what *Vandover* cannot: it completes the aestheticized portrait of the global, disclosing the geopolitical effects of art and beauty.

A contradiction emerges at precisely this point since Norris's overblown art seems a poor example of aesthetics. For this reason, I do not rely on *The Octopus* alone and instead engage other portraits of global aesthetics found in the work of early historians of Manifest Destiny, philosophers of aesthetics such as Benjamin and Schiller, and theorists of globalization. By revisiting the conflicts between the universal sensibility of *aisthētēs* and the centripetal attraction of national culture, this chapter offers a conclusion to the book as a whole. Sadly the trip back is never the same: as I accompany Norris and this eclectic set of fellow travelers in returning to scenes of global culture, I have come to suspect that the stirrings of internationalism and alternative aesthetics were never as pronounced as I initially imagined. What deflates the anarchic brio of global culture is nothing short of globalization itself: the awareness that beauty always contains its own antipodes is defeated by a geography so insistently capacious that no room seems left for heterogeneity or alterity. A global economy is but a poor substitute for the universal accord that, theoretically, is found in aesthetic judgment.

WORLDWIDE UNITY AND FORMALISM

Imperialism and empire have long been shown to have aesthetic dimensions. Support for this linkage comes in 2000 from Henry Schwarz, who suggests that aesthetics offers an "attractive tool" for staging an imperial enterprise.[6] In 1900, Pennsylvania State College President Edwin Sparks adduced a similar conclusion, citing Whitman's "Passage to India" as evidence of the creative spirit that had fueled four centuries of New World expansion.[7] If there is no evidence that Sparks consulted colleagues in the Philosophy or English departments as he worked on his history textbook, *The Expansion of the American People,* his archive and method nonetheless owe more than a little to lessons disseminated in the seminars and lectures of what I have dubbed "Aesthetics 101." Whether it is the implicit pun on "passage" as both navigational route and textual extract or Whitman's imagining of Christopher Columbus as a stage actor in a historical drama, Sparks' momentary blending of historiography and poetry responds to the sense that U.S. expansion supplies formal principles that give unity and coherence to the different spatialities and uneven temporalities of global development. A year later in 1901, *The Octopus* crossed this terrain where literature serves imperialism to convey a deeper lesson about how aesthetics facilitates the imagination and conceptualization of the globe as a single, perfect form. Turn-of-the-century globalization is an aesthetic project, which is not to say that it is beautiful but rather that globalization became a thinkable concept via certain criteria of wholeness and unified form. Considering the possibility of "world culture," Immanuel Wallerstein begins by discarding some definitions of culture, including "culture as the production of art-forms."[8] But one critic's trash is another's treasure: this essay sifts through the "art-forms" tossed aside by Wallerstein to explore globalization as a product of aesthetic imagination. When taken not as a pathway to a theoretical universal but as a sure route to global markets, formalist aesthetics allow economic and imperial interests to condense dispersed geographies into a single unified form as the beauty of empire.

Such a project offers U.S. industrial modernity no small thing: aesthetics hold out the promise of form, explaining how at the start of the twentieth century, for instance, the international crisscrossing of markets, commodities, and value comes to be conceptualized as a unified structure—the globe. The political economy of globalization literalizes the universal aspect of the aesthetic ideal. Once aesthetic judgment garners widespread accord, as Eagleton argues in his reading of Kant, it "come[s] mysteriously to assume all the compelling logic of a global decree."[9] Eagleton intends "global" as a stand-in for the philosophical universal, but we might well ask how it translates to the domain of political economy. When global aesthetics (as a heady fantasy of shared subjective judgment) encounters global economy (as an actuality of geopolitics), the formal principles of beauty and art not only buttress but help develop commerce and militarism on a previously unimaginable worldwide scale. The agreement of everyone, the unanimity of all judging subjects, *sensus communis,* and other notions of the universal are susceptible to the imperatives of political economy that misrecognize the globe as the universal. Aesthetics provide criteria of symmetry, unity, and balance that launch empire as a global idea, a geopolitical formation far beyond continental or hemispheric mappings. Ironically, then, symmetry, unity, and balance were invoked in ways that were completely asymmetrical, partisan, and lopsided in favor of an incipient globalization that U.S. interests were intent on pushing to every corner of the earth. Such skewed formalism becomes routine once a prototypical stage of globalization seemed inevitable in the 1890s as the West was won and the American frontier closed. Expansionism was at a dead end until the U.S. reconceived of itself as a unifying power that would make coherent sense of the world by defining it as a globe, that is, as a perfect sphere. An emerging aesthetic sense of the Pacific Rim—a sensibility as local and historically specific as a San Francisco bar named the Imperial—proved indispensable to this process.

Early twentieth-century histories of Manifest Destiny shoulder much of the burden in allowing aesthetic formalism to go global. As William Griffis asserted in *The Romance of Conquest: The Story of American Expansion through Arms and Diplomacy* (1899), "The United States of America have become, in the full sense of the word, a World Power, and in a double sense, 'the great Pacific Power.'" Aesthetics run deeper than formatting historiography in the fictive mode of "romance" and "story," however. What makes U.S. incursions in the Pacific so peaceful is an overall harmony of empire that resolves contradiction by treating differences as isolated, particularistic content that achieves greater unity at the structural remove of form. International tension, even hemispheric conflict, seems mere content that can be bracketed off in the realization of a larger isomorphism of form: "The Far East has become the Near West."[10] This formula of complete and total identity had been expressed a generation earlier in *Hunt's Merchant Magazine* of 1845 as a purely geometric precept: "For the last three centuries, the civilized world has been rolling westward; and Americans of the present age will complete the circle."[11] As ideal form, the circle provides a figure for the imagination both to comprehend the world as a globe and to manage international commerce as globalization.

Historiography is not alone in translating the aesthetic universal as the globe. The imagination does its share too, but for theorists such as Arjun Appadurai, its role is potentially less ideologically benighted. Appadurai seeks to retool the imagination as "no longer a matter of individual genius, escapism from ordinary life, or just a dimension of aesthetics. It is a faculty that informs the daily lives of ordinary people in myriad ways," enabling subjects to contemplate forms of collective life that are not dictated by states or corporate interests. Even though Appadurai takes steps to avoid what he deems simply aesthetic, his rhetoric itself seems prone to this accusation, as it acquires an imagistic hue in describing how a "world-generating optic," "world pictures," and "our fantasies" create a grassroots dialogue about globalization that overlaps territorial and geopolitical divisions.[12] Operating within "just a dimension of aesthetics" is well-nigh impossible since aesthetics are seldom limited to a single dimension but are instead traversed by multiple vectors of the specific and the abstract, the familiar and its antipode, the national and the universal.

Aesthetic imagination always contains materials that are other to it. This heteronomy ensures that the terrain of aesthetics includes, in Adorno's words, "not only art but something foreign and opposed to it."[13] In the imagining of a global economy, these antipodes are often bluntly geographic, roping off an externality for the universal to absorb as a new market. Adorno seems more comfortable in the philosophical stratosphere than on the ground of political economy, but it would be a mistake to assume that *Aesthetic Theory* does not worry about art's place in the social world. Adorno's translator makes the case that the overall project of *Aesthetic Theory* responds to Benjamin's artwork essay, which condemns the aestheticization of politics but without giving up on utopian hopes that aesthetics can promote the democratization of culture.[14] Against the destructive tendencies of spectacle, demagoguery, and imperialism that render fascism pleasurable and even beautiful, the politicization of aesthetics offers a redeeming prospect. This optimism rests on a chiasmus in which Benjamin opposes the fascist takeover of politics to the demystified consciousness of communism that politicizes art. No doubt, framing the conjunction of aesthetics and politics with such stark oppositions seems out of date.[15] Communism no longer appears as a workable alternative since the collapse of the Berlin Wall in 1989, and fascism, it is said, was stamped out with the Allies' victory in World War II. These categories seem anachronistic for globalization, even when dealing with its incipient American forms at start of the twentieth century.

With the history of fascism supposedly behind us, we may safely wish for democratic art, but Benjamin reminds us to be careful about what we wish for. What has all the trappings of democratization can devolve into fascist spectacle. In seeking global aesthetics we may instead get democracy as a mechanically reproduced art form in which the people become monolithic, their heterogeneity standardized. Even if we create democratic art, how do we then evaluate it—on political or aesthetic terms? Speaking at the Institute for the Study of Fascism in 1934, Benjamin wondered if progressive or emancipatory writing could also be "literarily correct." Can art and politics usefully share the same criteria without, on the one hand, dispensing with aesthetic questions altogether, or on the other, submerging political content under formalist considerations? Benjamin views this line of questioning as misguided, built on false oppositions between literary and political criteria; instead, he fuses the two in the conviction that the "more correct . . . the political tendency" of a work, then, by necessity "the higher [its] technical quality."[16] But this implosion of aesthetic merit and political evaluation also recalls the rise of National Socialism—and it is this history of mass deception and popular unfreedom that troubles the universal horizon that globalization and aesthetics envision in common.

Since globalization "counters older notions of the literary as purely aesthetic," according to Paul Jay, critics would do well to abandon the "essentially aestheticized national character" of literary tradition, a necessary move if indeed cultural production no longer orbits the state so tightly.[17] While this perspective repeats Appadurai's undervaluing of aesthetics as though some "purely aesthetic" terrain could be cordoned off and the constitutive antimonies of art and beauty forgotten, it does stress the fact that national literature is profoundly transformed by the flows and pressures of a world system. Literature may be global instead of national, but the more pressing point is that globalization is aesthetic and the political task is to figure out how the aestheticization of the *state* perceived by Benjamin lends itself to and differs from the aestheticization of the *globe*.

The problem with this political task is that progressive commentary often casts democracy in anti-aesthetic terms. "With socialism there will be no need for art because the people will become their own art," runs an apothegm that Anthony Easthope attributes to Raymond Williams.[18] But until this day arrives, according to Easthope, aesthetics and art exude political ambivalence, in bed with the social norms that they also critique. With the arrival of a counteraesthetic orientation that puts an end to this waffling, the *demos* no longer need choose between the seductive pleasures of artistic representation and the tedium of political representation: the polis is unified as an *objet d'art*. Once the tendrils of art are cut back, politics presumably will have no need for mediation and will represent the popular directly and immanently. A similar counteraesthetic appeal braces *The Octopus* in its story of a young poet turned young socialist who protests the triumph of organized capital by scorning art. Although hardly the first literary treatment of socialism in the U.S., this political orientation still seemed new enough to Norris that it appears in the novel only in its adjectival form and capitalized as "Socialistic."[19] Its message, though, may sound familiar: the rough-and-tumble virtue of "the people" will be rejuvenated by twin attacks on corporate greed and genteel humanism. This counteraesthetic impetus correlates exactly with the young poet's design to politicize the literary in ways that will advance democracy. But as *The Octopus* collapses aesthetics and politics it jumbles fascism and democracy. Norris provides *avant la lettre* a theoretical sequel to Benjamin's account of the forces of authoritarianism, spectacle, and reproduction that propel the populace toward fascism. These forces are global in nature: *The Octopus* locates aesthetics/politics at the site of transnational markets, and it is this expansionist geography that unifies fascist representation and democratic desire under a totalizing form.

Fueled by this counteraesthetic impetus, the political novel represents democracy in ways that seem a lot like fascism. Richard Chase first remarked on the eerie intimacy between Norris "the ardent democrat" and Norris "the protofascist."[20] Norris falls short of full-blown fascism because his demagogues are not in bed with any official bureaucratic apparatus. Rather, they remain hopelessly devoted to the people and their art; the poet in *The Octopus*, for instance, seeks no state or elite organs to transmit his Homeric ode of the West. He instead participates in a world poetics of commerce, sailing off to India to fold East into West. It is precisely where the *state* drops out of the picture that the *global* enters in the form of the Anglo-Saxon "race" expanding across the Pacific. The *proto*fascist is more properly a *post*fascist who retools the aesthetic politics of unity to a global world where state channels are outmoded by the new connections of world culture. Norris's vision of a universal "white city" that emerges without any help of the state has a strange currency in our global era when, as many would have it, the state has become increasingly less relevant.[21] For the postfascist committed to democratic forms, political aesthetics and aesthetic politics converge in images of the people as a once disorganized mass that acquires unity under the spectacle of world markets backed up by imperialist aggression.

Under this schema that is both *avant* and *après la lettre* of Benjamin's artwork essay, aesthetics operate as global discourse in a twofold sense. In a formalist sense, aesthetic judgment aspires to wholeness and unity, criteria that in a geopolitical sense supply the logic for the expansion of world markets underwritten by U.S. militarism. Aesthetic judgment ("this tastes sweet" or "everyone agrees *X* is beautiful") rests on globalizing claims that connect with historical developments in international capital and U.S. naval power at the turn of the century. When Norris wrote in *World's Work* of December 1901 that a "whole Literature goes marching by, clamoring for a leader and a master hand to guide it," his desire to see aesthetic potential—here cast as a disorganized popular mass—placed under the control of a consummate artist is satisfied by the demagogue who moonlights as a novelist.[22] As this fantasy unfolds in *The Octopus*, literature is no longer marching aimlessly: the aesthetic imagination turns to Asia, its mission to sublimate crass empire-building under the emergence of world culture.

The aestheticization of politics that puts democracy on a slippery slope toward fascism is not simply a domestic event but an international episode. Before Norris sat down in San Francisco and penned manifestos about implementing literature to serve the masses' economic and political interests, he sailed as a correspondent to South Africa during the Boer War and then two years later to Cuba when the U.S. military invaded the island. Global aesthetics for Norris have their roots in imperial adventure. "I really should love to visit you . . . but I think that the course of my Empire will take its way westward," wrote Norris to decline a friend's offer to journey to New York after his Cuba expedition.[23] "Empire" translates to the plan of becoming a novelist: Norris's career in global aesthetics aspires to expansive and unified forms by positioning itself against and finally encompassing elements deemed alien or foreign.

In his letter to "My Dear Mr. Howells" describing his plan to capture "this huge Niagara of wheat rolling from West to East," Norris left little doubt that the global flood of commodities was pioneered by a thoroughgoing Americanism.[24] Although the divide separating aesthetics and politics, like the gulf between fascism and democracy or East and West, narrows considerably under a global perspective committed to the unity of form, this collapse is inherent to the origins of aesthetic theory. Frank Norris completes the journey that leads to the art of what he called "my Empire"; Friedrich Schiller stands at the beginnings of the aestheticization of world culture. Schiller adopts this perspective reluctantly, perhaps even inadvertently, as his understanding of art and beauty seems defensive and national, a fallback position against the foreign terror unfolding across the German border in France. National aesthetics always bear a constitutive relation to non-national contexts: while Schiller and Norris map different regions, they rely equally on aesthetics to envision the furthest limits of the nation. The aesthetic imagination never escapes its antipodes that supply not merely a construct of otherness but also a literal geography, which, for Schiller, is the political upheaval across the border in France, and, for Norris, is the economic panorama of the Pacific Rim. Schiller, it might be said, looked at the unfamiliar political landscape of revolutionary France and saw terror incognito; Norris, in contrast, approached the economic unknown of the "Orient" as though it were simply the newest franchise of the market he already knew. I turn to Schiller, then, to reveal how national aesthetics stoke a global desire to encompass borders so fully that there would be no borders left, obliterating any difference between global and national culture.

ART AND TERROR

In 1792, the French National Assembly declared Schiller an honorary citizen of a republic sprung from revolution. But memory of the Terror suggested a need for distance, which Schiller found in an aesthetic experience immune to the excesses and upheavals of the political world. Although his *Letters on the Aesthetic Education of Man* (1794–95) mobilizes "the spirit of philosophical enquiry" to discover formal principles behind "the most perfect of all works of art, the building up of the true political freedom," Schiller takes pains to safeguard the art of freedom from the contagion of politics.[25]

When aesthetic criteria determine the course of political action, violence often ensues. Yet violence can be reshaped into beautiful forms: the freedom that seemed so threatening in revolutionary France is channeled into art where it acquires order and predictability. "Aesthetics are meant to give a differentiated apparatus of domination the look of unified and resolute action," Lutz Koepnick argues.[26] But not only does art clean up the traces of domination; it also acts as domination. Coherence, unity, and beauty contribute to an artwork's perfection, but these same qualities invite authoritarian control when translated to a political register. Schiller uses the analogy of a sculptor and a block of stone to suggest the dangers of conducting politics with an eye toward the overarching unity of form. To lend form to the "formless block," the sculptor resorts to violence, splintering and chipping away at parts of the stone deemed incongruent with the ideal design housed in the artist's brain. At a governmental level, this concern with form sacrifices the citizen to the overall work of the state. In order to achieve perfect functionality and unity, the state "must ruthlessly trample underfoot any such hostile individuality."[27] The annihilation of particularity is the tradeoff for political unity.

Once the final product—either in the form of artwork or the state—is unveiled, all traces of violence disappear. The sculptor who chisels the block "only forbears to show" his attack upon formlessness.[28] Gentle lines and polished curves erase memory of the fragments of marble become worthless, shards swept up as so much trash. The state, in turn, forgets its trampling of individuality by celebrating the aftereffects of the struggle for social order, taking pleasure in the sight of a regulated and coordinated citizenry. The state behaves as ruthlessly as the sculptor insofar as each metonymically represents the whole at the expense of the part. Unlike Schiller's mechanical artist who labors without an idea of the total artwork and cannot see beyond the individual parts, the fine artist ignores the broken parts scattered on the floor and instead concentrates on the whole. So, too, the state is "able to produce unity only by suppressing variety": aesthetics and politics are incommensurate, and permitting them to appear as equivalent expressions is to court violence and then destroy all evidence of that trespass.[29] Schiller's analogy stresses the need to maintain clear lines between the worlds of art and statecraft—but it is often an impossible effort.

Although the terror of revolution sends Schiller fleeing toward aesthetics, he does not renounce the project of "true political freedom," but rather reconceptualizes freedom as an artwork governed by order and unity. By routing political desire through aesthetics, citizens purify politics: formalist criteria ensure that irregularities or imperfections at the specific level of content are reconciled to an overall unity. Art provides a crucible to siphon off an excrescent influx of human passion. A beautiful state emerges at the end of aesthetic education, a perfectly ordered and law-loving republic ruled by an ethos of implicit consent. Properly instructed in aesthetics, citizens enter the arena of political commotion to introduce form where before there was none; the apparent formlessness of politics takes form as the state. "The communication of the Beautiful unites society," writes Schiller.[30]

Schiller is not thinking of mass "communication" here. Aesthetic education instead targets the individual, engendering a subject who channels emotion into well-regulated expression. Law operates as an interior ethical program rather than an external disciplinary operation. This lesson is cultivated with the development of aesthetic consciousness as self-governance; art interpellates "the inward man" who "begins finally to take possession of himself" by approaching his own subjectivity with the coolness of the bourgeois merchant who appreciates his possessions, including his own self. Just as the sculptor liberates a pleasing shape from the amorphous, unwieldy block of stone, the citizen judiciously crafts ethical, socially utile behavior from an undifferentiated realm of affect: "The lawless leap of joy becomes a dance, the shapeless gesture a graceful and harmonious miming of speech; the confused noises of perception unfold themselves, begin to obey a rhythm and weld themselves into song."[31] Where the sculptor manipulates an exterior object, the citizen molds an interior subject. Aesthetically trained citizens aspire to a generic identity that squelches difference by bracketing off particularistic human experiences and distinctive human accents. Caution sets the tone of the dance distilled from "lawless leap of joy" that once animated the subject; a melancholy note of restraint echoes through the lyrical form that once was "confused noises." As Eagleton remarks, "Schiller's 'aesthetic' is . . . Gramsci's 'hegemony' in a different key." [32] Consensus hinges on a formalist transcendence that represses the specific content of social antagonism as an impediment to the totalizing beauty of political freedom.

Despite the promise of mass involvement—any person can fill the capacious shoes of universal political form—the capacity to realize perfect freedom is as limited as the select few invited to become citizens of the aesthetic republic. In this way, the radical impulse of *Aesthetic Education* is also its most conservative effect. The beauty of freedom is theoretically available to everyone, but ultimately, most subjects fail to qualify as generic enough to stand in for the individual that Schiller has in mind. The desire for aesthetic form "exists in every finely tuned soul," but how many such souls can a discordant populace boast? Not too many, fears Schiller. "Only in a few select circles where it is not the spiritless imitation of foreign manners [*fremde Sitten*] but people's own lovely nature that governs conduct, where mankind passes through the most complex situations with eager simplicity and tranquil innocence" can we hope to encounter freedom in its purest form. [33] Freedom is a work of art, but are the people cultivated enough to appreciate—or create—it?

Not nearly as gung-ho as Norris's dream of "Anglo-Saxon" culture belting the globe, this prototype of the state as artwork nonetheless mandates a type of "foreign" service, even if only by way of rejection. The aesthetic republic demands cultural self-reliance that when translated to the mass dimensions of "the People" looks a lot like nativism. Its citizens relate to globalism in paranoid fashion. As Schiller warns of things *fremd* or alien, he tiptoes around the turmoil of the French Revolution that prompted his initial retrenchment to subsume political freedom under aesthetics. But aesthetics never escape from the unfamiliar and foreign—even if that contact is primarily negative. Although Schiller urges an aesthetic experience that stays safely on the shore of national homogeneity, his thoughts compulsively return to the terror of radical republicanism across the border. In constructing *fremde Sitten* as inimical to the beauty of the State, Schiller practices what Kojin Karatani calls "aestheticentrism" by locating beauty, not in the object itself, but in the repression of any feelings of alterity or strangeness that the object produces. A clampdown upon affect is necessary to an aesthetic stance that "gets pleasure not from its object but by bracketing various reactions to the object."[34] When the object in question is a "foreign" culture, the subject gets pleasure in foreignness by ignoring the less than ideologically beautiful effects of inassimilable difference. All that remains after purging the state of extraneous material are the generic outlines of an aesthetic nation whose form, paradoxically, allows for only limited access. *Aesthetic Education* at first seeks a type of cosmopolitan pleasure in the freedom erupting in revolutionary France. But the Terror threatens to particularize this pleasure in highly politicized and destructive ways. Schiller responds by quarantining freedom, dislocating it from any historical context infected either by *fremde Sitten* or the political. By lodging freedom in a contextual vacuum that removes all particles of foreignness and alterity, the citizen distills freedom, pure and simple, a politics so wholly formal that it has no content, no alien customs, no history that need be recognized.

These destructive implications have left Schiller prone to fascist misreadings, most horrifically in *Michael,* a novel written by Joseph Goebbels, who would later become Hitler's Reich Minister for Public Enlightenment and Propaganda. Goebbels takes advantage of Schiller's image of the sculptor to portray the fascist leader as a hero who perceives that "the statesman is an artist, too. Human beings are for him what stone is for the sculptor. Leader and masses are as little of a problem to each other as color is a problem for the painter. Politics are the plastic arts of the state."[35] Political freedom is rendered subordinate to the beautiful idea of the state that dictates the form "the people" must take. The bracketing process is thrown into high gear, a citizenry's particularities repressed until it takes generic form as the mass, which becomes intelligible only with the herculean efforts of the aesthetically minded politician. Norris, as we will see, also dubiously celebrated "the people" as a mass unit. In *The Octopus,* his Homeric representation of farmers, laborers, and railroad workers as a popular front that challenges robber barons who lay siege to the Western landscape uncomfortably slides into a portrait of Anglo-Saxon merchants bent on establishing an outpost of economic imperium in Asia.

The foreign precipitates this slippage: as aesthetic projects, both state governance and self-governance define themselves in opposition to *fremde Sitten,* that is, to particular meanings that disrupt sovereignty by insisting that governance is never completely an insular undertaking and, in fact, always entails contact with unharmonious contents that seem alien to the "organic" form of self or people. The exclusive circle around political membership is drawn tighter to distinguish a "people's own lovely conduct" from things unfamiliar. The implicit contrast between one's own behavior and the unfamiliarity of the *fremd* reveals *Aesthetic Education* as always on guard against things foreign, its author's privileging of a select ethos negatively articulated against what lies beyond the horizon of a unified self or homogenous populace. No matter how vigilant this sort of border patrol, the campaign against outside influence ignores the fundamental heteronomy that is an inescapable aspect of aesthetics. The universal simply cannot avoid the foreign; the global pull of aesthetics always runs into trouble at the antipodes. The only question is whether to delineate that border more sharply and build a higher fence, making a society that is still more select, or whether to absorb foreign difference as more of the same.

LITERATURE "AS SUCH"

Unapologetically political, Norris's fiction can hardly be termed aesthetic in Schiller's sense. Generations of readers have found plenty to wince at in Norris's prose, beginning with Van Wyck Brooks who a half-century ago labeled him the progenitor of "the 'cave-man' tendency in American writing."[36] Norris would hardly take offense at such a judgment, perhaps even salvaging some masculinist pride from the accusation. He often boasted of his work's *counter*aesthetic qualities and its rejection of putatively effeminate standards of taste and respectability. For Norris, the literary artist's uncouth reaction to aesthetic education aligns itself with the rough-and-tumble of the popular in a democratic maneuver against a simpering highbrow culture. Arnoldian aesthetics strike him as bloated by elitism and self-indulgence, unequal to the task of expressing democratic culture.

In adopting a counteraesthetic position, Norris is not too distant from theorists who dismiss traditional aesthetics and instead advocate revisionist aesthetics as an avenue for democratic social change. To this end, Laura Kipnis locates hopes for a "radical democratic Left" in "radical aesthetics" that transforms commodity culture into popular culture, though, of course, she has little use for testosterone-enhanced visions of art such as Norris's.[37] Progressive politics invite the contradiction of an aesthetics opposed to art: democracy necessitates a counteraesthetic response. Even as aesthetic ideology provides a last refuge to bourgeois apologists and other scoundrels, it also potentially supplies, according to Herbert Marcuse, a "counter-consciousness" that deconstructs "dominant consciousness."[38] Adorno similarly describes art as a "counterpressure to the force exerted by the *body social.*"[39] The "need for a 'counter-image' of a given everyday life" is supplied by art, according to Agnes Heller and Ferenc Fehér.[40] While Norris's cultivation of the middlebrow presents a serious obstacle to what these theorists, particularly Adorno, mean by art, *The Octopus* exerts considerable counterpressure on a social body in which dominant consciousness and everyday life are manipulated by the antidemocratic conniving of railroads and trusts.

For all his supposed inattention to the delicacies of form and style, Norris's deficiencies come across as democratic impulses. Deriding art for its cloying imitation and effeminacy, Norris cultivates a counteraesthetic steeped in a masculinist style cocky enough to represent "the People" in all its less-than-genteel behaviors. Just as Professor Gayley at Berkeley was complaining that American literary criticism had not yet entered "the 'cocksure' period of its development," Norris, a former Cal student (class of 1894), was working to correct a similar deficiency with his Epic of the Wheat. Literary criticism must consider "social problems" and "social progress," Gayley and his collaborator at the University of Michigan, Fred Scott, assert in their work on the "bases in aesthetics and poetics"; otherwise only a select circle of critics will have their say while the judgment of the "multitude of men" will go unnoticed. The popular criteria that Gayley and Scott saw as lacking in salon aesthetics are supplied in crudely biological fashion by Norris's naturalism, which portrays the *demos* as a race of fiercely independent farmers of Anglo-Saxon stock. Appearing at jackrabbit hunts, barn dances, and political protests, "the People" (this capitalization is Norris's throughout the novel) in *The Octopus* exhibit tastes that cannot be satisfied with snobby art produced by what Gayley and Scott disparage as "the coterie."[41] Democratic sensibilities require an aesthetics that defies art.

This opposition recalls the distinction that Du Bois, as I argued in chapter 3, cuts between art and aesthetics, although it is difficult to see where the "darker races" fit into Norris's epic, which is not shy about casting Mexicans as lazy and degenerate. Still, the December 1911 "What to Read" column of *The Crisis* classed *The Octopus* and *The Quest of the Silver*

Fleece as kindred expressions of naturalism: "To Frank Norris' commercial epic of wheat . . . Dr. Du Bois now adds the spiritual epic of cotton." *The Crisis* has a lot to say about how Du Bois uses the aesthetic form of the epic to reveal the "profound universality of human nature" but remains relatively silent about any horizon of universality in Norris's novel. It is not that Norris fails to share Du Bois's vision of "a great human oneness" but rather that Norris sees fundamental sameness as a salutary effect of worldwide commodity exchange.[42] The commercial terrain in which counteraesthetic bravado emerges ultimately becomes political quicksand as the contents of Norris's naturalist image of democracy—"the People"—acquire totalizing and global form.

The poet in *The Octopus,* Presley, comes West with the mission of contributing to political aesthetics by writing an epic about "the People." But it is not immediately clear whether his "great poem of the West" will be a popular (and, in the political terms of the 1890s, Populist) performance or an expression of imperial power: "Oh, to put it all into hexameters; strike the great iron note; sing the vast, terrible song; the song of the People; the forerunners of empire!" exclaims Presley as he imagines—but fails to write—his masterpiece.[43] Indecision about the purpose of modern epic poetry stems from Presley's lack of clarity about his own purpose: will his makeover from fawning aesthete to hardy champion of Populism be successful? Or, will he go too far, becoming a proponent of anarchist socialism? This uncertainty derives from the uneasy transit between aesthetics and politics: if a people's poetry is politicized, what should its politics be? As art becomes a medium for democracy, should it expand to spread still further westward across the Pacific Rim to wind up in the East? *The Octopus* never settles whether "the People" or "empire" should be advanced, because these two political projects—one about nurturing a people's capacity for self-government and the other about denying self-government to other people—converge in the misrecognition of a global market as universal culture.

Despite a trajectory that impels Presley from California's San Joaquin Valley to a clipper ship bound for India, his epic limits its compass to circles no more expansive than the select society Schiller invites to an aesthetic state. Eager to compose a paean to the toilers of the land, he settles down in an artist's garret at the swank ranch of the county's largest landowner. While assiduously loafing about the valley's farms, the poet renounces art. Abandoning genteel verse along with the "cluttered brica-brac and meaningless *objets d'art*" associated with the feminine world of the landowner's wife, Presley cultivates counteraesthetics and pens a "Socialistic poem" (371, 394). Where he once sent verses to small literary journals, he now prints his manifesto in the popular press, specifically a daily newspaper. As he imbibes radicalism from a saloonkeeper who quotes Mill and Bakunin, Presley's emerging political consciousness derails his artistic tendencies to write dainty verses. Aesthetics become the site of political affect. Denouncing the corrupt tactics of the railroad, Presley "saw red," his emotion (or is it a political orientation, a codeword for communism?) finding outlet in poetic creation. But the poet as producer finds his aesthetic labor appropriated when his socialist composition becomes the topic of literary debate, fodder for political speeches, and copy for advertising slogans. The more universal his message becomes, the more it relies on the market for its dissemination.

The Octopus opens up a rift in the logic of representation by virtue of its counteraesthetic stance. If aesthetics traditionally bracket material and cultural considerations in its articulation of a disinterested universal subject, then the "anti-aesthetic logic of naturalism," according to Donald Pease, recuperates once disavowed contexts of race, class, ethnicity, sexuality, and gender. The beauty of generic identity, unfettered by historical contingencies or social associations, collides with an anti-aesthetic orientation that wrests the subject away from a fantasy of hermetic identity to "multiple sites wherein alternative social, political, and economic identities have emerged."[44] The anti-aesthetic performs radical democratic critique. In Pease's eyes, Jack London's *Martin Eden* exemplifies an alternative form of aesthetic judgment that does not blindly reproduce the ideals of disinterest and transcendence that allow people to cozy up to the state. For Norris's *The Octopus* the theoretical payoff is less clear: a narrative written to protest the power of corporate capital mounts a counteraesthetic assault that in the end abides by aesthetic criteria consistent with the political economic interests of U.S. transnationalism. Unity manages the popular, subsuming heterogeneity under the falsely universal placeholder of "the People." However wide the rift between counteraesthetics and aesthetics, a deeper unity negates the contested, unpredictable nature of popular democracy by romanticizing the *demos* as a total work of art whose allure consists in adherence to formal principles that everyone can find beautiful.

Although counteraesthetics impel Presley to political action, he lapses back into a complacent and uncritical disposition. Even as he composes his

"Socialistic" poem, "the artist in him reasserted itself. He became more interested in his poem, as such, than in the cause that had inspired it" (372). Literature's formal properties—its "as such-ness"—outweigh the specific history of its contents. The avant-garde sensibility that allows Presley to distinguish counteraesthetics from traditional aesthetic concerns for unity, echoed in the economic landscape by the railroad's totalizing control of markets, also leads him paradoxically to adjust his "red" social vision to the safe criteria of formal order. Unable to control his indignation at the railroad's monopoly, searching for a vessel to manage his outrage, Presley begins to write. Much as Schiller's aesthetic education guides citizens to route ecstatic movement into dance or to shape untutored expression into song, Presley's denunciation of corporate capital takes poetic form as "The Toilers." "As his prose grew more exalted, it passed easily into the domain of poetry," writes Norris. "Soon the cadence of his paragraphs settled to an ordered beat and rhythm, and in the end Presley . . . was once more writing verse" (372). Out on a radical limb farther than anything rhyme has prepared him for, Presley yearns for the safety of aesthetic formalism where regularity reels in any affect too close to the red end of the spectrum. The routing of aesthetics into global commerce is hardly unexpected, given the scene where Presley first weds social protest to the beautiful: stumbling across a painting owned by a trans-Pacific shipping magnate, he is inspired to shape populism into a poetic form. His composition engenders radicalism along with conservatism, its phrases quoted in "revolutionary sermons" as well as "reactionary speeches" (394). Also "distorted so as to read as an advertisement for patented cereals and infants' foods," his socialist ode is appropriated by consumer capitalism to reveal how the divided lines of politics/aesthetics are united at a single location—the market (394). If, as Walter Benn Michaels has argued, the logic of the corporation permeates all things, even the act of writing itself, then the revolt against aesthetics appears as just another episode in the production of corporate consciousness.[45]

Fed up with poetry, the poet turns anarchist and attempts a synthesis of counteraesthetics and revolution. Where he once moped about the landscape seeking inspiration, he now delivers impassioned speeches denouncing a monopoly that feeds on "the People"; where he once wrote verse, he now tosses a pipe-bomb into the dining room of a railroad official. His reaction against aesthetics seems complete. Still, something remains missing from these incendiary acts. What they lack, The Octopus implies, is poetry.

At a protest against the strong-arm tactics of the railroad, Presley jumps on an opera house stage, lays out a case against the plutocrats' oppression of the populace, and invokes the American, French, and Russian revolutions as precedents of popular democratic uprisings. Yet highbrow aestheticism still wraps radical politics in formal structures: elevated above the crowd in an institution of upper-class culture, he warns against political excess, lest liberty personified as "the Man in the Street" be seduced by "the Red terror" (552). His call for a new insurgency takes familiar form as a tragic aria. Amid the cheers of the overflowing opera house, Presley remains indifferent about political activities organized loosely on socialist principles—much as he has been ambivalent about his poetic activities all along. His speech falls short of raising the crowd's political consciousness precisely because its reliance on radical affect and spectacle numbs the more measured aesthetic judgment that Schiller, at the time of a different revolution, sought to instill in citizens:

> A prolonged explosion of applause followed, the Opera House roaring to the roof, men cheering, stamping, waving their hats. But it was not intelligent applause. Instinctively as he made his way out, Presley knew that, after all, he had not once held the hearts of his audience. He had talked as he would have written; for all his scorn of literature, he had been literary. (552)

The interlude with demagoguery is both not enough and too much: his performance is too aesthetic to be appropriately democratic *and* too political to educate the people. Trembling at the specter of popular turmoil, Presley seeks refuge in art as a means of restraining sentiment. While he upbraids himself for not electrifying the people, the poet is secretly pleased that he has not done so. His "scorn of literature" enables a retreat to a predictable aesthetic posture; counteraesthetic impulses slide easily enough into the managed domain of the "literary." Although Presley's emotional alienation from the crowd betrays his distance from popular democracy, his estrangement and detachment lend form and order to an otherwise frenetic social outcry. He brackets democratic energy long enough to appreciate politics solely as an aesthetic effect: lukewarm about popular will, the formalist as politician invokes politics—the "Red terror"—only as a last resort. Far better to have mediocre speeches than revolutionary unrest. In a world where "the people" of California threaten to repeat the cry "à la Bastille" that "unleashes Revolution," just as Schiller feared, and democratic politics seem a powder keg waiting to explode, art provides a bunker of safety (550). The judicious citizen looks to aestheticize—to make "literary" in Presley's case—the popular and the democratic.[46]

Without the "literary," the art of political freedom, like a populist speech delivered at an opera house, is liable to erupt into anarchy and terror. According to this phobic logic, the final destination of affect should be nonpolitical: only by recognizing the awesome power of politics—and this is what aesthetic education warns citizens about—can we be spared the excesses of democracy incarnate. Although Norris never gives the text of Presley's socialist composition, he draws on a historical collision of the literary and the popular by basing this protest ode on Edward Markham's "The Man with the Hoe" (1899), a populist poem written "after seeing Millet's World-Famous Painting." Intended as a demotic protest, Presley's "The Toilers" is nonetheless several steps removed from working-class life, its provenance stemming from an art gallery, not from direct contact with the laborers who are its putative subject. When Presley gives his creation to the newspapers, he merely follows the example of his historic prototype, who sent his poem to the *San Francisco Examiner* and used the popular press as an organ of protest. Presley's performance at the opera house repeats the lesson of Markham's poem, which seems calculated not to rouse the oppressed or court the "Red terror" but rather to throw the masses a bone by gently scolding the privileged. The final stanza seeks to delay agitation in the present by invoking a vision of the Last Judgment:

> O masters, lords and rulers in all lands
> How will the Future reckon with this Man?
> How answer his brute question in that hour
> When whirlwinds of rebellion shake the world?
>
> .   .   .   .
>
> When this dumb Terror shall reply to God,
> After the silence of the centuries?[47]

Like Schiller, who feared *le Terreur*, and Presley, who halfheartedly invokes the "Red terror," Markham ominously casts revolution as "the dumb Terror" waiting to articulate an unspeakable message. At least one prominent aesthetic theorist saw Markham's poem suffused with affect that seemed ready to bleed over into the realm of the social. In a 1908 scholarly paper on "Pragmatism in Aesthetics" written in honor of William James, Kate Gordon hypothesized that Markham's poem must "inspire" its "public with a sense of social responsibility" whose result "should be some bettering of social conditions." At this point her argument breaks off, as she wonders how exactly art will produce these conditions. Her answer is that by itself art cannot effect change. What it can do, however, is prepare "the emotional stage of reform." Once let loose, emotion may lead beyond concrete plans for reform to the uncertainties of wider action, what Schiller fears will spark a political chain reaction otherwise known as revolution. Gordon admits that "aesthetic absorption" is incalculable, and it is this unknown that proves so disturbing in "The Man with the Hoe," which, with its barrage of unanswered questions, begins to sound like an interrogation of the social order as a whole.[48] Terror—whether French, Red, or dumb—is an uncertain and therefore scary political prospect that in each case is tamed by a counteraesthetic sensibility that scorns literature but prefers the literary, that hates art but loves its form.

GEO-AESTHETICS

"The Man with the Hoe had no spark in his brain," Vachel Lindsay would later charge in *The Art of the Moving Picture* (1915). On the lookout for the next new thing, Lindsay implies that old-fashioned media such as literature lack the flash to ignite the fuse of democratic art. Cinema is his alternative: insofar as motion pictures excite popular feelings, Lindsay hopes that "films of a more beautiful United States" will summon national loyalty and international friendship where militarism once compelled it. One might thus adapt Presley's self-condemnation to Lindsay: for all his scorn of conventional representation, he had been predictably nationalistic. The horizon of film is global, and *The Art of the Moving Picture* envisions American cinema as a "Permanent World's Fair" that will endlessly advertise the U.S. across the globe.[49] Lindsay only updates the tradition of appropriation that spins Presley's great socialist ode to peddle baby formula.

Having seen his poem absorbed into commercial advertisements, Presley turns to dynamite in the belief that he can at last renounce aesthetics in favor of militant anarchy. Like theorists of globalization who set up aesthetics as a straw figure, Presley undervalues and depoliticizes aesthetics by limiting literature to a single dimension of ineffectiveness. Aesthetics need not be wholly aligned with class privilege (salons and private art galleries), futility and miscalculation (Presley's jejune socialist ode), or reactionary formalism (Schiller's, Markham's and Norris's arguments against various forms of terror). Nor should aesthetics be considered as simple grist for the advertising mill and other corporate interests, even if those interests amount to a monopoly, as in *The Octopus*, where the railroad has its hand in everything from price fixing to the pockets of elected officials. Controlling all levels of society, the railroad may have a virtual lock on political reality but not on the aesthetic possibility that exists as a theoretically universal zone of shared subjective judgment. Although aesthetics do not figure centrally in Kant's later writings on world citizenship, he stipulates that this ideal prospect exists only as inner sensibility. His *Religion within the Limits of Reason Alone* cautions that utopian ideas about collectivity are traduced time and again by external structures of government. The sole place that these prospects are not compromised or co-opted, as happens to Presley's poem of social collectivity, is within subjects. We fool ourselves, Kant implies, if we think that an institution like the state or church can ordain an "ethical commonwealth." We are equally misled if we think that human beings can ever achieve this utopia. Kant stresses that an ethical commonwealth is "never wholly attainable," imbuing the concept with a weak messianic power that points the way to but never arrives at complete social commonality.[50] By first narrowing and then giving up on aesthetics, Presley also gives up on the world—quite literally. He replaces the world with the globe, a singular geo-economic unit that requires all sorts of fallible external structures and institutions.

Presley's failure of aesthetic imagination so crucial to world citizenship leads him to the ways of Johann Most (see chapter 2) and anarchist violence. But bombing the dining room of a capitalist meets with even less success than writing poems or delivering impassioned political speeches. As Presley wraps up loose ends before sailing to Asia, his path crosses the railroad flunky, S. Behrman, who escaped the blast. Suspecting the poet as the culprit, Behrman seems amused by the botched attempt on his life and offers only a mild rebuke: "Well, that don't show any common sense, Presley. . . . What could you have gained by killing me?" (626). He evaluates the poet's bomb-throwing as an aesthetic performance, critiquing the act for its overblown quality, its ostentatious and useless display of political passion. Appealing to "common sense," perhaps more in Paine's terms than as Kant's ideal of *sensus communis,* Behrman judges Presley's extremism as a sorry show. As this critique weighs political action in terms of aesthetic value, the specific causes of social unrest melt into air. Formalist considerations empty politics of history and content (in the poet's case, a protest against corrupt governmental machinery and economic exploitation) to leave only a dehistoricized scaffolding with no context to explain anarchism. For his part, Presley takes this misapplication of Kantian judgment to heart by agreeing that his actions lack the beauty of common sense:

> It don't seem as though you could be brought to book, S. Behrman, by anybody, or by any means, does it? They can't get at you through the courts,—the law can't get you . . . and you even escaped . . . six inches of plugged gas pipe. Just what are we going to do with you? (626–27)

Justice remains a literary proposition, as Presley's idiomatic use of "book" to signal the despair of ever finding legal redress implies. The capitalist cannot "be brought to book," and in a different sense neither can the poet who remains as far as ever from completing his epic to "the People" at the end of *The Octopus.*

This is not the first time that Presley agrees with the formalist criteria of capitalists. Earlier, Presley visits the central offices of the P. S. and W. railroad, where the corporation's president dismisses the poet's socialist ode not because of its radical message but because of its aesthetic deficiency. The landscape that inspired Presley receives higher marks because it is an original painting rather than a knockoff in verse. "You might just as well have kept quiet," he tells Presley, who not unexpectedly agrees with this critique of his futility and lack of common sense (574). But the railroad president overstates his case; "The Toilers" is not without social effects. Straight from the P. S. and W. headquarters to a soiree thrown by the wife of yet another railroad mucky-muck, Presley is told: "Just because of that poem, [we] have started a movement to send a whole shipload of wheat to the starving people in India. Now, you horrid *réactionnaire,* are you satisfied?" (605). Presley should be satisfied: poetry in the salons of the elite produces results, which, no matter how self-serving, eludes partisan agitation on an opera house stage. Whereas the aimless emotion at the populist rally soon dissipates, famine relief plays a stabilizing role in a cosmopolitan theater of supply and demand. At the opera house become mob meeting, the people overflow the highbrow aesthetic institution that shapes them as a mass; in contrast, India is far away enough that its specific content is already bracketed, trivialized as a minor distraction to the overall humanitarian project conducted in the name of world civilization. India—as it exists in the aesthete philanthropic imagination—is the incarnation of *fremde Sitten,* a geography of the foreign that falls outside the aesthetic state.

But contexts that fall outside the aesthetic state are also a fundamental part of its order. "What is heterogeneous in artworks is immanent to them," writes Adorno.[51] In the political economy of the turn-of-the-century U.S., the difference between aesthetic state and artwork is, finally, not that great a difference: the foreign elements that each identifies are not so much external as organic to its form and existence. The constant presence of the antipode is strategic for market expansion, indicating zones of future development and incorporation. As a dubious provocation toward global awareness, Presley's poem impels the select few of drawing room society to look toward the foreign, to sympathize with it, and catch it up within a world system of commodity exchange. Literature motivates these society women to understand scarcity as a question of adjusting—but always on their terms—the balance and symmetry between themselves and people from the antipodes. These criteria find their geopolitical analogue in U.S. expansion into Asia that establishes equilibrium between the starving East and the overproducing West.

Although *The Octopus* takes a dim view of the elite and its latest *cause célèbre,* Norris suggests the opening of Asian markets as the ultimate achievement of the aesthetic state. In fact, this success encourages the state to supersede itself in the appearance of a world system. Humanity forms a perfect circle: as Western-style capitalism reaches the "Orient," the Anglo-Saxon finds himself back at the birthplace of civilization. Manifest Destiny appears on the Pacific Rim not so much as an imperial mission but as a transhistoric return in which nationality and race pale before the great idea of a new human unity engineered by world markets. Not surprisingly, it is the shipping magnate whose art collection inspires Presley's "The Toilers" who first spouts this idea: "The great word of the twentieth century will be—listen to me, you youngsters—Markets" (305). As the U.S. pushes empire-capitalism so far westward that East and West, antipode and homeland, seem confluent, the globe achieves unity under a political economy so orderly and totalizing that it seems a work of art.

Turn-of-the-century globalization, with its drive toward consolidation and coordination of markets, adheres to principles of unity and balance.

Aesthetics have always shaped globalization: from Schiller's "foreign manners" to Norris's utopian sense of "Markets," criteria of wholeness and proportion resonate with fin-de-siècle concerns that frame U.S. interests as transnational. The geopolitical effects of aesthetics derive from the imperatives of form, but it is not just that aesthetics hinge on "global claims" and the "totalization of culture" to justify universalist claims for what is in actuality the particularity of the state.[52] More to the point, aesthetics envision the globe as both a unified shape and beautiful concept, creating an impression of wholeness, synthesis, and perfect completion carried out on a world scale. Literature "as such," as the formalist enterprise derided by *The Octopus*, is also the specific historical expression of what we might think of as "geo-aesthetics" at the start of the twentieth century. Norris's image of world trade that pours the bounty of American wheat into the gaping mouths of Indian peasants initially crops up at an art gallery where landowners, captains of industry, and aesthetes brainstorm about ways to reinvigorate American enterprise and art in a single stroke. The devotees of art intuit that excess is a political problem (as it is in the opera house) unless it is redefined as economic surplus (as it is within the new religion of "Markets") and shipped off to Asia. Equilibrium of form prevails: excess meets up with scarcity, famine solves the problem of overproduction, and East folds into West in a series of transnational flows.

Dejected by the railroad's victory, Presley stows aboard a clipper ship laden with California wheat bound for Calcutta. The world market has its aesthetic representative; under the poet's guidance, global trade takes shape as an artwork. As the owner of the shipping line predicts, "We'll carry our wheat into Asia yet. The Anglo-Saxon started from there at the beginning of everything and it's manifest destiny that he must circle the globe and fetch up where he began his march" (647). This long awaited white homecoming represents unity as the achievement of a global project—just as Norris would later cast global aspirations in aesthetic terms when he wrote about the future of the novel at the start of the twentieth century. Norris's blueprint for literary production anticipates the structure of what Michael Hardt and Antonio Negri in the twenty-first century theorize as the force of imperial sovereignty: "The concept of Empire united juridical categories and universal ethical values, making them work together as an organic whole." As Norris contemplates the state of the American novel, he imagines human civilization as a single continuum where the only unit of geography is the globe as West meets up with East and the only unit of time is a human history that unfolds like chapters in a novel. While this literary formula seems a lot like Hardt and Negri's formula for empire, it is also the case that empire echoes Norris's aesthetics. Like Norris's literary crusade, empire in Hardt and Negri's description "exhausts historical time, suspends history, and summons the past and future within its own ethical order."[53] No clash of cultures erupts from this total vision because there is no conflict to begin with: rather, an aesthetic sensibility ensures horizons of greater unity. The "beauty" that lingers in Hardt and Negri's account of empire is matched by the global form that suffuses Norris's literary manifestos.

In a series of essays written in the wake of *The Octopus,* Norris identifies the lack of a global horizon as a major obstacle to the expansion and future development of American literature. While he grumbles that the novel narrowly focuses on the parlor and not the workaday world of the street, Norris also intends his complaint as a call-to-arms for a national literature that has run out of room. Mindful of the frontier's closing, Norris wonders where the novel—like the nation—will expand and flex its muscle. He takes heart in a view of civilization as organically bent on empire, eternally moving westward until it ends up back in the East where, presumably, the seeds of Anglo-Saxon cultural superiority first sprouted. After sweeping across the Middle East into Europe and then leapfrogging to North America, Anglo-Saxons stand on the shores of the Pacific, a step away from belting the globe with Western culture. Humanity is realized as a perfect circle:

> Suddenly we have found that there is no longer any Frontier. . . . At last after so many centuries, after so many marches, after so much fighting, so much spilled blood . . . the Anglo-Saxon in his course of empire had circled the globe and had brought the new civilization to the old civilization, had reached the starting point of history, the place from which the migrations began. So as soon as the marines landed there was no longer any West, and the equation of the horizon, the problem of the centuries for the Anglo-Saxon was solved.

Like the balanced image of world markets supported by Presley the poet, the idea of a single cosmopolitanism finds a champion in Norris the novelist. This unity may at first require blood and aggression, but eventually militarism transcends war itself and becomes an aesthetic project. In elaborating his vision, Norris refers to U.S. forces that entered Peking in June 1900 to confront anticolonialist Boxers laying siege to foreign legations. The "day when the first United States marines landed in China" signals the arrival of a new dawn when the last bit of untamed frontier along the Pacific Rim is brought within the orbit of a global plan.[54] Nothing foreign remains to be bracketed; the globe exists as a unified work of art. As U.S. troops force a transnational unity that has been centuries in the making, empire winds up clustered about the future of the American novel.

Although Norris conceives of the global village as an armed camp, he looks forward to a day when an aestheticized global consciousness will break free of jingoism to be replaced by the nascent harmony of cosmopolitan capital unifying cultures. A "new patriotism, one that shall include all peoples," he predicts, will become the dominant force in a world where not only the American frontier but also national frontiers have lost significance.[55] *The Octopus* expresses this hope as jocular Yankee optimism for profit that sees commodities as the building blocks of world citizenship. As the shipping magnate bids farewell to Presley, he licks his chops over the new markets that the poet will encounter on Asian shores:

> My respects to the hungry Hindoo. Tell him "we're coming." . . . Tell the men of the East to look out for the men of the West. The irrepressible Yank is knocking at the doors of their temples and he will want to sell 'em carpet-sweepers for their harems and electric light plants for their temple shrines. (648)

Cosmopolitan promise masks orientalist threat; humanitarian mission primes the development of overseas markets. *The Octopus* employs aestheticentrism to sweep the conflictual nature of empire capital under the rug of organic unity. "As the West disappears into the market, it melts and solidifies at once," writes Fernando Coronil. "The image of a unified globe dispenses with the notion of an outside."[56] Norris's jaunty prediction of 1901 anticipates Coronil's analysis but without perceiving that the blending of West and East occurs on the West's terms. Imagined as a unified form, globalized culture incorporates difference within a single fabricated community, in effect, representing civilization as a total system. By virtue of the electricity, wheat, and other commodities bound for Asia, the Orient will become more like the West; the antipodes are brought home under a single geo-economic unit that fulfils the promise of a global aesthetic. In contrast to the worldwide ethical commonwealth that, according to Kant, will forever elude men and women, this work of geopolitical art seems within reach of anyone with a cargo ship and a ton of wheat.

The trans-Pacific circulation of commodities pivots on the work of geopolitical art. Not to be confused with the universal social collectivity envisioned by aesthetics, "geo-aesthetics" depend on commercial arrangements that configure the antipodes, heterogeneity, *fremde Sitten*, foreignness—all the constitutive antagonism that energizes aesthetic imagination—as untapped markets ready for development. This global perspective asks little in the way of ethical interiority, requiring only a boatload of commodities. As opposed to the theoretical ether of an ethical commonwealth, implementing community through the impersonality of commodity exchange seems feasible and commonsensical, but it is worthwhile to remember Kant's brooding over the fact that the idea of world solidarity "dwindles markedly under men's hands."[57] In Norris's world, ruthless business tactics and military intervention in the Pacific are swept aside by the infinite circle of global exchange. "Geo-aesthetics" envelop any unharmonious matter in his novel's final image of wheat pouring out of a grain chute into an "ever-reforming cone . . . the rushing of the Wheat that continued to plunge incessantly from the iron chute in a prolonged roar, persistent, steady, inevitable" (646). Whether it is the marines who opened China's door or wheat-growers hurt by international destabilizations of the 1890s, the never-ending formalism of the cone of wheat eliminates tension and discord. Totalizing and complete, this cone is global in more ways than one: the mound of wheat rises in the hold of a ship bound for the East. Flowing over the asphyxiated body of S. Behrman, the wheat prioritizes a unitary, global form over the discordant horror of political content suggested by the capitalist's corpse. The materials of global economy—for Norris, grain is the fundamental stuff of exchange—hold together as a geopolitical artwork, exemplifying how aestheticization "becomes the means through which the discontents in contemporary civilization are to be answered—or stifled."[58] Nothing can stop the cone from returning to the form of a cone just as nothing can prevent Anglo-Saxon civilization from advancing westward until arriving at the East, in effect, returning civilization to its birthplace. "The space of imperial sovereignty," write Hardt and Negri, "is smooth."[59] Like the cone of wheat that suffers neither break nor interruption, West flows into East without a trace of suture or conflict.

POSTFASCIST FORM

Geo-aesthetics shape populations into a single conceptual unit. Meanwhile, imperial expansion seems as beautiful as an "ever-reforming cone," assembling the detritus of cultures and the ruin of centuries into the grander project of civilization. An unstoppable market force, the invasion of Asia occurs with neither clash nor antagonism, since the migration of capitalism and militarism only augurs the return of the West to its ultimate origins in the East. This prehistoric unity reveals the world system as an *objet d'art*.

No useless piece of art is this. Global aesthetics educate citizens in an inclusive politics, its lessons encapsulated in the wheat that provides "the sustenance of a whole world, the food of an entire People" (177). Discrete peoples become "the People," their bodies and spirits sustained not so much by a single vision as a single commodity. Global form installs the *demos* as the crucial criterion of production and distribution. The "entire People" are unified and beautiful: they represent the only demographic that unites aesthetic judgment, economic rationality, and moral sense. When *The Octopus* celebrates the wheat's ability to feed the masses, it assumes Presley's abortive epic to represent "the voice of an entire people, wherein all people should be included" (9–10). If the world is hungry, let it eat wheat and seek satisfaction in an unwritten poem of the West. The aestheticized globe—a development far beyond Schiller's aesthetic state—need not fear the distractions of *fremde Sitten* because foreignness no longer signifies when the people attain an all-inclusive form that permits no outside. This appeal to the *demos* prettifies a system that exploits the people, as Norris's portrait of rampant corruption shows. Beneath this schizophrenic logic that alternately redeems global capitalism and indicts its antidemocratic mechanisms lies the deeper unity of an "entire People" nourished and abused by production. At once the beneficiary of industrial production and the victim of markets, the *demos* as an aesthetic category achieves a unity that proves elusive in the material terrain of history.

This literary take on early twentieth-century globalization claims the activities of the consummate artist as the ethos of the world citizen. As Norris surveyed the possibility of a world without frontiers, he looked forward to a dawning cosmopolitanism when "we who now arrogantly boast ourselves as Americans . . . may realize that the true patriotism is the brotherhood of man and know that the whole world is our nation."[60] This world citizen is the artist whose global sensibility allows for conceptualization of humanity as a single united form. Like the shipping magnate who heralds "Markets" as the watchword of a new era of international capital, Norris locates the future of the American novel in the writer who "would have sounded the world-note; he would be a writer not national, but international, and his countrymen would be all humanity, not the citizens of any one nation."[61] Norris's prescription for international literature cannot avoid imperialist calculation. With its comprehensive pretensions that make nation-states anachronistic, the novelist's "world-note" of mass democracy echoes with postfascist tones. His utopia that includes "all people" is also an obligatory order that leaves no choice to opt out of a total system of representation. As the sole locus of political identity, the global conception of humanity reduces multivocality to the singularity of voice that herds the *demos* into the enclave of "all." Democracy is mobilized for authoritarian purposes under the spectacle of the popular as a global unit.

Such is Benjamin's worry in observing how potentially egalitarian forms of technological reproduction eventuate in fascist representation. The newsreel that elevates "everyone . . . from passer-by to movie extra" also de-individuates the *demos* by capturing persons as a mass movement.[62] Form predominates: it only matters that the people are united and not what they are united for or against; the people exist simply as an aesthetic object to be shaped by an artist as potentially unscrupulous as Schiller's sculptor. Wholeness and unity do not relate to the content of history; instead these formal properties, as Schiller first recognized, answer to the impassive criteria of the beautiful:

> In a truly beautiful work of art the content should do nothing, the form everything. . . . Only from the form is true aesthetic freedom to be expected. Therefore, the real artistic secret of the master consists in his *annihilating the material by means of the form.*[63]

The people display a capacity for freedom only when the content of their specific identities are encapsulated, managed, and subordinated to formal considerations. Form, as Norris would later insist, establishes totalizing criteria in which abstract aesthetic principles converge with the historical conditions of international commodities at the turn of the century: just as "everything" flows into the formal properties of the artwork, the pressures of globalization force every political tendency from democracy to fascism into alignment.

Yet the question of force remains—but only its erasure. The struggle for global form turns on a power of annihilation that reveals itself when all traces of materiality are effaced. Although Norris's *The Octopus* originates around an actual 1889 shootout between railroad deputies and ranchers, the final economy of the novel envisions the beauty of trade and markets—the "ever-reforming cone"—as the sublimation of violence. Such is the final challenge of a critique of aesthetic politics: to recognize that the threat of annihilation, while ever present, disappears under globalization's postfascist form.

AFTERWORD

The form of the beautiful often rests on violence. When translated from an evaluation of art into a description of democracy, the beautiful just as often implies a nightmarish will to realize political governance as a total work of art, a vision that in the eyes of many rather uncomfortably approximates agendas based on brutality, destruction, and fascism. An awareness that democracy contains many ugly episodes, like the realization that an aesthetic approach to political society courts the dangers of misrepresentation and violence, can provide a sort of masochistic pleasure. This satisfaction, akin to the comfort that the clichéd leftist finds in the pointless truism that "things must become worse before they get better," invokes beautiful democracy only to await its negative fulfillment.

The intrusion of aesthetic criteria into the political field is frequently met with alarm, anxiously read as a signature effect of fascism. But it is also worthwhile remembering that Benjamin begins the second version of his artwork essay by stressing that art and aesthetics, while nowadays "manipulated in the interests of fascism," remain viable in creating *Kunstpolitik*, that is, a politics of art primed for "the formulation of revolutionary demands."[1] This dual potentiality—or is it deep-seated ambivalence?—characterizes the conceptual complexity of aesthetics. If beautiful democracy is ever to be anything more than a negative invocation, its prospect depends on a historical understanding of aesthetics that recognizes the contradictions of the beautiful as a social, political, and philosophical discourse from its lessons about ethical virtue to its embellishment of urban crime, from its use in establishing a reactive national idiom to its promotion of translation and internationalism, from its global economic functions to its utopian universalism. Studied in universities but also associated with crowds and other popular elements, beauty transforms from context to context. This mutability thwarts purely abstract discussions of aesthetics and instead suggests that every theorization of art and every invocation of beauty depends on its social history and discursive situation.

Even though aesthetics aspire to a universal discourse, variability is always a problem and a possibility within perceptions of the beautiful whether we recognize it or not (most often we do not). Aesthetic qualities do not inhere in the object but in the feelings and imagination of the judging subject. Imaginations, we know, are hardly calculable, susceptible to a range of forces, from free play to suggestion to force itself. I want to stress this point about changeability, even unpredictability, because I think it complicates attitudes about the conjunction of aesthetics and politics. We regularly forget the subjective substratum of aesthetics by saying, as in the example that Kant provides, "Canary wine is pleasant" when the speaker really should say that canary wine "is pleasant *to me*." Translate this set of circumstances to the question posed at the very beginning of this book: how does democracy taste? Democracy is beautiful, we assert, never pausing to consider that its attractiveness is no more an inherent characteristic of the nation that calls itself democratic than is pleasant-ness an essential attribute of sweet-tasting wine. If universal agreement is a central component of aesthetic judgment, then, a beautiful democracy cannot rest on a form so limited as the nation-state, which is why this book encounters histories of foreignness, translation, and anarchy. But because rewriting and alteration are intrinsic to each of these configurations, the universal horizon in works of international socialism or at the movies can often seem wavering and mobile. It is no doubt the case that not everyone shares, for instance, Norris's image of world culture—a variation for which we should be thankful. Time and again, universal horizons are scaled back to particular economic renditions of the global that serve the interests of U.S. culture.

Kant reminds us that the pleasant and the beautiful are not the same and that it "would be laughable" for someone to proclaim, "This object (the house we see, the coat that person wears, the concert we hear, the poem submitted to our judgment, [or the political order we inhabit]) is beauti-ful *for me*."[2] The beautiful, unlike the pleasant, comes hardwired with a presumption of collectivity, namely, that since everyone agrees upon the beautiful it makes sense to speak of beauty as though it were an intrinsic attribute of this house, that coat, or our democracy. Granted, the impulse to claim this judgment on behalf of everyone stems from a collective desire to share our impression of the world, but it also can echo with compulsion, implicitly demanding that all others subscribe to this belief while blaming those who do not. If, however, we pause to consider that democracy's beauty is not a property of the state or nation but rather a subjective determination, we might then see political taste as a matter of discussion for various and competing collectivities, an ongoing project, a work-in-progress, anything but a foregone conclusion. As I have tried to show, democracy is less a formal governmental system than a cultural practice that involves the participation of people at all levels from the popular to the non-national, from Jane Addams's city street to the globe.

Even though a good deal of the aesthetic theory produced around the turn of the nineteenth century sought to establish an unchanging and formal system of judgment, revision and transformation well up everywhere in the archive of beauty. In the case of college professors' lecture notes and aesthetic textbooks, traces of this unsettledness appear as hastily penciled additions between the lines or in reader's comments at the margins. In one of his notebooks compiled while lecturing at Yale at the start of the twentieth century, Henry Davies conjoined "art" and "revolt." Uncomfortable with this formulation, Davies crossed out the passage, not to disavow it, but to rework it four pages later by stating that radical aesthetics, while perhaps wild and undisciplined, produced social effects that were "democratic and widespread."[3] In the case of a different college professor who in 1910 left his position at Atlanta University to take up work with the NAACP and *The Crisis,* Du Bois put a definitive spin on a phrase buried deep within the pages of Stowe's *We and Our Neighbors,* a book I used in the Introduction to evidence the social work attributed to beauty's influence. An unrequited lover in Stowe's novel describes the sweet anguish of never being able to forget his object of adoration as "a double consciousness" in which he imagines his beloved's absence as an abiding, almost spectral, presence. It is hard to imagine that such a book as Stowe's, one in which a "fanaticism of the beautiful" possesses domestic housekeepers who position their antimacassars just so in an effort to keep a gritty social world beyond the threshold, could make something unexpected from this white sentimental rendition of double consciousness.[4] Du Bois, as we know, transfigured this concept, investing it with an ontological vigor that resonates as forcefully as ever.

These small-scale reworkings, one to aesthetic theory from a century ago and the other to a "minor" novel by a major writer, are not insignificant. They remind us that beauty does not necessarily require a state of completion—or even a state. To describe democracy as beautiful, then, is to declare the priority of subjectivity in determining the shape and hue of the political world, no more so than when we describe it to others and redescribe it to ourselves. We hope that everyone else will like our description (we may even demand that accord) but we are also forced to admit that even universal judgment has its limits. When it comes to describing U.S. democracy as beautiful, these limits materialize most readily in the times and spaces where strikes, crowds, the popular, and other anarchies trouble the conceptual borders of the nation-state. The prospect of beautiful democracy need not result in negative imaginings if its promise is freed from the criteria and judgment of a particular nation-state.

NOTES

INTRODUCTION

1. Raymond Williams, *Marxism and Literature* (New York: Oxford University Press, 1977), 151. In terms similar to Williams's, Adorno states that aesthetics are "more than a rhapsodic back and forth between the two standpoints [with meaning as either intrinsic or external to the artwork] by developing their reciprocal mediation in the artwork itself" (*Aesthetic Theory*, trans. Robert Hullot-Kentor [Minneapolis: University of Minnesota Press, 1997], 350).

2. Michael Bérubé offers an insightful (and entertaining) account of the imagined standoff between cultural studies and aesthetics: it was "as if the House of Aesthetics had been wronged by the House of Cultural Studies and was now about to exact its measure of justice by serving Cultural Studies' children in the form of a pie" ("Introduction: Engaging the Aesthetic," in *The Aesthetics of Cultural Studies*, ed. Michael Bérubé [Malden, Mass.: Blackwell, 2005], 3). See also from the same volume Rita Felski, "The Role of Aesthetics in Cultural Studies."

3. Richard Shusterman, *Performing Live: Aesthetic Alternatives for the End of Art* (Ithaca: Cornell University Press, 2000), 24; Terry Eagleton, *The Ideology of the Aesthetic* (Oxford: Blackwell, 1990), 95.

4. Harriet Beecher Stowe, *We and Our Neighbors: Or, The Records of an Unfashionable Street (Sequel to "My Wife and I")* (New York: J. B. Ford, 1875), 52, 294.

5. Friedrich Schiller, *On the Aesthetic Education of Man in a Series of Letters*, trans. Reginald Snell (New Haven: Yale University Press, 1954), 68n.

6. Shusterman, *Performing Live*, 9.

7. Hannah Arendt, *Between Past and Future: Six Exercises in Political Thought* (Cleveland: World Publishing, 1963), 224. For more on the importance of aesthetics to Arendt's political theory, see her *Lectures on Kant's Political Philosophy* (Chicago: University of Chicago Press, 1982).

8. F. R. Ankersmit, *Aesthetic Politics: Political Philosophy Beyond Fact and Value* (Stanford: Stanford University Press, 1996), 16.

9.   Jane Addams, *The Spirit of Youth and the City Streets* (New York: Macmillan, 1909), 76–77.

10.   See, for instance, Giles Gunn, "The Pragmatics of the Aesthetic," in *Aesthetics in a Multicultural Age*, ed. Emory Elliot, Louis Freitas Caton, Jeffrey Rhyne (New York: Oxford University Press, 2002), 67. The American pragmatist John Dewey who, along with his student Kate Gordon, appears in several spots in this book, theorized the transformative aspect of aesthetics. See Gordon, "Pragmatism in Aesthetics," in *Essays Philosophical and Psychological in Honor of William James, by His Colleagues at Columbia University* (New York: Longmans, Green, and Co., 1908), 461–82.

11.   For more on Benjamin in this context, see Richard Wolin, *Walter Benjamin: An Aesthetic of Redemption* (New York: Columbia University Press, 1982), 159–61. Benjamin's and Adorno's respective reservations about a "beautiful" politics entail more nuance than can be examined here. For starters, see Lutz Koepnick, *Walter Benjamin and the Aesthetics of Power* (Lincoln: University of Nebraska Press, 1999) and Michael Rothberg, "After Adorno: Culture in the Wake of Catastrophe," *New German Critique* 72 (Fall 1997): 45–81.

12.   Walter Benjamin, "The Work of Art in the Age of Mechanical Reproduction," in *Illuminations: Essays and Reflections*, ed. Hannah Arendt (New York: Schocken, 1968), 241. Benjamin is quoting Filippo Marinetti on the Italo-Ethiopian War of 1935–36.

13.   "Attacks Called Great Art," *New York Times*, Sept. 19, 2001: E6.

14.   Marx approached the convergence of aesthetics and politics with considerable suspicion that "art forms" act as "self-deceptions" that allow citizens to take pleasure in lying to themselves about the state of political reality. But there's more to Marx than the belief that bourgeois art forms traduce democratic revolution. As chapter 2 shows by reading *The Eighteenth Brumaire* as an international product of the American Renaissance, Marx left open the possibility that aesthetics could be the wellspring of political newness (*The Eighteenth Brumaire of Louis Bonaparte* [New York: International Publishers, 1963], 16).

15.   See Charles Musser in collaboration with Carol Nelson, *High-Class Moving Pictures: Lyman H. Howe and the Forgotten Era of Traveling Exhibition, 1880–1920* (Princeton: Princeton University Press, 1991).

16.   Elizabeth Kemper Adams, *The Aesthetic Experience: Its Meaning in Functional Psychology* (Chicago: University of Chicago Press, 1907), 40, 46, 110. According to *Doctors of Philosophy June, 1893–April, 1931* (Chicago: University of Chicago Press, 1931), the dissertation was filed in 1904.

17.   Phyllis Ackerman, "Plato's Aesthetics" (M.A. thesis, University of California, Berkeley, 1915), 76, 79.

18.   Adams, *The Aesthetic Experience*, 52.

19.   William Davis Furry, "The Aesthetic Experience: Its Nature and Function in Epistemology," *The Psychological Review: The Johns Hopkins Studies in Philosophy and Psychology* 1 (1908): 154–55.

20.   James Hayden Tufts, "Beauty and the Beautiful," in James Mark Baldwin, *Diction-*

ary of philosophy and psychology, including many of the principal conceptions of ethics, logic, aesthetics, philosophy of religion, mental pathology, anthropology, biology, neurology, physiology, economics, political and social philosophy, philology, physical science and education, and giving a terminology in English, French, German and Italian. Written by many hands and edited by James Mark Baldwin with the co-operation and assistance of an international board of consulting editors (1901; rpt. Gloucester, Mass: Peter Smith, 1960), 104.

21. Henry Davies, *Art in Education and Life: A Plea for the More Systematic Culture of the Sense of Beauty* (Columbus, Ohio: R. G. Adams, 1914), ix–x. Davies taught at Yale from 1896 to 1904.

22. Fred N. Scott, "The Interpretation of Art," 5, 10. This syllabus is appended to the copy of his *Aesthetics: Its Problems and Literature* (Ann Arbor: Inland Press, 1890) that I consulted in the Northern Regional Library Facility of the University of California.

23. On connections between aesthetic judgment and liberalism, see David Cook, "The Last Days of Liberalism" in *Postmodernism: A Reader* (New York: Columbia University Press, 1993), 121–22.

24. Henry Davies, "Introduction to Philosophy," Box 1, folder 5, Henry Davies Papers, Yale University Divinity Library, Archives and Manuscripts, n.p.. To my dismay, I discovered that Davies's notes rely on Pitman shorthand abbreviations. It was slow going at first but after a while I was able to make sense of how his circles, dots, slashes, and apostrophes substitute for frequently used words. In most cases, I have rendered passages from Davies back into longhand. Needless to say, all transliterations are mine.

25. Davies, "Philosophical Aesthetics. Theory of Art. 1. Principles of Art," Box 3, folder 14, 35.

26. Davies, "Data of Aesthetics. Normative Aesthetics. Principles of Fine Art," Box 3, folder 16, 34.

27. Ibid., 35.

28. Furry, "The Aesthetic Experience," 123.

29. Arendt, *Lectures on Kant's Political Philosophy,* 27.

30. Immanuel Kant, *The Critique of Judgment,* trans. J. H. Bernard (New York: Hafner, 1951), 6.

31. John Crowe Ransom, "Forms and Citizens," in *The World's Body* (1938; rpt. Baton Rouge: Louisiana State University Press, 1968), 45.

32. See Elaine Scarry, *On Beauty and Being Just* (Princeton: Princeton University Press, 1999). Also suggestive is Virgil Nemoianu's claim that "aesthetic formalism would be a minimum of ruling necessary for the smooth functioning of a community" in light of his fuller argument that while right-wing regimes have been suspicious of aesthetics, antifascists and leftist humanists have sided with formalist projects that promote "plurality, skepticism, and the general freedom of existence" (Virgil Nemoianu, "Hating and Loving Aesthetic Formalism: Some Reasons," *MLQ* 61 [2000]: 54, 57). Leaving aside questions about the desirability for communities to function smoothly, we might still pause over the incommensurability of aesthetic

formalism and political practice. Aesthetic formalism may indeed encourage subjects to consider multiple perspectives, but does this attitude decelerate action?

33. "Art for the People," *Literary Digest* 10 (1894–95): 402.

34. Vachel Lindsay, *The Art of the Moving Picture* (1915; rpt., New York: Liveright, 1970), 261.

35. William James, "How Can Lynching Be Stopped," *Literary Digest* 27 (1903): 156.

36. George H. Calvert, *Essays Aesthetical* (Boston: Lee and Shepard, 1875), 262.

37. James C. Moffat, *An Introduction to the Study of Aesthetics* (Cincinnati: Moore, Wilstach, Keys, 1856), 10.

38. Susan Buck-Morss, "Aesthetics and Anaesthetics: Walter Benjamin's Artwork Essay Reconsidered," *October* 62 (1992): 5. Serving as a synonym for beauty, denoting the philosophy of art, and implying the range of human sensation, "the aesthetic" is hardly a fixed term. On account of this instability, I speak of aesthetics as opposed to "the aesthetic." As Noël Carroll cautions, critics and theorists often confuse aesthetics, reducing the philosophy of art to the more narrow terrain of beauty (*Beyond Aesthetics: Philosophical Essays* [Cambridge: Cambridge University Press, 2001], 20–41). Others claim aesthetics as an expansive field concerned not just with the study of beauty but with "the whole process of human perception and sensation—ideas about the body, imagination and feeling" (John J. Joughin and Simon Malpas, "The New Aestheticism: An Introduction," in *The New Aestheticism*, ed. John J. Joughin and Simon Malpas [Manchester: Manchester University Press, 2003], 11). Also see Steffen Gross, who takes the first use of "aesthetics" in Baumgarten's *Aesthetica* as a broad provocation in "the art of beautiful thinking" that would reconnect rational faculties and sensuous experience ("The Neglected Programme of Aesthetics," *British Journal of Aesthetics* 42 [October 2002]: 411). These definitions are crucial in attempts to employ the term with consistency and clarity. In the history of sociopolitical practice, however, those calling for aesthetics (or beauty or art) rarely pause to sort out these competing and overlapping senses.

39. Thomas Paine, *Common Sense and Other Political Writings* (Indianapolis: Bobbs-Merrill, 1953), 3, 51. Of course, Paine's more immediate reference is Scottish Common Sense philosophy. On connections between Scottish Common Sense and aesthetics, see Elizabeth Maddock Dillon, "Sentimental Aesthetics," *American Literature* 76 (September 2004): 495–523.

40. Walter Benjamin, "Theses on the Philosophy of History," in *Illuminations*, 264. Susan Gillman employs Benjamin's intervention into temporality to describe an "occult history" (*Blood Talk: American Race Melodrama and the Culture of the Occult* [Chicago: University of Chicago Press, 2003], 202).

41. Theodor Adorno, *Aesthetic Theory*, trans. Robert Hullot-Kentor (Minneapolis: University of Minnesota Press, 1997), 1

CHAPTER ONE

1. Elaine Scarry, *On Beauty and Being Just* (Princeton: Princeton University Press 1999), 123.

2. William Dean Howells, "The What and the How of Art," in *Literature and Life: The Man of Letters as a Man of Business* (New York: Harper, 1902), 286, 288.

3. Scarry, *On Beauty and Being Just*, 98. For a related discussion, see John Brenkman's argument that the subject's perception that "*this is beautiful*" is a corollary to the citizen's statement that "*this is unjust*": each declaration pivots on an awareness that other selves in public life have value and should be credited with "self-realizing citizenship" (John Brenkman, "Extreme Criticism," in *What's Left of Theory: New Work in the Politics of Literary Theory,* ed. Judith Butler, John Guillory, and Kendall Thomas [New York: Routledge, 2000], 133). Henk E. S. Woldring, arguing from a different intellectual tradition, states that "social justice is a work of art" ("Social Justice as a Work of Art in Action," in *Beauty, Art, and the Polis,* ed. Alice Ramos [Washington, D.C.: American Maritain Association, 2000], 298).

4. Jeanne M. Heffernan, "Art: A 'Political' Good?," in *Beauty, Art, and the Polis,* 267; Sean McCann, "The Ambiguous Politics of Politicizing, or De-Politicizing the Aesthetic," in *Poetics/Politics: Radical Aesthetics for the Classroom,* ed. Amitava Kumar (New York: St. Martins, 1999), 50; E. E. Sleinis, *Art and Freedom* (Urbana: University of Illinois Press, 2003), 2; James Solderholm, "Introduction," in *Beauty and the Critic: Aesthetics in an Age of Cultural Studies,* ed. James Solderholm (Tuscaloosa: University of Alabama Press, 1997), 11.

5. Scarry, *On Beauty and Being Just*, 114.

6. F. R. Ankersmit, *Aesthetic Politics: Political Philosophy Beyond Fact and Value* (Stanford: Stanford University Press, 1996), 56.

7. Terry Eagleton, *The Ideology of the Aesthetic* (Oxford: Blackwell, 1990), 9.

8. Tony Bennett, *Outside Literature* (London: Routledge, 1990), 148.

9. See "The Princeton Lecture Course," *New York Times,* January 13, 1888, 3 and "New Courses in Aesthetics," *New York Times,* January 18, 1891, 9.

10. Edwin Lee Norton, "The Concepts of Harmony and Organism in Ethics" (Ph.D. diss., Harvard University, 1900), 152. A laudatory note signed by Professors S. H. Palmer, Hugo Münsterberg, and George Santayana is attached to the inside cover of Norton's thesis. Münsterberg and Santayana make fuller appearances in later chapters of my book. Martha Banta discusses efforts to apply scientific principles to aesthetics ("Raw, Ripe, Rot: Nineteenth-Century Pathologies of the American Aesthetic," *ALH* 17 [2005]: 666–86).

11. See Roswell Parker Angier, "The Aesthetics of Unequal Division" (Ph.D. diss., Harvard University, 1903), 78.

12. Edgar Pierce, "The Aesthetics of Simple Forms" (Ph.D. diss., Harvard University, 1895), 1.

13. *Division of Philosophy, 1902–03* (Cambridge, Mass.: Harvard University, 1902), 5.

14. "Notes of Ballou for Philosophy 10" (Box 695, Harvard University Archives, 1899–1900).

15. J. W. Stearns, *Aesthetics: Syllabus of a Course of Six Lectures* (Madison: Tracy, Gibbs, 1895), 4.

16. *University of Wisconsin: University Extension, 1907–1908* (Madison: University of Wisconsin, 1907), 3.

17. William Angus Knight, *The Philosophy of the Beautiful, Being Outlines of the History of Aesthetics,* 2 vols. (New York: Charles Scribner's Sons, 1891), 1: n.p, 29. Reference to Great Britain indicates that aesthetic discourse was an Anglo-American phenomenon in which cultural heavyweights such as William Morris and Matthew Arnold influenced—and were influenced by—the supposedly more provincial currents of the U.S. Thus Morris played upon Abraham Lincoln's Gettysburg Address to imbue art with popular principles, calling for a mode of expression that would result in "an *art which is to be made by the people and for the people, as a happiness to the maker and the user*" ("The Art of the People," in *Hopes and Fears for Art* [Boston: Roberts Brothers, 1882], 66). Arnold's judgment was harsher. In an 1888 essay, he conceded that while the U.S. may enjoy all sorts of success in solving political and social problems, it remained deficient in addressing "the human problem" because of "a great void exists in the civilization over there; a want of what is elevated and beautiful, of what is interesting" ("Civilization in the United States," in *Civilization in the United States: First and Last Impressions of America* [Boston: DeWolfe, Fiske, 1900], 181).

18. Arthur Weiss, "Introduction to the Philosophy of Art," *University of California Publications in Modern Philology* 1 (January 1910): 296. Gayley was Weiss's advisor as well as co-editor of *Modern Philology* when Weiss's dissertation was published in its pages.

19. Charles Mills Gayley, "Lectures on the Aesthetics of Literature Delivered at the University of California, 1890–91" (ms. Bancroft Library, University of California, Berkeley), 9, 32. See Charles Mills Gayley and Fred Newton Scott, *An Introduction to the Methods and Materials of Literary Criticism: The Bases in Aesthetics and Poetics* (Boston: Ginn, [1899] 1901), 86–87.

20. Charles Mulford Robinson, "Improvement in City Life: Educational Progress," *Atlantic Monthly* 83 (1899): 664. The last article in the series is subtitled "Aesthetic Progress." A key figure in the City Beautiful movement, Robinson brought his ideas about civic planning and embellishment to cities across the U.S., including Denver, Dubuque, Ft. Wayne, Santa Barbara, Honolulu, and Pittsburgh. When he came West, the *Los Angeles Sunday Times* of December 1, 1907 went with a headline acclaiming how his "rare vision of city beautiful" would entail parks, wide boulevards, and an "artistic grouping of public buildings." He later held one of the first positions in urban planning as Professor of Civic Design at the University of Illinois. Robinson's career fits into what Paul Boyer calls "the positive environmentalism of the Progressive years" (*Urban Masses and Moral Order in America, 1820–1920* [Cambridge, Mass.: Harvard University Press, 1978], 235).

21. Charles Mulford Robinson, "Improvement in City Life: Aesthetic Progress," *Atlantic Monthly* 83 (1899): 784. Though I have been unable to find the exact translation that Robinson is using, he is most likely citing Pericles' funeral oration as given in Thucydides' *The Peloponnesian War.* The classical bent of the City Beautiful movement retains its currency in contemporary aesthetic theory. Richard Shusterman states: "With its integration of rich variety into the unity of a single *polis,* the city has always promoted aesthetic experience by fostering the creation of great art-

works and often constituting in itself an aesthetic masterpiece that all its citizens could in some way enjoy" (*Performing Live: Aesthetic Alternatives for the End of Art* [Ithaca: Cornell University Press, 2000], 9).

22. Robinson, "Improvement in City Life: Aesthetic Progress," 785. On the authority of the *Atlantic* in promoting such cultural prescriptions, see Nancy Glazener, *Reading for Realism: The History of a U.S. Literary Institution, 1850–1910* (Durham: Duke University Press, 1997), 5.

23. Michel Foucault, "An Aesthetics of Existence," *Politics, Philosophy, Culture: Interviews and Other Writings, 1977–1984*, ed. Lawrence D. Kritzman, trans. Alan Sheridan et al. (New York: Routledge, 1988), 47–53.

24. Thucydides, *The Peloponnesian War*, trans. Richard Crawley (New York: Random House, 1982), 107–8.

25. Jacob A. Riis, "The Tenement House Blight," *Atlantic Monthly* 83 (1899): 762.

26. Ibid., 761, 769.

27. Hannah Arendt, *The Human Condition* (Chicago: University of Chicago Press, 1958), 179.

28. William Dean Howells, "Wild Flowers of the Asphalt," in *Literature and Life*, 94.

29. Henry Rutgers Marshall, *Aesthetic Principles* (New York: Macmillan, 1895), 81.

30. Francis Sparshott, *The Future of Aesthetics: The 1996 Ryle Lectures* (Toronto: University of Toronto Press, 1998), 6, 83.

31. Marshall, *Aesthetic Principles*, 81.

32. Scarry, *On Beauty and Being Just*, 4.

33. Marshall, *Aesthetic Principles*, 55, 82, 178.

34. See Thorstein Veblen, "Kant's *Critique of Judgment*," *The Journal of Speculative Philosophy* 18 (July 1884): 260–74; Henry Davies Papers, Box 3, folder 14 (40).

35. Ethel Dench Puffer, *The Psychology of Beauty* (Boston: Houghton, Mifflin, 1905), 18.

36. Ibid., 6, 24–25.

37. Ethel Dench Puffer, "Criticism and Aesthetics," *Atlantic Monthly* 87 (1901): 843.

38. Grant Allen, *Physiological Aesthetics* (London: Henry S. King, 1877), viii, 29, 46. While biology may stress common natural instincts and traits, aesthetics as a physiological and evolutionary matter are decidedly uneven and hierarchical. "The purest and most cultivated of our contemporaries" exercise judgment and taste that "will at any rate be far truer and higher than that of the masses," writes Allen (48).

39. "Esthetic Nature of Thugs to be Subjected to Old Art," *New York Times*, April 24, 1927: 20.

40. George Lansing Raymond, *The Essentials of Aesthetics in Music, Poetry, Painting, Sculpture and Architecture* (New York: G. P. Putnam's Sons, 1906), 248.

41. Ellis Gray, "The Flower Mission," *Harper's New Monthly Magazine* 48 (May 1874): 791.

42. Jacob A. Riis, *How the Other Half Lives: Studies among the Tenements of New York* (New York: Charles Scribner's Sons, 1890; rpt. New York: Dover, 1971), 138.

43. Hugo Münsterberg, "Psychology and Art," *North American Review* 82 (1898): 635, 643.

44. Jacob A. Riis, "Light in Dark Places: A Study of the Better New York," *The Century: A Popular Quarterly* 53 (December 1896): 251.

45. Riis, *How the Other Half Lives*, 124–26.

46. See Helen Campbell, Thomas W. Knox, Thomas Byrnes, *Darkness and Daylight; or, Lights and Shadows of New York Life. A Pictorial Record of Personal Experiences by Day and Night in the Great Metropolis with Hundreds of Thrilling Anecdotes and Incidents, Sketches of Life and Character, Humorous Stories, Touching Home Scenes, and Tales of Tender Pathos, Drawn from the Bright and Shady Sides of the Great Under World of New York* (Hartford, Conn: Hartford Publishing Co., 1897), 313; Kate Gannett Wells, "Free Summer Pleasures for the People in Boston" *The New England Magazine* 12 (August 1892): 793.

47. Wells, "Free Summer Pleasures," 793.

48. Gray, "The Flower Mission," 791.

49. A Working Girl, "An Aesthetic Idea," *Harper's New Monthly Magazine* 67 (June 1883): 139. I have found another *Harper's* short story by "A Working Girl," which also subscribes to the regenerative force of beauty. In this tale, "a handful of arbutus, fragrant and fresh" given to a former felon inspire him with enough optimism to offer marriage and a home to a working girl (A Working Girl, "A New Cinderella," *Harper's New Monthly Magazine* 66 [April 1883]: 767).

50. Riis, "Light in Dark Places," 252.

51. Riis, *How the Other Half Lives*, 124.

52. Isobel Armstrong, *The Radical Aesthetic* (Oxford: Blackwell, 2000), 167.

53. Shusterman, *Performing Live*, 5.

54. Charles Loring Brace, *The Dangerous Classes of New York, and Twenty Years' Work among Them* (New York: Wynkoop & Hallenbeck, 1872), 331–32.

55. Immanuel Kant, *The Critique of Judgment*, trans. J. H. Bernard (New York: Hafner, 1951), 44.

56. Eagleton, *The Ideology of the Aesthetic*, 28.

57. Riis, *How the Other Half Lives*, 59. As Maren Stange argues, "the idea of photography as surveillance, the controlling gaze as a middle-class right and tool, is woven throughout Riis's lectures and writings" (*Symbols of Ideal Life: Social Documentary Photography in America, 1890–1950* [Cambridge: Cambridge University Press, 1989], 23). But see Keith Gandal, who credits Riis as an aesthetic innovator in slum representation (*The Virtues of the Vicious: Jacob Riis, Stephen Crane, and the Spectacle of the Slum* [New York: Oxford University Press, 1997], 65). Gandal claims Riis as a proponent of "a new ethics and a corresponding politics of self-esteem," a conclusion that somewhat obscures the social dimension of Riis's ethics (118). On portraits of the slum that Riis offered his middle-class auditors and readers, see Gregory S. Jackson, "Cultivating Spiritual Sight: Jacob Riis's Virtual-Tour Narrative and the Visual Modernization of Protestant Homiletics," *Representations* 83 (Summer 2003): 126–66. Jackson argues that Riis "intended to bridge the epistemological and geographical gaps that separated middle-class reformers from the individuals they sought to know and help" (134). I question whether Riis and other middle-class reformers were able to see "individuals" as opposed to masses of people that could be understood and managed through large categorizations based on class, race, and ethnicity. Through repeated and strategic use of foreground in photographs,

Riis's shots accentuate the distance between the viewer and subject. Such disagreements have enlivened my work on Riis, making this a good time to repeat my thanks to Greg.

58. Jacob A. Riis, *The Making of an American: A New Edition with an Epilogue by His Grandson, J. Riis Owre* (London: Macmillan, 1970), 173, 175.

59. Arthur Pember, *The Mysteries and Miseries of the Great Metropolis, with Some Adventures in the Country: Being the Disguises and Surprises of a New-York Journalist* (New York: D. Appleton and Company, 1874), 284–85, 290–94. Pember's often cheeky work deserves to be classed momentarily alongside Riis's more serious and sociologically minded analysis if only because his preface describes his sketches as efforts "investigating how the other half lives" (iii).

60. Riis, *The Making of an American*, 118–19.

61. Veblen, "Kant's *Critique of Judgment*," 268, 272.

62. Hjalmar Hjorth Boyeson, *Social Strugglers* (New York: Charles Scribner's Sons, 1893), 263–64. Boyeson deplored the use of art to shore up snobbishness. In "American Literary Criticism and Its Value," he prized literature, not for its effects on the rarefied circle of critics, but for "its influence upon the public" (Boyeson, "American Literary Criticism and Its Value," *Forum* 15 [1893]: 460).

63. Boyeson, *Social Strugglers*, 272 (my emphasis).

64. Boyeson, "American Literary Criticism and Its Value," 461.

65. Riis, *The Making of an American*, 119.

66. Ibid., 121.

67. Governor Lucius Robinson's proclamation is quoted in full by J. A. Daucus, *Annals of the Great Strike in the United States: A Reliable History and Graphic Description of the Causes and Thrilling Events of the Labor Strikes and Riots of 1877* (Chicago: L. T. Palmer, 1877), 162.

68. Riis, *The Making of an American*, 120. At the time of this incident in 1877, Riis was powerless to disavow his putative link to the strikers. Retelling this incident in 1901, he does not allow for a second misinterpretation as to where his loyalties ultimately lie: "It was the only time I have been suspected of sympathy with violence in the settlement of labor disputes" (*The Making of an American*, 121).

69. Ibid., 121.

70. Eagleton, *Ideology of the Aesthetic*, 13.

71. George Trumbull Ladd, *Introduction to Philosophy: An Inquiry after a Rational System of Scientific Principles in Their Relation to Ultimate Reality* (New York: Charles Scribner's Sons, 1890), 332.

72. Henry Noble Day, *The Science of Aesthetics; or, The Nature, Kinds, Laws and Uses of Beauty* (New Haven: Charles C. Chatfield, 1872), 25, 76.

73. Knight, *Philosophy of the Beautiful*, 2:29.

74. Gayley and Scott, *Introduction to the Methods and Materials of Literary Criticism*, 87.

75. John Dewey, *Art as Experience* (1934; New York: Capricorn Books, 1958), 107, 134, 345–46. Dewey's book is based on lectures he gave in 1931, but he had been thinking about aesthetics for several decades.

76. Riis, *The Making of an American*, 273.

77. "Beauty in Art," *New York Times*, June 24, 1905, BR 417.

78. Kate Gordon, *Esthetics* (New York: H. Holt, 1909), 304, 309. The status of Gordon's work as a textbook is confirmed in letters that Harvard faculty member, Herbert Sidney Langfeld, exchanged with Houghton Mifflin about a project to develop his own textbook on aesthetics. Included with these letters are Langfeld's handwritten notes providing chapter breakdowns and estimated word counts. At the bottom of one page, he identifies "Kate Gordon Esthetics" as his "competitor." See "Three Letters from Houghton Mifflin to Herbert Sidney Langfeld" (bMS Am 1925 [1046], Houghton Library, 1919; quoted by permission of the Houghton Library, Harvard University). Langfeld's *The Aesthetic Attitude* was published in 1920.

79. Gordon, *Esthetics*, 309.

80. Michel Foucault, "An Aesthetics of Existence," 49.

81. Michel Foucault, "On the Genealogy of Ethics: An Overview of Work in Progress," in *The Essential Works of Michel Foucault, 1954–1984*, 3 vols., ed. Paul Rabinow, trans. Robert Hurley (New York: The New Press, 1997), 1:260.

82. Michel Foucault, *The Care of the Self*, vol. 3 of *The History of Sexuality*, trans. Robert Hurley (New York: Pantheon, 1978), 53.

83. Ibid., 53. Ethics imply an aesthetic sort of activity "in which the work of oneself on oneself and connection with others were linked" (51).

84. Foucault, "On the Genealogy of Ethics," 267.

85. Ibid., 255, 261.

86. Thomas Augst, *The Clerk's Tale: Young Men and Moral Life in Nineteenth-Century America* (Chicago: University of Chicago Press, 2003), 34.

87. Campbell, Knox, and Byrnes, *Darkness and Daylight*, 173.

88. Gray, "The Flower Mission," 794.

89. William Dean Howells, *The Minister's Charge or The Apprenticeship of Lemuel Barker*, in *Novels, 1886–1888: The Ministers Charge; April Hopes; Annie Kilburn* (New York: Library of America, 1989), 21.

90. Ernest Nusse, "The Protection of Children," *The Bay State Monthly* 2 (November 1884): 92.

91. Riis, *The Battle with the Slum* (1902; rpt., Montclair, N.J.: Patterson Smith, 1969), 231. In this context, see reporting on "what may be called the aesthetics of crime" ("Artistic Crime," *New York Times*, April 8, 1873: 4).

92. Riis, *The Battle with the Slum*, 157. A tintype or ferrotype is a positive photograph produced on a dark background of, respectively, tin or iron.

93. Riis, *How the Other Half Lives*, 174.

CHAPTER TWO

1. See the courses taught by George Howison in *Annual Announcement of Courses of Instruction in the Colleges at Berkeley for the Academic Year 1896–97* (Berkeley: University of California, 1896), 4.

2. Henry Davies, "Data of Aesthetics. Psychological Data (Experimental Introspective)," Box 3, folder 17 (34).

3.   William Dean Howells, "Criticism and Fiction," in *Criticism and Fiction and Other Essays* (New York: New York University Press, 1959), 38.

4.   Ibid., 66–67. It is useful to remember, as Marc Redfield does, that the Hyde Park riots along with Arnold's longstanding opposition to "working-class agitation for an extension of the franchise" motivate *Culture and Anarchy* (*The Politics of Aesthetics: Nationalism, Gender, Romanticism* [Stanford: Stanford University Press, 2003], 13). Whitman and Twain were much more barbed in their rejection of Arnold; see John Henry Raleigh, *Matthew Arnold and American Culture* (Berkeley and Los Angeles: University of California Press, 1957), 58–66.

5.   Amy Kaplan, *The Social Construction of American Realism* (Chicago: University of Chicago Press, 1988), 21. See also Kenneth Warren on Howells's "aestheticization of the everyday" (*Black and White Strangers: Race and American Literary Realism* [Chicago: University of Chicago Press, 1993], 49).

6.   James H. Tufts, *On the Genesis of the Aesthetic Categories* (Chicago: University of Chicago Press, 1902), 3, 9. *Curricular of Information: The Departments of Art, Literature, and Science* (Chicago: University of Chicago, 1902), 18.

7.   William Dean Howells, "Editor's Study" (September 1886), reprinted in William Dean Howells, *Editor's Study*, ed. James W. Simpson (Troy, N.Y.: Whitson, 1983), 40–41.

8.   Gore Vidal, *At Home: Essays 1982–1988* (New York: Random House, 1988), 164. The most comprehensive account of the effect that Howells's remarks had on his reputation and subsequent creative process comes from John W. Crowley, "The Unsmiling Aspects of Life: *A Hazard Of New Fortunes*," in *Biographies of Books: The Compositional Histories of Notable American Writings*, ed. James Barbour and Tom Quirk (Columbia: University of Missouri Press, 1996).

9.   Johann Most, *Science of Revolutionary Warfare* (1885; rpt., El Dorado, Ariz: Desert Publications, 1978), 1, 12, 14, 20, 39. The price of 10 cents a copy made *Science of Revolutionary Warfare* popularly affordable and, as Paul Avrich reports, it "gained a wide circulation during the months preceding the Haymarket incident. . . . It was sold at picnics and meetings. . . . Its contents were serialized in the anarchist press" (*The Haymarket Tragedy* [Princeton: Princeton University Press, 1984], 165). The gravity of the threat posed by Most's manual was made clear by the prosecution's case against the accused Haymarket anarchists. "People's Exhibit 62" consists of a page from *Science of Revolutionary Warfare* detailing how firebombs can be made from ordinary fruit jars; see "Illinois vs. August Spies et al. trial evidence book" at www.chicagohistory.org/hadc/transcripts/exhibits/X051-100/X0620.htm (accessed July 22, 2004).

10.   Johann Most, "The Beast of Property" ca. 1884, atwww.eclipse.net/~basket42/ beast.html (accessed July 13, 2006). Describing the Commune that would emerge after the annihilation not just of capitalism but also of capitalists, Most stipulated that "theaters and concert halls will offer free seats to all."

11.   Dick Hebdige, *Subculture: The Meaning of Style* (1979; rpt., London: Routledge, 1991), 107, 110.

12. Howells, "Editor's Study," 41. For Howells's erasure of Most, compare this passage of his "Editor's Study" with *Criticism and Fiction* (62).

13. Terry Eagleton, *The Ideology of the Aesthetic* (Oxford: Blackwell, 1990), 28.

14. James Hayden Tufts, *On the Genesis of the Aesthetic Categories* (Chicago: University of Chicago Press, 1902), 3 (from the copy at Joseph Regenstein Library at the University of Chicago).

15. Henry Davies, "Notes on Art," Box 4, folder 20 (24), Henry Davies Papers, Yale University Divinity Library.

16. Walter Benjamin, "The Task of the Translator," in *Illuminations: Essays and Reflections,* ed. Hannah Arendt (New York: Schocken, 1968), 73.

17. Benjamin, "Translation: For and Against," in *Walter Benjamin: Selected Writings, 1935–1938,* ed. Michael W. Jennings (Cambridge, Mass.: Harvard University Press, 2002), 3:249–50.

18. "German Socialism in America," *North American Review* 128 (April 1879): 374.

19. Karl Marx, "Inaugural Address of the International Working Men's Association," in *Inaugural Address and Provisional Rules of the International Working Men's Association, along with the "General Rules"* published in London in 1864 and available at www.marxists.org/archive/marx/works/1864/10/27.htm (accessed August 10, 2004).

20. Benjamin, "The Task of the Translator," 76, 78. Colleen Glenney Boggs connects "transnational" and "translational" in the work of Margaret Fuller ("Margaret Fuller's American Translation," *American Literature* 76 [March 2004]: 33).

21. Howells quoted in Paul Avrich, *The Haymarket Tragedy* (Princeton: Princeton University Press, 1984), 340. See also John W. Crowely, "The Unsmiling Aspects of Life: *A Hazard Of New Fortunes,*" in *Biographies of Books: The Compositional Histories of Notable American Writings,* ed. James Barbour and Tom Quirk (Columbia: University of Missouri Press 1996), 82.

22. Undated letter from Eleanor Marx-Aveling is reproduced in Sender Garlin, *William Dean Howells and the Haymarket Era* (New York: American Institute for Marxist Studies, 1979), 38–39.

23. Jenny Marx to Weydemeyer, February 27, 1852, in Karl Marx and Frederick Engels, *Letters to Americans, 1848–1895: A Selection,* ed. Alexander Trachtenberg (New York: International Publishers, 1953), 43. Trachtenberg states that Weydemeyer "may be considered the first American Marxist leader" ("Editor's Preface," 3).

24. Wai Chee Dimock, "A Theory of Resonance," *PMLA* 112 (1997): 1060–71.

25. Terrell Carver, "Imagery/Writing, Imagination/Politics: Reading Marx through the *Eighteenth Brumaire,*" in *Marx's "Eighteenth Brumaire": Post(modern) Interpretations,* ed. Mark Cowling and James Martin (London: Pluto Press, 2002), 118, 119.

26. Karl Marx, *The Eighteenth Brumaire of Louis Bonaparte* (New York: International Publishers, 1963), 15, 76.

27. Jacques Derrida, *Specters of Marx: The State of the Debt, the Work of Mourning, and the New International,* trans. Peggy Kamuf (New York: Routledge, 1994), 10.

28. Marx, *Eighteenth Brumaire,* 15–16.

29. Benjamin, "The Task of the Translator," 71.

30. Karl Marx, *Der achtzehnte Brumaire des Louis Bonaparte,* http://www.marxists.org/

deutsch/archiv/marx-engels/1852/brumaire/kapitel1.htm (accessed August 12, 2004).

31. Marx, *Eighteenth Brumaire*, 15.

32. Thomas M. Kemple, *Reading Marx Writing: Melodrama, the Market, and the "Grundisse"* (Stanford: Stanford University Press, 1995), 7.

33. Carver, "Imagery/Writing," 122.

34. Peter Bellis, *Writing Revolution: Aesthetics and Politics in Hawthorne, Whitman, and Thoreau* (Athens: University of Georgia Press, 2003), 3.

35. Robert William Chambers, *The Red Republic: A Romance of the Commune*, 5th ed. (1895; rpt., New York: G. P. Putnam's Sons, 1898), 170. Larry J. Reynolds (*European Revolutions and the American Literary Renaissance* [New Haven: Yale University Press, 1988]) and Philip M. Katz (*From Appomattox to Montmartre: Americans and the Paris Commune* [Cambridge, Mass.: Harvard University Press, 1998]) examine connections between U.S. culture and French revolutionary activity of 1848 and 1871.

36. Marx, "Address of the International Workingmen's Association to Abraham Lincoln" (January 7, 1865), in *Letters to Americans*, 66.

37. See Avrich, *The Haymarket Tragedy*, 160.

38. Marx, *Eighteenth Brumaire*, 121; Margreta de Grazia, "Teleology, Delay, and the 'Old Mole,'" *Shakespeare Quarterly* 50 (Autumn 1999): 251–52. The citation from *Hamlet* is to 1.5.162.

39. "All of this can be thought," writes Derrida, "only in a dis-located time of the present, at the joining of a radically dis-jointed time" (*Specters of Marx*, 17). The "this" seems to indicate the entirety of possibility, an openness to ideas that do not belong together, ideas that exist nowhere in the present but instead are possible only in "the radical experience of the *perhaps*" (35).

40. Ralph Waldo Emerson, "The American Scholar," in *Essays and Lectures* (New York: Library of America, 1983), 68–69.

41. J. A. Daucus, *Annals of the Great Strike in the United States: A Reliable History and Graphic Description of the Causes and Thrilling Events of the Labor Strikes and Riots of 1877* (Chicago: L. T. Palmer, 1877), 82–83. Benedict Anderson's work on José Rizal suggests the reach of the International as global, spreading across Europe, the Americas, and Asia ("In the World-Shadow of Bismarck and Nobel: José Rizal: Paris, Havana, Barcelona, Berlin—2," *New Left Review* 28 [July/August 2004]: 85–129).

42. Karl Marx, *The Civil War in France*, in *The Marx-Engels Reader*, ed. Robert C. Tucker (New York: Norton, 1972), 560, 573.

43. Marx, "Inaugural Address of the International Working Men's Association."

44. Alan Pinkerton, *Strikers, Communists, Tramps, and Detectives* (New York: G. W. Carleton, 1878), 396–97.

45. Daucus, *Annals of the Great Strike*, 89–90. The condemned Haymarket martyrs reportedly sang the Marseillaise from their jail cells (Kristin Boudreau, "Elegies for the Haymarket Anarchists," *American Literature* 77 [June 2005]: 333). On the *pétroleuses* and U.S. class and gender conflicts, see chapter 1 of David A. Zimmer-

man, *Panic! Markets, Crises, and Crowds in American Fiction* (Chapel Hill: University of North Carolina Press, 2006).

46. Robert V. Bruce, *1877: Year of Violence* (Indianapolis: Bobbs-Merrill, 1959). Even as this violence was attributed to foreign influences, the number of U.S. workers killed in labor disputes was a dubious domestic accomplishment. "Between 1872 and 1914, according to one count, seven workers were killed in labour disputes in Britain, 16 were killed in Germany, and 35 were killed in France. Yet at least 500 to 800 were killed in the United States" (Daniel Lazare, "America the Undemocratic," *New Left Review* 232 [November/December 1998]: 3–40).

47. Pinkerton, *Strikers, Communists, Tramps, and Detectives*, 86.

48. Joseba Zulaika and William A. Douglass, *Terror and Taboo: The Follies, Fables, and Faces of Terrorism* (New York: Routledge, 1996), 31.

49. Pinkerton, *Strikers, Communists, Tramps, and Detectives*, 81, 88, 229.

50. Howard Lay, "'Beau Geste!' (On the Readability of Terrorism)," *Yale French Studies* 101 (2001): 80.

51. Jeffory Clymer, *America's Culture of Terrorism: Violence, Capitalism, and the Written Word* (Chapel Hill: University of North Carolina Press, 2003), 62.

52. Zulaika and Doulgass, *Terror and Taboo*, 31.

53. Daucus, *Annals of the Great Strike*, 17. Daucus labels adherents of the American Commune "socialist disorganizers" (90).

54. Archibald Forbes, "What I Saw of the Paris Commune. II," *Century Magazine* 45 (November 1892): 52.

55. "What an American Girl Saw of the Commune," *Century Magazine* 45 (November 1892): 63.

56. Quoted in Bruce, *1877: Year of Violence*, 90.

57. "Four years after the Great Strike raised the possibility of violent upheaval, 130,000 workers were involved in 477 work stoppages. In 1886 there were 1,572 strikes or walkouts involving 610,000. . . . Only once in the remainder of the century did the number of strikes fall below 1,000" (Daniel Borus, *Writing Realism: Howells, James, and Norris in the Mass Market* [Chapel Hill: University of North Carolina Press, 1989], 153). Paul Gilje sums up the situation vividly: "To list all labor riots would be almost impossible; it would entail cataloguing every cracked head found along countless miles of picket lines" (*Rioting in America* [Bloomington: Indiana University Press, 1996], 117).

58. James Livingston, *Pragmatism and the Political Economy of Cultural Revolution, 1850–1940* (Chapel Hill: University of North Carolina Press, 1994), 46.

59. Walter Crane, "Why Socialism Appeals to Artists," *Atlantic Monthly* 69 (January 1892): 110.

60. Walt Whitman, *Democratic Vistas*, in *Complete Poetry and Collected Prose* (New York: Library of America, 1982), 933, 961. Whitman's references to his service as a wartime nurse in the makeshift hospital at the Washington Patent Office serve as a visceral reminder that the polity has not fully healed.

61. Betsy Erkkilä, *Whitman the Political Poet* (New York: Oxford University Press, 1989), 82.

62. Whitman, *Democratic Vistas*, 960, 963.

63. George Santayana, *The Sense of Beauty: Being the Outlines of Aesthetic Theory* (1896; Cambridge, Mass: MIT Press, 1988), 73.

64. Walt Whitman, *Leaves of Grass*, in *Complete Poetry and Collected Prose*, 73, 121.

65. Santayana, *Sense of Beauty*, 72.

66. "President Bush's Proclamation for National Arts and Humanities Month 2001," October 25, 2001, http://www.collegeart.org/advocacy/000068 (accessed November 5, 2006). I would like to thank Cathy Davidson for bringing Bush's remarks to my attention.

67. "President Bush's Proclamation."

68. Letter from Marx to Sorge, October 19, 1877, in *The American Journalism of Marx and Engels: A Selection from the New York Daily Tribune* (New York: New American Library, 1966), 117. On the Pennsylvania strike as an emanation of the Commune, see Katz, *From Appomattox to Montmartre*, 166.

69. Brace, *The Dangerous Classes*, 27, 29. Foreignness was common: "By 1900, 60% of the residents of the nation's 12 largest urban centers were either foreign-born or of foreign parentage, and in many cities—Saint Louis, Cleveland, Detroit, Milwaukee, Chicago, New York—the figure approached and sometimes exceeded 80%" (Paul Boyer, *Urban Masses and Moral Order in America, 1820–1920* [Cambridge, Mass.: Harvard University Press, 1978], 123–24). Katz discusses plans to repatriate French Communards to the U.S. (*From Appomattox*, 131).

70. Jane Addams, *Twenty Years at Hull-House with Autobiographical Notes* (New York: Signet, 1961), 284. Addams is here explaining the purpose behind a Shakespeare Club at the settlement house, which also served as a venue for art exhibitions, musical concerts, dancing lessons, magic lantern shows, and motion pictures.

71. J. S. McClelland, *The Crowd and the Mob: From Plato to Canetti* (London: Unwin Hyman, 1989), 155.

72. Gustave Le Bon, *The Crowd: A Study of the Popular Mind* (New Jersey: Transaction, 1995), 37, 77.

73. G. T. W. Patrick, "The Psychology of Crazes," *Popular Science Monthly* 57 (1900): 285, 287, 292–93.

74. Charles H. Cooley, *Social Organization: A Study of the Larger Mind* (1909), in *Two Major Works of Charles H. Cooley: "Social Organization" and "Human Nature and the Social Order"* (Glencoe, Ill.: The Free Press, 1962), 153. Like the books on aesthetics that I examine, *Social Organization* was, according to Cooley, "rather widely used as a text-book" (421) and he developed "study questions" for each chapter.

75. Le Bon, *The Crowd*, 27, 61, 77.

76. Immanuel Kant, *The Critique of Judgment*, trans. J. H. Bernard (New York: Hafner, 1951), 37.

77. Part III of Cooley's *Social Organization* is entitled "the democratic mind."

78. Michael Warner, "The Mass Public and the Mass Subject," in *The Phantom Public Sphere*, ed. Bruce Robbins (Minneapolis: University of Minnesota Press, 1993), 251.

79. Kant, *Critique of Judgment*, 74.

80. Le Bon, *The Crowd,* 83 (my emphasis), 89.

81. Robert E. Park, *The Crowd and the Public and Other Essays,* trans. Charlotte Elsner (Chicago: University of Chicago Press, 1972), 16, 22, 47, 81. Mary Esteve also discusses this era of crowds and public unrest, but her argument proceeds by disentangling the political from the aesthetic in scenes of mass subjectivity. See *The Aesthetics and Politics of the Crowd in American Literature* (Cambridge: Cambridge University Press, 2003).

82. Gerald Stanley Lee, *Crowds: A Moving Picture of Democracy* (New York: Garden City, 1913) 30, 32, 271, 337–38, 533. On Lee's commercial success and popularity, see Gregory W. Bush, *Lord of Attention: Gerald Stanley and the Crowd Metaphor in Industrializing America* (Amherst: University of Massachusetts Press, 1991).

83. Gerald Stanley Lee, "Making the Crowd Beautiful," *Atlantic Monthly* 87 (February 1901): 245.

84. Lee, *Crowds,* 337–38, 551, 553. Lee considers labor stoppages as a vehicle for change, calling strikes "an invention for making crowds think," but ultimately, in his opinion, such actions are hijacked by socialist schemers advocating class warfare (*Crowds,* 49).

85. Lee, "Making the Crowd Beautiful," 249.

86. Howells, *Criticism and Fiction,* 87.

87. Lee, *Crowds,* 271.

88. Quoted in Timothy Parrish, "Haymarket and *Hazard:* The Lonely Politics of William Dean Howells," *Journal of American Culture* 17 (Winter 1994): 29. Parrish describes Howells inadvertent complicity with Most (26).

89. William Dean Howells, *A Hazard of New Fortunes* (New York: Penguin, 2001), 64. All further references are to this edition and are cited parenthetically. *Hazard* was serialized in *Harper's Weekly* from March 23 to November 16, 1889, published in Scotland in 1889, and produced as a book for the U.S. market in 1890. For a discussion of the novel's magazine run, see Gib Prettyman, "The Serial Illustrations of *A Hazard of New Fortunes,*" *Resources for American Literary Study* 27 (2001): 179–95. On connections of *Hazard* to "the internationalist hum of the aesthetic arts movement," particularly in its use of and allusions to risqué illustration, see Brad Evans, "Howellsian Chic: The Local Color of Cosmpolitanism," *ELH* 71 (2004): 801.

90. Kaplan, *Social Construction of American Realism,* 59. Cynthia Stretch discusses the importance of the streetcar strike to Howells's novel in "Illusions of a Public, Locations of Conflict: Feeling Like Populace in William Dean Howells's *A Hazard of New Fortunes,*" *American Literary Realism* 35 (Spring 2003): 233–46.

91. Clymer, *America's Culture of Terrorism,* 58.

92. Miles Orvell states that the novel allows Howells to "affirm his radicalism, and also to deny it, containing it safely within the margins of bourgeois tolerance" (*The Real Thing: Imitation and Authenticity in American Culture, 1880–1940* [Chapel Hill: University of North Carolina Press, 1989], 112). See also Crowley, who concludes that "Howells's 'socialism' became a relatively innocuous 'altruism': not political but educational" ("The Unsmiling Aspects of Life," 90).

93. UrbanDictionary.com confirms the comments of students in English 629 (Fall 2004) by defining "the shit" as "Something that kicks ass. Not to be confused with *shit*, which is something that sucks ass. . . . When the word 'the' is taken away, it has a completely opposite meaning" (http://www.urbandictionary.com/define. php?term=the+shit&r=f, accessed January 20, 2005).

94. Boggs, "Margaret Fuller's American Translation," 46. March's fear of translation impacts his triangular relationship with Lindau and Dryfoos, the capitalist who backs his magazine venture. At a celebratory dinner, Lindau speaks German to denounce Dryfoos as a "traitor and a tyrant," thinking that Dryfoos will not understand. Because Dryfoos spoke German as a boy, he is spared none of Lindau's attack. March apologizes, "I didn't know that you understood Lindau's German, or I shouldn't have allowed him—he wouldn't have allowed himself—to go on" (405). Between the hypothetical combination of March's censorship and Lindau's self-censorship, the critique of capital never would have been translated into everyday speech. Brook Thomas registers the irony of this scene, showing how Howells's belief that translation leads to "communicative harmony" is undone by "Dryfoos's successful translation [which] increases conflict" (*American Literary Realism and the Failed Promise of Contract* [Berkeley and Los Angeles: University of California Press, 1997], 285). In contexts of internationalism and anarchy, is "communicative harmony" even desirable? Such harmony might very well depend on the mutual intelligibility of the old and the new in ways that constrain the new, sapping it of its conflictual force.

95. See Thomas, *American Literary Realism and the Failed Promise of Contract,* 279–83.

CHAPTER THREE

1. *The Crisis: A Record of the Darker Races* 7 (February 1914): 163.

2. Ibid.

3. Wilson Jeremiah Moses, *The Golden Age of Black Nationalism, 1850–1925* (Hamden, Conn.: Archon Books, 1978), 11.

4. William Stanley Braithwaite, "The Negro in Literature," *The Crisis* 28 (September 1924): 207.

5. Claude McKay to W. E. B. Du Bois, June 18, 1928 in *The Correspondence of W. E. B. Du Bois,* ed. Herbert Aptheker (Amherst: University of Massachusetts Press, 1973), 1:375.

6. Darwin T. Turner, "W. E. B. Du Bois and the Theory of a Black Aesthetic," in *The Harlem Renaissance Re-examined: A Revised and Expanded Edition,* ed. Victor A. Kramer and Robert A. Russ (Troy, N.Y.: Whitson Publishing, 1997), 53.

7. W. E. B Du Bois, "Criteria of Negro Art," in *The Norton Anthology of African American Literature,* ed. Henry Louis Gates Jr and Nellie Y. McKay (New York: Norton, 1997), 757.

8. Nathan Irvin Huggins, *Harlem Renaissance* (New York: Oxford University Press, 1971), 196.

9. James Weldon Johnson, *The Autobiography of an Ex-Colored Man,* in *Three Negro Classics* (New York: Avon, 1965), 472, 474.

10. Elizabeth Maddock Dillon, "Fear of Formalism: Kant, Twain, and Cultural Studies in American Literature," *Diacritics* 27 (1998): 67.

11. David Levering Lewis, *W. E. B. Du Bois: Biography of a Race, 1868–1919* (New York: Henry Holt, 1993), 410.

12. Thus Kant: "A negro must necessarily (under these empirical conditions) have a different normal idea of the beauty of forms from what a white man has, and the Chinaman one different from the European" (*The Critique of Judgment*, trans. J. H. Bernard [New York: Hafner, 1951], 78). In fairness to Kant, it must be noted that he wants to bracket such "empirical conditions" so as to leave open the possibility of another realm, a nonverifiable reality, in which there would be no differences in beauty created by race. Earlier, Edmund Burke in detailing the sublime provided the following anecdote about a boy whose sight had been restored: "The first time the boy saw a black object, it gave him great uneasiness; and that some time after, upon accidentally seeing a negro woman, he was struck with great horror at the sight" (Edmund Burke, *A Philosophical Enquiry into the Origin of our Ideas of the Sublime and the Beautiful* [London: Routledge and Kegan Paul, 1958], 144). Academics in the U.S. tended to accept these distinctions by correlating beauty and anthropologically inflected ideas about "race." Dewey, as we will see below, offers an important exception.

13. Lewis, *W. E. B. Du Bois: Biography of a Race*, 424. On the publication history of *The Crisis*, see the fine research of Anne Carroll, "Protest and Affirmation: Composite Texts in the *Crisis*," *American Literature* 76 (2004): 89–116.

14. See Lewis, *W. E. B. Du Bois*, 413–16.

15. *The Crisis* 7 (February 1914): 163–64, 170.

16. William Morris, *Hopes and Fears for Art* (Boston: Roberts Brothers, 1882), 9.

17. John Ruskin, "The Lamp of Beauty," in *The Seven Lamps of Architecture* (1849; rpt., London: J. M. Dent and Sons, 1907), 124.

18. Johnson, *Autobiography of an Ex-Colored Man*, 510.

19. Huggins, *Harlem Renaissance*, 199.

20. Du Bois, "Criteria of Negro Art," 752 (emphasis added).

21. Arnold Rampersad, *The Art and Imagination of W. E. B. Du Bois* (Cambridge, Mass.: Harvard University Press, 1976), 188. Commentators have noted the imperiousness to the parameters Du Bois proposed in "Criteria of Negro Art." According Turner, the essay "reflected his assumption that his standards were the standard for all blacks—at least for all cultivated blacks" ("W. E. B. Du Bois and the Theory of a Black Aesthetic," 53).

22. See Du Bois writing with Alain Locke in 1924, critiquing Toomer's "apparently undue striving for effect" ("The Younger Literary Movement," in *The Crisis Reader*, ed. Sandra Kathryn Wilson [New York: Modern Library, 1999], 289).

23. Arnold Rampersad, "Foreword" to W. E. B. Du Bois, *The Quest of the Silver Fleece* (1911; Boston: Northeastern University Press, 1989), 5; *Art and Imagination*, 126.

24. Adolph L. Reed Jr, *W.E.B. Du Bois and American Political Thought: Fabianism and the Color Line* (New York: Oxford University Press, 1997), 130, 150, 177.

25. Carroll, "Protest and Affirmation," 89.

26. Kant, *Critique of Judgment,* 47.

27. Hannah Arendt, *Between Past and Future: Six Exercises in Political Thought* (Cleveland: World Publishing, 1963), 221.

28. Du Bois, "Criteria," 759.

29. Henry Rutgers Marshall, *Aesthetic Principles* (New York: Macmillan, 1895), 45. This view percolated down to mass-market publications. Thus *The Literary Digest* pointed out that what is "esthetically lovely" varies by climate and race ("Different Types of Beauty," *Literary Digest* 13 [1896]: 124).

30. William Angus Knight, *The Philosophy of the Beautiful, Being Outlines of the History of Aesthetics,* 2 vols. (New York: Charles Scribner's Sons, 1895), 2:2, 7, 35.

31. Kobena Mercer, "Looking for Trouble," *Transition* 51 (1991): 191–92.

32. Stewart E. Tolnay and E. M. Beck, *A Festival of Violence: An Analysis of Southern Lynchings, 1882–1930* (Urbana: University of Illinois Press, 1995), ix. Exact numbers are hard to come by when tabulating the victims of lynching. As Robert Zangrando writes, "tables include only recorded lynchings, and one can merely guess how widespread the phenomenon actually was" (*The NAACP Crusade Against Lynching, 1909–1950* [Philadelphia: Temple University Press, 1980], 4). Not all lynchings were public exhibitions replete with photographers, reporters, banner headlines in the press "advertising" the event, and hundreds to thousands of spectators brought to town by specially run trains. As activists such as Ida B. Wells-Barnett and organizations such as the NAACP pushed for antilynching legislation, terror against blacks may have become less public. Statistics may also fail to take into account those who died at the hands of mobs during race riots in cities such as Wilmington, East St. Louis, and Atlanta. In determining the number of victims, it is therefore difficult to find agreement in the historical record: "Estimates made by the NAACP and by anti-lynching activists such as James Elbert Cutler and Ida B. Wells suggest that the number of black victims ranged from 3,337 to 10,000" (Sandra Gunning, *Race, Rape, and Lynching: The Red Record of American Literature, 1890–1912* [New York: Oxford University Press, 1996], 5). Finally, how far back do historians look when amassing figures about lynching? Philip Dray makes this question a troubling one by conjecturing that "lynchings may well have been a common feature of Southern life during Reconstruction, even though historians have traditionally (and understandably) 'started the clock' on the practice in the early 1880s, when it became a recorded public phenomenon" (*At the Hands of Persons Unknown: The Lynching of Black America* [New York: Random House, 2002], 48).

33. Du Bois, "Criteria," 754.

34. Walter Benjamin, "The Work of Art in the Age of Mechanical Reproduction," in *Illuminations: Essays and Reflections,* ed. Hannah Arendt (New York: Schocken, 1968), 242.

35. Du Bois, "Criteria," 755.

36. Ibid., 752.

37. See, for instance, Dray, *At the Hands of Persons Unknown*, xii, 77, and Tolnay and Beck, *Festival of Violence*.

38. James K. Allen, *Without Sanctuary: Lynching Photography in America* (Santa Fe, N.Mex.: Twin Palms, 2000). The allusion to *nature morte* is found at a website featuring a photographic montage and voice narration by Allen, http://www.journale .com/withoutsanctuary/main.html (accessed February 7, 2003). The danger that examination of lynching as aesthetic practice will do violence to historical memory is exemplified in one reader's online review of *Without Sanctuary*: "If you are a collector of early photos, and you also collect books on early photo collections, this book is a must as an extremely important part of your collection. It contains several pages of readable text on some noted lynching events in small but sufficient enough detail, descriptions of plates and their photo types in the back, and what other early historical photo collection book are you going such a wealth of this type of portrait? [*sic*]" (http://www.amazon.com/exec/obidos/tg/detail/-/0944092691/ ref=lib_rd_btb/103-4684391-2536604?v=glance&s=books#product-details, accessed February 7, 2003).

39. Michael Hatt, "Race, Ritual, and Responsibility: Performativity and the Southern Lynching," in *Performing the Body/Performing the Text*, ed. Amelia Jones and Andrew Stephenson (London: Routledge, 1999), 81.

40. Dray, *At the Hands of Persons Unknown*, 4, 77 (emphasis added).

41. Johnson, *Autobiography of an Ex-Colored Man*, 497. Such compulsion—that is, the experience of having to look—seems thoroughly aesthetic. Consider the similarities between Johnson's description and Satya P. Mohanty's account of aesthetic experience: "Cathedrals and temples, sunsets and deserts, even horrific spectacles that we cannot tear our eyes away from, all have formed the bases for social cohesion" ("Can Our Values Be Objective? On Ethics, Aesthetics, and Progressive Politics," in *Aesthetics in a Multicultural Age*, ed. Emory Elliot, Louis Freitas Caton, Jeffrey Rhyne [New York: Oxford University Press, 2002], 49–50).

42. Hannah Arendt, *Lectures on Kant's Political Philosophy* (Chicago: University of Chicago Press 1982), 63.

43. "Topics of the Times: Lynched on Stage; Shots Came From Pit," *New York Times*, April 21, 1911. Dray drew my attention to the reportage in the *Times*.

44. "A Lynching of a New Sort," *New York Times*, April 22, 1911. *The Crisis* reported that "it was said admission was charged and spectators were allowed to shoot one or more bullets at the victim, according to the location" and price of the seat (*The Crisis* 2 [June 1911]: 61). The *Times* article of April 12 disputed this account about paying for admission, as did a reply from Kentucky Governor Augustus E. Wilson printed in *The Crisis*.

45. For more on this 1919 riot and lynchings in Phillips County, Arkansas, especially White's role in the investigation, see Dray, *At the Hands of Persons Unknown*, 238–43.

46. Walter Francis White, *Rope and Faggot: A Biography of Judge Lynch* (New York: Arno Press, 1969), 9.

47. Du Bois, *Dusk of Dawn: An Essay Toward the Autobiography of a Race Concept* (New

York: Harcourt, Brace, 1940), 240. The NAACP quickly perceived the aesthetic politics of film. As Dray observes of the organization's response to *Birth of a Nation*, "When the film, at that point still titled *The Clansman*, was screened in Los Angeles in February 1915, that city's branch of the NAACP alerted Villard, Du Bois, and the New York office that 'every resource of a magnificent new art' was being employed 'to picture Negroes in the worst possible light' (*At the Hands of Persons Unknown*, 192).

48. White, *Rope and Faggot*, vii, 19. William James remarked similarly upon the popularization of lynching in U.S. newspapers: "The hoodlums in our cities are being turned by the newspapers into as knowing critics of the lynching game as they long have been of the prize-fight and football" ("How Can Lynching Be Stopped?" *Literary Digest* 27 [1903]: 156).

49. W. E. B. Du Bois to Carl Van Vechten, November 5, 1925, *Correspondence*, 1:325.

50. Braithwaite, "The Negro in Literature," 207.

51. W. S. Scarborough, *The Birds of Aristophanes: A Theory of Interpretation. A Paper Read before the American Philosophical Association at Its Annual Meeting at Sage College, Cornell University, Ithaca, N.Y., July 13, 1886* (Boston: J. S. Cushing, 1886), 3, 24, 20. Although Scarborough is an understudied figure, Steven Mailloux devotes a chapter to Scarborough's role in professional humanities organizations (*Disciplinary Identities: Rhetorical Paths of English, Speech, and Composition* [New York: MLA, 2006], 83–100).

52. W. S. Scarborough, *An Address Delivered by Prof. W. S. Scarborough, or Wilberforce University on Our Political Status, at the Colored Men's Inter-State Conference, in the City of Pittsburgh, PA., Tuesday, April 29, 1884* (Xenia, Ohio: Torchlight Job Rooms, 1884), 11. Given Scarborough's prominence as university president, *The Crisis* often mentioned this "scholar and teacher" (*The Crisis* 20 [August 1920]: 177). But these mentions were often critical: Du Bois implied that the "scholar and teacher" was too retiring to act as leader of an institution of higher education, perhaps judging Scarborough against his own leadership role at the NAACP. Scarborough was not so retiring not to fire back a response that called *The Crisis* to task for its "malicious desire" to trash Wilberforce University.

53. *The Crisis* takes note of this "exhibit of small pieces of sculpture" and then cites a reviewer from the *Boston Transcript* (*The Crisis* 17:135). Using another publication to make an aesthetic pronouncement, *The Crisis* here gives proof of Braithwaite's claim about the paucity of African American contributions to aesthetic theory.

54. *The Crisis* 17:135–36.

55. William Stanley Braithwaite, "Democracy and Art," *The Crisis* 10 (August 1915): 186.

56. John Dewey, *Art as Experience* (1934; New York: Capricorn Books, 1958), 349.

57. Ibid., 334.

58. Herbert Sidney Langfeld, *The Aesthetic Attitude* (New York: Harcourt, Brace, 1920), 3–4. Langfeld's research aspires to university course use and is "intended for the general reader as well as for the student in aesthetics" (vi). Though "it is not a text-

book in the sense of complete and systematic survey of all the problems of beauty," Langfeld's contribution surveys prior aesthetic textbooks including those of Puffer and Gordon (vi). Langfeld also taught at Harvard.

59. Ibid., 59, 104.

60. Du Bois, "Criteria," 754.

61. Ibid., 754. Du Bois's reluctance here ("may be," "humble disciple," "cannot presume") reflects his larger doubts whether art and literary forums were the best use of *The Crisis'* limited space and resources. Jessie Fauset wore away the editor's opposition as she "set about . . . softening, at least temporarily, Du Bois's deep suspicion about combining official civil rights activities with the arts," writes Lewis (*W. E. B. Du Bois,* 123). After a falling out between Du Bois and Fauset about the place of literature and art should have in a journal that had made its mark by commenting on civil rights and imperialism, *The Crisis* by 1928 had resumed its former course, downplaying aesthetics to concentrate on economics, sociology, and international affairs.

62. Claude McKay, "Soviet Russia and the Negro," *The Crisis* 27 (December 1923): 61–62. Relations between McKay and Du Bois were strained, especially when it came to sorting out the differences between art and propaganda. McKay blasted the editor of *The Crisis* for his tendency to "mistake the art of life for nonsense and to try to pass off propaganda as life in art" (Du Bois, *Correspondence,* 1:375). For more on the antagonisms between McKay and Du Bois, see Rampersad, *Art and Imagination,* 190.

63. *The Crisis* 27 (January 1924): 105.

64. Braithwaite, "Negro in Literature," 205.

65. Rampersad, *Art and Imagination,* 190–91.

66. Du Bois, "The Black Man and the Wounded World," *The Crisis* 27 (January 1924): 111.

67. Du Bois, *Dusk of Dawn,* 94.

68. Walter White, "The Success of Negro Migration" *The Crisis* 19 (January 1920): 112, 115.

69. Du Bois, "Fall Books," *The Crisis* 29 (November 1924): 25. For more on class position, whiteness, and lynching, see Leon F. Litwack, "Hellhounds," in *Without Sanctuary,* 17–20.

    The Fire in the Flint most reads like propaganda when the doctor reflects on his literary tastes: "Perhaps best of all he admired the writing of Du Bois—the fiery, burning philippics of one of his own race against the proscriptions of race prejudice. He read them with a curious sort of detachment—as being something which touched him in a more or less remote way but not as a factor in forming his own opinions as a Negro in a land where democracy often stopped dead at the color line" (Walter Francis White, *The Fire in the Flint* [1924; New York: Negro University Press, 1969], 46). The doctor's reading of Du Bois seems confined to personal insight, absorbing potential lessons about democracy into private, inner conviction.

This passage functions as calculated flattery, that is, as personal propaganda directed at the man who was for a time White's boss. Relations between the two were often tense, raising the possibility that the problem may lie not with the doctor's "detachment" but instead with Du Bois's rhetoric as somehow itself productive of political repose and indifference. Ross Posnock identifies White as a "mainstream liberal and a foe of Du Bois" (*Color and Culture: Black Writers and the Making of the Modern Intellectual* [Cambridge, Mass.: Harvard University Press, 1998], 127). Discussing the post-World War II era and the black popular front, Nikhil Pal Singh places their mutual animosity in larger context. Unlike Du Bois's commitment to reading the racial question as a global dilemma endemic to "the imperialist history of modern capitalism," White was "selectively drafted into the cold war" by viewing race as a national issue ("Culture/Wars: Recoding Democracy in an Age of Empire," *American Quarterly* 50 [1998]: 485, 487).

70. White, *Fire in the Flint*, 39.

71. White, *Fire in the Flint*, 44; *Flight* (1926; New York: Negro University Press, 1969), 94.

72. White, *Flight*, 94.

73. Ibid., 195. The novel concludes with Mimi rushing out of—fleeing?—a concert hall upon encountering a hybrid art that combines European Romantic music with African American spirituals. As she "whispered exultantly" the words, "Free! Free! Free," is Mimi only prolonging her flight that has led her away from her child and her people (300)?

74. Fauset, "The Sleeper Wakes: A Novelette in Three Installments," *The Crisis* 20 (September 1920): 229.

75. Ibid.

76. Elaine Scarry, *On Beauty and Being Just* (Princeton: Princeton University Press, 1999), 4.

77. Fauset, "The Sleeper Wakes," *The Crisis* 20 (October 1920): 267. Disillusionment with beauty appears Fauset's *There is Confusion* (1924). Although the danseuse, Joanna, wants to believe that "if there's anything that will break down prejudice it will be equality or perhaps even superiority on the part of the colored people in the arts," she ends up renouncing art as public intervention to devote herself to "Love," that is, the privacy of heteronormativity (*There is Confusion* [New York: Boni and Liveright, 1924], 97, 283).

78. Du Bois, "Krigwa, 1926," *The Crisis* (January 1926): 115. Although this notice is not signed by Du Bois, its style and message suggest him as its likely author.

79. Du Bois, *Dusk of Dawn*, 269.

80. W. E. B. Du Bois, *Dark Princess: A Romance* (1928; rpt., Millwood, N.Y.: Kraus-Thomson, 1974), 25, 147, 193.

81. Ibid., 280.

82. See Wai Chee Dimock, "Aesthetics at the Limit of the Nation: Kant, Pound, and the *Saturday Review*," *American Literature* 76 (September 2004): 526.

83.   Du Bois, *The Quest of the Silver Fleece*, 52, 141, 348. As both commodity and object of beauty, cotton never exists simply for its own sake. Bles and Zora intend to sell the cotton to finance Zora's education. Their plan is to put beauty to use.

84.   Ibid., 29, 31–32.

CHAPTER FOUR

1.   Jacob Riis, *The Making of an American: A New Edition with an Epilogue by His Grandson, J. Riis Owre* (London: Macmillan, 1970), 184–85.

2.   William Dean Howells, "Editor's Easy Chair," *Harper's Monthly Magazine* 125 (1912): 634–37.

3.   Ibid., 637.

4.   William Uricchio and Roberta Pearson, *Reframing Culture: The Case of the Vitagraph Quality Films* (Princeton: Princeton University Press, 1993), 21.

5.   Charlie Keil, *Early American Cinema in Transition: History, Style, and Filmmaking, 1907–1913* (Madison: University of Wisconsin Press, 2001), 10. See also Ben Brewster, "Periodization of Early Cinema," in *American Cinema's Transitional Era: Audiences, Institutions, Practices,* ed. Charlie Keil and Shelley Stamp (Berkeley and Los Angeles: University of California Press, 2004), 70–71.

6.   Charles Musser, with Carol Nelson, *High-Class Moving Pictures: Lyman H. Howe and the Forgotten Era of Traveling Exhibition, 1880–1920* (Princeton: Princeton University Press, 1991), 171.

7.   See Paul Starr, *The Creation of the Media: The Political Origins of Modern Communications* (New York: Basic Books, 2004), 297.

8.   Tom Gunning, *D. W. Griffith and the Origins of American Narrative Film: The Early Years at Biograph* (Urbana: University of Illinois Press, 1991), 6. Other dates emerge with a change of focus that takes into account audience composition, methods of distribution, and exhibition practices. The years 1907–13 are significant for Urrichio and Pearson in marking a moment when cultural authorities, film producers, moviegoers, and censorship boards tussled over the themes and images that were appropriate for the screen (*Reframing Culture,* 5).

9.   Brewster, "Periodization of Early Cinema," 71, 74.

10.   Jonathan Auerbach, "Chasing Film Narrative: Repetition, Recursion, and the Body in Early Cinema," *Critical Inquiry* 26 (Summer 2000): 798–820, and " 'Wonderful Apparatus,' or *Life of an American Fireman,*" *American Literature* 77 (December 2005): 669–98; Jane Gaines, *Fire and Desire: Mixed-Race Movies in the Silent Era* (Chicago: University of Chicago Press, 2001); Miriam Hansen, *Babel and Babylon: Spectatorship in American Silent Film* (Cambridge, Mass.: Harvard University Press, 1991).

11.   See Hansen, *Babel and Babylon,* 43–44.

12.   Terry Ramsaye, *A Million and One Nights: A History of the Motion Picture* (New York: Simon and Schuster, 1926), xi.

13.   Starr provides this figure of weekly attendance (*Creation of the Media,* 319).

14.   Hugo Münsterberg, *The Photoplay: A Psychological Study* (1916; New York: Arno

Press, 1970), 233. Despite Münsterberg's assertions, an enduring rap against film has been that it is not a "true" art form. See Berys Gaut, "Cinematic Art," *Journal of Aesthetics and Art Criticism* 60 (Fall 2002): 299–312.

15.   Horace M. Kallen, "The Dramatic Picture Versus the Pictorial Drama: A Study of the Influences of the Cinematograph on the Stage," *The Harvard Monthly* 50 (March 1910): 24, 31.

16.   Howells, "Editor's Easy Chair," 637.

17.   Quoted in Myron Osborn Lounsbury, *The Origins of American Film Criticism, 1909–1939* (New York: Arno, 1973), 32.

18.   See Starr, *Creation of the Media*, 303. In an ironic bit of nostalgia, Nathaniel West recalls the spiritedness of early filmgoers, describing how viewers at a private screening "imitated a rowdy audience in the days of the nickelodeon" (*Day of the Locust* [New York: Signet, 1983], 44).

19.   On the relationship between crowds and movies, see Amy Kaplan, *The Anarchy of Empire in the Making of U.S. Culture* (Cambridge, Mass.: Harvard University Press, 2003), 149, and Michael Tratner, "Working the Crowd: Movies and Mass Politics," *Criticism* 45 (Winter 2003): 57. Gaines intensifies these connections by examining the racial aspects of movie crowds (*Fire and Desire*, 245–50).

20.   Roy Rosenzweig, *Eight Hours For What We Will: Workers and Leisure in an Industrial City, 1870–1920* (Cambridge: Cambridge University Press, 1983), 201. See also Gunning, *D. W. Griffith and the Origins of American Narrative Film*, 86.

21.   Gunning, *D. W. Griffith*, 87.

22.   Gilbert Seldes, *The Seven Lively Arts* (New York: Harper, 1924), 9.

23.   Hansen, *Babel and Babylon*, 60. Still, early cinema had its share of detractors who feared that it would spread moral contagion. Howells caustically represents the reactionary stance of those who see "birds of prey hovering in the standing-room and the foyers of the theaters" ("Editor's Easy Chair," 634). That these "predacious fowl," to use a bit more of Howells's language, came to the moving-picture show with licentiousness in mind seemed clear enough to one reformer in 1915 who cautioned: "Under cover of dimness evil communications readily pass and bad habits are taught. Moving picture theaters are favorite places for the teaching of homosexual practices" (quoted in Garth Jowett, *Film: The Democratic Art* [Boston: Little, Brown, 1976], 82). Even critics who admitted film's aesthetic qualities were troubled, since "the rape-like tactics of the lustful villain have been reincarnated and made 'artistic'" by cinema (Harmon B. Stephens, "The Relation of the Motion Picture to Changing Moral Standards," *Annals of the American Academy* 128 [November 1926]: 153). Oversight was needed, reformers insisted. When New York City Mayor George B. McClellan shut down the nickelodeons in 1908, the film industry responded, not by challenging his edict, but by voluntarily establishing its own National Board of Censorship (Gunning, *D. W. Griffith*, 151–56). It was not so much that censorship represented a threat to freedom of expression (though it did have this effect) but rather that the film industry's ability to create its own censorship board and uphold nationwide standards was possible "only because the consolida-

tion of the movie industry had reduced it to a tight oligopoly" (Starr, *Creation of the Media*, 325). An industry in the hands of the few hardly amounts to democracy; hence the need for Hollywood's counter-myth about democratic art.

After 1908, the rhetoric of film as an art form intensified in an effort to make the movies more respectable and middle class. Film adapted classical themes and melodrama to the screen, pushing raucous subjects—white slavery, dementia, kooch-dancing, and crime—to the edge of the frame. Narrative, as Gunning states, brought film in line with the concerns of "the middle-class guardians of culture" for whom "the movies represented a working-class pastime" sorely in need of control and custodianship (*D. W. Griffith*, 89).

24. Quoted in Stanley Kauffman, "Introduction," in Vachel Lindsay, *The Art of the Moving Picture* (1915; rpt., New York: Liveright, 1970), ix.

25. Larry May, *Screening Out the Past: The Birth of Mass Culture and the Motion Picture Industry* (New York: Oxford University Press, 1980), 38.

26. Musser and Nelson's *High-Class Moving Pictures* explores efforts to present pictures that would transcend popular entertainment. Uricchio and Pearson examine Vitagraph "quality films" from 1907 to 1913 that sought "the approval of many who had formerly castigated moving pictures for fomenting disorder among the 'lower orders'" (*Reframing Culture*, 5). For a study of how uncertainty over cinema's status (was it a popular or a mass form?) animates early U.S. film criticism, see Jonathan Auerbach, "American Studies and Film, Blindness and Insight," *American Quarterly* 58 (March 2006): 31–50.

27. Jane Addams, *The Spirit of Youth and the City Streets* (New York: Macmillan, 1920), 21, 85.

28. James Lastra, *Sound Technology and the American Cinema: Perception, Representation, Modernity* (New York: Columbia University Press, 2000), 4.

29. Addams, *Spirit of Youth*, 101.

30. Addams, *Democracy and Social Ethics* (1902; rpt., New York: Macmillan, 1920), 2, 216, 221, 223. Addams's thoughts about the unifying aspects of commercialism echo Howells's assertion that the interests of collectivity require writers to engage the economic world. "At present business is the only human solidarity," Howells writes regretfully (*Literature and Life: The Man of Letters as a Man of Business* [New York: Harper, 1902; rpt., Boston: IndyPublish.com, n.d.], 3).

31. Addams, *Spirit of Youth*, 85.

32. Ibid., 16–17.

33. Thomas Cravern, "The Great American Art," *The Dial* 81 (December 1926): 485. Validation of film as a classic aesthetic continues. Describing silent feature films as "Etruscan vases, artifacts of a departed culture," Robert Sklar endows cinema with a longstanding ability to balance common appreciation and refined taste. Alluding to a different epoch of classicism, he next likens U.S. film to Elizabethan drama for its ability to showcase a "truly popular culture, accessible to all social groups" (*Movie-Made America: A Cultural History of the Movies*, revised and updated [New York: Vintage, 1994], 32, 86). See also Uricchio and Pearson, who examine "qual-

ity films" based on Shakespeare, which give evidence of the film industry's interest in garnering the imprimatur of high cultural institutions with products that remained "polysemic enough to appeal to a broad spectrum of viewers" (*Reframing Culture*, 64).

34. See Cravern, "The Great American Art," 484. Other estimates about film's popularity are just as effusive. According to Münsterberg, "Enthusiasts claim that in the United States ten million people are daily attending picture houses. Sceptics believe that 'only' two or three millions form the daily attendance. But in any case 'the movies' have become the most popular entertainment of the country, nay, of the world, and their influence is one of the strongest social energies of our time" (*Photoplay*, 215). Ramsaye, too, speaks of U.S. film as "world market merchandise." Such "internationalism," he suggests, is itself a product of homegrown U.S. diversity, giving American filmmakers an edge in global competition (*A Million and One Nights*, 823).

35. Addams, *Spirit of Youth*, 5, 19.

36. Hansen, *Babel and Babylon*, 13. No congratulatory Americanism circulates through Hansen's assessment. She offers these comments on the classical public sphere in light of Alexander Kluge's work on European media. For more on the possibility that meaningful political experience lies within mass culture, whether as art, entertainment, or some mixture of the two, see Miriam Hansen, "Introduction," in Siegfried Kracauer, *Theory of Film: The Redemption of Physical Reality* (Princeton: Princeton University Press, 1997), xi–xii, and Lastra, *Sound Technology and the American Cinema*, 4–7.

37. "The White Slave Films," *The Outlook* 106 (January 17, 1914): 121.

38. Münsterberg, *The Photoplay*, 29–30. On Münsterberg's importance to theories of spectatorship, see Hansen, *Babel and Babylon*, 83, and May, *Screening Out the Past*, 41.

39. "White Slave Films," 122.

40. Münsterberg, *The Photoplay*, 29, 39.

41. See Hansen, *Babel and Babylon*, 78.

42. Benjamin, "The Work of Art in the Age of Mechanical Reproduction," in *Illuminations: Essays and Reflections*, ed. Hannah Arendt (New York: Schocken, 1968), 221.

43. Uricchio and Pearson, *Reframing Culture*, 24. By the time Münsterberg's study appeared, the pursuit of bourgeois approbation had already succeeded in making motion pictures less of a working-class venue. Behind this shift, as Gilbert Seldes would remember in 1924, lay "the remorseless hostility of the genteel" to anything that smacked of sex, liberatory fantasy, or the flouting of authority (*The Seven Lively Arts*, 3).

44. Münsterberg, *The Photoplay*, 38, 43.

45. Ibid., 144, 181.

46. Hansen describes the invention of the spectator in terms of "a shift from a collective, plural notion of the film viewer to a singular, unified but potentially universal category, the commodity form of reception" (*Babel and Babylon*, 85).

47. George William Eggers, "Foreword," in Lindsay, *The Art of the Moving Picture,* xxiv. On his book's use in university curricula, Lindsay writes that the "1915 edition was used . . . as one of the text-books in the Columbia University School of Journalism" (30).

48. Lindsay, *The Art of the Moving Picture,* 199, 215. Benjamin debunks comparisons of film and hieroglyphics ("Mechanical Reproduction," 227).

49. W. E. B. Du Bois, *Darkwater: Voices from within the Veil* (New York: AMS Press, 1969), 222.

50. Ibid., 247.

51. Ibid., 223.

52. See Jacqueline Najuma Stewart, *Migrating to the Movies: Cinema and Black Urban Modernity* (Berkeley and Los Angeles: University of California Press, 2005), xiii–xviii.

53. This passage does not appear in the "second version" of the essay, unpublished during Benjamin's lifetime. Compare "The Work of Art in the Age of Its Technological Reproducibility," in *Walter Benjamin: Selected Writings, 1935–1938,* ed. Michael W. Jennings (Cambridge, Mass.: Harvard University Press, 2003), 3:114, with "Mechanical Reproduction" (231). On the different versions of this artwork essay, see Miriam Hansen, "Benjamin, Cinema, and Experience: 'The Blue Flower in the Land of Technology,'" *New German Critique* 40 (Winter 1987): 179–224.

54. Benjamin, "Mechanical Reproduction," 231.

55. Du Bois, *Darkwater,* 224.

56. Jacqueline Stewart, *Migrating to the Movies,* 101.

57. W. E. B. Du Bois, *The Souls of Black Folk,* in *Three Negro Classics* (New York: Avon, 1965), 368.

58. Ibid., 377.

59. Du Bois, *Darkwater,* 224, 247.

60. Ibid., 226, 228, 230. Since Du Bois continues in this section of *Darkwater* to speak of Beauty, Truth, and the eternal, it should not be implied that his rejection of idealist aesthetics is complete. On the links between German aesthetic idealism and ethics, see chapter 3 of Toril Moi, *Henrik Ibsen and the Birth of Modernism: Art, Theater, Philosophy* (Oxford and New York: Oxford University Press, 2006).

61. Gunning, *D. W. Griffith,* 85.

62. Du Bois, *Darkwater,* 246–47.

63. Walter Benjamin, "A Look at Chaplin," trans. John McKay, *Yale Journal of Criticism* 9 (1996): 311.

64. The film industry often had a theoretical impetus: "Explicitly theoretical debates about the general nature of technological representation were central to the development of Hollywood representational norms" (Lastra, *Sound Technology and the American Cinema,* 123). On the origins of U.S. film theory and criticism, see Lounsbury, *Origins of American Film Criticism.*

65. W. Dodgson Bowman, *Charlie Chaplin: His Life and Art* (New York: John Day Company, 1931), 36, 44. Bowman gives 1889 as the date of Edison's invention probably

more to set up a convenient parallel between Chaplin and the birth of film than to provide accuracy. Although Edison's laboratory was working on the kinetoscope as early at the late 1880s, he did not file a patent for device until 1891. On the history of the kinetoscope, see http://memory.loc.gov/ammem/edhtml/edmvhist.html (accessed May 13, 2004).

66.   Bowman, *Charlie Chaplin*, 118. For another view of Chaplin in grandly humanistic terms, see Lewis Jacobs, *The Rise of American Film: A Critical History* (1939; rpt., New York: Teachers College, Columbia University, 1968), 247.

67.   Charles Chaplin, *My Autobiography* (New York: Pocket Books, 1966), 91. All further references to this edition are noted parenthetically. Taking Chaplin's memoir as a history of film, François Truffaut writes: "If one had only one book to read to understand a century of cinema, I would recommend *My Autobiography*" ("Charlie Chaplin Was a Man Just Like Any Other Man," in André Bazin, *Essays on Chaplin*, ed. and trans. by Jean Bodon [New Haven: University of New Haven Press, 1985], 94).

68.   Douglas Fairbanks Jr, "Foreword," in Bowman, *Charlie Chaplin*, 9.

69.   Minnie Maddern Fiske, "The Art of Charles Chaplin," in *Focus on Chaplin*, ed. Donald W. McCaffrey (Englewood Cliffs, N.J.: Prentice Hall, 1971), 70.

70.   Charles Chaplin, *A Comedian Sees the World* (http://www.cinemaweb.com/ silentfilm/bookshelf, accessed April 9, 2004, n.p.). Chaplin's articles about his world tour were originally published serially in the *Women's Home Companion* (1933–34).

71.   Chaplin, *A Comedian Sees the World*, n.p.

72.   Jacobs, *Rise of American Film*, 237. For Chaplin's reading of Whitman (and Emerson), see *My Autobiography*, 137–38.

73.   Lorenzo Turrent Rozas, "Charlie Chaplin's Decline," *Living Age* 396 (June 1934): 320–21. The article is translated from *ruta*. Connections between film and explosives are not simply figurative. Gun cotton, the same material that Johann Most recommended to anarchists for making dynamite (see chapter 2), is the raw material for nitrate film. During World War I, as Kristin Thompson notes, Britain was anxious to prohibit German imports of nitrate, which stunted Germany's film industry, one of the many factors that led to the eventual U.S. dominance in global movie production (*Exporting Entertainment: America in the World Film Market* [London: British Film Institute, 1985], 67).

74.   Rozas, "Charlie Chaplin's Decline," 320.

75.   Ibid., 322.

76.   Fairbanks, "Foreword," 8.

77.   Chaplin, *A Comedian Sees the World*, n.p.

78.   Rozas, "Charlie Chaplin's Decline," 320. For more on Rozas and proletarian art, see his *Hacía una literatura proletaria*, which seeks a form of expression commensurate with "esta nueva modilidad de nuestra vida revolucionaria" [this new modality of our revolutionary life] that cannot be found in nationalist themes (*Hacía una literatura proletaria* [Jalapa. Mexico: La Economica, 1932], 8).

79. Quoted in Philip G. Rosen, "The Chaplin World-View," *Cinema Journal* 12 (Fall 1969): 11. Even as the studios were downplaying "bolshevism," radical film critics commenting on revolutionary cinema used the debates and issues raised by Russian filmmaking to express "a common feeling of deep resentment against the commercial American movie, the symbol of comfortable middle class values" (Lounsbury, *Origins of American Film Criticism*, 227–28). Charles Maland describes the ideologically charged atmosphere surrounding the production of *Modern Times* (*Chaplin and American Culture: The Evolution of a Star Image* [Princeton: Princeton University Press, 1989], 144–46).

80. André Bazin, "Time Validates Modern Times," in *Essays on Chaplin*, 5. On U.S. movies that participated in propaganda campaigns against labor radicalism and union activities, see Steven J. Ross, "Cinema and Class Conflict: Labor, Capital, the State, and American Silent Film," in *Resisting Images: Essays on Cinema and History*, ed. Robert Sklar and Charles Musser (Philadelphia: Temple University Press, 1990), 81–83.

81. Garrett Stewart, "Modern Hard Times: Chaplin and the Cinema of Self-Reflection," *Critical Inquiry* 3 (1976): 298.

82. Charles Musser, "Work, Ideology, and Chaplin's Tramp," in *Resisting Images: Essays on Cinema and History*, ed. Robert Sklar and Charles Musser (Philadelphia: Temple University Press, 1990), 37.

83. Siegfried Kracauer, *Theory of Film: The Redemption of Physical Reality* (Princeton: Princeton University Press, 1997), 108.

84. For authoritative treatment of this issue, see Hansen who describes how "the nickelodeon offered structural conditions around which older forms of working-class and ethnic culture could crystallize and responses to social pressures, individual displacement, and alienation could be articulated in a communal setting. The relative autonomy of the nickelodeon from both a genteel high-culture and the 'big-time' entertainment was short-lived and precarious" (*Babel and Babylon*, 94).

85. "Sealing Wax, Cabbages, and Kings," *New York Times*, September 30, 1934.

86. Neither is *City Lights* a silent movie. Before the statue is undraped and Chaplin disturbed from his nap, the dignitaries take turns in blathering into a microphone. The voices amplified are thin, tinny, and unintelligible. It matters not what the officials say because the audience recognizes that their rhetoric is full of bombast just as we know that they are speaking English although all the words, except "Thank you," are muddled. Sound is predictable, accessible only to the few, and strangely uncommunicative. As Kracauer notes, "When first incorporating the spoken word, Chaplin aimed at corroding it" (*Theory of Film*, 107). The Tramp, expert slacker that he is, has no difficulty in tuning out these speeches, no matter how loud or grating. Sound lacks eloquence and performs no public function. In contrast, the Tramp's passive-aggressive tango with the frozen marble figures serves up a much more instructive commentary on the usefulness (or lack thereof) of civic art.

87. Jonathan Sterne, *The Audible Past: Cultural Origins of Sound Reproduction* (Durham, N.C.: Duke University Press, 2003), 24. Lastra documents how sound technology

made "acoustic experiences . . . available for mass consumption and private possession" (*Sound Technology and the American Cinema*, 22).

88. Jane Addams, *Twenty Years at Hull-House with Autobiographical Notes* (1911; New
York: Signet, 1961), 246.

89. The clash of silent film and sound is still more complex. The Tramp and the gamin
silently rehearse his number while the music of the singing waiters intrudes from
off-screen. Even though this scene is framed by sound, Chaplin and Goddard
are "not only bobbing about in a much livelier silent rhythm, they are convers-
ing in titles. Here sound has been allowed to proclaim itself dominant" (Walter
Kerr, *The Silent Clowns* [New York: Knopf, 1975], 355). But, as Lastra states, in the
nickelodeon era, image frequently played second fiddle to sound. Always much
more than a film, nickelodeon programs included music, lectures, and sing-alongs,
which made "visual presentation . . . decidedly secondary. . . . In economic, conceptual, and structural terms, the song—sound—was clearly dominant over the
image" (*Sound Technology*, 100). From this view, Chaplin's portrait of image threatened by sound eclipses an earlier history in which visual matter was instrumental
in standardizing and retracting audience participation at the movies.

90. Garrett Stewart, "Modern Hard Times," 313.

91. James A. Bland, "In the Evening by the Moonlight," in *James A. Bland's Great Ethiopian Songs* (New York: Hitchcock's Music Store, 1880). Accessed at www.stephen-
foster-songs.de/Amsong22.htm, May 22, 2006.

92. Theodor Adorno and Max Horkheimer, *Dialectic of Enlightenment* (Stanford: Stanford University Press, 2002), 112.

93. According to Maland, *Modern Times* "grossed only $1.4 million domestically, at
least a half-million dollars less than each of Chaplin's previous three films" and
did not recoup production costs until foreign distribution (*Chaplin and American
Culture*, 157).

94. Bowman, *Charlie Chaplin*, 130. According to Garrett Stewart, Chaplin "was well
known as the most ardent reactionary of the silent film," viewing synchronized
sound as a threat to "emotive artistry" ("Modern Hard Times," 308).

95. Brooks Atkinson, "Beloved Vagabond: Charlie Chaplin Canonized Out of a Sentimental Memory Book," *New York Times*, February 16, 1936: sec. 9:1.

96. Lyrics quoted from Donald W. McCaffrey, "An Evaluation of Chaplin's Silent
Comedy Films, 1916–36," in *Focus on Chaplin*, 94–95. Esperantists encouraged
performers to develop "universal" songs: "Singers are therefore strongly recommended to add Esperanto songs to their repertoire, and it is certain that not only
they but their audiences will be quick to appreciate the musical charms of the
international language" (Bernard Long, *Esperanto: Its Aims and Claims: A Discussion
of the Language Problem and Its Solution* [London: Esperanto Publishing, 1930], 59).

97. Lillian Gish, "A Universal Language," *Encyclopedia Britannica*, 14th ed. (1929),
www.britannica.com/women/classic/C0026.html (accessed April 16, 2004, n.p.).
Chaplin returned to Esperanto in *The Great Dictator* (1940) in which Esperanto-
language signs are featured in the "Jewish" ghetto. Hitler was suspicious of Espe-

ranto most likely because its inventor, Ludwik Lazar Zamenhof, was a Polish Jew and because the notion of an international language posed a threat to the "beautiful" language of the fatherland.

98.   Long, *Esperanto*, 31.

99.   Dr. Esperanto [Ludwik Lazar Zamenhof], *An Attempt towards an International Language*, trans. Henry Phillips Jr (New York: Henry Holt, 1889), 7.

100.   Winston Churchill, "Everybody's Language," in *Focus on Chaplin*, 76–77.

101.   General Secretariat of the League of Nations, *Esperanto as an International Auxiliary Language* (Paris: Imprimerie des Presses Universitaires de France, 1922), 32. Meanwhile, studio executives exhorted the League of Nations that "the problems of mankind could be settled within three generations" by turning to film as a means of worldwide education (Benjamin B. Hampton, *A History of the Movies* (New York: Covici, Freide, 1931, 431).

102.   General Secretariat of the League of Nations, *Esperanto*, 6, 27–28. *La Komunista Manifesto de Karl Marx kaj Friedrich Engels* was translated by Emil Pfeffer and published in Leipzig in 1923.

103.   E. M. Chapelier and Gassy Marin, *Anarchists and the International Language, Esperanto. With an Appendix Explaining the Elements of the Language* (London: "Freedom" Office, 1908), 3–4, 10.

104.   Charlie Chaplin, "A Rejection of the Talkies," in *Focus on Chaplin*, 63.

105.   Bowman, *Charlie Chaplin*, 132.

106.   Charles Chaplin, "Making Fun," *Soil* 1 (1916): 5.

107.   Karl K. Kitchen, "Chaplin and 'The Masses,'" *New York Times*, March 17, 1935.

108.   Zamenhof, *An Attempt towards an International Language*, 9.

109.   Hampton, *History of the Movies*, 430.

CHAPTER FIVE

1.   "Dollar Wheat," *The Literary Digest* 15 (1897): 654.

2.   Richard Hofstader, *The Age of Reform: From Bryan to F. D. R.* (New York: Vintage, 1955), 51.

3.   Conant's influence is suggested by Jack London's *The Assassination Bureau, Ltd.*, which places the book in the library of the Ivan Dragomiloff, the head of the international firm of contract murderers who kill as a matter of social ethics. Conant illustrates that many of the same pressures characterized fin-de-siècle globalization as now: "International finance has become a power which disregards boundaries, takes scant account of personal and class feelings, and sometimes dictates terms to nations" (*The United States in the Orient: The Nature of the Economic Problem* [Boston: Houghton, Mifflin, 1900], 173).

4.   William Dean Howells, "A Case in Point," in *Criticism and Fiction and Other Essays* (New York: New York University Press, 1959), 282.

5.   Frank Norris, Letter to Howells, in *Criticism and Fiction*, 277.

6.   Henry Schwarz, "Aesthetic Imperialism: Literature and the Conquest of India," *MLQ* 61 (December 2000): 580. See also Amy Kaplan, "Nation, Region, and Empire," in *The Columbia History of the American Novel*, ed. Emory Elliot (New York:

Columbia University Press, 1991), 240–66, and John Carlos Rowe, *Literary Culture and U.S. Imperialism* (New York: Oxford University Press, 2000). Thomas Peyser argues "*the nation is replaced with the globe as the fundamental unit of human association*" at the turn of the century (Thomas Peyser, *Utopia and Cosmopolis: Globalization in the Era of American Literary Realism* [Durham: Duke University Press, 1998], x).

7.   Edwin Erle Sparks, *The Expansion of the American People, Social and Territorial* (Chicago: Scott, Foresman, 1900), 13. Study questions at the end of the book imply its use as a textbook.

8.   Immanuel Wallerstein, "The National and the Universal: Can There Be Such a Thing as World Culture," in *Culture, Globalization, and the World-System,* ed. Anthony D. King (Minneapolis: University of Minnesota Press, 1997), 91–92.

9.   Terry Eagleton, *The Ideology of the Aesthetic* (Oxford: Blackwell, 1990), 95.

10.   William Elliot Griffis, *The Romance of Conquest: The Story of American Expansion through Arms and Diplomacy* (Boston: W. A. Wilde, 1899), 14.

11.   Quoted in Norman A. Graebner, *Empire on the Pacific: A Study in American Continental Expansion* (New York: Ronald Press, 1955), 98.

12.   Arjun Appadurai, "Grassroots Globalization and the Research Imagination," *Public Culture* 12 (Winter 2000): 6, 8. In addition to Appadurai on the democratic strains within globalization, Polly Toynbee claims that global exchange redistributes real, cultural, and symbolic capital, "making the elites distraught but improving the lot of the rest" ("Who's Afraid of Global Culture," in *Global Capitalism,* ed. Will Hutton and Anthony Giddens [New York: The New Press, 2000], 194). James Rosenau suggests that globalization creates "functional equivalents," including NGOs, city-spaces, and the worldwide web, that act as democratic mechanisms ("Governance and Democracy in a Globalizing World," in *Re-imagining Political Community: Studies in Cosmopolitan Democracy,* ed. Danielle Archibugi, David Held, and Martin Köhler [Stanford: Stanford University Press, 1998], 41–46). David Held supplies evidence for such assertions: "In the mid-1970s, over two-thirds of all states could reasonably be called authoritarian. This percentage has fallen dramatically; less than a third of all states are now authoritarian, and the number of democracies is growing rapidly" ("Democracy and Globalization," in *Re-imagining Political Community,* 11). Even those who would dispute the centrality of the state in an era of globalization still see democracy on the horizon. Hutton and Giddens examine "new forms of global agency" with the potential to "reproduce globally" democratic forms that arose in nation-states in the eighteenth and nineteenth centuries ("Fighting Back," in *Global Capitalism,* ed. Will Hutton and Anthony Giddens [New York: The New Press, 2000], 216, 223). Appadurai contests the idea that easily recognizable currents of globalization—such as the worldwide web—can be heralded as democratic. He never forgets "the gigantic corporate machineries that celebrate globalization" while remaining committed to the possibility of "globalization from below" in which democratic meanings circulate at lower frequencies of exchange (1, 3).

13.   Theodor Adorno, *Aesthetic Theory,* trans. Robert Hullot-Kentor (Minneapolis: University of Minnesota Press, 1997), 4.

14. See Robert Hullot-Kentor, "Translator's Introduction," in *Aesthetic Theory*, xvi.

15. Application of Benjamin's argument to U.S. culture requires important stipula-tions. First, the relevance of the artwork essay depends on its historical specificity to National Socialism. As Lutz Koepnick asks, "how can Benjamin be of use today to evaluate contemporary attractions and simulations without advocating impetu-ous comparisons or belittling the historical uniqueness of Nazi terror?" (*Walter Benjamin and the Aesthetics of Power* [Lincoln: University of Nebraska Press, 1999], 185). Second, the dislocation of aesthetic politics to U.S. contexts can aestheticize the critical impetus of Benjamin's argument by suppressing its historical speci-ficity, thereby construing fascism as an empty, ahistorical form. Such reasons explain why Andrew Hewitt is "wary of any presumption that . . . might lead to the construction of a transhistorical or even transnational phenomenology of fascism" (*Fascist Modernism: Aesthetics, Politics, and the Avant-Garde* [Stanford: Stanford University Press, 1993], 3).

16. Walter Benjamin, "The Author as Producer," in *Reflections: Essays, Aphorisms, Auto-biographical Writings* (New York: Schocken Books, 1986), 221, 237.

17. Paul Jay, "Beyond Discipline? Globalization and the Future of English," *PMLA* 116 (January 2001): 36, 43.

18. Anthony Easthope, "The Pleasures of Labour: Marxist Aesthetics in a Post-Marx-ist World," in *Post-Theory: New Directions in Criticism*, ed. Martin McQuillan et al. (Edinburgh: Edinburgh University Press, 1999), 63.

19. Upton Sinclair captures the novelty of "Socialist" allegiance in the following exchange: "'But—but—' gasped the boy, 'then am I a Socialist?' 'Nine tenths of the people in the country are Socialists . . . only they haven't found it out yet'" (*Samuel the Seeker* [Racine, Wisconsin: Western Printing and Lithographing, 1910], 289).

20. Richard Chase, *The American Novel and Its Tradition* (New York: Doubleday, 1957), 198.

21. Malcolm Waters proposes deterritorialization as a prime effect of globalization (*Globalization*, 2d ed. [London: Routledge, 2001], 182–92). The idea of a weak-ened state has been met with dismay by John Gray, who sees global laissez-fare as the new order (*False Dawn: The Delusions of Global Capitalism* [New York: The New Press, 1998], 100, 207), and Benjamin Barber, who argues that citizenship becomes meaningless if it is pried apart from the state (*Jihad vs. McWorld* [New York: Random House, 1995], 6–8). More nuance is provided by Fernando Coronil, who perceives that "the unregulated production and free circulation of primary commodities in the open market [which] requires a significant dismantling of state control" is a neoliberal project that still requires "the helping hand of the state" ("Towards a Critique of Globalcentrism: Speculations on Capitalism's Nature," *Public Culture* 12 [Spring 2000]: 363–64). On the role of the "white city" at the 1893 Chicago World's Fair in producing an image of a "frictionless global order," see Curtis M. Hinsley, "Strolling Through the Colonies," in *Walter Benjamin and the Demands of History*, ed. Michael P. Steinberg (Ithaca: Cornell University Press, 1996), 133.

22. Frank Norris, "The Need of a Literary Conscience," in *Frank Norris: Novels and Essays* (New York: Library of America, 1986), 1159.

23. Norris, *The Letters of Frank Norris*, ed. Franklin Walker (San Francisco: Book Club of California, 1956) 19. Norris was kicked out of South Africa by the Boer government in the wake of failed Uitlander insurrection in 1896. Norris saw the conflict as spectacle, describing the face-off between the Boers and the British as a "situation [that] was almost theatrical . . . a tremendous story" ("A Christmas in the Transvaal," in Robert C. Letiz III, "'A Christmas in the Transvaal': An Addition to the Norris Canon," *Studies in American Fiction* 14 [Autumn 1986]: 222). In Cuba, restraint was harder to come by, as Norris wrote after one battle, "Santiago was ours—was ours, ours, by the sword we had acquired, we, Americans, with no one to help—and the Anglo-Saxon blood of us" (quoted in Franklin Walker, *Frank Norris: A Biography* [Garden City: Doubleday, 1932], 199).

24. Norris, Letter to Howells, 277.

25. Friedrich Schiller, *On the Aesthetic Education of Man in a Series of Letters*, trans. Reginald Snell (New Haven: Yale University Press, 1954), 25. On Schiller's relationship to the French Revolution, see Josef Chytry, *The Aesthetic State: A Quest in Modern German Thought* (Berkeley and Los Angeles: University of California Press, 1989), 75–76, and Rainer Stollman, "Fascist Tendencies as a Total Work of Art: Tendencies of the Aesthetization of Political Life in National Socialism," *New German Critique* 14 (Spring 1978): 47.

26. Koepnick, *Walter Benjamin and the Aesthetics of Power*, 89.

27. Schiller, *Aesthetic Education*, 32–33.

28. Ibid., 32.

29. Ibid.

30. Ibid., 138.

31. Ibid., 136. The disciplinary nature of such beautiful freedom has rightly given critics pause; see David Lloyd, "Arnold, Ferguson, Schiller: Aesthetic Culture and the Politics of Aesthetics," *Cultural Critique* 2 (Winter 1985–86): 165–66.

32. Eagleton, *Ideology of the Aesthetic*, 106.

33. Schiller, *Aesthetic Education*, 139.

34. Kojin Karatani, "Uses of Aesthetics: After Orientalism," trans. Sabu Kosho, *boundary 2* 25 (1998): 151.

35. Goebbels, quoted in Paul de Man, *Aesthetic Ideology* (Minneapolis: University of Minnesota Press, 1996), 154–55. See also Stollman, "Fascist Tendencies as a Total Work of Art," 47–48.

36. Van Wyck Brooks, *The Confident Years: 1885–1915* (New York: E. P. Dutton, 1952), 218.

37. Laura Kipnis, *Ecstasy Unlimited: On Sex, Capital, Gender, and Aesthetics* (Minneapolis: University of Minnesota Press, 1993), 29.

38. Herbert Marcuse, *The Aesthetic Dimension: Toward a Critique of Marxist Aesthetics* (Boston: Beacon, 1978), ix, 8.

39. Adorno, *Aesthetic Theory*, 33. Where Marcuse comes closer to idealizing art as

distinct from ideology, Adorno situates art as always within it and always bound up with "extra-aesthetic productive forces" (33). Adorno moves beyond static oppositions between art and politics to claim aesthetic discourse as always connected to the socius, even if that connection is to critique the established order and expose its empty individualism.

40. Agnes Heller and Ferenc Fehér, "The Necessity and Irreformability of Aesthetics," in *Reconstructing Aesthetics: Writings of the Budapest School*, ed. Agnes Heller and Ferenc Fehér (Oxford: Basil Blackwell, 1986), 3.

41. Charles Mills Gayley and Fred Newton Scott, *An Introduction to the Methods and Materials of Literary Criticism: The Bases in Aesthetics and Poetics* (1899; rpt., Boston: Ginn, 1901), iii, 3, 86.

42. William Stanley Braithwaite, "What to Read," *The Crisis* (December 1911): 77–78. Rampersad notes that wheat and cotton signify very differently. "For Norris, wheat is the symbol of a natural force; to the socialist-minded Du Bois, cotton is basically the labor of the people who produce it. Thus, cotton as a symbol stands closer to human representation, and Du Bois is able to explore this association to a degree impossible in Norris, who abhorred socialism" (Arnold Rampersad, *The Art and Imagination of W. E. B. Du Bois* [Cambridge, Mass.: Harvard University Press, 1976], 120).

43. Frank Norris, *The Octopus: A Story of California* (1901; New York: Penguin, 1986), 40. All further references are to this edition and cited parenthetically.

44. Donald E. Pease, "*Martin Eden* and the Limits of Aesthetic Experience," *boundary 2* 25 (Spring 1998): 144, 151.

45. See Walter Benn Michaels, *The Gold Standard and the Logic of Naturalism: American Literature at the Turn of the Century* (Berkeley and Los Angeles: University of California Press, 1987), 189–90, 211–13.

46. The "Red terror" endangers political stability because it has the status of *fremde Sitten*, a foreign influence that disrupts a sovereign republic. As Paul Buhle argues, socialism in the U.S. was a "multi-ethnic" movement developed and sustained by immigrant populations (*Marxism in the United States: Remapping the History of the American Left* [London: Verso, 1987], 49). In contrast, John Diggins states that the "American Left was born in United States. Contrary to popular belief, it was not the product of foreign powers and alien ideologies" (*The Rise and Fall of the American Left* [New York: Norton, 1992], 17). Diggins's claims about homegrown radicalism, however, sound a lot like Schiller's desire to preserve the aesthetic state from "foreign manners." To what extent do aesthetic notions shape Diggins's historical narrative?

47. Edward Markham, *The Man with the Hoe and Other Poems* (New York: Doubleday, 1899), 5, 17–18.

48. Kate Gordon, "Pragmatism in Aesthetics," in *Essays Philosophical and Psychological in Honor of William James, by His Colleagues at Columbia University* (New York: Longmans, Green, and Co., 1908), 469, 479.

49. Vachel Lindsay, *The Art of the Moving Picture* (1915; rpt., New York: Liveright, 1970), 274, 276, 291.

50. Immanuel Kant, *Religion within the Limits of Reason Alone,* trans. Theodore M. Greene and Hoyt H. Hudson (New York: Harper, 1960), 91. How unattainable are an ethical commonwealth and world citizenship? In *Perpetual Peace,* Kant sees universal accord as possible only within "the vast burial ground of the human race" (*Perpetual Peace,* trans. Lewis White Beck [New York: Macmillan, 1957], 8).

51. Adorno, *Aesthetic Theory,* 89.

52. See Lloyd, "Arnold, Ferguson, Schiller," 139, 166.

53. Michael Hardt and Antonio Negri, *Empire* (Cambridge, Mass.: Harvard University Press, 2000), 10–11.

54. Frank Norris, "The Frontier Gone at Last: How Our Race Pushed It Westward around the World and Now Moves Eastward Again—The Broader Conception of Patriotism as the Age of Conquest Ends," in *Frank Norris: Novels and Essays,* 1183, 1184–85. Later in the essay, Norris expresses the same faith in "Markets" as the shipping magnate in *The Octopus:* "The great word of our century is no longer War but Trade" (1185).

55. Norris, "Frontier Gone at Last," 1188.

56. Coronil, "Towards a Critique of Globalcentrism," 368.

57. Kant, *Religion within the Limits of Reason Alone,* 91.

58. Russell Berman, *Modern Culture and Critical Theory: Art, Politics, and the Legacy of the Frankfurt School* (Madison: University of Wisconsin Press, 1989), 32.

59. Hardt and Negri, *Empire,* 11.

60. Norris, "Frontier Gone at Last," 1189–90.

61. Frank Norris, "The Great American Novelist," in *Frank Norris: Novels and Essays,* 1181–82.

62. Walter Benjamin, "The Work of Art in the Age of Mechanical Reproduction," in *Illuminations: Essays and Reflections,* edited by Hannah Arendt (New York: Schocken, 1968), 231.

63. Schiller, *Aesthetic Education,* 106.

AFTERWORD

1. Walter Benjamin, "The Work of Art in the Age of Its Technological Reproducibility," in *Walter Benjamin: Selected Writings, 1935–1938,* ed. Michael W. Jennings (Cambridge, Mass.: Harvard University Press, 2002), 3:101–102.

2. Immanuel Kant, *Critique of Judgment,* trans. J. H. Bernard (New York: Hafner, 1951), 46–47.

3. "Notes on Art," Henry Davies Papers, Box 4, folder 20 (44, 48).

4. Harriet Beecher Stowe, *We and our Neighbors: Or, The Records of an Unfashionable Street (Sequel to "My Wife and I")* (New York: J. B. Ford, 1875), 178, 214.

WORKS CITED

Ackerman, Phyllis. "Plato's Aesthetics." M.A. thesis. University of California, Berkeley, 1915.

Adams, Elizabeth Kemper. *The Aesthetic Experience: Its Meaning in Functional Psychology.* Chicago: University of Chicago Press, 1907.

Addams, Jane. *Democracy and Social Ethics.* 1902. Rpt., New York: Macmillan, 1920.

———. *The Spirit of Youth and the City Streets.* New York: Macmillan, 1920.

———. *Twenty Years at Hull-House with Autobiographical Notes.* 1911. Rpt., New York: Signet, 1961.

Adorno, Theodor. *Aesthetic Theory.* Translated by Robert Hullot-Kentor. Minneapolis: University of Minnesota Press, 1997.

Adorno, Theodor, and Max Horkheimer. *Dialectic of Enlightenment.* Stanford: Stanford University Press, 2002.

Allen, Grant. *Physiological Aesthetics.* London: Henry S. King, 1877.

Allen, James K. *Without Sanctuary: Lynching Photography in America.* Santa Fe, N.M.: Twin Palms, 2000.

Anderson, Benedict. "In the World-Shadow of Bismarck and Nobel: José Rizal: Paris, Havana, Barcelona, Berlin—2." *New Left Review* 28 (July/August 2004): 85–129.

Angier, Roswell Parker. "The Aesthetics of Unequal Division." Ph.D. diss., Harvard University, 1903.

Ankersmit, F. R. *Aesthetic Politics: Political Philosophy Beyond Fact and Value.* Stanford: Stanford University Press, 1996.

Annual Announcement of Courses of Instruction in the Colleges at Berkeley for the Academic Year 1896–97. Berkeley: University of California, 1896.

Appadurai, Arjun. "Grassroots Globalization and the Research Imagination." *Public Culture* 12, no. 1 (Winter 2000): 1–19.

Arendt, Hannah. *Between Past and Future: Six Exercises in Political Thought.* Cleveland: World Publishing, 1963.

———. *Lectures on Kant's Political Philosophy.* Chicago: University of Chicago Press, 1982.

——. *The Human Condition*. Chicago: University of Chicago Press, 1958.

Armstrong, Isobel. *The Radical Aesthetic*. Oxford: Blackwell, 2000.

Arnold, Matthew. *Civilization in the United States: First and Last Impressions of America*. Boston: DeWolfe, Fiske, 1900.

"Art for the People." *Literary Digest* 10 (1894–95): 402.

"Artistic Crime." *New York Times*, April 8, 1873: 4.

Atkinson, Brooks. "Beloved Vagabond: Charlie Chaplin Canonized Out of a Sentimental Memory Book." *New York Times*, February 16, 1936: sec. 9:1.

"Attacks Called Great Art." *New York Times*, September 19, 2001: E6.

Auerbach, Jonathan. "American Studies and Film, Blindness and Insight." *American Quarterly* 58 (March 2006): 31–50.

——. "Chasing Film Narrative: Repetition, Recursion, and the Body in Early Cinema." *Critical Inquiry* 26 (Summer 2000): 798–820.

——. "'Wonderful Apparatus,' or *Life of an American Fireman*." *American Literature* 77 (December 2005): 669–98.

Augst, Thomas. *The Clerk's Tale: Young Men and Moral Life in Nineteenth-Century America*. Chicago: University of Chicago Press, 2003.

Avrich, Paul. *The Haymarket Tragedy*. Princeton: Princeton University Press, 1984.

Banta, Martha. "Raw, Ripe, Rot: Nineteenth-Century Pathologies of the American Aesthetic." *ALH* 17 (2005): 666–86.

Barber, Benjamin. *Jihad vs. McWorld*. New York: Random House, 1995.

Bazin, André. *Essays on Chaplin*. Edited and translated by Jean Bodon. New Haven: University of New Haven Press, 1985.

"Beauty in Art." *New York Times*, June 24, 1905: BR 417.

Bellis, Peter. *Writing Revolution: Aesthetics and Politics in Hawthorne, Whitman, and Thoreau*. Athens: University of Georgia Press, 2003.

Benjamin, Walter. *Illuminations: Essays and Reflections*. Edited by Hannah Arendt. New York: Schocken, 1968.

——. "A Look at Chaplin." Translated by John McKay. *Yale Journal of Criticism* 9 (1996): 309–14.

——. *Reflections: Essays, Aphorisms, Autobiographical Writings*. Edited by Peter Demetz. New York: Schocken Books, 1986.

——. *Walter Benjamin: Selected Writings, 1935–1938*. 4 vols. Edited by Michael W. Jennings. Cambridge, Mass.: Harvard University Press, 2003.

Bennett, Tony. *Outside Literature*. London: Routledge, 1990.

Berman, Russell. *Modern Culture and Critical Theory: Art, Politics, and the Legacy of the Frankfurt School*. Madison: University of Wisconsin Press, 1989.

Bérubé, Michael. "Introduction: Engaging the Aesthetic." In *The Aesthetics of Cultural Studies*, edited by Michael Bérubé, 1–27. Malden, Mass.: Blackwell, 2005.

Bland, James A. "In the Evening by the Moonlight." In *James A. Bland's Great Ethiopian Songs*. New York: Hitchcock's Music Store, 1880.

Boggs, Colleen Glenney. "Margaret Fuller's American Translation." *American Literature* 76 (March 2004): 31–58.

Borus, Daniel. *Writing Realism: Howells, James, and Norris in the Mass Market.* Chapel Hill: University of North Carolina Press, 1989.

Boudreau, Kristin. "Elegies for the Haymarket Anarchists." *American Literature* 77 (June 2005): 319–47.

Bowman, W. Dodgson. *Charlie Chaplin: His Life and Art.* New York: John Day Company, 1931.

Boyer, Paul. *Urban Masses and Moral Order in America, 1820–1920.* Cambridge, Mass.: Harvard University Press, 1978.

Boyeson, Hjalmar Hjorth. "American Literary Criticism and Its Value." *Forum* 15 (1893): 459–66.

———. *Social Strugglers.* New York: Charles Scribner's Sons, 1893.

Brace, Charles Loring. *The Dangerous Classes of New York, and Twenty Years' Work among Them.* New York: Wynkoop & Hallenbeck, 1872.

Braithwaite, William Stanley. "Democracy and Art." *The Crisis* 10 (August 1915): 186.

———. "The Negro in Literature." *The Crisis* 28 (September 1924): 208–10.

———. "What to Read." *The Crisis* (December 1911): 77–78.

Brenkman, John. "Extreme Criticism." In *What's Left of Theory: New Work in the Politics of Literary Theory,* edited by Judith Butler, John Guillory, and Kendall Thomas, 114–36. New York: Routledge, 2000.

Brewster, Ben. "Periodization of Early Cinema." In *American Cinema's Transitional Era: Audiences, Institutions, Practices,* edited by Charlie Keil and Shelley Stamp, 66–75. Berkeley and Los Angeles: University of California Press, 2004.

Brooks, Van Wyck. *The Confident Years: 1885–1915.* New York: E. P. Dutton, 1952.

Bruce, Robert V. *1877: Year of Violence.* Indianapolis: Bobbs-Merrill, 1959.

Buck-Morss, Susan. "Aesthetics and Anaesthetics: Walter Benjamin's Artwork Essay Reconsidered." *October* 62 (1992): 3–41.

Buhle, Paul. *Marxism in the United States: Remapping the History of the American Left.* London: Verso, 1987.

Burke, Edmund. *A Philosophical Enquiry into the Origin of our Ideas of the Sublime and the Beautiful.* London: Routledge and Kegan Paul, 1958.

Bush, George W. "President Bush's Proclamation for National Arts and Humanities Month 2001. " http://www.collegeart.org/advocacy/000068. Accessed November 5, 2006.

Bush, Gregory W. *Lord of Attention: Gerald Stanley and the Crowd Metaphor in Industrializing America.* Amherst: University of Massachusetts Press, 1991.

Calvert, George H. *Essays Aesthetical.* Boston: Lee and Shepard, 1875.

Campbell, Helen, Thomas W. Knox, and Thomas Byrnes. *Darkness and Daylight; or, Lights and Shadows of New York Life. A Pictorial Record of Personal Experiences by Day and Night in the Great Metropolis with Hundreds of Thrilling Anecdotes and Incidents, Sketches of Life and Character, Humorous Stories, Touching Home Scenes, and Tales of Tender Pathos, Drawn from the Bright and Shady Sides of the Great Under World of New York.* Hartford, Conn: Hartford Publishing Co., 1897.

Carroll, Anne. "Protest and Affirmation: Composite Texts in the *Crisis.*" *American Literature* 76 (2004): 89–116.

Carroll, Noël. *Beyond Aesthetics: Philosophical Essays.* Cambridge: Cambridge University Press, 2001.

Carver, Terrell. "Imagery/Writing, Imagination/Politics: Reading Marx through the *Eighteenth Brumaire.*" In *Marx's "Eighteenth Brumaire": Post(modern) Interpretations,* edited by Mark Cowling and James Martin, 113–28. London: Pluto Press, 2002.

Chambers, Robert William. *The Red Republic: A Romance of the Commune.* 5th edition. New York: G. P. Putnam's Sons, 1895.

Chapelier, E. M., and Gassy Marin. *Anarchists and the International Language, Esperanto. With an Appendix Explaining the Elements of the Language.* London: "Freedom" Office, 1908.

Chaplin, Charles. *A Comedian Sees the World.* http://www.cinemaweb.com/silentfilm/ bookshelf. Accessed April 9, 2004.

———. "Making Fun." *Soil* 1 (1916): 5–7.

———. *My Autobiography.* New York: Pocket Books, 1966.

———. "A Rejection of the Talkies." In *Focus on Chaplin,* edited by Donald W. McCaffrey, 63–65. Englewood Cliffs, N.J.: Prentice Hall, 1971.

Chase, Richard. *The American Novel and Its Tradition.* New York: Doubleday, 1957.

Churchill, Winston. "Everybody's Language." In *Focus on Chaplin,* edited by Donald W. McCaffrey, 74–78. Englewood Cliffs, N.J.: Prentice Hall, 1971.

Chytry, Joseph. *The Aesthetic State: A Quest in Modern German Thought.* Berkeley and Los Angeles: University of California Press, 1989.

Clymer, Jeffory. *America's Culture of Terrorism: Violence, Capitalism, and the Written Word.* Chapel Hill: University of North Carolina Press, 2003.

Conant, Charles. *The United States in the Orient: The Nature of the Economic Problem.* Boston: Houghton, Mifflin, 1900.

Cook, David. "The Last Days of Liberalism." In *Postmodernism: A Reader,* edited by Thomas Docherty, 120–27. New York: Columbia University Press, 1993.

Cooley, Charles H. *Social Organization: A Study of the Larger Mind. In Two Major Works of Charles H. Cooley: "Social Organization" and "Human Nature and the Social Order."* Glencoe, Ill.: The Free Press, 1962.

Coronil, Fernando. "Towards a Critique of Globalcentrism: Speculations on Capitalism's Nature." *Public Culture* 12 (Spring 2000): 351–74.

Crane, Walter. "Why Socialism Appeals to Artists." *Atlantic Monthly* 69 (January 1892): 110–15.

Cravern, Thomas. "The Great American Art." *The Dial* 18 (December 1926): 483–92.

Crowley, John W. "The Unsmiling Aspects of Life: *A Hazard Of New Fortunes.*" In *Biographies of Books: The Compositional Histories of Notable American Writings,* edited by James Barbour and Tom Quirk, 78–109. Columbia: University of Missouri Press, 1996.

Curricular of Information: The Departments of Art, Literature, and Science. Chicago: University of Chicago, May 15, 1902.

Daucus, J. A. *Annals of the Great Strike in the United States: A Reliable History and Graphic Description of the Causes and Thrilling Events of the Labor Strikes and Riots of 1877.* Chicago: L. T. Palmer, 1877.

Davies, Henry. *Art in Education and Life: A Plea for the More Systematic Culture of the Sense of Beauty.* Columbus, Ohio: R. G. Adams, 1914.

———. Henry Davies Papers, Yale University Divinity Library, Archives and Manuscripts.

Day, Henry Noble. *The Science of Aesthetics; or, The Nature, Kinds, Laws and Uses of Beauty.* New Haven: Charles C. Chatfield, 1872.

de Grazia, Margreta. "Teleology, Delay, and the 'Old Mole.'" *Shakespeare Quarterly* 50 (Autumn 1999): 251–67.

de Man, Paul. *Aesthetic Ideology.* Minneapolis: University of Minnesota Press, 1996.

Derrida, Jacques. *Specters of Marx: The State of the Debt, the Work of Mourning, and the New International.* Translated by Peggy Kamuf. New York: Routledge, 1994.

Dewey, John. *Art as Experience.* 1934. New York: Capricorn Books, 1958.

"Different Types of Beauty." *Literary Digest* 13 (1896): 124.

Diggins, John Patrick. *The Rise and Fall of the American Left.* New York: Norton, 1992.

Dillon, Elizabeth Maddock. "Fear of Formalism: Kant, Twain, and Cultural Studies in American Literature." *Diacritics* 27 (1998): 46–69.

———. "Sentimental Aesthetics." *American Literature* 76 (September 2004): 495–523.

Dimock, Wai Chee. "Aesthetics at the Limit of the Nation: Kant, Pound, and the *Saturday Review.*" *American Literature* 76 (September 2004): 525–47.

———. "A Theory of Resonance." *PMLA* 112 (1997): 1060–71.

Division of Philosophy, 1902–03. Cambridge, Mass.: Harvard University, 1902.

Doctors of Philosophy June, 1893–April, 1931. Chicago: University of Chicago Press, 1931.

"Dollar Wheat." *The Literary Digest* 15 (1897): 654

Dray, Philip. *At the Hands of Persons Unknown: The Lynching of Black America.* New York: Random House, 2002.

Du Bois, W. E. B. *The Correspondence of W.E.B. Du Bois.* 3 vols. Edited by Herbert Aptheker. Amherst: University of Massachusetts Press, 1973.

———. The Black Man and the Wounded World." *The Crisis* 27 (January 1924): 110–14.

———. "Criteria of Negro Art." In *The Norton Anthology of African American Literature,* edited by Henry Louis Gates Jr and Nellie Y. McKay, 753–59. New York: Norton, 1997.

———. *Dark Princess: A Romance.* 1928. Millwood, N.Y.: Kraus-Thomson, 1974.

———. *Darkwater: Voices from within the Veil.* New York: AMS Press, 1969.

———. *Dusk of Dawn: An Essay Toward the Autobiography of a Race Concept.* New York: Harcourt, Brace, 1940.

———. "Fall Books." *The Crisis* 29 (November 1924): 25.

———. "Krigwa, 1926." *The Crisis* (January 1926): 115.

———. *The Quest of the Silver Fleece.* 1911. Boston: Northeastern University Press 1989.

———. *The Souls of Black Folk.* With an introduction by John Hope Franklin. In *Three Negro Classics.* New York: Avon, 1965.

Du Bois, W. E. B., and Alain Locke. "The Younger Literary Movement." In *The Crisis Reader,* edited by Sandra Kathryn Wilson, 288–303. New York: Modern Library, 1999.

Eagleton, Terry. *The Ideology of the Aesthetic.* Oxford: Blackwell, 1990.

Easthope, Anthony. "The Pleasures of Labour: Marxist Aesthetics in a Post-Marxist World." In *Post-Theory: New Directions in Criticism,* edited by Martin McQuillan et al., 63–77. Edinburgh: Edinburgh University Press, 1999.

Eggers, George William. "Foreword." In Vachel Lindsay, *The Art of the Moving Picture,* xxi–xxv. New York: Liveright, 1970.

Emerson, Ralph Waldo. *Essays and Lectures.* New York: Library of America, 1983.

Erkkilä, Betsy. *Whitman the Political Poet.* New York: Oxford University Press, 1989.

Esperanto, Dr. *See* Zamenhof.

Esteve, Mary. *The Aesthetics and Politics of the Crowd in American Literature.* Cambridge: Cambridge University Press, 2003.

"Esthetic Nature of Thugs to be Subjected to Old Art." *New York Times,* April 24, 1927: 20.

Evans, Brad. "Howellsian Chic: The Local Color of Cosmpolitanism." *ELH* 71 (2004): 775–812.

Fairbanks, Douglas, Jr. "Foreword." In W. Dodgson Bowman, *Charlie Chaplin: His Life and Art,* 7–10. New York: John Day Company, 1931.

Fauset, Jessie Redmon. "The Sleeper Wakes: A Novelette in Three Installments." *The Crisis* 20 (Aug.–Oct. 1920): 168–73, 226–29, 267–74.

———. *There is Confusion.* New York: Boni and Liveright, 1924.

Felski, Rita. "The Role of Aesthetics in Cultural Studies." In *The Aesthetics of Cultural Studies,* edited by Michael Bérubé, 28–43. Malden, Mass.: Blackwell, 2005.

Fiske, Minnie Maddern. "The Art of Charles Chaplin." In *Focus on Chaplin,* edited by Donald W. McCaffrey, 69–70. Englewood Cliffs, N.J.: Prentice Hall, 1971.

Forbes, Archibald. "What I Saw of the Paris Commune. II." *Century Magazine* 45 (November 1892): 48–61.

Foucault, Michel. "An Aesthetics of Existence." In *Politics, Philosophy, Culture: Interviews and Other Writings, 1977–1984,* edited by Lawrence D. Kritzman, translated by Alan Sheridan, 47–53. New York: Routledge, 1988.

———. *The Care of the Self.* Volume 3 of *The History of Sexuality.* Translated by Robert Hurley. New York: Pantheon, 1978.

———. "On the Genealogy of Ethics: An Overview of Work in Progress. " In *The Essential Works of Michel Foucault, 1954–1984,* 3 vols., edited by Paul Rabinow, translated by Robert Hurley, 1:102–25. New York: The New Press, 1997.

Furry, William Davis. "The Aesthetic Experience: Its Nature and Function in Epistemology." *The Psychological Review: The Johns Hopkins Studies in Philosophy and Psychology* 1 (1908): v–155.

Gaines, Jane. *Fire and Desire: Mixed-Race Movies in the Silent Era.* Chicago: University of Chicago Press, 2001.

Gandal, Keith. *The Virtues of the Vicious: Jacob Riis, Stephen Crane, and the Spectacle of the Slum.* New York: Oxford University Press, 1997.

Garlin, Sender. *William Dean Howells and the Haymarket Era.* New York: American Institute for Marxist Studies, 1979.

Gaut, Berys. "Cinematic Art." *Journal of Aesthetics and Art Criticism* 60 (Fall 2002): 299–312.

Gayley, Charles Mills. "Lectures on the Aesthetics of Literature Delivered at the University of California, 1890–91." Ms. Bancroft Library, University of California, Berkeley.

Gayley, Charles Mills, and Fred Newton Scott. *An Introduction to the Methods and Materials of Literary Criticism: The Bases in Aesthetics and Poetics.* 1899. Rpt., Boston: Ginn, 1901.

General Secretariat of the League of Nations. *Esperanto as an International Auxiliary Language.* Paris: Imprimerie des Presses Universitaires de France, 1922.

"German Socialism in America." *North American Review* 128 (April 1879): 372–88.

Giddens, Anthony, and Will Hutton. "Fighting Back." In *Global Capitalism,* edited by Will Hutton and Anthony Giddens, 213–33. New York: The New Press, 2000.

Gilje, Paul. *Rioting in America.* Bloomington: Indiana University Press, 1996.

Gillman, Susan. *Blood Talk: American Race Melodrama and the Culture of the Occult.* Chicago: University of Chicago Press, 2003.

Gish, Lillian. "A Universal Language." *Encyclopedia Britannica,* 14th ed. www.britannica.com/women/classic/C0026.html. Accessed April 16, 2004.

Glazener, Nancy. *Reading for Realism: The History of a U.S. Literary Institution, 1850–1910.* Durham: Duke University Press, 1997.

Gordon, Kate. *Esthetics.* New York: H. Holt, 1909.

———. "Pragmatism in Aesthetics." In *Essays Philosophical and Psychological in Honor of William James, by His Colleagues at Columbia University,* 461–82. New York: Longmans, Green, and Co., 1908.

Graebner, Norman A. *Empire on the Pacific: A Study in American Continental Expansion.* New York: Ronald Press, 1955.

"Grand Concourse Dominant Idea in Rare Vision of City Beautiful." *Los Angeles Times,* December 1, 1907. Accessed at http://www.ulwaf.com/LA-1900s/07.12.html#CityBeautiful, July 10, 2006.

Gray, Ellis. "The Flower Mission." *Harper's New Monthly Magazine* 48 (May 1874): 787–95.

Gray, John. *False Dawn: The Delusions of Global Capitalism.* New York: The New Press, 1998.

Griffis, William Elliot. *The Romance of Conquest: The Story of American Expansion through Arms and Diplomacy.* Boston: W. A. Wilde, 1899.

Gross, Steffan. "The Neglected Programme of Aesthetics." *British Journal of Aesthetics* 42 (October 2002): 403–14.

Gunn, Giles. "The Pragmatics of the Aesthetic." In *Aesthetics in a Multicultural Age,* edited by Emory Elliot, Louis Freitas Caton, and Jeffrey Rhyne, 61–77. New York: Oxford University Press, 2002.

Gunning, Sandra. *Race, Rape, and Lynching: The Red Record of American Literature, 1890–1912.* New York: Oxford University Press 1996.

Gunning, Tom. *D. W. Griffith and the Origins of American Narrative Film: The Early Years at Biograph.* Urbana: University of Illinois Press, 1991.

Hampton, Benjamin B. *A History of the Movies.* New York: Covici, Freide, 1931.

Hansen, Miriam. *Babel and Babylon: Spectatorship in American Silent Film.* Cambridge, Mass.: Harvard University Press, 1991.

———. "Benjamin, Cinema, and Experience: 'The Blue Flower in the Land of Technology.'" *New German Critique* 40 (Winter 1987): 179–224.

————. "Introduction." In Siegfried Kracauer, *Theory of Film: The Redemption of Physical Reality*, vii–xlv. Princeton: Princeton University Press, 1997.

Hardt, Michael, and Antonio Negri. *Empire*. Cambridge, Mass.: Harvard University Press, 2000.

Hatt, Michael. "Race, Ritual, and Responsibility: Performativity and the Southern Lynching." In *Performing the Body/Performing the Text*, edited by Amelia Jones and Andrew Stephenson, 76–88. London: Routledge, 1999.

Hebdige, Dick. *Subculture: The Meaning of Style*. 1979. Rpt., London: Routledge, 1991.

Heffernan, Jeanne M. "Art: A 'Political' Good?" In *Beauty, Art, and the Polis*, edited by Alice Ramos, 259–68. Washington, D.C.: American Maritain Association, 2000.

Held, David. "Democracy and Globalization." In *Re-imagining Political Community: Studies in Cosmopolitan Democracy*, edited by Danielle Archibugi, David Held, and Martin Köhler, 11–27. Stanford: Stanford University Press, 1998.

Heller, Agnes, and Ferenc Fehér. "The Necessity and Irreformability of Aesthetics." In *Reconstructing Aesthetics: Writings of the Budapest School*, ed. Agnes Heller and Ferenc Fehér, 1–22. Oxford: Basil Blackwell, 1986.

Hewitt, Andrew. *Fascist Modernism: Aesthetics, Politics, and the Avant-Garde*. Stanford: Stanford University Press, 1993.

Hinsley, Curtis M. "Strolling Through the Colonies." In *Walter Benjamin and the Demands of History*, edited by Michael P. Steinberg, 119–40. Ithaca: Cornell University Press, 1996.

Hofstader, Richard. *The Age of Reform: From Bryan to F.D.R.* New York: Vintage, 1955.

Howells, William Dean. *Criticism and Fiction and Other Essays*. New York: New York University Press, 1959.

————. "Editor's Easy Chair." *Harper's Monthly Magazine* 125 (1912): 634–37.

————. *Editor's Study*. Edited by James W. Simpson. Troy, N.Y.: Whitson, 1983.

————. *A Hazard of New Fortunes*. 1889. New York: Penguin, 2001.

————. *Literature and Life: The Man of Letters as a Man of Business*. New York: Harper, 1902. Rpt., Boston: IndyPublish.com, n.d.

————. *The Minister's Charge or The Apprenticeship of Lemuel Barker*. 1887. In *Novels, 1886–1888: The Ministers Charge; April Hopes; Annie Kilburn*. New York: Library of America, 1989.

Hullot-Kentor, Robert. "Translator's Introduction." In Theodor Adorno, *Aesthetic Theory*, translated by Robert Hullot-Kentor, xi–xxi. Minneapolis: University of Minnesota Press, 1997.

Huggins, Nathan Irvin. *Harlem Renaissance*. New York: Oxford University Press, 1971.

"Illinois vs. August Spies et al. trial evidence book." www.chicagohistory.org/hadc/transcripts/exhibits/X051-100/X0620.html. Accessed July 22, 2004.

Jackson, Gregory S. "Cultivating Spiritual Sight: Jacob Riis's Virtual-Tour Narrative and the Visual Modernization of Protestant Homiletics." *Representations* 83 (Summer 2003): 126–66.

Jacobs, Lewis. *The Rise of American Film: A Critical History*. 1939. Rpt., New York: Teachers College, Columbia University, 1968.

James, William. "How Can Lynching Be Stopped?" *Literary Digest* 27 (1903): 156.

Jay, Paul. "Beyond Discipline? Globalization and the Future of English." *PMLA* 116 (January 2001): 32–47.

Johnson, James Weldon. *The Autobiography of an Ex-Colored Man.* 1912. In *Three Negro Classics.* New York: Avon, 1965.

Joughin, John J., and Simon Malpas. "The New Aestheticism: An Introduction." In *The New Aestheticism,* edited by John J. Joughin and Simon Malpas, 1–19. Manchester: Manchester University Press, 2003.

Jowett, Garth. *Film: The Democratic Art.* Boston: Little, Brown, 1976.

Kallen, Horace M. "The Dramatic Picture Versus the Pictorial Drama: A Study of the Influences of the Cinematograph on the Stage." *The Harvard Monthly* 50 (March 1910): 22–31.

Kant, Immanuel. *The Critique of Judgment.* Translated by J. H. Bernard. New York: Hafner, 1951.

———. *Religion within the Limits of Reason Alone.* Translated by Theodore M. Greene and Hoyt H. Hudson. New York: Harper, 1960.

———. *Perpetual Peace.* Translated by Lewis White Beck. New York: Macmillan, 1957.

Kaplan, Amy. *The Anarchy of Empire in the Making of U.S. Culture.* Cambridge, Mass.: Harvard University Press, 2003.

———. "Nation, Region, and Empire." In *The Columbia History of the American Novel,* edited by Emory Elliot, 240–66. New York: Columbia University Press, 1991.

———. *The Social Construction of American Realism.* Chicago: University of Chicago Press, 1988.

Karatani, Kojin. "Uses of Aesthetics: After Orientalism." Translated by Sabu Kosho. *boundary 2* 25 (1998): 145–60.

Katz, Philip M. *From Appomattox to Montmartre: Americans and the Paris Commune.* Cambridge, Mass.: Harvard University Press, 1998.

Kauffman, Stanley. "Introduction." In Vachel Lindsay, *The Art of the Moving Picture,* ix–xix. New York: Liveright, 1970.

Keil, Charlie. *Early American Cinema in Transition: History, Style, and Filmmaking, 1907–1913.* Madison: University of Wisconsin Press, 2001.

Kemple, Thomas M. *Reading Marx Writing: Melodrama, the Market, and the "Grundisse."* Stanford: Stanford University Press, 1995.

Kerr, Walter. *The Silent Clowns.* New York: Knopf, 1975.

Kipnis, Laura. *Ecstasy Unlimited: On Sex, Capital, Gender, and Aesthetics.* Minneapolis: University of Minnesota Press, 1993.

Kitchen, Karl K. "Chaplin and 'The Masses.'" *New York Times,* March 17, 1935: sec. 8:4.

Knight, William Angus. *The Philosophy of the Beautiful, Being Outlines of the History of Aesthetics.* 2 vols. New York: Charles Scribner's Sons, 1891.

Koepnick, Lutz. *Walter Benjamin and the Aesthetics of Power.* Lincoln: University of Nebraska Press, 1999.

Kracauer, Siegfried. *Theory of Film: The Redemption of Physical Reality.* Princeton: Princeton University Press, 1997.

Ladd, George Trumbull. *Introduction to Philosophy: An Inquiry after a Rational System of Scientific Principles in Their Relation to Ultimate Reality*. New York: Charles Scribner's Sons, 1890.

Langfeld, Herbert Sidney. *The Aesthetic Attitude*. New York: Harcourt, Brace, 1920.

———. "Three Letters from Houghton Mifflin to Herbert Sidney Langfeld." Houghton Library, 1919.

Lay, Howard. "'Beau Geste!' (On the Readability of Terrorism)." *Yale French Studies* 101 (2001): 79–100.

Lastra, James. *Sound Technology and the American Cinema: Perception, Representation, Modernity*. New York: Columbia University Press, 2000.

Lazare, Daniel. "America the Undemocratic." *New Left Review* 232 (November/December 1998): 3–40.

Le Bon, Gustave. *The Crowd: A Study of the Popular Mind*. New Jersey: Transaction, 1995.

Lee, Gerald Stanley. *Crowds: A Moving Picture of Democracy*. New York: Garden City, 1913.

———. "Making the Crowd Beautiful." *Atlantic Monthly* 87 (February 1901): 240–53.

Lewis, David Levering. *W. E. B. Du Bois: Biography of a Race, 1868–1919*. New York: Henry Holt, 1993.

Lindsay, Vachel. *The Art of the Moving Picture*. 1915. Rpt., New York: Liveright, 1970.

Litwack, Leon F. "Hellhounds." In *Without Sanctuary: Lynching Photography in America*, 8–37. Santa Fe, N.M.: Twin Palms, 2000.

Livingston, James. *Pragmatism and the Political Economy of Cultural Revolution, 1850–1940*. Chapel Hill: University of North Carolina Press, 1994.

Lloyd, David. "Arnold, Ferguson, Schiller: Aesthetic Culture and the Politics of Aesthetics." *Cultural Critique* 2 (Winter 1985–86): 137–69.

Long, Bernard. *Esperanto: Its Aims and Claims: A Discussion of the Language Problem and Its Solution*. London: Esperanto Publishing, 1930.

Lounsbury, Myron Osborn. *The Origins of American Film Criticism, 1909–1939*. New York: Arno, 1973.

"A Lynching of a New Sort," *New York Times*, April 22, 1911: 1.

McCaffrey, Donald W. "An Evaluation of Chaplin's Silent Comedy Films, 1916–36." In *Focus on Chaplin*, edited by Donald W. McCaffrey, 82–95. Englewood Cliffs, N.J.: Prentice Hall, 1971.

McCann, Sean. "The Ambiguous Politics of Politicizing, or De-Politicizing the Aesthetic." In *Poetics/Politics: Radical Aesthetics for the Classroom*, edited by Amitava Kumar, 39–70. New York: St. Martins, 1999.

McClelland, J. S. *The Crowd and the Mob: From Plato to Canetti*. London: Unwin Hyman, 1989.

McKay, Claude. "Soviet Russia and the Negro." *The Crisis* 27 (December 1923): 61–65.

Mailloux, Steven. *Disciplinary Identities: Rhetorical Paths of English, Speech, and Composition*. New York: MLA, 2006.

Maland, Charles. *Chaplin and American Culture: The Evolution of a Star Image*. Princeton: Princeton University Press, 1989.

Marcuse, Herbert. *The Aesthetic Dimension: Toward a Critique of Marxist Aesthetics.* Boston: Beacon, 1978.

Markham, Edward. *The Man with the Hoe and Other Poems.* New York: Doubleday, 1899.

Marshall, Henry Rutgers. *Aesthetic Principles.* New York: Macmillan, 1895.

———. *Pain, Pleasure, and Aesthetics: An Essay Concerning the Psychology of Pain and Pleasure.* New York: Macmillan, 1894.

Marx, Karl. *The Civil War in France.* In *The Marx-Engels Reader,* edited by Robert C. Tucker, 526–76. Norton: New York, 1972.

———. *Der achtzehnte Brumaire des Louis Bonaparte.* http://www.marxists.org/deutsch/ archiv/marx-engels/1852/brumaire/kapitel1.htm. Accessed August 12, 2004.

———. *The Eighteenth Brumaire of Louis Bonaparte.* New York: International Publishers, 1963.

———. "Inaugural Address of the International Working Men's Association." 1864. http:// www.marxists.org/archive/marx/works/1864/10/27.htm. Accessed August 10, 2004.

Marx, Karl, and Frederick Engels. *The American Journalism of Marx and Engels: A Selection from the New York Daily Tribune.* Edited by Henry M. Christman. New York: New American Library, 1966.

———. *Letters to Americans, 1848–1895: A Selection.* Edited by Alexander Trachtenberg. New York: International Publishers, 1953.

May, Larry. *Screening Out the Past: The Birth of Mass Culture and the Motion Picture Industry.* New York: Oxford University Press, 1980.

Mercer, Kobena. "Looking for Trouble." *Transition* 51 (1991): 184–97.

Michaels, Walter Benn. *The Gold Standard and the Logic of Naturalism: American Literature at the Turn of the Century.* Berkeley and Los Angeles: University of California Press, 1987.

Moffat, James C. *An Introduction to the Study of Aesthetics.* Cincinnati: Moore, Wilstach, Keys, 1856.

Mohanty, Satya P. "Can Our Values Be Objective?: On Ethics, Aesthetics, and Progressive Politics." In *Aesthetics in a Multicultural Age,* edited by Emory Elliot, Louis Freitas Caton, and Jeffrey Rhyne, 31–59. New York: Oxford University Press, 2002.

Moi, Toril. *Henrik Ibsen and the Birth of Modernism: Art, Theater, Philosophy.* Oxford and New York: Oxford University Press, 2006.

Morris, William. *Hopes and Fears for Art.* Boston: Roberts Brothers, 1882.

Moses, Wilson Jeremiah. *The Golden Age of Black Nationalism, 1850–1925.* Hamden, Conn.: Archon Books, 1978.

Most, Johann. "The Beast of Property." ca. 1884. http://www.eclipse.net/~basket42/ beast.html. Accessed July 12, 2006.

———. *Science of Revolutionary Warfare.* 1885. El Dorado, Ariz: Desert Publications, 1978.

Münsterberg, Hugo. *The Photoplay: A Psychological Study.* 1916. New York: Arno Press, 1970.

———. "Psychology and Art." *North American Review* 82 (1898): 632–43.

Musser, Charles, in collaboration with Carol Nelson. *High-Class Moving Pictures: Lyman H. Howe and the Forgotten Era of Traveling Exhibition, 1880–1920.* Princeton: Princeton University Press, 1991.

———."Work, Ideology, and Chaplin's Tramp." In *Resisting Images: Essays on Cinema and History,* edited by Robert Sklar and Charles Musser, 36–67. Philadelphia: Temple University Press, 1990.

Nemoianu, Virgil. "Hating and Loving Aesthetic Formalism: Some Reasons." *MLQ* 61 (March 2000): 41–57.

"New Courses in Aesthetics." *New York Times,* January 18, 1891: 9.

Nietzsche, Friedrich. *The Gay Science: with a Prelude in German Rhymes and an Appendix of Songs.* Translated by Josefine Nauckhoff. Cambridge: Cambridge University Press, 2001.

"Notes of Ballou for Philosophy 10." Box 695, Harvard University Archives, 1899–1900.

Norris, Frank. "A Christmas in the Transvaal." In Robert C. Letiz III, "'A Christmas in the Transvaal': An Addition to the Norris Canon." *Studies in American Fiction* 14 (Autumn 1986): 221–24.

———. *Frank Norris: Novels and Essays.* New York: Library of America, 1986.

———. *The Letters of Frank Norris.* Edited by Franklin Walker. San Francisco: Book Club of California, 1956.

———. *The Octopus: A Story of California.* 1901. New York: Penguin, 1986.

Norton, Edwin Lee. "The Concepts of Harmony and Organism in Ethics." Ph.D. diss, Harvard University, 1900.

Nusse, Ernest. "The Protection of Children." *The Bay State Monthly* 2 (November 1884): 89–96.

Orvell, Miles. *The Real Thing: Imitation and Authenticity in American Culture, 1880–1940.* Chapel Hill: University of North Carolina Press, 1989.

Paine, Thomas. *Common Sense and Other Political Writings.* Indianapolis: Bobbs-Merrill, 1953.

Park, Robert E. *The Crowd and the Public and Other Essays.* Translated by Charlotte Elsner. Chicago: University of Chicago Press, 1972.

Parrish, Timothy. "Haymarket and *Hazard:* The Lonely Politics of William Dean Howells." *Journal of American Culture* 17 (Winter 1994): 23–32.

Patrick, G. T. W. "The Psychology of Crazes." *Popular Science Monthly* 57 (1900): 285–94.

Pease, Donald E. "*Martin Eden* and the Limits of Aesthetic Experience." *boundary 2* 25 (Spring 1998): 139–60.

Pember, Arthur. *The Mysteries and Miseries of the Great Metropolis, with Some Adventures in the Country: Being the Disguises and Surprises of a New-York Journalist.* New York: D. Appleton and Company, 1874.

Peyser, Thomas. *Utopia and Cosmopolis: Globalization in the Era of American Literary Realism.* Durham: Duke University Press, 1998.

Pierce, Edgar. "The Aesthetics of Simple Forms." Ph.D. diss., Harvard University, 1895.

Pinkerton, Alan. *Strikers, Communists, Tramps, and Detectives.* New York: G. W. Carleton, 1878.

Posnock, Ross. *Color and Culture: Black Writers and the Making of the Modern Intellectual.* Cambridge, Mass.: Harvard University Press, 1998.

Prettyman, Gib. "The Serial Illustrations of *A Hazard of New Fortunes.*" *Resources for American Literary Study* 27 (2001): 179–95.

"The Princeton Lecture Course." *New York Times*, January 13, 1888: 3.

Puffer, Ethel Dench. "Criticism and Aesthetics." *Atlantic Monthly* 87 (1901): 839–48.

———. *The Psychology of Beauty.* Boston: Houghton, Mifflin, 1905.

Raleigh, John Henry. *Matthew Arnold and American Culture.* Berkeley and Los Angeles: University of California Press, 1957.

Rampersad, Arnold. *The Art and Imagination of W. E. B. Du Bois.* Cambridge, Mass.: Harvard University Press, 1976.

———. "Foreword." In W. E. B. Du Bois, *The Quest of the Silver Fleece*, 1–11. Boston: Northeastern University Press, 1989.

Ramsaye, Terry. *A Million and One Nights: A History of the Motion Picture.* New York: Simon and Schuster, 1926.

Ransom, John Crowe. "Forms and Citizens." In *The World's Body*, 29–54. 1938. Rpt., Baton Rouge: Louisiana State University Press, 1968.

Raymond, George Lansing. *The Essentials of Aesthetics in Music, Poetry, Painting, Sculpture and Architecture.* New York: G. P. Putnam's Sons, 1906.

Redfield, Marc. *The Politics of Aesthetics: Nationalism, Gender, Romanticism.* Stanford: Stanford University Press, 2003.

Reed, Adolph L., Jr. *W. E. B. Du Bois and American Political Thought: Fabianism and the Color Line.* New York: Oxford University Press, 1997.

Reynolds, Larry J. *European Revolutions and the American Literary Renaissance.* New Haven: Yale University Press, 1988.

Riis, Jacob A. *The Battle with the Slum.* 1902. Rpt., Montclair, N.J.: Patterson Smith, 1969.

———. *How the Other Half Lives: Studies among the Tenements of New York.* New York: Charles Scribner's Sons, 1890. Rpt., New York: Dover, 1971.

———. "Light in Dark Places: A Study of the Better New York." *The Century: A Popular Quarterly* 53 (December 1896): 246–53.

———. *The Making of an American: A New Edition with an Epilogue by His Grandson, J. Riis Owre.* London: Macmillan, 1970.

———. "The Tenement House Blight." *Atlantic Monthly* 83 (1899): 760–71.

Robinson, Charles Mulford. "Improvement in City Life: Aesthetic Progress." *Atlantic Monthly* 83 (1899): 771–85.

———. "Improvement in City Life: Educational Progress." *Atlantic Monthly* 83 (1899): 654–65.

Rosen, Philip G. "The Chaplin World-View." *Cinema Journal* 12 (Fall 1969): 2–12.

Rosenau, James. "Governance and Democracy in a Globalizing World." In *Re-imagining Political Community: Studies in Cosmopolitan Democracy*, edited by Danielle Archibugi, David Held, and Martin Köhler, 28–57. Stanford: Stanford University Press, 1998.

Rosenzweig, Roy. *Eight Hours For What We Will: Workers and Leisure in an Industrial City, 1870–1920.* Cambridge: Cambridge University Press, 1983.

Ross, Steven J. "Cinema and Class Conflict: Labor, Capital, the State, and American Silent Film." In *Resisting Images: Essays on Cinema and History*, edited by Robert Sklar and Charles Musser, 68–107. Philadelphia: Temple University Press, 1990.

Rothberg, Michael. "After Adorno: Culture in the Wake of Catastrophe." *New German Critique* 72 (Fall 1997): 45–81.

Rowe, John Carlos. *Literary Culture and U.S. Imperialism*. New York: Oxford University Press, 2000.

Rozas, Lorenzo Turrent. "Charlie Chaplin's Decline." *Living Age* 396 (June 1934): 319–23.

———. *Hacía una literatura proletaria*. Jalapa, Mexico: La Economica, 1932.

Ruskin, John. "The Lamp of Beauty." In *The Seven Lamps of Architecture*, 103–50. 1849. Rpt., London: J. M. Dent and Sons, 1907.

Santayana, George. *The Sense of Beauty: Being the Outlines of Aesthetic Theory*. 1896. Cambridge, Mass: MIT Press, 1988.

Scarborough, W. S. *An Address Delivered by Prof. W. S. Scarborough, or Wilberforce University on Our Political Status, at the Colored Men's Inter-State Conference, in the City of Pittsburgh, PA., Tuesday, April 29, 1884*. Xenia, Ohio: Torchlight Job Rooms, 1884.

———. *The Birds of Aristophanes: A Theory of Interpretation. A Paper Read before the American Philosophical Association at Its Annual Meeting at Sage College, Cornell University, Ithaca, N. Y., July 13, 1886*. Boston: J. S. Cushing, 1886.

Scarry, Elaine. *On Beauty and Being Just*. Princeton: Princeton University Press, 1999.

Schiller, Friedrich. *On the Aesthetic Education of Man in a Series of Letters*. Translated by Reginald Snell. New Haven: Yale University Press, 1954.

Schwarz, Henry. "Aesthetic Imperialism: Literature and the Conquest of India." *MLQ* 61 (December 2000): 563–86.

Scott, Fred N. *Aesthetics: Its Problems and Literature*. Ann Arbor: Inland Press, 1890.

"Sealing Wax, Cabbages, and Kings." *New York Times*, September 30, 1934: X5.

Seldes, Gilbert. *The Seven Lively Arts*. New York: Harper, 1924.

Shusterman, Richard. *Performing Live: Aesthetic Alternatives for the End of Art*. Ithaca: Cornell University Press, 2000.

Sinclair, Upton. *Samuel the Seeker*. Racine, Wisconsin: Western Printing and Lithographing, 1910.

Singh, Nikhil Pal. "Culture/Wars: Recoding Democracy in an Age of Empire." *American Quarterly* 50 (1998): 471–522.

Sklar, Robert. *Movie-Made America: A Cultural History of the Movies*. Revised and updated. New York: Vintage, 1994.

Sleinis, E. E. *Art and Freedom*. Urbana: University of Illinois Press, 2003.

Solderholm, James. "Introduction." In *Beauty and the Critic: Aesthetics in an Age of Cultural Studies*, edited by James Solderholm, 1–12. Tuscaloosa: University of Alabama Press, 1997.

Sparks, Edwin Erle. *The Expansion of the American People, Social and Territorial*. Chicago: Scott, Foresman, 1900.

Sparshott, Francis. *The Future of Aesthetics: The 1996 Ryle Lectures*. Toronto: University of Toronto Press, 1998.

Stange, Maren. *Symbols of Ideal Life: Social Documentary Photography in America, 1890–1950*. Cambridge: Cambridge University Press, 1989.

Starr, Paul. *The Creation of the Media: The Political Origins of Modern Communications*. New York: Basic Books, 2004.

Stearns, J. W. *Aesthetics: Syllabus of a Course of Six Lectures*. Madison: Tracy, Gibbs, 1895.

Sterne, Jonathan. *The Audible Past: Cultural Origins of Sound Reproduction.* Durham, N.C.: Duke University Press, 2003.

Stephens, Harmon B. "The Relation of the Motion Picture to Changing Moral Standards." *Annals of the American Academy* 128 (November 1926): 151–57.

Stewart, Garrett. "Modern Hard Times: Chaplin and the Cinema of Self-Reflection." *Critical Inquiry* 3 (1976): 295–314.

Stewart, Jacqueline Najuma. *Migrating to the Movies: Cinema and Black Urban Modernity.* Berkeley and Los Angeles: University of California Press, 2005.

Stollman, Rainer. "Fascist Tendencies as a Total Work of Art: Tendencies of the Aesthetization of Political Life in National Socialism." *New German Critique* 14 (Spring 1978): 41–60.

Stowe, Harriet Beecher. *We and Our Neighbors: Or, The Records of an Unfashionable Street (Sequel to "My Wife and I").* New York: J. B. Ford, 1875.

Stretch, Cynthia. "Illusions of a Public, Locations of Conflict: Feeling Like Populace in William Dean Howells's *A Hazard of New Fortunes.*" *American Literary Realism* 35 (Spring 2003): 233–46.

Thomas, Brook. *American Literary Realism and the Failed Promise of Contract.* Berkeley and Los Angeles: University of California Press, 1997.

Thompson, Kristin. *Exporting Entertainment: America in the World Film Market.* London: British Film Institute, 1985.

Thucydides. *The Peloponnesian War.* Translated by Richard Crawley. New York: Random House, 1982.

Tolnay, Stewart E., and E. M. Beck. *A Festival of Violence: An Analysis of Southern Lynchings, 1882–1930.* Urbana: University of Illinois Press, 1995.

"Topics of the Times: Lynched on Stage; Shots Came from Pit." *New York Times,* April 21, 1911: 1.

Toynbee, Polly. "Who's Afraid of Global Culture." In *Global Capitalism,* edited by Will Hutton and Anthony Giddens, 191–212. New York: The New Press, 2000.

Tratner, Michael. "Working the Crowd: Movies and Mass Politics." *Criticism* 45 (Winter 2003): 53–73.

Tufts, James Hayden. "Beauty and the Beautiful." In James Mark Baldwin, *Dictionary of philosophy and psychology, including many of the principal conceptions of ethics, logic, aesthetics, philosophy of religion, mental pathology, anthropology, biology, neurology, physiology, economics, political and social philosophy, philology, physical science and education, and giving a terminology in English, French, German and Italian. Written by many hands and edited by James Mark Baldwin with the co-operation and assistance of an international board of consulting editors,* 104–109. 1901. Rpt., Gloucester, Mass: Peter Smith, 1960.

———. *On the Genesis of the Aesthetic Categories.* Chicago: University of Chicago Press, 1902.

Turner, Darwin T. "W. E. B. Du Bois and the Theory of a Black Aesthetic." In *The Harlem Renaissance Re-examined: A Revised and Expanded Edition,* edited by Victor A. Kramer and Robert A. Russ, 45–63. Troy, N.Y.: Whitson Publishing, 1997.

University of Wisconsin: University Extension, 1907–1908. Madison: University of Wisconsin, 1907.

Uricchio, William, and Roberta Pearson. *Reframing Culture: The Case of the Vitagraph Quality Films.* Princeton: Princeton University Press, 1993.

Veblen, Thorstein. "Kant's *Critique of Judgment.*" *The Journal of Speculative Philosophy* 18 (July 1884): 260–74.

Vidal, Gore. *At Home: Essays 1982–1988.* New York: Random House, 1988.

Walker, Franklin. *Frank Norris: A Biography.* Garden City: Doubleday, 1932.

Wallerstein, Immanuel. "The National and the Universal: Can There Be Such a Thing as World Culture?" In *Culture, Globalization, and the World-System: Contemporary Conditions for the Representation of Identity,* edited by Anthony D. King, 91–105. Minneapolis: University of Minnesota Press, 1997.

Walters, Malcolm. *Globalization.* 2d ed. London: Routledge, 2001.

Warner, Michael. "The Mass Public and the Mass Subject." In *The Phantom Public Sphere,* edited by Bruce Robbins, 234–56. Minneapolis: University of Minnesota Press, 1993.

Warren, Kenneth. *Black and White Strangers: Race and American Literary Realism.* Chicago: University of Chicago Press, 1993.

Weiss, Arthur. "Introduction to the Philosophy of Art." *University of California Publications in Modern Philology* 1 (January 1910): 245–302.

Wells, Kate Gannett. "Free Summer Pleasures for the People in Boston." *The New England Magazine* 12 (August 1892): 790–95.

West, Nathaniel. *Day of the Locust.* New York: Signet, 1983.

"What an American Girl Saw of the Commune." *Century Magazine* 45 (November 1892): 61–66.

White, Walter Francis. *The Fire in the Flint.* 1924. New York: Negro University Press, 1969.

———. *Flight.* 1926. New York: Negro University Press, 1969.

———. *Rope and Faggot: A Biography of Judge Lynch.* New York: Arno Press, 1969.

———. "The Success of Negro Migration." *The Crisis* 19 (January 1920): 112–15.

Whitman, Walt. *Complete Poetry and Collected Prose.* New York: Library of America, 1982.

Williams, Raymond. *Marxism and Literature.* New York: Oxford University Press, 1977.

Woldring, Henk E. S. "Social Justice as a Work of Art in Action." In *Beauty, Art, and the Polis,* edited by Alice Ramos, 287–300. Washington, D.C.: American Maritain Association, 2000.

Wolin, Richard. *Walter Benjamin: An Aesthetic of Redemption.* New York: Columbia University Press, 1982.

A Working Girl. "An Aesthetic Idea." *Harper's New Monthly Magazine* 67 (June 1883): 136–42.

———. "A New Cinderella." *Harper's New Monthly Magazine* 66 (April 1883): 765–70.

Zamenhof, Ludwik Lazar [Dr. Esperanto]. *An Attempt towards an International Language.* Translated by Henry Phillips Jr. New York: Henry Holt, 1889.

Zangrando, Robert. *The NAACP Crusade Against Lynching, 1909–1950.* Philadelphia: Temple University Press, 1980.

Zimmerman, David A. *Panic! Markets, Crises, and Crowds in American Fiction.* Chapel Hill: University of North Carolina Press, 2006.

Zulaika, Joseba, and William A. Douglass. *Terror and Taboo: The Follies, Fables, and Faces of Terrorism.* New York: Routledge, 1996.

INDEX

Uncle Tom's Cabin (Stowe), 127
United States in the Orient (Conant), 181
universal: aesthetics, 1–4, 14–15, 17–18,
20–21, 24, 29–30, 55, 100, 174,
183–87, 194; art, 109; beauty and, 117,
155, 214; as biological, 37–38; commodities as, 179, 181, 197; consensus,
36, 55; false, 122, 134, 197; judgment,
124, 202; language, 23, 139, 170,
173–79, 181; location of, 115, 135; motion pictures as, 137–38, 141, 145, 151,
153, 160, 166, 170; redeployments of,
115; taste, 20, 33, 46, 71
Universala Esperanto Asocio, 176
"Universal Language" (Gish), 173
university extension, 9, 11, 13, 17–18, 37,
70; film as, 20; at the University of
Wisconsin, 31
University of California, Berkeley, 10–12,
30, 32, 43, 65, 195
University of Chicago, 11–12, 16, 67
University of Heidelberg, 96
University of Illinois, 222n20
University of Iowa, 94
University of Michigan, 14, 30, 55, 94,
195
University of Wisconsin–Madison, xi, 12
urban reform, 9, 15, 20, 33–45, 48, 64,
88, 222n20; repressive aspects,
92–93
Uricchio, William, 240n4, 242n26,
242–43n33, 243n43

Vandover and the Brute (Norris), 180
vaudeville, 142–43, 146, 148, 159, 166,
168, 170
Veblen, Thorstein, 36, 51, 223n34,
225n61
Vidal, Gore, 68, 227n8
violence, 3, 5–6, 8–9, 18; aestheticized,
117–22; beauty and, 37, 53–54, 64,
111, 116–22, 190–91, 211, 213; as class

antagonism, 30, 54, 101, 202; during
"The Great Strike," 22, 53, 82–88;
linguistic aspects, 84–86; photography and, 48, 63–64; racial, 107–10,
117–22, 125–26, 129–35. *See also*
lynching; strikes (and strikers)

Wagner, Richard, 154
Wallerstein, Immanuel, 184
Warner, Michael, 94
Warren, Kenneth, 227n5
Washington, Booker T., 110
Waters, Malcolm, 250n21
Watteau, Antoine, 7
We and Our Neighbors (Stowe), 4–5, 215
Weiss, Arthur, 32, 43, 222n18
Wellesley College, 30, 37, 57
Wells, H. G., 161
Wells, Kate Gannett, 224nn46–47
Wells-Barnett, Ida B., 235n32
West, Nathaniel, 241n18
Weydemeyer, Joseph, 73, 223n23
wheat: as global commodity, 181–82,
205, 207–9; epic of, 195, 252n42
White, Walter, 11, 110, 118, 121–22,
128–30, 236nn44–45, 238–39n69
whiteness. *See* Anglo-Saxonism
white slave films, 148
Whitman, Walt, 66, 78, 89–91, 96, 161,
227n4, 230n60, 245n72; *Democratic
Vistas*, 89–90, 231n62; "Passage to
India," 183
Whittier, John Greenleaf, 98
Wilberforce University, 123, 251n52
Williams, Raymond, 3, 187, 217n1
Woldring, Henk E. S., 221n3
Wolin, Richard, 218n11
women: professors, 11–12; and right to
vote, 123–24; Southern white, 135;
and strikes, 83
workers, 138–39, 162–64, 181; art and
leisure for, 21, 93, 98, 142; interests